THOMAS COKE

Apostle of Methodism

THE WESLEY HISTORICAL SOCIETY LECTURE NO. 30
METHODIST CONFERENCE 1964
A SYNOPSIS OF WHICH WAS DELIVERED AT
MILLHOUSES METHODIST CHURCH, SHEFFIELD
ON 8 JULY 1964

THOMAS COKE
1747-1814

JOHN VICKERS

THOMAS COKE
Apostle of Methodism

WIPF & STOCK · Eugene, Oregon

Wipf and Stock Publishers
199 W 8th Ave, Suite 3
Eugene, OR 97401

Thomas Coke
Apostle of Methodism
By Vickers, John A.
Copyright©1969 by Vickers, John A.
ISBN 13: 978-1-62032-975-7
Publication date 3/15/2013
Previously published by Epworth, 1969

For
VIVIENNE
with my love

CONTENTS

CONTENTS

ABBREVIATIONS USED IN THE NOTES

Candler ⎫	
Crowther	Biographies of Thomas Coke:
Drew ⎬	for details, see Bibliography Section (A)
Etheridge	
Sutcliffe ⎭	
Archives Centre	Methodist Archives and Research Centre, London
Asbury, *Journal*	*The Journal and Letters of Francis Asbury*, 1958, volumes 1–2
Asbury, *Letters*	Ibid., volume 3
B.M.	British Museum
Coke's *Journal*	Collected edition, 1816: see Bibliography
Coke's *Journal*, (American edition)	Journal of first visit to America, printed in *Arminian Magazine* (Philadelphia), 1789
D.N.B.	*Dictionary of National Biography*
Drinkhouse	*History of Methodist Reform*, 1898
E.M.P.	*Lives of the Early Methodist Preachers*, 3rd edn, 1865
Findlay & Holdsworth	*History of the Wesleyan Methodist Missionary Society*, 1921–4
L.Q.R.	*London Quarterly and Holborn Review*
M.E.C.	Methodist Episcopal Church
M.M.S.	Methodist Missionary Society
Minutes	Minutes of the British Conference, collected edition, 1862
N.L.W.	National Library of Wales
O.D.C.C.	*Oxford Dictionary of the Christian Church*, 1957
P.R.O.	Public Record Office, London
Tyerman	L. Tyerman, *Life and Times of John Wesley*, 1870–1
W.H.S. *Proc.*	*Proceedings of the Wesley Historical Society*
Wesley, *Works*	*Works of John Wesley*, 3rd edn., 1829–31

PREFACE

This book owes its existence in the first place to the late Rev. Wesley F. Swift who, as Editor of *The Proceedings of the Wesley Historical Society*, was responsible for the invitation to deliver the Society's annual Lecture at the Methodist Conference of 1964. For this honour and the stimulus it gave to my work on Thomas Coke I am glad to record my gratitude. Sadly, Mr Swift did not live to see the Lecture delivered as part of the commemoration of the 150th anniversary of Coke's death.

In another sense, the book is a by-product of my work on the *General Index* to the *Proceedings of the Wesley Historical Society*, Volumes I–XXX, in the course of which I discovered that the name of Thomas Coke was occurring with considerable regularity and in a variety of contexts. Here, evidently, was a key figure in the early history of Methodism, with a finger in many pies. Yet, seeking further information, I found that the only twentieth-century study of Coke was that of the American Bishop Candler (1923), while the most recent British biography appeared as long ago as 1861. Like their predecessors, these were largely undocumented. Further search located several hundred of Coke's letters and other unpublished material, and the present study began to take shape.

Although Coke appears in a supporting role in many Methodist histories and biographies of Wesley, it cannot be denied that he has, on the whole, been unsympathetically handled. The criticisms levelled at him in his own day, notably that of worldly ambition, have been endlessly repeated by later writers who, so far as I can see, have made little attempt to examine the evidence in any detail. The view set out in the present book is that, for all his faults, Coke has generally been misrepresented, and even maligned, on certain important counts. Thus, the most persistent charge against him, that of ambitious self-seeking, is clearly crucial for any assessment of his character. There is, of course, more than one kind of ambition. Coke certainly possessed his share of the ambition which is essential to all worthwhile achievement and which provokes the mediocre to jealousy; but that he was motivated largely by self-seeking ambition is a very different assertion which I do not believe to be consistent with the evidence when it is examined in full.

In a recent study of *John Wesley and the Christian Ministry* (1963), Dr A. B. Lawson perpetuates this traditional view of Coke's 'ambitious and wilful nature'. Coke, not Wesley, was the culprit responsible for the indiscretions committed in Bristol in September 1784; subsequently, in America, he deliberately misrepresented Wesley's intentions and adopted the title of Bishop for self-aggrandisement. My own reading of the admittedly incomplete and ambiguous facts is to be found in Chapters 5, 7 and 8 below.

Still more recently, the early pages of Dr Robert Currie's *Methodism Divided* (1968) contain references to Coke which exemplify the unsatisfactory basis of so much that has been written about him. Thus on p. 27 he is content to quote without substantiating evidence the statement of T. P. Bunting that Coke 'never quite dispossessed himself of the notion . . . that he was the true successor of Wesley'. On p. 29 he states that 'Coke, who deplored these concessions [of 1795 and 1797], prevented the insertion of the crucial Plan of Pacification and the Leeds Regulations in the Conference Journal.' It was one thing for Samuel Warren and his followers to accept Coke's complicity in this matter in the heat of the controversy of 1836, but we are now concerned with dispassionate scholarship, not with polemics. The verifiable fact here is that these two items *were* omitted from the Conference Journal; whether by negligence or deliberately (and, if the latter, for what motives) is a matter for dispute. But that Coke had any direct hand in the omission seems at variance with the facts that (*a*) it was he who took the initiative in drafting what was in due course adopted by the Conference as the Plan of Pacification, and (*b*) at the Conference of 1797, far from 'deploring these concessions', it was he who proposed, unsuccessfully, that Circuit Stewards should be admitted to the District Meeting. Finally, we are told (p. 32) that in 1804 Coke 'may have exiled' Bunting to the provinces 'for his temerity' in sorting out the missionary accounts, and that in 1813 the Missionary affairs were 'still languishing under Coke'. The evidence that this is a serious misreading of the facts is, I hope, writ large in the later pages of this book and need not be repeated here.

I have tried to spare my successors the chore of hunting down the sources of information about Coke by quoting extensively from my

sources and by giving the fullest possible documentation. For this
I make no apology to those who prefer their history at secondhand
or are irritated by footnotes. (It may discourage them from skipping
if I mention that the very few jokes in an otherwise dull book are
mostly in the footnotes.) Where I have drawn on printed material
such as the early *Lives* of Crowther, Sutcliffe and Drew to fill gaps
in the primary sources, this is indicated in the footnotes.

Publication of the Lecture has been so long delayed that at least
one would-be reader suspects me of seeking to emulate one of my
predecessors by repeating it, after a decent interval, as a Fernley-
Hartley Lecture! The delay has a simpler and less sinister explanation in the need for extensive revision of the original draft before it
was fit for publication. I am grateful to the Epworth and Abingdon
Presses for their readiness to consider a full-scale biography instead
of the usual monograph. For helpful advice and criticism (not
always heeded) in this lengthy process of revision, I am particularly
grateful to the Rev. Dr Frank Baker, the Rev. Dr F. E. Maser and
my former colleague Mr G. R. Steel.

One of the pleasantest aspects of writing such a book as this is
that it puts the author in the debt of so many knowledgeable and
helpful people. It is a pleasure to acknowledge in particular the
encouragement and help received from the following: Miss Joan
M. Anderson; the Rev. Dr J. Hamby Barton Jr.; the Rev. Dr John
C. Bowmer; the Rev. R. Lee Cole; Prof. D. J. Davies; Mr
Christopher Fyfe; the Rev. A. Raymond George; Mrs Irving E.
Gray; Mr W. A. Green; Mr and Mrs Arthur Hill; the Rev. R. T.
Jenkins; the Rev. J. Jones-Davies; the Rev. George Lawton; Mr
Idwal Lewis; the Rev. Dr Arthur Bruce Moss; the Rev. W. Stanley
Rose; the Rev. Dr W. Thomas Smith; Mr A. F. Walls; Mrs John
H. Warnick; Mr A. H. Williams; and the Rev. Max W. Woodward.

Permission to quote from manuscripts has been given by: the
Methodist Archives and Research Centre, London; the Archives of
the Methodist Missionary Society; Wesley's Chapel, London; the
Library of the Wesley Historical Society; the New Room, Bristol;
Wantage Methodist Church; Wesley College, Headingley; the
British Museum; the Public Record Office; the National Library of
Wales; the London Missionary Society; Mr T. H. C. Squance;
World Methodist Headquarters, Lake Junaluska; Baltimore
Methodist Historical Society; the New England Methodist
Historical Society; the Historical Society of Pennsylvania; Rose

Memorial Library, Drew University; Emory University; Garrett Theological Seminary; Bridwell Library, Southern Methodist University; and Duke University Library. The location of unpublished records, particularly letters, is given in brackets in the footnotes.

Finally I would record my gratitude to the Rev. G. Thackray Eddy, now General Secretary of the Methodist Missionary Society, who honoured and delighted me by taking the chair at the Conference Lecture; to my wife, whose valiant assistance in typing, retyping and proof-reading at least excuses her from any obligation to read it through yet again; and to Mr A. Curwen whose maps embellish the endpapers.

PROLOGUE

On the evening of 13th August, 1776, in the pleasant but undramatic setting of the Somersetshire village of Kingston St Mary, occurred the first meeting between two men, John Wesley and Thomas Coke, which was to have far-reaching consequences for the history of Methodism. Wesley was now an ageing, though still active, man of seventy-three who had asserted in his *Journal* earlier that summer that he was now 'far abler to preach than . . . at three and twenty'. Be that as it may, he was increasingly concerned for the fate of the Methodist Connexion after his death. He had hoped that John Fletcher, the vicar of Madeley, might prove a suitable successor, but Fletcher was already a sick man, as Wesley found when he met him in Bristol just after the Conference. It was the very next day that Wesley rode on to Taunton and, after preaching in the town, accompanied the Rev. James Brown to the 'large, old parsonage-house . . . pleasantly situated close to the churchyard' at Kingston St Mary. 'Here', his *Journal* records, 'I found a clergyman, Dr Coke, late Gentleman Commoner of Jesus College in Oxford, who came twenty miles on purpose.'

For once 'the time and the place and the loved one' had come together. Mr Wesley's Connexion was moving steadily towards that established respectability which was to mark the Wesleyanism of the early nineteenth century. There were plans to build a new chapel in London to replace the old Foundery, and already the first thousand pounds had been subscribed. Almost the only cloud that overhung the Conference of that year was the anxiety felt for the rapidly developing work in America. It was three years since the famous incident in Boston harbour. The revolt to which this gave rise was proving a serious embarrassment to the Methodist preachers in the colonies there, and the final day of the Conference was devoted to fasting and prayer 'as well for our own nation as for our brethren in America'.[1]

Thomas Coke was the man to match this hour. He had been reading

[1] *Journal of John Wesley*, vi. 98, 117–19.

some of the works of Wesley and Fletcher lent to him by James Brown, and rode over from his parish of South Petherton on hearing that Wesley was in the neighbourhood. The two men had 'much conversation' together and Wesley summed up their meeting in words that are scarcely less prophetic for having been penned several years later: 'A union then began which I trust shall never end.'[1] Before long the younger man was to throw in his lot with the Methodists and to become not only the right-hand man Wesley had long been seeking, but also joint-superintendent with Asbury of the Methodist Episcopal Church in America, a leader of British Methodism in the formative years after Wesley's death, and the pioneer of its missionary work, both at home and overseas.

Yet the figure of Thomas Coke has suffered neglect: in America, because of the overshadowing presence of Francis Asbury; and in England, because our minds tend to leap from the age of Wesley to that of Jabez Bunting. In the words of Cyril Davey at the time of the Bicentenary in 1947: 'No man in Methodism had a greater significance for his own age, for Methodism, and for the Missionary movement, than Thomas Coke. No man, deserving to be remembered, has been more completely forgotten.'[2]

[1] Ibid., pp. 119f.   [2] C. J. Davey, in *L.Q.R.*, July 1947.

CHAPTER I

EARLY YEARS: BRECON AND OXFORD

Thomas Coke was born on 28th September 1747 (O.S.),[1] the third but only surviving son of Bartholomew and Anne Coke of Brecon. Just six months before this, his parents had buried their three-year-old firstborn son, named after his father; while a second son, John, baptized in November 1745, had survived only a few days. This no doubt explains why they hastened to baptize their third son when only a week old, and why he was cherished as the one ewe-lamb of parents who were no longer young.

Of his maternal ancestry we know very little, beyond the fact that Anne Coke was the daughter of Thomas Phillips of Trosdre, Cantref. She was remembered as 'a plain, motherly woman, well suited to promote the comfort of her husband'.[2] Bartholomew Coke was descended from a Henry Cooke of Gwern y Fuwch, Radnorshire, whose son Edward and grandson Jeffrey had each held the living of Llanfrynach near Brecon.[3] The Rev. Edward Cooke had a son of the same name, to the confusion of later students of the family; and he in turn was the father of Bartholomew and grandfather of the Thomas Coke with whom we are immediately concerned.[4]

---

[1] Considerable confusion has arisen over this date. Some writers, following Coke himself (*Journal*, p. 184), have given it as 9th October; others, influenced by the fact that the baptismal entry at St Mary's, Brecon, is dated 5th October, have concluded that Coke made an error of a month and suggest 9th *September*. It is more natural to assume that in later life Coke observed his birthday on 9th October (N.S.) i.e. 28th September (O.S.).

[2] Etheridge, p. 5, quoting a witness who had known her.

[3] None of the printed sources is reliable on this matter of Coke's ancestry. A double confusion has arisen, between the two Edwards, father and son, and between the two members of the family who were rectors of Llanfrynach. For a more detailed survey of the available evidence, see my article in *Brycheiniog*, 1964.

[4] The spelling 'Coke' superseded the earlier form about the beginning of the eighteenth century, but the pronunciation was unaffected. Hence the spelling 'Cook(e)' occurs several times in connexion with Thomas Coke, even in his later years, and Charles Wesley invariably rhymes the name with such words as 'took' and 'forsook'.

Bartholomew Coke was an apothecary who, at a time when the medical profession was both less skilled and less highly organized than it is today, did not confine himself to the dispensing of prescribed medicines, but gained a considerable reputation for his medical skill throughout the neighbourhood. Though not the 'eminent surgeon' of Samuel Drew's description,[1] he certainly deserved the more sober tribute engraved by his son on his memorial tablet, which states that 'his great medical knowledge was well known in this county so that very rarely did anyone under his care employ a physician'. Among his clients he numbered the Gwynne family of Garth, and Howell Harris at Trevecca, although neither of these associations seems to have provoked any Methodist leanings in him: as befits so public a figure, everything points to his having remained a staunch churchman to the end.

Even before his early retirement from business, Bartholomew Coke found time to play a very active part in public life. He was for many years a Common Councilman of the borough, and was elected bailiff (i.e. mayor) in 1737 and again in 1758, having served meanwhile as alderman.[2]

Thomas Coke, as warm-hearted in boyhood as he was in later life, had a deep affection for his parents, though he spoke of them only on rare occasions. From Bartholomew he inherited a life-long interest in medicine, a profession which he was not, however, to adopt.[3] In the memorial inscription he describes his father as 'a man of most amiable temper, and . . . beloved of all who knew him', and mentions in particular 'his great benevolence, generosity and hospitality'.[4] These were characteristics which can certainly be traced in the son. Years later, in a letter to one of the Methodist preachers, John Burdsall, who had withdrawn his offer to go as a missionary to Bermuda because of paternal opposition, Coke wrote: 'I assure you, I . . . can in some degree enter into the feelings of a son and a father.

[1] Drew, p. 3; cf F. D. Leete, *Methodist Bishops*, p. 47, where Coke's father becomes 'an eminent surgeon . . . who died early'. (Bartholomew was, in fact, 72 when he died in May 1773.)

[2] T. Jones, *History of Brecknockshire* (4th edn.), iv. 307; E. Poole, *History of Brecknockshire*, p. 371.

[3] When the London Electrical Dispensary was instituted in 1793, Thomas Coke became one of its first vice-presidents. (*W.H.S. Proc.* xxvii. 24). See also his *Journal*, pp. 162, 169, 238; and letter to John Holloway, 25th March 1812 (copy among the Deaville Walker papers, M.M.S. Archives).

[4] Memorial tablet in the Coke Memorial Church, Brecon.

I once had a father, the tenderest parent, methinks, that ever lived!
I could not have found it in my heart to grieve him, unless duty to
God bound me so to do, in the clearest and most coercive manner.'[1]
It was perhaps as well that Bartholomew died in 1773, while his son
was still a faithful, if unusually zealous, parish priest. Although Anne
Coke had little difficulty in accepting her son's defection to Metho-
dism, it might have been a very different matter with the worthy
Bartholomew.

The Brecon of Thomas Coke's boyhood was a bustling centre of
provincial life, which had been described in 1720 as 'the richest town
in Wales'.[2] The coming of the railway and the development of South
Wales industry had not yet diverted both traffic and wealth to
Cardiff, which in the second half of the century still had a population of only 2,000 compared with Brecon's 2,700. Lying on the busy
post-road from London to Carmarthen, Brecon was important in a
variety of ways. Until 1885, the borough returned its own M.P. As
the centre of a rich agricultural area, which Wesley once said could
compare with any in all England 'for fields, meadows, woods, brooks,
and gently rising mountains, fruitful to the very top',[3] it had two
weekly markets in addition to the annual fairs. Its Agricultural
Society, established in 1755, was the first in Wales. Wilkins's Brecon
Old Bank played a vital part in financing the early development of the
South Wales iron industry. Besides the Quarter Sessions, there were
the Great Sessions, or Assizes, which were held twice a year in the
town. The lawyers and financiers had their spacious houses, and
many of the county gentry had town-houses there. Social occasions
abounded for those privileged to share in them. The theatre flourished: we remember that in 1755, a child who was to become famous
as Sarah Siddons was born in the *Shoulder of Mutton* inn, almost
next door to the Cokes' home, while her father's company was play-
ing in the town.

Although not yet a cathedral town, Brecon had also a strong
ecclesiastical element in its population. There was the College of

---

[1] Quoted, without date, in Lyth, *Glimpses of Early Methodism in York*, 1885,
p. 174. Many years later, Coke told Andrew Hamilton that the news of his
father's death so overwhelmed him that he was unable to weep until, travelling
homeward by night, he heard a nightingale's song and his pent-up grief was
released (*The Faithful Servant*, p. 26).

[2] For this paragraph, I am indebted to an article on John Hughes by R. T.
Jenkins, in *Brycheiniog*, Vol. viii, 67ff.

[3] *Journal of John Wesley*, v. 25 (20th August 1763).

Christ, a collegium of non-resident prebendaries, from which the present grammar school derives. It was to Christ College, early in the headmastership of the Rev. David Griffith, that Thomas Coke went for the earliest part of his formal education. One of his schoolfellows, a month or two younger than himself, was Walter Churchey. Churchey too was to become a Methodist, though unlike Coke he never strayed far from home; and their friendship was maintained, largely through spasmodic correspondence, for many years.[1]

Some reflections on his own education may be gleaned from the sermon Coke preached on Education while at South Petherton.[2] Asserting that there was no reason why boys should be confined to the study of the Greeks and Romans, he said, 'It is far from my intention to decry the best of the Classick-writers, they are excellent in their way, and very proper for the instruction of youth'. But he spoke, with obvious feeling, of having to translate into Latin or Greek 'an expedition of Alexander the Great or a lewd story of the heathen gods and goddesses', asserting that many schoolmasters 'regard nothing but the elegance of the language, and are as well pleased to hear their boys translate the lewd odes of Anacreon (which tend only to teach them drunkenness and debauchery,) as the moral writings of Plato or Cicero'. At the same time he allowed the value of moral examples taken from 'profane writers, particularly historians', provided they were prudently chosen.[3] Though it would clearly be unfair to form any judgement on David Griffith from these words, Coke is certainly drawing on memories of his own still recent schooldays.

The England of Thomas Coke's youth was busy extending its dominion in India and in North America, at the expense of the French. He had scarcely attained years of comprehension when the news of Robert Clive's successful defence of Arcot in 1751 came through; but by the time Plassey was fought, he was ten years old and able to appreciate such heroism. The Seven Years' War, begun in 1756, had

[1] In a letter to Churchey, quoted in Etheridge, p. 72, Coke refers to him as 'my dear old schoolfellow'. By profession an attorney, Churchey lived much of his life at Hay. He wrote, and published, a good deal of indifferent poetry, and claimed a part in having suggested the idea of the *Arminian Magazine*. Towards the end of his life he became an ardent millenarian. (*D.N.B.*; *Dictionary of Welsh Biography*; Tyerman, *John Wesley*, iii. 579.)

[2] Preached at Crewkerne, 14th September, 1773, and published early in 1774, this was Coke's first venture into print.

[3] Ibid., pp. 15-17.

brought the elder Pitt to power. Britain found herself in Protestant alliance with the Prussia of Frederick the Great against France, Russia, Austria and others. As a counterpart to Clive's victories in the East, the French stranglehold in America was being broken. The defeat of General Braddock's expedition in 1755 was avenged by successive victories at Louisburg and Quebec in 1758–9, and the defeat of the French navy at Quiberon. The reports of these events would stir the schoolboy patriotism and hero-worship of Thomas Coke and Walter Churchey as they explored the Breconshire mountains together and fished in the waters of the Usk. When George III came to the throne in 1760, it seemed certain that British sovereignty was as firmly established in the West as in the East. There was as yet no warning hint of revolt among the American colonies, or of the revolution in France with all its repercussions. But the storm was to break soon enough.

At the Brecon Assizes in 1744 it was stated that the Methodists were a threat to 'the peace of our sovereign Lord the King', and that 'unless their proceedings are timely suppressed, they may endanger the peace of the kingdom in general'.[1] The reference is probably to the Calvinistic Methodism of Howell Harris. At the time of Thomas Coke's birth, there may not have been a single follower of Wesley in Brecon. Within six months, however, in February 1748, John Wesley passed through the town, travelling through deep snow to visit Garth with his brother Charles.[2] A year later, he passed that way again to his brother's wedding, but he does not seem to have preached in Brecon until March 1756. 'The town-hall, in which I was desired to preach, is a large and commodious place,' he wrote, 'and the whole congregation (one poor gentleman excepted) behaved with seriousness and decency.' After visiting Howell Harris at Trevecca, he decided to stay a day or two longer in Brecon, before going on to Holyhead. There was a gathering of the Justices and Commissioners in the town, 'and curiosity (if no better motive) brought most of the gentlemen to the preaching. Such another opportunity could not have been of speaking to all the rich and great of the county; and they all appeared to be serious and attentive. Perhaps one or two,' he added characteristically, 'may lay it to heart.'[3] By this time a Methodist

---

[1] *W.H.S. Proc.*, xxxiii. 95; cf R. F. Wearmouth, *Methodism and the Common People*, 1945, pp. 250f.

[2] *Journal of John Wesley*, iii. 333 (17th February 1748).

[3] Ibid., iv. 152 (18–20th March 1756).

society, probably the result of Charles Wesley's visits to the neighbourhood, already existed in the town.[1] No doubt Bartholomew Coke was among Wesley's hearers. Whether Thomas, now eight years old, was with him we cannot be certain; but there is little doubt that he would be among the crowd who heard Wesley preach on his next visit, seven years later. This time the Town Hall was not available because of the Assizes, so he preached 'at Mr James's door' and next day near the market-place.[2] This was in August 1763, and Thomas Coke was within a year of going up to Oxford.

Through his father Thomas would have free entry into the provincial, but none the less urbane, society life of Brecon. In this respect, his social and cultural background was very different from that of the great majority of the Methodist people and preachers, with whom he was eventually to cast his lot. The sincere, but narrow, piety of his early biographers was readily shocked by his manner of life from his youth up. Samuel Drew, for example, probably drawing on Coke's own recollections, speaks of 'the frivolities incident to youth' and his attachment to 'the prevailing amusements'. This, says Drew, 'exposed him to much company; and as he was peculiarly handsome, he became an object of admiration among the thoughtless and the gay, and was a singular favourite among his female associates, to whose charms his heart was by no means insensible'.[3] Which is to say no more than that in his teens Thomas Coke was 'a bit of a lad', with an eye for the girls, whose enjoyment of high life was likely to shock no one who has not entirely forgotten the days of his own youth. He was a warm-hearted, friendly person, witty in conversation, his broad features made attractive by the eager eyes and ready smile, despite a stocky figure that was later to turn to portliness. Given an average run of luck, he might easily have settled down as a respectable and respected dignitary of the Church. And no doubt it

[1] T. Wynne Jones, *Wesleyan Methodism in Brecon Circuit*, pp. 33f. The society met at first in the homes of William Gilbert and Thomas James. The first chapel was built in 1770 on the corner of Little Free Street, on a site given by Gilbert. (But cf John Prickard, in *E.M.P.* iv. 178f., who implies that the chapel had been built some time before 1770.) It was at first used for both English and Welsh services.

[2] *Journal of John Wesley*, v. 25 (18–19th August 1763).

[3] Drew, pp. 4f. The same writer hastens to relieve this picture of incipient debauchery by telling how Coke's sense of divine providence was strengthened by his being saved from danger, once when crossing a river, and again after accidentally swallowing a sixpence!

did his father's heart good to watch his son growing up so auspiciously.

Though his incessant travelling in later years prevented Coke from frequently revisiting his birthplace,[1] he retained to the end a special affection for his native land—'my Wales' as he called it in a letter towards the end of his life.[2] He himself, like most others in the upper levels of society in Brecon at that time, spoke no more Welsh than would enable him to announce, parrot-wise, one verse of the hymn 'Come, let us join our cheerful songs', and to repeat the traditional words at the distribution of the elements at the Lord's Supper.[3] But this did not prevent his realizing the urgent need for Welsh-speaking missions which, in due course, he was to advocate with an undisguised warmth. On his later journeyings, particularly in the West Indies and America, he must often have carried with him memories of his boyhood exploration of his native mountains, and occasionally these find their way into his printed *Journals*. During his first visit to America the mountains of Virginia brought the memories crowding back. 'I prefer this country to any in America,' he wrote. 'It is so like Wales, my native country.' Passing through St Anne's parish, Jamaica, in 1790, he admired the wide, fertile plain lying between the mountains and the sea, as 'more like the vale of *Glamorgan*, in *Wales*, than any other place I can recollect'; and a little later, we find him comparing the rugged mountains near Spanish Town to the cliffs at Dover and Penmaenmawr.[4]

On 6th April, 1764, Thomas Coke entered Jesus College, Oxford, as a gentleman commoner. He was sixteen years old, but this was not

[1] After his return from America in 1789, he preached a missionary sermon in the old Town Hall on his favourite text, Psalm 68:31; this deeply impressed John Hughes, then still a schoolboy. (A. H. Williams, *Welsh Wesleyan Methodism*, p. 88.) Poole, op. cit., p. 373, records an amusing anecdote of one of his visits to the town. Coke was the guest of Squire Meredith in the Watton. About to go to the Town Church where he was to preach, his appearance in gown and cassock alarmed the house dog, Lion, who attacked him. Coke took refuge in the wood shed next to the street. 'The late Miss Matthews, who lived opposite, hearing an appealing voice calling "Miss! Miss!" crossed to the shed, through the trellis work of which she saw the imprisoned doctor. He meekly explained his situation, and besought her protection from the enemy . . . and soon the anxious doctor, whose cassock was literally saturated with the perspiration which had poured down his face in his fright, hurried away to his preaching appointment.'

[2] Letter to Robert Johnson, 22nd September 1808 (M.M.S.).

[3] John Hughes, in *Wesleyan Methodist Magazine*, 1832, p. 541.

[4] Coke's *Journal*, pp. 70, 154, 155.

unusually young for Oxford students of that period.[1] The Oxford to which he came was still largely contained within its medieval walls and gates, and hemmed in by water-meadows. Though considerably better than it has frequently been painted, it was not, at this time, notable for either its high morality or its academic standards. In neither respect had there been much improvement since the Wesley brothers were in residence. There was little serious concern either to teach or to learn, and examinations were non-existent or quite inadequate. Many of the youthful undergraduates, particularly the gentlemen commoners, released from the restrictions of home and school life, gave themselves more to the enjoyment of their newly-found freedom than to any sustained academic pursuits.[2]

The moral condition of the university had improved to some extent since the disastrous effect of the residence of Charles II and the Court, when London was visited by the plague a century earlier. But this improvement was, at best, a relative one. Wesley's scathing castigation of the Oxford of 1744 in the 'plain, practical application' of his sermon on 'Scriptural Christianity'—the last he was permitted to preach in St Mary's Church—had aroused little response beyond the immediate indignation of those to whom the truth was unpalatable. Coming up in 1751, Edward Gibbon found himself a member of a venerable body which, he said, was 'sufficiently old to partake of all the prejudices and infirmities of age', and the period he spent there he dismisses as 'the most idle and unprofitable of my whole life'. Just twenty years later, a writer who knew both Oxford and Cambridge declared that the opportunities for vice were such that it was 'next to an impossibility for lively young men to resist the temptation'. And Thomas Coke was undoubtedly a 'lively young man'.

In religious matters, Oxford was still marked by an intense loyalty to the King and the Established Church. Dissenters were rigidly excluded, and recollections of the abhorrent 'reign of the saints' during the Commonwealth period still aroused violent hostility to the least suggestion of enthusiasm or methodistical leanings. The original Holy Club had not long survived the departure of the Wesleys for Georgia in 1735. In the early years of the revival

[1] Entry in the Battel book of Jesus College. The entry in the University Register of Admissions is dated 11th April. Cf J. S. Simon, *John Wesley & The Religious Societies*, 1921, p. 69.

[2] A. D. Godley, *Oxford in the 18th Century*; V. H. H. Green, *The Young Mr. Wesley*, esp. Ch. 2.

Wesley preached in the town a number of times, but after 1751, when he resigned his Lincoln College fellowship, his visits became infrequent. By the time Thomas Coke came up in 1764, a fresh wave of 'enthusiasm' had led to the formation of a 'second Holy Club' under the leadership of Thomas Haweis and James Stillingfleet. Its members were Calvinistic Methodists who 'met regularly to read the Greek Testament, discuss theology, share their Christian experience, and join in prayers'.[1] Though they continued to do so through most of Coke's time at Oxford, we have no evidence that he had any personal contact with any of this group. Certainly, he would follow with interest, if with little sympathy, the events in March 1768, when six of them, students of St Edmund Hall, were expelled from the University for holding 'Methodistical principles' and attending 'illicit conventicles' in private houses. Thomas Coke's sympathies were no doubt with the authorities, the more so since he had by then become an earnest Churchman who was probably already contemplating Holy Orders.

Jesus College, founded in 1571 by Dr Hugh Ap Rice primarily for his fellow Welshmen, had been described earlier in the eighteenth century as the college where 'everyone is a gentleman born'.[2] Among its former members it boasted Beau Nash. The Coke family already had a link with the college through Thomas's uncle, John Coke of Llanfrynach, who had matriculated there in 1723, at the age of 19, though he does not seem to have graduated.[3] Thomas, on the other hand, was to obtain his B.A. on 4th February 1768, become a Fellow Commoner the following day, and proceed to his M.A. on 15th June 1770. Subsequently he also succeeded in obtaining a doctorate in Civil Law.

Of Coke's academic studies we know almost nothing except by surmise. In later life he had at least enough Greek to read his Greek Testament and the Septuagint; but it is difficult to determine how far his knowledge of the Hebrew Old Testament depended on other commentators. Latin he read with sufficient fluency to enable him to enjoy Virgil on his first voyage to America. Modern languages, however, had not then attained their present academic status, and he does not appear to have begun to learn French until his voyage out in

[1] A. Skevington Wood, in *W.H.S. Proc.* xxix. 73.

[2] Godley, op. cit., p. 196.

[3] Foster, *Alumni Oxonienses*. John Coke's father is given as Edward, i.e. Edward Coke junr. John was thus a younger brother of Bartholomew.

1786.[1] Among the English poets, Milton and Spenser seem to have been his favourites;[2] if it were safe to argue from silence, we might assume that his acquaintance with Shakespeare was confined to Portia's speech on the quality of mercy![3] Beyond this, we have to fall back on a single reminiscence recorded by Andrew Hamilton: 'In the sciences he particularly delighted. [This is to some extent borne out by the alert observation of natural phenomena in the *Journals* of his travels.] I recollect hearing him tell a very pleasing anecdote, concerning his love for mathematics, during his residence at College. Having had a problem of more than ordinary difficulty under consideration, he found his mind for a long time greatly exercised: at last, in the happy moment, he saw the solution of the problem, and for joy got up and danced about his room, crying out with the celebrated Greek philosopher on a nearly similar occasion, εὕρηκα, εὕρηκα, i.e. *I have found it, I have found it.*'[4]

The social life into which Coke was immediately flung by virtue of his being a Gentleman Commoner was quite as gay as that of Brecon, but far less restrained by custom or parental oversight. He found that, as Gibbon says, the velvet cap which, with the silk gown, distinguished a gentleman commoner from 'a plebeian student', was a 'cap of liberty', freeing him from the duties and discipline imposed upon the 'poor scholars'. 'He fell an easy prey to the fashionable follies', says Drew, instancing such card games as whist and quadrille; but, he hastens to add, neither gambling nor drinking were indulged in to excess. His natural sociability and an unwillingness to differ from the majority inclined him to enjoy to the full the pleasures of his new environment.[5] We remember how, forty years before, the young John Wesley, even after he had begun to order his life methodistically, found the time and inclination for a game of cards or backgammon, for dancing and the social life of the coffee house. Coke was young and inexperienced enough to have fallen from grace; but he does not seem to have gone seriously astray. For

---

[1] Coke's *Journal*, p. 80; cf letter to Arthur Keene of Dublin, 6th June 1786 (Marriott MSS, copy via Dr Frank Baker), in which he speaks of profiting 'from the kind instruction of sister Ward during my few days residence in Cork'.

[2] Ibid., pp. 157, 80. Of Spenser, the 'English Virgil', he says: 'His genius and strength of imagination were amazing; and from his allegories may be extracted some of the most instructive lessons of religion'.

[3] Letter to Joseph Entwisle, 29th October 1804 (M.M.S.); cf letter to the Missionary Committee, 2nd December 1807 (M.M.S.).

[4] Hamilton, op. cit., p. 14.   [5] Drew, p. 7.

a time he enjoyed the company of 'the young Bucks and Bloods of the town',[1] but his nature was soon repelled by their open debauchery. His early upbringing and religious beliefs, wholly inadequate as they may have appeared from an evangelical standpoint,[2] were sufficient to keep him from any gross immorality, though he came perilously near it on one occasion when persuaded to go with some of his fellow students to a brothel in the town. 'But here', says his early biographer, 'the blushing modesty of an unspotted youth, the remains of the law written on the heart, and a God in whom he scarcely believed, shook him on the precipice, and withheld him from sin.'[3]

The Methodist Coke of later years did not look back on his student days with as much antipathy as did his biographers. True, he took little pride or pleasure in recollecting the worldly delights in which he had for a time indulged. (Though in Barbados in 1792, when he unexpectedly renewed acquaintance with an old friend of his Oxford days, a Mr Henry, they spent the greater part of two days together, 'repeating old adventures'.)[4] No doubt he had his own adolescence in mind when he told his South Petherton flock, in a sermon on the Parable of the Sower, that 'the soul finds no comfort in reflecting on a life spent in a round of sensual pleasures and carnal satisfactions: in the end it is all a bubble, vanity of vanities: the glass breaks, and the giddy meteors all perish . . . Tho' they leave no sweetness, yet they leave much gall in the cup.'[5] For Oxford itself on the other hand, he retained a grateful affection. In the sermon he

[1] Coke's *Journal*, p. 160.

[2] Looking back in 1773, he said of the neglect of religious and moral training in the public schools of his day, that many pupils, 'before they have arrived at the age of sixteen or seventeen, have been perfect masters of the vile arts of debauchery, drunkenness, and almost every kind of immorality. One would think', he adds, 'their masters looked upon Heaven and Hell as only old women's tales, or that the knowledge of Latin and Greek were sufficient to secure their everlasting salvation.' (*Sermon upon Education*, pp. 23f.)

[3] The incident is given by Sutcliffe (Coke's *Journal*, p. 5) as related by Coke himself. Sutcliffe's phrase is 'a house which of all others he ought to have shunned'. Etheridge, whose account of these years makes up in verbosity what it lacks in factual detail, records that Coke told a friend in after years that 'at the midnight revel . . . he frequently witnessed scenes of depravity which were not to be described' (Etheridge, p. 11).

[4] Coke's *Journal*, p. 204. The reference is probably to Ellis Henry of Wrexham, who took his B.A. in 1763 at Brasenose (*Alumni Oxonienses*).

[5] MS sermon on Luke 8:15, (Wesley's Chapel).

preached in America in 1791 on the death of John Wesley, he emphasized, none too tactfully, all that Wesley had sacrificed in abandoning Oxford for Georgia in 1735. There is little doubt where his own inclinations lay. 'Those who are acquainted (as I have been)', he said, 'with the difference between one of the most elegant Universities in the world, and a country just laid out for colonization,—between the varieties and luxuries of life in the former instance, and the vast simplicity of living in the latter:—and above all, between a converse with some of the first Literati in the world, and in general with men of very improved understandings, on the one hand; and only with a few honest planters, living within a mile or two's distance of each other, in the midst of immeasurable forests, on the other,—will estimate the sacrifice made by Mr Wesley in the present case as not inconsiderable.'[1]

Early in his undergraduate career, Coke came under the influence of the prevalent deist philosophy, which rejected the supernatural element in Christianity, casting doubts on the authority of Scripture and the validity of revelation. In this he was not helped by his tutor, who according to Henry Moore was a drunken cynic. '"Eh! Coke," he would say, as well as he could, "do you believe the Adam and Eve story, eh?" And thus get rid of the Bible with a foolborn jest.'[2] By way of contrast, William Newcome, fellow of Hertford College until his removal to Ireland in 1766, was a tutor who stood out among his contemporaries for integrity and learning, and Coke long cherished the memory of his acquaintance with this 'man of a very amiable disposition and of great learning'.[3] Thirty years before, Bishop Butler had attacked the deist position in his *Analogy of Religion*; but it was through a humbler work, now virtually forgotten but then enjoying a popularity that was maintained through numerous editions into the nineteenth century, that Coke was brought back to more orthodox beliefs. This was Bishop Sherlock's *Trial of the Witnesses of Jesus*, 'a highly characteristic apologetic writing of its

---

[1] *Sermon on the Death of John Wesley*, pp. 9f.

[2] H. Moore, *Life of Wesley*, ii. 308.

[3] Coke's *Journal*, p. 257. In 1797 Coke visited the Archbishop's palace at Armagh and spoke highly of Newcome's commentary on the Minor Prophets. William Newcome, 1727–1800, became fellow of Hertford in 1753. In 1766 he was appointed chaplain to the Earl of Hertford, who had just become Lord Lieutenant of Ireland. His elevation to the Primacy was 'the reward of character, principles and erudition'. His biblical studies were mainly exegetical, and directed particularly at the revision of the A.V. (D.N.B.).

age'. Since[1] it dealt persuasively with an issue which was crucial for his views on miracles, the life after death and the authority of Scripture, Coke's reading of this book weaned him completely from his addiction to Deism. Henceforth, its standpoint was as abhorrent to him as was Calvinism itself. It was the deists whom he no doubt had in mind when he referred in a sermon at South Petherton to 'the atheistic crew', characterizing them as 'a set of men, in this prophane age, who endeavour to jeer all devotion out of the world, making the whole business of the returns and answer of prayer, . . . a mere piece of fancy, the effect of an over-heated brain, attributing all the events which come either upon the good or upon the bad, either to chance or necessity, or mechanical powers as blind as that'.[2] The vigour of his attack certainly owed something to the nearness of his own approach to the abyss. Years later, in 1796, his deist phase was unexpectedly to stand him in good stead. Striving to reach Baltimore in time for the General Conference, he found himself on the St Mary's River, in a sloop with two companions who 'had embraced the opinions of *Thomas Payne*, and the other modern Infidels'. 'Having been once a Deist myself, (O what a Miracle of Grace now!) I perhaps was better qualified on that account to meet their various arguments . . . Indeed they seemed to be candid inquirers after Truth: but whether my arguments were sufficient to proselyte them, or not, I cannot say.'[3] It is significant that his sermon on the Godhead of Christ preached at the first General Conference in Baltimore, was more frequently preached and published than any other, and that he was quick to suspect other preachers of heresy on this point.[4]

The intellectual conversion brought about by reading Bishop Sherlock did not lead immediately to a personal renewal of faith. He was as yet only a 'theoretical believer'. As with John Wesley, a long pilgrimage lay before him, which would be far from over when he took Holy Orders. The next step forward came when he read Witherspoon's treatise on Regeneration: then the 'stranger to the religion of the heart' realized that if he was to see the kingdom of God he must be born again.[5] However spasmodically, the search had begun, though

[1] O.D.C.C., article on Thomas Sherlock. *The Trial of the Witnesses of Jesus*, 1729, went into a fifteenth edition in 1794, and continued to be reprinted in the nineteenth century.

[2] MS sermon on Prayer; text, Philippians 4:6.

[3] Coke's *Journal*, p. 226; cf p. 243.   [4] See below, p. 44 and Bibliography.

[5] John Witherspoon, 1723–94; Presbyterian divine and statesman; principal of Princeton College, N.J., 1768. His *Essay on the Connection between the Doctrine*

he was still very far from anything that would be recognized, in Methodist circles, as an experience of conversion.

After becoming a Fellow Commoner in 1768, Coke probably spent most of his time at home in Brecon. Though barely twenty-one, he was already beginning to follow in his father's footsteps: on 24th September 1769, he was elected burgess of the borough and a member of the Common Council, in place of Thomas Morgan deceased.[1] He accordingly took the Oaths of Allegiance and Supremacy, and attended his first Council meeting on 3rd October. It may be an indication of the esteem in which his father was held in the town that only a year later, in September 1770, at the age of twenty-three, Thomas was elected Bailiff for the ensuing year.[2] By this time he had been ordained deacon, and a new phase in his life was beginning.

---

of Justification by the imputed Righteousness of Christ and Holiness of Life (1756) was frequently reprinted.

[1] Minutes of the Common Council, at the Town Clerk's Office, Brecon.

[2] Council minutes, 24th September 1770. The title of Bailiff was altered to that of Mayor under the Municipal Reform Act of 1835.

CHAPTER 2

SOUTH PETHERTON

On Trinity Sunday, 1770, Thomas Coke was ordained deacon by the Bishop of Oxford in the Cathedral Church of Christ, five days before proceeding to his M.A. Two years later, on Sunday, 23rd August 1772, he was ordained to the priesthood by the Bishop of St David's, at a General Ordination in the Chapel of St John the Baptist in the Episcopal Palace at Abergwili, near Carmarthen.[1] There is little doubt that at this stage Coke was confident of preferment in the Church through promises made by influential friends.[2] One of these appears to have been the M.P. for Brecon—presumably John Morgan, returned as Member for Brecon Borough on 15th May 1769—who had obtained his seat through the support of the Coke family. Another, variously described as a 'gentleman, still more exalted in rank'[3] and 'a certain Nobleman',[4] was probably Lord North, from whose friendship Coke continued to hope for preferment, at least until he obtained his doctorate in 1775, and perhaps even up to the time he joined the Methodists.[5]

Whatever promises were made to Coke, and whoever may have made them, they came to nothing; and before long we find him setting foot on the lowest rung of the ecclesiastical ladder. He appears to have officiated occasionally at Rode, near Frome, though there is no evidence that he was ever curate there.[6] In due course, though still

[1] The original ordination certificates are in the M.M.S. Archives, and are printed by Etheridge, pp. 427f. Etheridge quotes Coke as saying, 'My examination for deacon's orders in Oxford, and for priest's orders at Abergwilly, were both of them oral. I was examined both times in the Greek Testament, not in the grammatical department. At Oxford I translated a Latin article into English; at Abergwilly an English article into Latin; and at both places was asked some general questions in divinity' (Ibid., p. 22).

[2] Drew, p. 10, refers specifically to a prebendaryship at Worcester.

[3] Drew, p. 10.   [4] Crowther, p. 102.

[5] In his reply to the anonymous *Strictures* of 1785, Coke admits he had been promised 'some Crown-preferment'.

[6] Crowther, p. 103: 'He became curate of Rodd near Bath'. Cf similar statements in the memorial sermons of Samuel Warren and Samuel Woolmer. Later

17

anticipating eventual preferment through his influential acquaintances, he was appointed assistant curate to the Rev. Robert Twyford, vicar of South Petherton, Somerset.

South Petherton was a market-town of rather more than 1,500 souls, once the capital of the West Saxon kingdom. The parish was an extensive one, including several outlying hamlets, the Strattons, Yeobridge, Compton Durville and West Lambrook.

In this part of Somerset, Nonconformity was strong, and many of the Independent congregations trace their origin to the time of the Restoration. Not far to the north lies Sedgemoor, and South Petherton contributed to Monmouth's ill-fated army, three of Judge Jeffreys's victims being hanged in the town. The earliest regular congregation of Dissenters was established in 1688, and the present Congregational Church was an offshoot of this 'Old Meeting', which like so many Independent causes was veering towards Unitarianism. Their 'New Meeting House', in Roundwell Street, was built in 1775, towards the end of Coke's curacy; and in response to an appeal for help, the Countess of Huntingdon sent Richard Herdsman to be their first minister. Herdsman was to prove a man after Coke's own heart as an instigator of the London Missionary Society; but it is doubtful whether he and Coke had any personal dealings at South Petherton, so rigid was Coke's churchmanship even to the end of his curacy.

We know from the Burials Register that Coke had taken up his duties as curate by 14th July 1771, while still in the middle of his year of office in Brecon. No doubt his mayoral duties were light and did not involve more than an occasional ride from Somerset. On 23rd September he was in Brecon, and as bailiff presided over the meeting at which his successor was elected. The Council elected Coke as one of the two aldermen, but on 19th July in the following year he requested leave to resign his office because he was now 'residing abroad'. His name does not recur in the Minutes, although he remained a Common Councillor and was scrupulous in paying his share of the expenses for Corporation dinners for many years.[1]

---

biographers repeat Crowther's statement; but Coke's name does not appear in the parish registers, and in 1770 the curate at Rode was a John Martin. (Deaville Walker papers, in M.M.S. Archives.) Sutcliffe is probably nearer the mark when he says that Coke 'had preached occasionally for his friends, and at Road, near Frome' (p. 7).

[1] He intended submitting his resignation in 1797, in preparation for settling

18

When Coke came to South Petherton, his vicar, the Rev. Robert Twyford, was also new, having taken over earlier in the year from a predecessor who had held the living for thirty-four years. Renovations, and also innovations, were probably both urgently needed and unwelcome in the parish. There was already one curate, a J. N. Thomas who signed the minutes of the Easter Vestry with the vicar in 1771 and 1772, and who reappears later in the story as curate of Shepton Beauchamp, a neighbouring parish.

Twyford disappears into the background after the Easter Vestry in 1773, perhaps because of ill-health. Thenceforth Coke, still in the first flush of youthful enthusiasm, was for practical purposes in charge of the parish, at any rate until the appointment of a new vicar after Twyford's death in 1776. There was as yet no taint of Methodism in him, but he entered eagerly and earnestly upon his parochial duties, with a confidence born of his experience in public affairs at Brecon. It would not have been surprising if there had been an immediate clash between this young newcomer of twenty-three and the stolid Somerset farmers who dominated the church-going section of the South Petherton population. In fact, perhaps because his responsibilities were at first limited, the collision was delayed for several years. Meanwhile he continued faithful in his parochial duties, including some that were widely neglected by the parish clergy of his day, and gave long hours to his intensive studies, often working on his sermons far into the night.[1] There is no direct evidence of the effect which his labours had on the parish during this early part of his ministry. The nearest we can get is in the sermons which he preached at the time, a few of which have survived.[2] At this time he read his

---

in America (letter to Thomas Williams, 5th April 1797 [M.M.S. Archives]); but a year later was requesting Williams to pay his quota of 'the Subscription which the Corporation of Brecon subscribed for the defence of our King and Country' (letter of 5th May, 1798 [Wesley's Chapel, London]). In 1801 he was still paying his 'usual fees at dinners, &c. in the Corporation' through Williams (letter of 10th March 1801 [Wesley's Chapel, London]; cf another of 1st May 1802 [Duke University, Durham N.C.]).

[1] T. Roberts, *The Burning and Shining Light*, p. 13.
[2] Three MS sermons are in the M.M.S. Archives:
1. On Matthew 7:24.
2. On Luke 15:17–18, dated 6th September 1772.
3. On Proverbs 3:17.
Two are in the Lamplough Collection, Methodist Archives and Research Centre:
4. On Philippians 4:6. Endorsed: 'Sermon by Dr Coke when at South

sermons from a manuscript, and did not scruple, we are told, to make use of choice passages from the pen of others when these suited his purpose. Despite this, it is hard to believe that some of the fiery eloquence of his Welsh ancestry did not at times break through, to the edification or consternation of his parishioners.

Those sermons which have survived, though a random selection which cannot all be exactly dated, are probably typical of his earliest preaching. While there is little that could be labelled evangelical and no appeal to personal experience, they have a whole-hearted earnestness which must have embarrassed some of the more complacent or casual of his congregation. A good example of the kind of moral exhortation which characterizes all these sermons is that on Proverbs 3:17, 'Her ways are ways of pleasantness, and all her paths are peace'. In this, he sets out to refute 'two opinions which the inconsiderate are apt to take upon trust'—namely, that 'a vicious life is a life of liberty, pleasure and happy advantages', and, conversely, that 'a religious life is a servile and most uncomfortable state'.

These were opinions into which, as an 'inconsiderate' undergraduate, Coke had himself strayed in his early days at Oxford. His theme was one which might have furnished a more evangelical preacher with the opportunity of waxing eloquent over the true liberty of the sons of God. Coke's treatment was quite different. If the hopes of eternal life were our only motive for doing good, he argues, most of us would find this too remote a prospect of reward. The Bible, in this text, authorizes us to take a shorter view and to look for more immediate gain. Virtue, in fact, is rewarded in this life, not only by a clear conscience, but by such outward advantages as a greater chance of preferment in business or public life (he still

---

Petherton a clergyman authenticated by Revd. S. Brocksop Wes. Min'.

5. On Acts 10:4. Endorsed: 'South Petherton Somersetshire. Sept. 27. 1772'.

In the Julia Hall Bequest at Wesley's Chapel is:

6. On Luke 8:15. This is in Coke's hand, though mistakenly described on the cover as by Charles Wesley. Endorsed at the end: 'South Petherton Somersetshire. Feb. 7. 1773
      Feb. 19. 1775 M:'

In the possession of Dr Elmer T. Clark (and printed in *World Parish*, October 1960):

7. On John 16:6-11.

None of these MSS gives any support to Etheridge's statement (p. 36) that as he grew in knowledge of the saving truths of the Gospel Coke 'made repeated alterations in his manuscript sermons, interlining here, and interleaving there' before eventually discarding them altogether.

had one eye at least on the main chance), and the support of friends in time of need.

This causal relationship between virtue and present happiness is one to which he repeatedly returns. At the conclusion of his series of discourses on the Sermon on the Mount, he goes so far as to assert that 'Everyone, in proportion to his moral worth, in proportion to his goodness, according as he keeps within the lines of his duty, is proportionately happy.'[1] Nor does he consider these things as beyond man's attainment: it is thoughtlessness, rather than sin, which is the inherent flaw in human nature. In a sermon on the Prodigal Son, he tells his parishioners, 'that it is want of thinking and reflecting . . . that hath been the great occasion of all your past sins and follies,' and consequently, 'that wherever serious thinking and reflection is practised and continued, it never fails to produce reformation in the man that useth it . . . In a word, it is stupidity and unthinkingness that undoes us all.' Three weeks after this, it is true, he was proclaiming that 'Bare morality or honesty, without a right faith, will not save a man's soul'; but his conception of this saving faith is still very formal and intellectual—the acceptance of revealed truth, rather than trust in a saviour.[2] Coke was as yet, in September 1772, seeing only through a glass, darkly; he still had far to go towards a full knowledge either of himself or of the grace of God.

By way of contrast, the sermon on John 16: 6–11, though undated, must belong to a rather later period, perhaps when he was already under Methodist influences. On the work of the Spirit in convicting us of sin, he speaks of 'the infinite heinousness, infinite guilt, and desert of sin; and also of the depravity which it brings into the soul'. The Spirit 'gives us a knowledge of ourselves; convinces the sinner that "from the sole of the foot even unto the head there is no soundness in" him'.[3] Coke had already moved a long way from his former

[1] Sermon on Matthew 7:24. We may compare these words from his published *Sermon upon Education*, pp. 29f.: 'The recollection of a life entirely devoted to the service of God must at any period of it give an inexpressible satisfaction; . . . The grief, anxiety, and sorrow, which are the necessary attendants of deep repentance, will hardly be known to him, who has spent the chief part of his life in well-doing'. This last sentence is an eloquent reminder of how short a way Coke had as yet travelled in his spiritual experience.

[2] Sermon on Acts 10:4.

[3] Compare the *Sermon upon Education*, p. 10. In both cases, the writings of Fletcher were perhaps the decisive influence at work: see his letter to Fletcher, p. 24 below.

21

position. He knew now that the 'great means of salvation' was 'saving, operative faith, without which nothing can be pleasing to God, as every thing without it flows from a most corrupt fountain'. There is, consequently, 'no ground for mercy, no hope of salvation, but in and through the death of Christ'. Whereas he had formerly exhorted his congregation to more diligent attendance at Church and keeping of the Law, now he bids them to 'rest not in systems of opinions, in outward works or in attendance upon ordinances', but to 'be content with nothing less than a heart purified and adorned for the God of Love'. 'The end of the Gospel,' he had proclaimed in an earlier sermon on the Parable of the Sower, 'is never answered unless it produce holiness of heart and life.' He seems to have believed at that time that 'constant watchfulness' and 'serious self-examination' were sufficient means to that desirable end. But now he realized that only the Holy Spirit 'is sufficient for these things'.[1]

Perhaps this realization was the fruit of failure. South Petherton was not immediately transformed by the fervent preaching of its curate. There were those who shrugged their shoulders, and others who shook their heads in disapproval. His sermon on the Parable of the Sower reveals that he was already aware of the seed falling on stony or thorny ground. 'Do not think it enough,' he warned them, 'merely to have heard [the Word] in the house of God, and then forget it as soon as you depart thence . . . Too many, by a neglect of self-examination after service, in the churchyard or in their own families, by idle conversation, and many other like methods, lose all advantage, as neglecting all improvement of the Word.' Had he not seen and overheard them for himself, gathering in knots for idle gossip, as he passed through the churchyard and down the steps to his lodging after the service? Their complacence lay heavily on his heart, so that there was almost a touch of peevishness in the concern which he expressed for them in his conclusion: 'You see your duty: you see your danger: the rest now remains with you. I have done all I can in sincerity, to convince, persuade, advise, awaken and admonish you: it is not in the power of your Ministers to do more: Would God it were! for then not one of you should depart hence unpersuaded and unconvinced . . .'[2] The note of impatient chiding which can be detected in these words was to contribute to the final clash between Coke and his flock.

We should be spared the necessity for a great deal of speculation

[1] *World Parish*, October 1960, pp. 28–37.   [2] Sermon on Luke 8:15.

about Coke's spiritual pilgrimage during his days at South Petherton, had he kept a diary or revealed his struggles and triumphs in correspondence with some intimate friend. In the absence of more than fragmentary—and often conflicting—evidence, we can do no more than note certain milestones. Responsibility for the cure of souls no doubt made his own quest for truth, and for the God of truth, all the more urgent and eager, as he became increasingly aware of his own spiritual deficiency. Henry Moore had it from Coke himself that he drew comfort at this period from reading in private the prayers composed for William III by Archbishop Tillotson.[1] But the book which took him a decisive step forward was Alleine's *Alarm to the Unconverted*, the reading of which underlined the need for personal commitment of which Witherspoon had first made him aware.[2]

Somewhere about this point the influence of good books and the influence of friends coalesced in the person of the Rev. James Brown, rector of Portishead and vicar of Kingston St Mary, near Taunton, who introduced him to the writings of Wesley and Fletcher.[3] In particular, he lent him Fletcher's *Appeal to Matter of Fact and Common Sense*, published in 1772, and his four *Checks to Antinomianism* (1771–2). Years later, Coke wrote of Fletcher as 'the dear saint of God', whose acquaintance he valued 'as one of the greatest external privileges' of his life.[4] The reading of Fletcher's works was, he said, 'the blessed means of bringing me among that despised people called Methodists, with whom, God being my helper, I am determined to live and die'.[5] To this influence for good, we owe a letter which Coke wrote to Fletcher later in his curacy at South Petherton, and which reveals something both of his own spiritual progress and of his parish activities.[6]

[1] H. Moore, *Life of John Wesley*, ii. 309.

[2] Years later, in 1787, Alleine's *Alarm* and Baxter's *Call* were included by Coke among the books with which each of the West Indies missionaries was furnished (Mission Report, 1794, p. 16).

[3] James Brown was rector of Portishead, 1764–91, vicar of Kingston, 1771–92. On friendly terms with Wesley and sympathetic towards the Methodists, he was one of the recipients of Wesley's famous appeal for union in 1764.

[4] Letter to Thomas Morrell, 23rd June 1790 (printed in *Christian Advocate*, 3rd April 1851, p. 53, and *World Parish*, October 1961, pp. 29f.). In his sermon on the death of Wesley Coke refers to Fletcher as 'that holy Saint and great polemical Divine' (op. cit., p. 19).

[5] Quoted by Drew, p. 18.

[6] Letter to Fletcher, 28th August 1775 (M.M.S. Archives).

Revd. Sir,

I take the liberty, tho' unknown to you, but not unacquainted with your admirable publications, of writing you a letter of sincerest thanks for the spiritual instruction as well as entertainment which they have afforded me; and the spirit of candour and Christian charity which breathed throughout your writings, as well as the charming character which my best of earthly friends (The Revd. Mr Brown of Kingston near Taunton) has given me of you, emboldens me to hope that, tho' my situation in life be only that of a poor Curate of a Parish, you will excuse this liberty I have taken of addressing you in the fullness of my heart.

You are, indubitably, Sir, a sincere friend of the Gospel of Jesus Christ; I am also an humble admirer of the blessed Jesus; and it is on that foundation only I would wish and it is on that only I am sure I can recommend myself to you. Your excellent Checks to Antinomianism have rivetted me in an abhorrence and detestation of the peculiar Tenets of Calvin: and the monstrous errors into which those great and good men Bishops Hopkins and Beveridge (whose memories I highly reverence) have run into, have frequently filled me with wonder. Your Essay on Truth has been more particularly blessed to me. Your Scripture Scales I am just going to read with great attention. Many thanks to you, Sir, for your treatise on the fallen state of man; it has been of service to me, and of much more I have reason to think to many of my congregation. O Sir, I have frequently prayed to my God that he will make you a great pillar of his Church; in return, I do humbly beg that you will pray for me: I am sure you will grant me that favour when I inform you that (as nearly as I can guess) a thousand or more immortal souls come to me on every Lord's Day in the afternoon to receive their portion of the manna of the word, of the bread of everlasting life.

I will so far transgress against the Publick and your dear flock, as to request an answer: I am almost afraid to ask for more. May the God who loves you—and whom you love—make you a great instrument of his Glory in this life, and grant you the height of your ambition in the next.

> I am, Revnd. Sir, with great respect,
> Your much obliged and very humble servant,
> Thomas Coke.

South Petherton,
near Crewkerne, Somerset.
28th August, 1775.

At the same time as he was finding help in this way from the friendship and writings of his fellow-Anglicans, Coke also made the acquaintance of at least one dissenter who was able to help him.

Christopher Hull was the Independent minister at Bower Hinton, near Martock, who as a student at Trevecca had himself come under the influence of Fletcher. Coke's preaching already had sufficient fervour to attract some of the dissenters to hear him in the parish church, and Hull was among these. Rightly divining Coke's spiritual condition, he sent him a 'friendly letter', which led to correspondence and eventually to an interview. Coke's churchmanship at this time was so inflexible, that he would not agree either to visit, or be visited by, a dissenter.[1] Accordingly, they met on neutral ground at a farm-house. Hull is described as 'reasonable, communicative, and ingenuous'; as willing to listen as to speak, and more inclined to uphold his beliefs by argument than by dogma. He was so far from being bigoted in his views, that when convinced of the truth of Arminianism he made a public avowal of his change of view.[2] Not the least result of their conversation was Coke's discovery that 'piety and knowledge' were to be found outside the Establishment, one of the facts of life from which his upbringing and career had hitherto sheltered him. This was further brought home to him when, on a visit to friends in Devon, he seized the opportunity to shed both his learning and his prejudice and sit at the feet of a Methodist farm-labourer and class-leader. This man had clearly found something for which Coke was still seeking. They talked freely and at length on such themes as the nature of forgiveness and the witness of the Spirit, and were led to pray together. As a result, Coke found himself wanting to know more about 'the people called Methodists', about whom so many rumours and scandals still circulated. 'It was to the pious and communicative simplicity of this happy rustic, that Dr Coke declared he owed greater obligations with respect to finding peace with God . . . than to any other person.'[3]

Drew places all these events during Coke's first three years in South Petherton, but in fact they are far more likely to have taken place towards the end of his curacy. Mrs Ann Stone of Cathanger Farm, where Coke first encountered the Methodist preachers, used to state that when he preached in her hall it was the first time he had done so outside a parish church. This cannot have been earlier than August 1775, when she was converted under the preaching of John

[1] 'The Doctor ingenuously confessed, that a while before, his high church prejudices were so strong, that had Mr Hull been dying, and needed the offices of devotion, he believed he should have declined the task' (Sutcliffe, p. 9).

[2] Drew, pp. 18f.; Sutcliffe, p. 9.   [3] Drew, p. 20.

Wesley at Taunton.[1] But whether early or late, under these various influences, his preaching and parochial activities had begun to show a greater evangelical fervour. He now began to augment the services in the parish church by holding weeknight meetings in the homes of friends and parishioners, particularly for the sake of the aged and infirm. One evening, walking to a service in an outlying part of his parish, he prayed earnestly for a fuller blessing; and later, while proclaiming the greatness of redeeming love, 'it pleased God to speak peace to his soul, to dispel all his fears, and to fill his heart with a joy unspeakable and full of glory'.[2] This was the moment which most deserves to be labelled his conversion, and the one to which, in later years, he was accustomed to refer as the very day and hour when he had received an 'instantaneous assurance of the pardon of sin'.[3]

As Coke's evangelical zeal increased, so too did both the size of his congregations and the hostility of his opponents. He was even taunted, prematurely, with being himself a Methodist, and his activities certainly lent some credibility to the accusation. He now began to preach extempore, and to win conversions, though it is doubtful whether his rigid churchmanship was sufficiently modified, before his encounter with Wesley, to allow him to preach out of doors.

Earlier in the century, in 1738, a former vicar, the Rev. James Harcourt D.D., had given to his successors an acre and a yard of land near the vicarage; he did this, so that 'the children of South Petherton might be instructed in the Church Catechism, and have the same expounded to them in the time of morning-prayer . . . at least once in every week, by the vicar or his curate, and that the common-Prayer might be read every Wednesday and Friday, and every Saint's day for ever'.[4] Should any vicar fail to perform these duties, the land was to revert to Harcourt's heirs during his incumbency. Robert Twyford certainly had no need to fear that this might happen while he had Thomas Coke as his curate. There was no part of his ordination vows he took more solemnly than the undertaking, with the help of God, 'to instruct the youth in the catechism'. The

---

[1] Drew, p. 21; *Wesleyan Methodist Magazine*, 1824, p. 568.
[2] Drew, p. 21. Drew is virtually the only evidence we have for the inner history of Coke's spiritual pilgrimage. He is rather unreliable for the chronology of this early period, but in other respects his evidence, deriving from Coke himself, is particularly useful.
[3] [George Booth], *A Key to Explore the Mystery.*
[4] J. Collinson, *History of the County of Somerset* (1791) iii. 113.

public catechizing of the children of the poor seemed to him of particular importance, and he was appalled by its neglect in other parishes round about.[1]

During the later part of his curacy, Coke's exertions were redoubled. As the congregations grew, so did the number of communicants, and it is likely that Coke tried to institute the weekly communion, at a time when it was customary for there to be no more than four or six celebrations a year in most parishes. This sacramental devotion, which was an integral part of his, as it was of the Wesleys', evangelicalism, is reflected in the Church accounts, in which we find the payments made for Communion wine rising from £2 2s in 1771 to £4 10s in 1776. Similarly, in the minutes of Vestry Meetings held on 10th March and 22nd September 1774, both signed by Coke, the Church Wardens are instructed to 'procure two new rails for the accommodation of the Communicants in the Chancel, . . . according to the plan of those which are there at present'; and that 'as soon as may be' they are to 'provide for the use of the Minister and other Communicants, a Silver Gilt Plate, of the same size and form with that which is at present used for the administration of the Bread in the Sacrament'.[2] In the following January, they are further 'empowered and ordered to provide in the Chancel and Belfry [i.e. under the crossing, where the Memorial Choir-stalls now stand], whatever rails may be necessary for the accommodation of the Communicants'. The reaction of those who objected to such frequent celebrations is reflected in the minute of a Vestry Meeting held on 17th January 1777 soon after Thomas Goddard had been instituted, at which it was 'agreed and ordered that the Churchwardens do provide Bread and Wine for the Communion in the church monthly as usual and not otherwise, and that they take proper care that no strangers be commonly admitted there'. Had Coke been welcoming 'all who love the Lord Jesus Christ', even if they were Dissenters or Methodists? Or had he merely admitted communicants from other men's parishes? Either way, such irregularities could not be allowed to continue.

The final clash, when it came, was over the curate's rank enthusiasm. Ought it to be tolerated any longer? But long before matters came to a head, the seeds of an underlying hostility had been sown.

[1] *Sermon upon Education*, pp. 18f.

[2] For this and other extracts from the Vestry Book, I am indebted to the Deaville Walker papers in the M.M.S. Archives.

In origin, the conflict was one of personalities, and had more to do with the parish-pump than with anything doctrinal or liturgical. Coke was an eager and, to his enemies, a headstrong young man, accustomed to assuming leadership and to getting things done. He is supposed to have built at his own expense and on his own initiative a new gallery to accommodate the increasing numbers who flocked to hear him preach. This anecdote is very poorly authenticated, and bears all the marks of a pious legend.[1] Nevertheless, quite apart from the question of its historicity, it epitomizes the main features of the conflict between Coke and those of his parishioners who, because they were rate-payers, had a say in the temporal affairs of the church.

We can trace the development of that conflict, at least in outline, in the South Petherton Vestry Book. Clearly Coke was keen to repair and improve the fabric of the church which had perhaps been neglected by the previous incumbent. In addition to the expenditure already noted in connexion with the Sacrament, we find various other expenses authorized, beginning with 'two brass sconces for the Reading Desk'. Some of the rate-payers obviously looked upon their curate as extravagant and too ready to take the law into his own hands. Things did not come to a head, however, until the autumn of 1775, and then the issue was over nothing more theologically significant than a new west door and a gilt weather-cock for the tower. A Vestry Meeting on 2nd November agreed, at Coke's instigation, to the necessary expenditure; but a week later a group of eleven other rate-payers, who had been absent from the first meeting, gathered in vigorous protest at what seemed to them the needless spending of money that would come from their pockets.

Twyford, the vicar, was probably too ill by then to take sides in the conflict. The Minute Book indifferently ministers justice by recording the resolutions of both factions. 'Whereas', the entry of 10th November begins, 'there is an order of Vestry on or about the 2nd day of November instant for making a new WEST DOOR for this parish church, which order was made *in a hasty and precipitate manner*, and signed only by a few persons being *very inconsiderable*

[1] The earliest statement regarding this is in Drew, pp. 15f. This is echoed by most later biographers, including Etheridge, p. 37, where, however, the incident is transferred to a later point in his curacy. There is no support for the story in the Vestry Minutes, nor can any record be found at the Diocesan Registry of the granting of the necessary Faculty for the erection of a gallery. Galleries undoubtedly existed in the Church until the restorations of 1861, but on their number and location the evidence is meagre and confused.

payers, and came to that meeting *merely at the request and to issue the purpose of a certain Individual who is not a payer*. . . . We therefore, whose Names are subscribed (Payers towards the Church Rates of this parish) being by far the majority of the persons and payers, . . . having ourselves viewed the present West Door of this Church, and likewise having consulted a very judicious and faithful workman as to what would be proper to be done relating to the said door, *are convinced that a new West Door for this Church is WHOLLY UNNECESSARY, and do hereby reverse and repeal the said order of Vestry dated the 2nd day of November instant*, and order and direct the Churchwardens to cause the present West Doors to be very well cased with good oak . . . AND WHEREAS the old WEATHER-COCK is sufficiently repaired, *we oppose the purchase of a new one.*' The meeting closed in a less intransigent mood by authorizing the repair of the church roof.

That some sort of compromise was reached is indicated by a further meeting on 15th November, attended by Coke and thirteen others, some of whom had been at the protest meeting on the 10th. This meeting authorized a rate of 2d. in the pound for the necessary repairs to be carried out; but how far the earlier proposals were implemented is not clear. The West Door no longer exists, though its outline can still be traced. A weathercock—whether the original or its proposed successor—still surmounts the octagonal tower, to all appearances serenely unaware of the *furore* of which it was once the innocent cause.

The parish had welcomed a curate who was also Bailiff of Brecon; they were to lose one who was a Doctor of Civil Law at Oxford. Earlier in 1775 Coke had obtained his doctorate with the support of no less a person than the Prime Minister, Lord North, who furnished a letter to the Convocation, requesting that, as Coke 'was prevented by circumstances from proceeding regularly to the Degree of Bachelor' in the Law Faculty, he might now 'be allowed to accumulate the Degrees of Bachelor and Doctor in Civil Law, paying Fees for both Degrees but doing exercise for that of Doctor only'.[1] The application was successful, and on 17th June, after whatever exercises were required of him, Thomas Coke became a Doctor of Civil Law.[2]

---

[1] Convocation, 14th June 1775: letter from Lord North, dated 'Downing Street, 8th June 1775' (copy among the Deaville Walker papers). The entry in the Register of Congress is dated June 17th.

[2] Oxford, unlike Cambridge, had no power to grant degrees in Canon Law,

One of his bitterest opponents at this time went so far as to assert in print that his 'embracing the dark and erroneous doctrines of Methodism' was chiefly the result of disappointed hopes of preferment in the Church.[1] But it is surely of some significance that a man of Coke's background, qualifications and connexions should have remained in his curacy in an unimportant Somerset parish as long as he did, and then should leave only when driven out by the concerted opposition of influential parishioners and a new vicar. Whatever hopes he entertained of rapid preferment, Coke did not allow these to determine his actions or impede his parochial duties: in the eyes of his enemies he was *too* conscientious in his performance of them. Though the hostility he encountered, coupled perhaps with the limited success of his pleadings from the pulpit, may well have tempted him to shake off the dust of South Petherton from his feet, it was something more compelling than financial necessity that kept him there. His doctorate secured, it was still more than a year before his meeting with John Wesley opened to him the prospect of wider spheres of service; even then the time was not fully ripe, and he submitted to the older man's judgement in returning to the duties of his parish until the hour came.

and it is therefore an error to describe Coke's doctorate as LL.D., though he himself often did so. (In his letter to Bishop Seabury, on the other hand, he speaks of 'having taken two degrees in Civil Law in the University of Oxford'.) In the eighteenth century, LL.D. and D.C.L. appear to have been used interchangeably. (See *W.H.S. Proc.* xi. 94, 144.)

[1] John Thomas, *Two Letters to the Rev. Thomas Coke*, p. iii.

CHAPTER 3

THE METHODIST

On 13th August 1776, Thomas Coke rode over to Kingston St Mary to meet John Wesley, with whose writings and activities he was already familiar.

It would be easy to draw too highly coloured a picture of the young parish priest, frustrated and disillusioned by his first experience of the cure of souls, perplexed that his attempts to share his newly-found faith should meet with so mixed a response, and rebelliously eager to find some wider and more rewarding sphere for the expenditure of his enthusiasm and energy.

The truth was less simple than that. For one thing it was not a question of choosing between two mutually exclusive loyalties. Methodism was still a religious movement within the Church of England, and Wesley for all his irregularities was to remain doggedly within the Establishment to the end of his life. More and more members of the Methodist societies were converts with little or no religious background, or with dissenting rather than Anglican connexions. The demand for the administration of the Sacraments in the Methodist chapels by the Methodist preachers had been voiced as early as 1755, and was to be heard again from time to time throughout Wesley's life. All these things are true, but they only modify the picture of a people who were still distinguishable from the rank and file of their fellow church-goers chiefly by their more regular and devout attendance, their greater devotion to the Sacrament, their personal self-discipline and keenness in evangelism. Although he did not win the degree of active support he had hoped for among the clergy, Wesley nevertheless had the sympathy and friendship of a number of evangelicals who, in varying degrees, in their own parishes and beyond, preached the Methodist doctrines and actively fostered the labours of Wesley's itinerant 'Assistants'. These were men such as Fletcher of Madeley, Grimshaw of Haworth, and Perronet of Shoreham, Kent. To be a Methodist did not yet mean to renounce Anglicanism.

'Nothing at this time,' says Drew, 'could be more repugnant to

[Coke's] feelings and judgement, than the thought of separating from the Establishment'; and he instances the fact that Coke would not agree to hear Wesley preach anywhere apart from in a parish church —so limited, it seems, had been the influence of Christopher Hull upon his churchmanship.[1] To bear out Drew's words we have the evidence of a correspondence on which Coke was engaged at the very time of his meeting with Wesley. In it he sought to persuade his friend Walter Churchey to take Holy Orders. Those letters which have survived reveal an interesting mixture of pious zeal for the furtherance of the Kingdom and acceptance of the existing 'machinery' within the Establishment, which hardly accords with the picture of Coke as already a Dissenter in the making. In one letter, after explaining the course to be adopted for admission as a literate, he wrote: 'I do it for the sake of Jesus Christ, because it appears to me that you will be an acquisition to the ministry; and an eternity of the most zealous service will not be sufficient to compensate for one drop of the blood He so freely spilt upon the cross. The harvest, my friend, is very great, and the faithful labourers very few.'[2]

Although already established in the legal profession, Churchey gave serious consideration to Coke's proposal, with the result that, early in August 1776, Coke was busily engaged in arranging for his friend to be ordained by the Bishop of Bath and Wells, with a view to his becoming curate at Exton in North Somerset.[3] It was only a few days after this that he went over to meet Wesley at Kingston St Mary.

Kingston lies in a pleasant fold of the Quantock Hills just north of Taunton. The parish church stands on rising ground above the village, with the long, low parsonage 'pleasantly situated' just beyond, 'just fit', says Wesley, 'for a contemplative man'.[4] Wesley had been preaching in Taunton and was to spend the night with James Brown. We can only imagine the course of the conversation that evening, and what passed between the two Oxonians, the one still groping towards the experience which had turned the other into

[1] Drew, pp. 28f. Compare the statement of Mrs Stone of Cathanger, quoted above, p. 25.

[2] Quoted by Etheridge, p. 426, as having been written some time in 1776.

[3] Letter to Churchey, 3rd August, 1776 (M.M.S. Archives).

[4] *Journal of John Wesley*, vi. 119f. The old vicarage is now a private house. Its successor, down in the village and next to the present, post-war vicarage, has sometimes been mistaken for the house in which Wesley and Coke met (e.g. in the commemorative issue of *Kingdom Overseas*, September 1947).

a veteran evangelist and founder of a connexion of religious societies throughout the land. Each, no doubt, was sizing up the other. They rose early next morning to continue their talk as they walked in the parsonage garden overlooking the churchyard and the roofs of the village to the hills beyond, bathed in the early sunlight. The fullest account we have is that of Henry Moore, who says he got it from Coke himself.

> In the morning, Mr. Wesley having walked into the garden, he joined him there, and made known his situation and enlarged desires. Mr. Wesley, with marked sobriety, gave him an account of the way in which he and his brother proceeded at Oxford, and advised the Doctor to go on in the same path, doing all the good he could, visiting from house to house, omitting no part of his clerical duty; and counselled him to avoid every reasonable ground of offence. The Doctor was exceedingly surprised, and, indeed, mortified. "I thought", said he when he related the account to me, "he would have said, *Come with me, and I will give you employment according to all that is in your heart.*"

Moore goes on to speak of Coke's disappointment at being thus put off and 'confined still to the work of a parish'.[1]

We must balance this disappointment against the correspondence with Churchey which we have already noted, and the fact that he *did* return to his parish and did his best to turn it into a Methodist parish, on the lines of Madeley or Haworth. The fact remains that his meeting with Wesley left Coke restless and eager for a more extensive sphere of activity. It was only a matter of time before the opposition which he had already encountered reached a climax, and, being dismissed from his curacy, he 'bid adieu to his honourable name, and determined to cast in his lot' with the people called Methodists.[2]

The final clash was hastened by the death of Coke's vicar, Robert Twyford. His successor, Thomas Goddard, was presented

---

[1] H. Moore, *Life of John Wesley*, ii. 3–9f. It is not altogether easy to reconcile this account, which nevertheless derives from Coke himself, with that of Mrs Stone of Cathanger Farm, who claimed to have been present at the first interview between Coke and Wesley. 'The Dr. expressing his doubts respecting the propriety of confining himself to one congregation, Mr. W. instantly, clasping his hands, with a manner peculiarly his own, rejoined, . . . "Brother, go out, go out, and preach the Gospel to all the world!" ' (*Wesleyan Methodist Magazine*, 1824, p. 568). This incident almost certainly belongs to their *second* meeting, after Coke's expulsion from South Petherton.

[2] *Journal of John Wesley*, vi. 169. Cf Coke's *History of the West Indies*, i. 411f.

to the living at the end of November 1776. In the interregnum Coke's enemies seized their opportunity of making their case heard in higher circles. Charles Moss, as Bishop of St David's, had ordained Coke to the priesthood four years earlier. He had since been translated to Bath and Wells and, on receiving complaints about Coke's activities, wrote him an admonitory letter. But Coke's reply appears to have satisfied him and he let the matter rest there.[1]

Meanwhile in Coke's ministry the influence of Methodism was becoming more and more pronounced. His preaching had long displayed an increasing fervour; he now began on Sundays, after the second lesson, to announce the times and places at which week-night preaching services would be held and to extend his activities to adjacent parishes, so annoying his fellow-clergy. When refused the use of the church at Shepton Beauchamp, he tactlessly held a preaching service in an unlicensed private house in the parish, and a nocturnal broil ensued between the Methodists and their opponents. Coke was accused of violating the canons of the Church by instigating such illegal conventicles, by encouraging unqualified laymen to preach and expound the Bible, by himself preaching in his parish church on weekdays without diocesan authority, and by taking upon himself to appoint 'Fasts and Exercises'.[2]

There were disturbances even during the services in the parish church at South Petherton, and for these Coke himself must bear at least as much of the blame as his opponents. One Sunday he announced that for the future Wesley's hymns would replace the Psalms for congregational singing, and anticipated trouble by invoking an Act of Mary I originally intended for the protection of popish priests. Armed with this 'ancient and rusty weapon', on the last Sunday in 1776 he proceeded to carry out his intention in the face of strong opposition from the pews, where part of his congregation set up the rival strains of Psalm 95. Not content with this indecorous and unedifying wrangle, their curate proceeded to harangue his recalcitrant flock, condemning them in heated terms as 'Devil's Trumpeters', 'Satan's Agents' and 'rattlesnakes', and forbidding them, with a wealth of anathemas, to approach the

---

[1] Drew, p. 23. Moss was Bishop of St David's, 1766–74, and of Bath and Wells, 1774–1802. The references in this context to Dr John Ross, Bishop of Exeter (Sutcliffe, p. 11; Drew, pp. 22f.; Etheridge, p. 38) appear to be an error, since he was not consecrated until the following year.

[2] John Thomas, *Two Letters to the Rev. Thomas Coke*, pp. 1ff.

Communion Table until they should see the error of their ways. Though the only contemporary account we have of this incident is from the pen of one of his sworn enemies, it is nevertheless clear that Thomas Coke's Welsh blood had reached boiling point, with the result that he handled the situation in an altogether inadvisable and indefensible way.[1]

A special vestry meeting early in the new year considered the explosive situation and passed a resolution that 'whosoever shall interrupt the congregation in the singing of David's Psalms to the Praise and Glory of God according to the immemorial usage in our Church, shall be deemed as a disturber or disturbers of the congregation and be brought to justice at the expense of the parish'.[2] The weapon was two-edged, but there is little doubt in whose direction it was being flourished. The same meeting gave instructions, as we have already noted, that the Communion was to be held 'monthly as usual, and not otherwise', and that no 'strangers' should be admitted to it. This marked, perhaps, the uneasy lull before the final storm. Though Goddard was not present at this new year vestry, Coke's enemies now enlisted the support of the new vicar, who no doubt found it an irritating embarrassment to have such a curate as young Coke entrenched in the parish and accustomed for so long to enjoying a free hand. He had every reason to side with those who were determined to oust Coke.

The end came swiftly and without warning. One Sunday, in the presence of the congregation, Coke was publicly dismissed from his curacy, and the pealing of the church bells added insult to injury as he left. A new curate, appointed without his knowledge, was waiting to step into the pulpit, where he preached a sermon directed against his predecessor.[3] Meanwhile, those who were so inclined celebrated their deliverance from this Methodistical curate by broaching several hogsheads of cider in the street.[4] The most probable date for this ignominious expulsion is 30th March, which was Easter Sunday.[5]

Deprived of any opportunity of vindicating himself in the parish church, Coke did not immediately quit the town. He determined to

[1] Ibid., pp. 16ff. [2] Vestry book, under the date 17th January, 1777.
[3] Drew, p. 23.
[4] H. Moore, *Life of John Wesley*, ii. 310. It is not clear whether this celebration marked Coke's expulsion from the curacy or his departure from the town.
[5] The marriage register shows that he was still officiating on 23rd March, when he published banns for the last time. He was not present, on the other hand, at the Easter Vestry.

remain, in the face of hostility and scorn, long enough to state his case in the open air. On the following Sunday he accordingly took his stand in the churchyard and addressed the retiring congregation, who showed sufficient sympathy to allow him to finish unmolested. There were, however, threats of stoning if he dared to repeat the performance. Coke must have known that it was no idle threat. Wesley himself had frequently been pelted with stones. The first Methodist martyr, William Seward, had died by such means at Hay, very near Coke's native Brecon. Nevertheless, he was determined to take his stand once more on the following Sunday, and his enemies prepared accordingly. Fortunately he was not without friends who shared his courage. Foremost among these were the son and daughter of a dissenting family named Edmonds, of Hayes End Manor on the edge of the town,[1] who had become regular members of his congregation. On the second Sunday after his dismissal, against the advice of their parents, these two young people took up their position on either side of Coke as he stood up in the churchyard; and their presence, with that of a number of his other supporters, caused his enemies to leave the stones untouched in the hampers in which they had brought them.[2]

At this turning-point in his career, Coke's trail almost peters out. There is scarcely any trace of his movements between his leaving South Petherton and the entry in Wesley's *Journal* on 19th August (1777), when after the Conference in Bristol he 'went forward with Dr Coke to Taunton'. A persistent tradition, uncorroborated by the parish records, says that Coke acted as curate to James Brown at Kingston;[3] if so, it may have been on quitting South Petherton. But this cannot have lasted long. By 25th June he had joined Wesley, who wrote to Walter Churchey from London on that date: 'Dr Coke promises fair, and gives us reason to hope that he will bring forth not only blossoms but fruit. He has hitherto behaved exceedingly well and seems to be aware of his grand enemy, applause.'[4]

[1] The original part of the farmhouse still fronts the road. Drew says that on subsequent visits Coke always stayed with the Edmonds. The site of the first Methodist chapel was conveyed to the trustees in 1809 from a John Baker Edmonds, no doubt a member of the same family, if not the son who stood by Coke in 1777.

[2] In describing this, Drew unbends sufficiently to speak of the '*hampered* proselytes' who were too irresolute to carry out their threat.

[3] E.g. *Journal of John Wesley*, vi. 119, footnote.

[4] *Letters of John Wesley*, vi. 267.

On 30th June, Wesley left London on a tour which brought him eventually into South Wales, and on 10th July he preached in Brecon, on the Bulwarks.[1] Possibly Coke accompanied him that far, since he seems to have paid at least one visit to Brecon at this time, during which he went over to see Walter Churchey at Hay.[2]

Coke's name does not make its first appearance in the *Minutes* until the Conference of 1778, although he was almost certainly present at the Bristol Conference of 1777.[3] Drew conjectures that Wesley may have feared that Coke would have second thoughts about 'bidding adieu to his honourable name', under the influence of some of his wealthy friends. Wesley's letter to Churchey, already quoted, lends some support to this. Saying that Coke will be 'in danger from offence', he adds, 'If you are acquainted with him, a friendly letter might be of use, and would be taken kindly. He now stands on slippery ground, and is in need of every help.' Henry Moore, on the other hand, dismisses the idea that Wesley kept Coke on unofficial probation after the Conference. While Coke was in Bristol, he says, 'among a people established in the true faith of the Gospel, the Doctor's gentlemanly manners, his manifest zeal for religion, and his attachment to Mr. Wesley, gained him universal love and esteem.' At the same time he discovered how far his own spiritual experience lagged behind that of even some of the humblest members of the Bristol society.[4]

The most plausible explanation of the absence of Coke's name from the 1777 Minutes is that his case was in some respects unique. Though a newcomer to Methodism and unknown to most of the preachers, he was on the other hand an ordained clergyman and had an Oxford doctorate. He could hardly be 'received on trial' with the other new preachers. To delay the insertion of his name was the most tactful way of dealing with the matter. By the next Conference he had made himself known and begun to prove his worth.

Coke stayed on in Bristol for some time after the Conference had

[1] *Journal of John Wesley*, vi. 162.

[2] Letter to Churchey, 25th September 1777, in which Coke says, 'When I visited you last, you did not seem to be so alive to God, and so dead to the world, as I expected to find you.' (*Wesleyan Methodist Magazine*, 1826, p. 387).

[3] Drew, p. 30. Pawson's *Chronological Catalogue of all the Travelling Preachers*, 1795, gives Coke's date as 1776; as does the memorial inscription in City Road Chapel.

[4] H. Moore, *Life of John Wesley*, pp. 310f.

ended,[1] and then rode over to Brecon to settle some of his personal affairs before proceeding to London. On 25th September, he was still in Brecon apologizing to Churchey that he has been too busy to pay him a visit at Hay. The new convert to Methodism was clearly disappointed that his friend had failed to respond to the call to the ministry and even seemed less wholeheartedly committed than he had formerly been. Protesting that he writes 'in all the sincerity and openness of friendship', Coke reveals something of his own frame of mind as he pauses on the threshold of his new life. 'Let us, my friend, keep our souls constantly turned towards God; and he will soon fill us with righteousness, peace and joy in the Holy Ghost. The Christian's life is hidden with Christ in God; but from that life flows a constant burning zeal for the good of others; it is his meat and drink to do his heavenly Father's will.' Coke was already becoming immersed in the humdrum affairs of the Connexion, and using some of its jargon with a newcomer's accent. 'I have sent you the proposals for the Arminian Magazine,' he writes to Churchey. 'Will you become a Subscriber? Brother Moon can give you further information concerning that work. Brother Benson's Sermons are not come out. It was made a rule at the last Conference that none but the travelling Preachers should have a copy of the Minutes.'

While in Bristol, Coke had sought consolation for his backwardness in the spiritual life by reassuring himself that, though his knowledge of God might be surpassed by that of the humblest member of the Methodist Society, yet he excelled 'in philanthropy, and in larger views for the good of mankind'. Moore preserves a curious anecdote of how he was stripped of what would once have been called 'these filthy rags of righteousness'. On the way from Bristol to London one of his fellow passengers in the coach was taken ill. Coke hurried to fetch water from a stream some way off; but realizing that his only means of carrying it was in 'the fine new beaver, decorated with an elegant rose, then common among clergymen', he returned empty-handed. 'A gentleman, who was assisting the afflicted man, and had observed with pleasure the Doctor's design, exclaimed with surprise and indignation, "What, Sir, have you brought no water?" and instantly ran himself to the brook and returned with his hat full.' Coke was thus rebuked for his com-

[1] Crowther, p. 104, surmises that after the Conference Coke accompanied Wesley on his tour of Devon and Cornwall; but we cannot be sure that he went any further than Taunton, or Kingston, as indicated in Wesley's *Journal*.

placency about the benevolence which still to some degree served him as a substitute for the 'righteousness which is of God by faith'.[1]

It was soon after his arrival in London that, according to Moore, Coke came under the beneficial influence of Thomas Maxfield, Wesley's first lay preacher who was later ordained by the Bishop of Londonderry to provide Wesley with a curate. Maxfield subsequently separated from Wesley and was at this time occupying a chapel in Moorfields, very near to the Foundery and the newly-built chapel in City Road. Maxfield and Coke struck up an intimate friendship which, for the younger man, led to a fuller knowledge of the deep things of God and, in particular, a realization of his need to be 'perfected in love'.[2]

In the year before Coke's arrival in the capital a young Scotsman named John Bruce had come to live in a house in City Road and joined the Foundery Society. He was soon introduced to Coke by Wesley, and the two men became close friends. Bruce later kept open house for the Methodist preachers, adding a comfortable study and a good theological library to his otherwise unpretentious hospitality. The house became a home and headquarters for Coke whenever he was in London.[3] The Foundery was still in use, but work on the new chapel in City Road was proceeding despite delays and setbacks. It was eventually opened in November 1778, a year or so after Coke's arrival. The unordained assistants were excluded from the City Road pulpit, as they had been from that of the Foundery, largely at the instigation of Charles Wesley; but Coke's Anglican orders qualified him to officiate there, as well as at West Street Chapel. This state of affairs would not contribute towards a happy relationship between the older preachers and this 'upstart crow'. The Foundery, and subsequently the house adjoining the new chapel, were Coke's first homes in London, and at an early date he moved his mother from Brecon, so that she could be nearer to him and his work. Writing from the Foundery on 23rd February 1779, to his relative Thomas Williams, chiefly on financial matters,

[1] Moore, op. cit., pp. 212–14.

[2] Ibid., p. 314. Drew, p. 16, antedates the influence of Maxfield to the South Petherton period (as does Thomas Roberts, *The Burning and Shining Light*, p. 14); but Moore dismisses this as 'an entire mistake'. There are very few detailed sources for the life of Maxfield, but all the evidence there is supports the view that he continued to preach in London. It is unlikely that he was ever near South Petherton.

[3] Stevenson, *City Road Chapel*, pp. 261, 494–6.

39

he reports that his mother is 'in tolerable health'.[1] Her death in 1783, at the age of seventy, removed the last close human tie which might have kept Coke from the wider work upon which he was then about to enter.

Coke's fame had gone before him, so that he soon found himself preaching to gratifyingly large congregations. 'The fashionable and rich took their places with the poor',[2] and though many no doubt came partly out of curiosity to see this young Welsh clergyman with an Oxford doctorate who had been so ignominiously driven from his parish, his popularity was sustained. He preached frequently at West Street, originally a Huguenot Chapel, near Seven Dials. Often, too, he took to the open air, a favourite spot being that now covered by Tavistock Square.

From 1778 until 1783, the Minutes show Coke as stationed in London, and although we are unable to trace his movements in detail, it is clear from the few letters that have survived from these years that he must have spent much of his time in the capital. Wesley reposed in him a degree of confidence he had not been able to place in some of his earlier assistants. 'Wesley himself told the Rev. Henry Moore, that while Mr Maxfield was with him, he could not, when himself absent from London, leave him there, unless Dr Jones was there also. For the first so limited his exhortation to the exercise of faith, that the presence of the other was necessary, whose peculiar talent it was to enforce the fruits of faith and the duties of the Gospel. With Dr Coke it was otherwise; he was equally "sound in the faith," and "zealous of good works".'[3] Thus did Wesley find the assistant he had been so long seeking.

[1] Letter to Thomas Williams, 23rd February 1779 (Drew University). Drew, p. 4, says that she joined the society, though he mistakenly refers to Bristol instead of London.

[2] So Telford, *Two West End Chapels*, p. 42, based on Drew, p. 31, where Coke's popularity as a preacher is ascribed in large measure to 'the harmony of his voice, the engaging smile which his countenance displayed, and the clerical character which he sustained'.

[3] Smith, *History of Wesleyan Methodism*, i. 417.

CHAPTER 4

RIGHT-HAND MAN

The portrait of Thomas Coke which embellished the pages of the *Arminian Magazine* in May 1779 is of an impetuous young man with animated features and a hint of devilry in his eye which suggests that he respected his elders only in so far as they showed themselves to be his betters. Jonathan Crowther, who first met him about this time, describes him as 'like Zaccheus, little of stature, being of about five feet and an inch in height; . . . strong, stout, vigorous and handsome'. 'The first time I saw him,' wrote Crowther, 'which was . . . when he was about thirty-two or thirty-three years of age, I thought him the most handsome man I had ever seen. His face was remarkably pleasing, and continued so, notwithstanding the increase of years, and fatiguing exercises, to the end of his days.'[1] Later on his short figure became more portly, but his dark hair, fresh complexion and bright, piercing eyes combined with his engaging smile to belie his years. Wilberforce once said of him, with a touch of wry affection, that 'he looked a mere boy when he was turned fifty, with such a smooth apple face, and little round mouth, that if it had been forgotten you might have made as good a one by thrusting in your thumb'.[2]

As a well-educated and widely-travelled man, he was never at a loss in conversation with strangers, and his polished manners and natural courtesy, even towards those who had maligned or ill-treated him, was widely remembered. There was another side to this picture, it is true, for as we have already seen, he could be carried away in the heat of the moment and was given to extravagant invective which he afterwards regretted. Those who knew him best, however, were unanimous in their view that his shortcomings were the defects of his virtues. 'He was said to have been precipitous [*sic*],' wrote Thomas Roberts. 'Yet surely never but on the principle of doing right. But were it not for his precipitousness, how many a

---

[1] Crowther, p. 511.   [2] *Life of Wilberforce* by his sons, iii. 389f.

golden opportunity had passed unimproved!'[1] His lack of sympathy for the half-heartedness of Laodicea won him enemies. 'He spared not those whom he thought lukewarm, and consequently they did not spare him. Complaints were sometimes made to Mr. Wesley against what was called his rash spirits and proceedings; but as those complaints were generally made by those who were known to be *lukewarm*, . . . [Wesley] took little notice' of them.[2] On the other hand, when shown to be in the wrong, Coke was open to reproof and as eager to admit his fault as he had been to do good. 'Seldom, if ever, did the sun go down upon his wrath. He studied no revenge, and cherished no resentment. Often would he stand corrected, and could beg pardon with a peculiar grace.'[3] Above all, his closest acquaintances bear witness to his freedom from uncharitable rancour. 'There was one thing in particular', wrote Andrew Hamilton, 'in which Dr. Coke excelled the most men I have known —viz. his never speaking evil of any person.'[4] This is confirmed by Thomas Roberts who, as his travelling companion for months at a time, wrote, 'I never knew him in a single instance to speak ill of an absent person; even when some have freely animadverted on those faults he had abundantly more cause to censure.'[5]

At the time of the Bristol Conference in 1777, Coke was nearing his thirtieth birthday. The new recruit would find himself in the company of veterans such as Christopher Hopper, who had entered the itinerancy in the year Coke was born, and of others such as Thomas Brisco, Thomas Olivers, Peter Jaco and Alexander Mather, who had been among Mr Wesley's 'assistants' for almost as long. There were, too, the men of a younger generation, such as John Pawson, Richard Whatcoat, Joseph Benson, Joseph Bradford and Samuel Bradburn, with whom Coke was to be closely associated in the crucial years that lay ahead.

It was perhaps inevitable that some who were his senior in the ranks of the preachers should look upon Coke as a young upstart who had usurped their place in Wesley's favour. For this Wesley himself was partly to blame. He did not easily confide in his lay-

[1] Thomas Roberts, *The Burning and Shining Light*, pp. 24f. Cf Boehm's *Reminiscences*, quoted in Stevens, *History of Methodist Episcopal Church*, iv. 171.

[2] Moore, *John Wesley*, ii. 315f.

[3] Crowther, pp. 511f. Cf Roberts, op. cit., pp. 16f.

[4] Andrew Hamilton, *The Faithful Servant receiving his Reward*, p. 25.

[5] Roberts, op. cit., pp. 15f. Cf Samuel Woolmer, *The Servant of the Lord*, p. 19.

assistants, or delegate to them matters of real importance: they remained assistants, to be consulted regularly, yet without being given a share in the government of the Connexion. In Wesley's eyes, Coke did not so much take the place hitherto occupied by others of his preachers, as fill a role which no one else had yet succeeded in filling—that of an ordained helper such as Charles Wesley had once been. When Charles married and settled down in Bristol none of John Wesley's other clerical sympathizers ever quite succeeded in taking his place. Even Grimshaw had confined himself to his 'Haworth Round', and he had now been dead for many years. John Jones, ordained in 1763 at Wesley's instigation by the pseudo-bishop Erasmus and later by the Bishop of London, had been driven out of the Connexion by Charles Wesley's implacable hostility to anything smacking of separation. Vincent Perronet was an old man; Fletcher, in whom Wesley had once thought to find a successor, was ill. So too was John Richardson, who after being driven from his curacy at Ewhurst in Sussex served as Wesley's 'curate' in London for thirty years.[1] Coke's youthful energy and enthusiasm, coupled with the fact that he was in regular Anglican orders, seemed the answer to a long-uttered prayer.

Wesley's feelings in the matter were expressed in a letter to Mrs Fletcher in July 1782: 'It seems to have been the will of God for many years that I should have none to share *my proper labour*. My brother never did. Thomas Walsh began to do it; so did John Jones. But one died and one fainted. Dr. Coke promises fair; at present I have none like minded.'[2] And at a later stage, in 1786, when Coke had set out on his second voyage to America, Wesley wrote to Freeborn Garrettson, 'I can exceedingly ill spare him from England, as I have no clergyman capable of supplying his lack of service; but I was convinced he was more wanted in America than in Europe.'[3] Drinkhouse was very wide of the mark, as we shall see, in supposing that when Wesley sent out Coke in 1784 to ordain Asbury, he intended him to stay in America permanently. He had been indispensable for too long.

[1] *W.H.S. Proc.* xxi. 97ff. Richardson joined Wesley in 1762. Coke preached his funeral sermon in 1792, stressing his continuing love for the Church of England.

[2] *Letters of John Wesley*, vii. 128. Cf Ibid., vii. 289, where Wesley tells his brother Charles that Coke 'is now such a right hand to me as Thomas Walsh was'.

[3] Ibid., vii. 343.

'He admitted me', said Coke, 'to his most secret councils, and in some things placed a confidence in me, the recollection of which even fills me with surprise.'[1] It is little wonder that the elder preachers should feel themselves ousted, especially after some of them had been omitted from the 'Legal Hundred' in 1784. But even those who resented his closeness to Wesley were sometimes glad to take advantage of it, so that Coke found himself speaking on behalf of other preachers, though not even his advocacy was always efficacious. In 1787 the three preachers ordained two years before for Scotland were brought back into English circuits and deprived of their right to administer the sacraments. This arbitrary treatment deeply distressed them, though they complied out of respect for Wesley. Thomas Hanby, however, wrote to Coke, begging him to use his influence with Wesley on their behalf. Coke sought the earliest opportunity to do so, and on 23rd January 1788 he replied to Hanby's letter, apologizing for the delay. 'I waited for some time in hopes of gaining a favourable opportunity of reading your Letter to Mr. Wesley, & conversing with him on the contents of it; tho' I had nothing to say, but what I have said or written to him over and over again; but the various pointed remarks he has been continually making convinced me that he was impregnable.'[2]

Coke's standing among his fellow-preachers was not enhanced by his outspokenness, even though it was matched by a readiness to admit his mistakes and to seek the forgiveness of those he had wronged. In particular, he showed far too much eagerness in suspecting heretical tendencies even in those who were his senior. Almost before he had established himself in the Connexion, in October 1779, he crossed swords with Joseph Benson and several other preachers over a matter of theological speculation. Benson had in his youth read Isaac Watts's *Glory of Christ*. 'I read it with great attention and much pleasure. I became a convert to his doctrine, and believed . . . the pre-existence of our Lord's human soul.' As late as September 1788, Wesley saw fit to warn him against abandoning the language and sentiment of Scripture in favour of unprofitable

---

[1] *Sermon on the Death of the Rev. John Wesley*, p. 5. Entries in Wesley's Journal and Diary (e.g. vi. 329, 437) confirm this.

[2] Letter to Thomas Hanby, 23rd January 1788 (Emory University). Hanby voiced his disappointment to James Oddie in a letter of 7th February, in which he speaks feelingly of being 'deprived of that precious ordinance' (Original in W.H.S. Library).

metaphysical reasonings about 'what God has not plainly revealed'.[1] Through speaking his mind too freely on such matters, which he acknowledged were not essential to salvation, Benson found himself widely suspected of Arianism, with Coke as his chief accuser.[2] His initial reply did not satisfy Coke, who wrote:

I have recd. (I cannot say, with Pleasure) your Letter: the fashionable way of talking & writing, which you take Notice of, arises from a too fashionable Opinion, and the Custom of wresting Scripture-terms from their Original Simplicity. I did not design to enter into a religious controversy with you, "for I am determined never to dispute at all, if I have no hope of convincing my Opponent". I will not wear a Mask, and therefore I will frankly own to you, that it is my full Resolution to bring this important Point on the Carpet at the next Conference.[3]

At the same time, it appears, Coke made similar charges against John Hampson, who was less eager to defend himself, and also against Samuel Bradburn, whose reply he found entirely satisfactory.[4] That Coke was not motivated merely by vindictiveness, but by a genuine and personal concern, is shown by the fact that he paid more than one visit to Benson, to discuss the matter fully with him. 'I bless the Lord,' Benson wrote, 'notwithstanding the manner in which he has used me, I found nothing in my heart towards him contrary to love.'[5] The matter was duly raised on the opening day of the 1780 Conference and a committee was appointed to look into it. The committee were unanimous in clearing Benson of the charge of Arianism, and declared that Coke had no grounds for speaking and writing as he had done. Coke immediately showed his readiness to acknowledge his fault before the assembled preachers, and the two men were accordingly reconciled.[6] In several subsequent publications[7] Benson demonstrated the orthodoxy of his belief in the divinity of Christ, and no more was heard of the charges against

[1] *Letters of John Wesley*, viii. 89f.

[2] J. Macdonald, *Memoirs of Joseph Benson*, pp. 98f., 106ff. Cf Coke's letter to Lancelot Harrison (quoted in Etheridge, pp. 65f.) in which he declares his esteem for the preachers as 'the most important and useful body of men in this kingdom'. He declares that he loves Benson 'not only with a love of pity on account of his error, but with a love of friendship and complacency on account of his many amiable qualities,' but adds nevertheless that he is 'a subtle casuist, and therefore . . . a very dangerous man'.

[3] Letter to Benson, 10th November 1779 (Archives Centre).

[4] *Letters of John Wesley*, vi. 358, 366.   [5] Macdonald, op. cit., p. 105.

[6] Ibid., p. 106.   [7] Ibid., pp. 205, 229.

him; and though the two men found themselves on opposite sides in the dispute at Bristol in 1794, they remained on friendly terms despite their differences.[1]

Wesley was not entirely blind to Coke's shortcomings. He knew him to be forgetful and sometimes careless of details,[2] even to the point of overlooking a matter such as Joseph Cownley's ordination certificate.[3] Yet he entrusted to him a great variety of administrative tasks and it is a measure of the skill and devotion with which Coke undertook them that we learn of some of these only through his temporary absence from his post.[4] Coke was, in fact, both Wesley's secretary[5] and his personal representative among the societies during the fourteen years when, despite all his disclaiming, Wesley's powers were suffering an inevitable decline.

Nor did the meticulous Wesley overlook the younger man's impulsiveness, a fault which was to lead him into hasty and some-times ill-considered decisions. 'The Doctor is often too hasty,' he wrote to Adam Clarke in 1788. 'He does not maturely consider all circumstances.'[6] 'Dr Coke and I,' said Wesley on one occasion, 'are like the French and the Dutch. The French have been compared to a flea, and the Dutch to a louse. I creep like a louse, and the ground I get I keep; but the Doctor leaps like a flea, and is sometimes obliged to leap back again.'[7]

[1] Sutcliffe's MS *History of Methodism*, iv. 265, asserts that there had been a distance between Coke and Benson ever since the Bristol dispute of 1794. Relations between the two were certainly strained then and again in 1804, but the evidence suggests that their personal relationship was not permanently affected. (See especially, Macdonald, op. cit., pp. 343, 440.)

[2] E.g. *Letters of John Wesley*, vii. 212.

[3] Ibid., viii. 98, letter to Cownley, 12th October 1788.

[4] 'Mr. Prickard keeps the money of the Contingent Fund in Dr. Coke's absence' (Ibid., vii. 146, written at a time when Coke was busy with the case of the Birstall preaching-house).

'J. Fenwick is to correct the press chiefly, in the absence of Dr. Coke, and to transcribe tracts for me' (Ibid., vii. 189).

[5] E.g. the body of Wesley's letter to Thomas Carlill, copies of which went to several of the preachers, is in Coke's writing, the signature alone being Wesley's (Ibid., vi. 356f.).

[6] Letter to Adam Clarke, 5th November, 1788 (Ibid., viii. 101).

[7] Crowther, pp. 233f. Adam Clarke, in a letter to Humphrey Sandwith, 16th June, 1829, refers this saying to the 1788 Conference, and gives it in the following form: 'Dr Coke puts me in mind of the German proverb, which I may apply to himself, and myself: He skips like a flea; I creep like a louse. He would tear all from top to bottom—I will not tear, but unstitch' (*W.H.S. Proc.* xviii. 26).

Relations between the two men were not always cordial, especially as Coke was capable at times of taking matters into his own hands, even to the point of defying his superior. In his youthful zeal, he was more ready than the ageing evangelist to follow out the implications of Wesley's dictum, 'The world is my parish'. No removable obstacle was allowed to hinder the progress of the missions, and he eagerly sought out the best of the preachers as volunteers for the work overseas. Wesley was provoked almost to jealousy. 'Ought we', he asked Peard Dickinson, with a touch of pique, 'to suffer Dr Coke to pick out one after another of the choicest of our young preachers?'[1] And when Coke applied himself to raising funds for the missions, Wesley answered a complaint from Thomas Taylor, 'I did not approve of Dr Coke's making collections either in yours or any other circuit. I told him so, and I am not well pleased with his doing it. It was very ill done.'[2] It took a bold man to incur Wesley's displeasure; but it took even more to deflect Thomas Coke from the tasks to which he believed himself to be called.

That Wesley for a time had reservations about Coke's spiritual maturity has been inferred from the fact that when his portrait was inserted in the *Arminian Magazine* for May 1779, no accompanying 'memoir' appeared. Instead Wesley printed this laconic note: 'As it is not thought advisable to insert any account of Dr Coke at present, the following account of a woman of long and deep experience will be deemed a good substitute by all lovers of real religion.' This substitute was a memoir of Sarah Ryan. However this may be, it did not deter Wesley from entrusting many weighty and delicate tasks into Coke's hands.

Coke's opinions of Wesley are most fully expressed in the memorial sermon he preached in Baltimore and Philadelphia in 1791, though we must make obvious allowances for the occasion on which they were expressed. (Thus, at the outset, he calls Wesley 'the greatest benefactor to mankind that later ages have known', a claim that even Mr Wesley's most devoted admirers might not admit without some hesitation.) Coke's text, 2 Kings 2:12, enabled him, some thought presumptuously, to compare his relationship to Wesley with that of Elisha to Elijah, and in the body of the sermon Wesley is compared with the older prophet in detail.

[1] Letter to Peard Dickinson, 11th April, 1789 (*Letters of John Wesley*, viii. 129).
[2] Letter to Taylor, 4th April 1790 (ibid., viii. 211).

I will by no means allow that the obligations of Elisha to Elijah could exceed mine to Mr. Wesley. For fourteen years I had the honour of enjoying an intimate acquaintance with him. He drew me forth into an extensive field of action, when confined within the limits of a little Parish; and instrumentally, under the Grace and Providence of God, gave me *that* which I value more than all the gold of the Indies, and for which alone I would desire to be absent a moment from my Lord—my usefulness in the Church of Christ.

Of his singleness of purpose he says, 'I can without hesitation declare that I never knew one, concerning whom I could form any mature judgment, that sacrificed ease, pleasure, profit, friends, to the welfare of the Church of Christ, with so much freedom as Mr. Wesley'. At the same time, Coke concludes, 'He was but a man. He had his defects: and those who were best acquainted with the earthen vessel knew them best'. Among these, no doubt, Coke would have included his unduly authoritarian attitude to those 'in connexion' with him, and that inflexibility of purpose which those who differed from him understandably called 'stubbornness'. 'But O! that Vessel contained most precious treasure; and its great Master did delight to make his Spirit of glory shine upon it.'[1]

The first of Coke's official excursions from London of which we have any details was about a year after his arrival in the capital. On 17th August 1778, soon after returning from the Conference in Leeds, Wesley and Coke set out together by coach for Bristol.[2] Almost certainly Coke accompanied Wesley throughout his subsequent tour of the West Country: his letter to George Gidley from Stroud on 24th November shows that he had recently visited Exeter and knew many of the members of the society there. He was aware of their plans for building a new chapel in Musgrave's Alley, and had pledged his support for their efforts to raise funds.[3]

The same letter makes a passing reference to South Petherton, a reminder that Coke had not forgotten his old parishioners, or washed his hands of them. On 3rd September of this year, returning from the West, Wesley preached in the village for the first and only time. Though he makes no mention in his *Journal* of the events of

[1] *Sermon on the Death of the Rev. John Wesley*, p. 4. Cf *History of the West Indies*, i. 411f.

[2] *Journal of John Wesley*, vi. 207.

[3] Letter to Gidley, 24th November 1778 (Archives Centre). Charles Wesley also accompanied them from Newbury to Bristol. (*Journal of Charles Wesley*, ed. T. Jackson, ii. 269.)

the previous year, Coke's association with the place must have been one of Wesley's reasons for the visit, and it seems likely that Coke was with him. It is possibly to this visit that the anecdote belongs which describes the triumphal welcome to the curate they had lately driven out. 'We *chimed* him out,' they said, 'and now we will atone for our error by *ringing* him in.'[1] One result of the visit was that Coke began planning to raise funds for the building of a chapel at South Petherton. His letter to Gidley shows that other commitments hampered the fulfilment of this project; but it was not immediately abandoned. In another letter, two years later, Coke asked Gidley, 'Will you give me leave to insert you as a trustee for my little preaching-house at South Petherton?'[2] Nevertheless, the scheme apparently came to nothing, as the first chapel was not built there until 1809,[3] shortly after another visit to his old parish had prompted Coke to persuade Conference to make it a home mission station.

In 1779 Coke began to travel a little further afield. On 7th July he wrote asking Thomas Williams to arrange for the payment of certain overdue rents, 'as I am going a long journey in the beginning of August, & shall want money'.[4] It was his custom to defray his own expenses in travelling on connexional business, though some incidental items were paid for by the societies he visited: thus on 11th November of this year, the stewards at Sheffield paid 1s 9d for 'washing for Dr. Coke' and 4s 2d, 'his expenses to Nottingham'.[5] Beyond such chance references, we know very little of this 'long journey'. On his way north in August, he was accompanied by Jeremiah Brettell. 'In passing through Stafford with Dr Coke,' he wrote, 'while dining at an inn, the bellman was sent about to say, that the Rev. Dr Coke, from Oxford, was going to preach at the

[1] Sutcliffe, pp. 13f., where no indication of date is given. The *Victoria County History*, ii. 64, dates the incident in 1782, but without adducing any authority. It is possible that the anecdote really belongs to a much later period; cf. the account of Coke's visit in 1807, p. 305 below.

[2] Etheridge, p. 63. A letter to Gidley dated 17th June 1779 (Archives Centre) shows that Coke had paid at least one visit to his old parish in the previous year.

[3] See Norris, *South Petherton in Olden Days*, where, however, the date of the first chapel is wrongly given as 1808. (The conveyance of the site to the trustees is dated 25 May 1809.)

[4] Letter to Williams, 7th July 1779 (Wesley's Chapel, London).

[5] T. A. Seed, *Norfolk Street Wesleyan Chapel, Sheffield*, p. 31. In January 1792 the Sheffield society paid for 6 yards of black cloth at 8s 6d a yard, plus £1 3s 0d for 'making and trimming' on Coke's behalf: presumably for a suit.

market-place. The Doctor mounted a table, which I took from the inn for the purpose: the people came, and looked at us from a distance: but shortly drew near, and heard with attention.' A little society was formed as a result of this.[1] In the course of this journey Coke also called on Joseph Benson in Manchester, and discussed their doctrinal differences.[2]

For the most part, Coke found himself preaching to large congregations, though many no doubt came out of curiosity at the unusual spectacle of a Methodist preacher in full canonicals and one, in addition, who possessed an Oxford doctorate. Occasionally, he faced the kind of treatment which the Wesleys had received in the early years of the revival, and which was still meted out to the itinerants by the mob. Thus at Ramsbury, in Wiltshire, where he took his stand under an ancient wych-elm in the village square, he met with spirited opposition, of which Etheridge gives this eye-witness account:

As soon as he had commenced the service, he and his audience were attacked by a turbulent mob, headed by the vicar of the parish. Stones and sticks were plentifully used. Dr Coke was violently pushed from his stand, and his gown torn into shreds. Nothing daunted, he continued the service. The vicar then thought of another expedient, and gave the order, 'Bring out the fire-engine.' The mandate was obeyed, and both preacher and congregation were compelled to retire before the well-directed volleys of this liquid artillery. But, while leaving the square, the Doctor turned, and remarked to the people, that there were other uses for the fire-engines, of which Providence might soon permit the perpetrators of this outrage to become well aware. His words were drowned by the cry of 'False prophet!' Yet, within a fortnight a fire broke out which destroyed nearly all the houses in the square, and extended a considerable distance down the street of the village.[3]

Before the end of the year, Coke found himself involved in the first of a series of disputes with which he was to be concerned as Wesley's trusted delegate. Trouble had broken out at Bath, and on 22nd November, John Wesley set out, with his brother, Brian Bury

[1] Brettell's autobiographical memoir in *Wesleyan Methodist Magazine*, 1830, p. 657; quoted in J. B. Dyson, *Wesleyan Methodism in Leek Circuit*, p. 19.

[2] Letter to Benson, 10th November 1779 (Archives Centre).

[3] Etheridge, p. 62, quoting an eye-witness account supplied by the Rev. William Edwards, whose grandfather had been present and helped to shield Coke from the mob.

Collins and Coke, to deal with it. At the previous Conference, the Scottish preacher, Alexander McNab, had been appointed to superintend the Bristol Circuit, to which Bath then belonged. Subsequently the Rev. Edward Smythe, an Anglican clergyman who had joined the Methodists in Northern Ireland in circumstances similar to Coke's, came to stay in Bath on account of his wife's health. Wesley had a high regard for Smythe and instructed that he was to occupy the pulpit at the recently opened chapel in King Street on Sunday evenings. To this McNab took exception, on the grounds that his own appointment, and that of his fellow-preachers, was by the Conference, so that Wesley was exceeding his authority in thus interfering with it. The society was quickly split into rival factions. Wesley went down in person and dealt with the matter with a degree of high-handedness unusual even for him; demanded submission to the Methodist rules (and, in particular, the twelfth of the 'Rules of a Helper' in a recension that appears to have been all his own); and next morning summarily dismissed McNab for not agreeing to 'our fundamental rule'.[1]

McNab was, by general consent, both an outstanding preacher and a man of irreproachable integrity: Wesley shared this estimate, though considering also that he was 'too warm and impatient of contradiction'.[2] There was general sympathy for him among the other preachers, although they were not prepared to make an issue of it. It was Charles Wesley whose influence lay behind his brother's intransigence. A similar issue had arisen earlier in the year in London, over the exclusion of the lay assistants from the pulpit of the new chapel at City Road.[3] Not unnaturally the sympathies of John Pawson, the superintendent of the London Circuit at that time, were on the side of McNab. He says that Charles Wesley 'made his brother believe, that Mr. McNab was only the tool of a violent party among the preachers, among whom there was a very

[1] *Journal of John Wesley*, vi. 262f., 289; Tyerman, *John Wesley*, iii. 303ff.; Simon, *The Last Phase*, 145ff.

[2] Letter to Lady Maxwell, 24th January, 1771 (*Letters of John Wesley*, v. 219).

[3] See Tyerman, op. cit., iii. 297–302, quoting Pawson's MS account at length. The unordained preachers in London protested that Charles Wesley was monopolizing the City Road pulpit and that they were excluded from it. Charles clearly thought that 'the passive Dr. Coke' sympathized with the preachers, but that he had left London for Bristol deliberately, to avoid being involved in the issue (Letter from Charles to John Wesley, 16th June 1779, in *Arminian Magazine*, 1789, p. 441).

powerful combination against his authority; and that, at the next Conference, they would show themselves'. Pawson denied that this was true. 'Not one preacher in the whole connexion was concerned in the business, save those who were stationed in the Bristol circuit. It is true, that the preachers in general thought that Mr. McNab was cruelly used; and so they do to this day.'[1] The general view is probably fairly expressed by the verdict of Thomas Taylor, who wrote: 'I cannot learn, that he [McNab] has merited such treatment. A man who has been a credit to our cause, whose moral character is unblameable, and whose abilities are considerable, is expelled for his integrity and uprightness.'[2] That Wesley may have had second thoughts on the matter and repented of his precipitate action seems a reasonable inference from the fact that, despite all the pressure which his brother could bring to bear on him, McNab was restored at the following Conference.

Where Thomas Coke's personal sympathies lay in all this we have no direct means of determining. Officially, in so far as he was one of the little group of Wesley's ordained helpers, his position was virtually determined for him; and his admiration for and loyalty towards Wesley led him to accept the extremely difficult role of mediator in the McNab dispute. Having delivered broadsides at both Bath and Bristol and issued his unconditional ultimatum, Wesley immediately withdrew, leaving Coke to salvage what he could of the two societies. We have Pawson's word for it that only Coke's exertions saved the Bristol society from being split like that at Bath.[3] On 15th December, 1779, he reported from Bristol such progress as he had managed to achieve: 'I am endeavouring to bring matters, respecting the Bath Chapel, to a conclusion. I find it very difficult to get money: yet, I hope, through the Divine blessing, it will be raised, and settled upon the plan prescribed in the Minutes. Brother B. shall be appointed steward, if you do not object to him. He is a man of peace, loves you, loves the Church of England, and is beloved by all the people.'[4]

[1] Pawson's MS account, quoted in Tyerman, op. cit., iii. 311. Simon, op. cit., 142, 147, refers to 'John *Dawson*', an error which is also transferred to the index.

[2] Quoted in Tyerman, op. cit., iii. 306.

[3] Ibid., iii. 310. See also the Address to the Bath Society by John Valton, who was stationed with McNab in the Bristol Circuit (MS at Methodist Archives Centre).

[4] Letter to Wesley, 15th December 1779 (*Arminian Magazine*, 1790, pp. 50f.).

The dispute at Bath was only the first of a series of difficult assignments entrusted to Coke by the ageing Wesley, so that before long he was increasingly out of London. In October 1781 he accompanied Wesley to the Isle of Wight for the opening of the new chapel at Newport.[1] In due course, it became the normal custom for the two men to follow an independent itinerary: Wesley, who had hitherto visited most of the societies annually, was now able to spread his round of visits over two years, while Coke took his place in alternate years. Replying to an invitation from Thomas Williams in Brecon, Coke wrote in 1783, 'I shall be happy to wait upon you, when I go to Brecon: but whether I can conveniently take a Bed with you, . . . I cannot at present determine. As Mr. Wesley is going into Wales for a little time this year, I shall not probably visit it till the next.'[2] In 1782 he paid the first of many visits to Ireland, where he presided over the Conference in Wesley's behalf. In September of the same year he set off for Scotland,[3] pausing on the way at Birstall, where another dispute demanded his conciliatory attention.[4]

The first preaching-house at Birstall had been built by John Nelson in 1751. Wesley's misgivings about the deeds on which the original building was settled were confirmed when the chapel was rebuilt in 1782. The new deed contained a clause providing that after the death of both John and Charles Wesley the choice and appointment of preachers should be in the hands of the trustees and certain local class-leaders; and, furthermore, that 'every person who shall be so appointed to preach in the said house shall enjoy the same office only during the good-will and pleasure of the major part of such trustees and classleaders as aforesaid and it may be lawful for the major part of the trustees and class leaders to deprive, remove or

[1] *Journal of John Wesley*, vi. 337 and note; also letter to Thomas Williams, 2nd November 1781 (Wesley's Chapel, London).

[2] Letter to Thomas Williams, 1st August, 1783 (Wesley's Chapel, London).

[3] Letter to Thomas Williams, 21st September 1782 (Wesley's Chapel, London): 'I am going to set off for *Scotland*, & shall not return much before Christmas.' During this tour he stayed for a few days with William Dodwell, rector of Welby, Lincs., a friend of his Oxford days, and introduced Methodism into the neighbouring village of Skillington. (T. Cocking, *Wesleyan Methodism in Grantham*, 1836, pp. 187f.)

[4] For the Birstall Chapel case, see: Tyerman, op. cit., iii. 373ff.; E. B. Perkins, *Methodist Preaching Houses*, pp. 25ff.; Wesley, *The Case of the Birstal House* (*Works*, xiii. 241ff.); *Minutes*, i. 157; Coke, *Address to the Inhabitants of Birstal*, 1782, etc.

suspend the preacher or pastor, for the time being, at their free will or pleasure . . .'[1]

It was this 'power to place or displace' the preachers, condemned by Wesley as Presbyterian, that was the crux of the matter. Put into the hands of the local trustees, it would quickly have disrupted the Methodist Connexion, whose unity rested upon the itinerant principle, and would have effectively gagged the preachers. Confronted by the new deed on 9th May Wesley refused to sign it, but later that day he was badgered by the trustees into capitulating, apparently under the persuasion that it was impossible to alter this clause from the deed of 1751. It was the act of an elderly man, tired out by a day filled with preaching and business affairs, and Wesley was not long in repenting of it. Towards the end of the month he wrote to his brother explaining how the trustees had 'got round' and 'worried him down'. He adds, rather pitifully, 'But I think they cannot worry *you*', and suggests that Charles should thwart the trustees by refusing to add his signature to the deed.[2]

The matter was then discussed at the Conference and it was decided that, if the trustees still refused to settle the chapel on 'the Methodist plan', two further steps were to be taken: '1. Let a plain state of the case be drawn up: 2. Let a collection be made throughout all England, in order to purchase ground, and to build another preaching-house as near the present as may be.' At this point Coke became actively involved, as the one deputed to put these resolutions into effect. Once again the situation was not of his making, and to that extent it would hardly be fair to blame him for any lack of success in his mission. However, Joseph Benson, for one, believed that Coke's handling of the matter was inept; and wrote that, if Wesley had dealt with it in person, then 'things would have been settled in an amicable manner; at least, they would not have been carried to such a length'.[3] We have little direct evidence on which to form a just estimate: but so far as the length to which matters went is concerned, we must bear in mind that Coke was acting on the Conference mandate we have already quoted. If a local schism threatened, it was precipitated quite as much by the Conference resolution as by anything he may have done or said on the spot.

On the evening of 17th October, Coke preached at Birstall. John Valton, the assistant there, described in his *Journal* how he 'signified

---

[1] E. B. Perkins, op. cit., p. 27.   [2] *Letters of John Wesley*, vii. 125.
[3] MS Life of Benson, quoted in *Letters of John Wesley*, vii. 148.

afterwards to the people that another house was to be built, on account of the Trustees of the other refusing to settle it upon the Conference plan. Immediately the waves lifted up their voice, and were ready to devour him . . . The next day the Attorney and a few of the Trustees met us, and such spirits were discovered as astonished me. But the Lord overruled the whole, for a proposal was made by Brother Charlesworth that was universally received and which ended the matter.'[1] Valton's hopes were, however, premature. What seemed a promising 'breakthrough' in the negotiations was thwarted by the trustees' insistence on retaining the power to determine whether or not the Conference had deviated from 'the grand Methodist plan'; and further approaches failed to produce any retraction on this point. Coke therefore proceeded to carry out the Conference instructions, first by issuing his *Address to the Inhabitants of Birstal*, in which, after a detailed account of the dispute, he asserted that the negotiations had proved fruitless largely because the trustees insisted on retaining the power of judging the fidelity of Conference to the principles of Methodism. He further pointed out that they had consistently refused to submit the case to arbitration. It appears that the reluctance of the trustees to come to terms with the Conference was based, at least in part, on financial considerations. In a letter to one of them, Joseph Charlesworth, Coke agreed that it was unfair that any who had loaned money on the new chapel should lose it and offered to guarantee that the interest on the loans would be paid regularly.[2] In the *Address* he went further, offering to repay both interest and principal, and to refund within two years the donations of any who disliked the 'Methodist-plan'. (Wesley himself later backed this offer with a promise of £100 towards clearing the £350 debt.) These overtures were bluntly rejected.

Coke's *Address* closes with an impassioned appeal to the members of the Birstall congregation. 'To whom, under God, are you indebted for your convictions?' he asks them. 'Were they the stones and mortar of the old House? Or the ground on which it stood? Were they the old or new Trustees? Or were they not the *Methodist Preachers*, those whom some of you would gladly subject to the caprice or mercy of men of like passions with yourselves?' And he

[1] Valton's MS Journal, quoted in *W.H.S. Proc.* viii. 23.
[2] Tyerman, op. cit., iii. 378, where the address of the letter is mistakenly given as 'Bristol'.

ends with a prayer to 'the Lover of Concord and Prince of Peace', which, unless we dismiss it as hypocritical cant, reveals a man who was more deeply concerned for the spiritual welfare of the flock than with bricks and mortar.[1] The matter was not finally settled until Wesley had again met the trustees in the autumn of 1783.

This particular storm in a Yorkshire teacup has been described in some detail partly because it is an illustration of the kind of mundane problem in which Coke found himself involved during these years. There is little doubt that he had no taste for such embroilments; but his personal loyalty to Wesley and his zeal for the kingdom of God both found expression in the care he lavished on the administrative details of the tasks assigned to him. He was not one of those who make spiritual-mindedness an excuse for inefficiency.

The settlement of the Birstall issue did not release Coke from preoccupation with such matters. The 1783 Conference, aware that an important principle was at stake, asked and answered the following question:

Q. 24. What can be done to get all our preaching-houses settled on the Conference Plan?

A. Let Dr Coke visit the Societies throughout England, as far as is necessary for the accomplishment of this design; and let the respective Assistants give him all the support in their power.[2]

Coke's legal background was clearly proving as useful to Wesley as his clerical status. It was an easy enough decision for the Conference to take: how much travelling and effort it cost Coke in implementing it we can do little more than guess. Certainly he would make enemies, some of them influential ones, in the process, and it would be easy enough for them to fling the accusation of authoritarianism at him. His impulsive nature was inclined to lead him into tactlessness; but of his sincerity and zeal only his sworn enemies could harbour any doubts. Among the further cases in which he found himself involved, the most notorious was that of the preaching-house at Daw Green, Dewsbury, only a short distance

---

[1] Similarly, in his *State of the Dewsbury House*, 1788, Coke concludes with a prayer that God 'may blast all the designs of Ahitophel' and 'bind the first author of this evil, the Devil', so as to preserve the unity of the company of the Methodist preachers.

[2] *Minutes*, i. 167.

from Birstall.[1] Here the rebuilding of the chapel had been begun in 1784, but the trustees subsequently refused to settle it on the Conference plan, claiming, in particular, the right both to try and to expel any preacher accused of immorality. They were encouraged in this by John Atlay, Wesley's book steward at the time, who promised to become their minister in the event of a separation. Wesley wrote to them on 30th July 1788, succinctly setting out the point at issue: 'The question between us is, "By whom shall the preachers sent, from time to time, to Dewsbury be judged?" You say, "By the trustees". I say, "By their peers—the preachers met in conference." '[2]

A few days later Coke wrote on behalf of the Conference then meeting in London, expressing their determination 'to be judged by their peers in respect to their appointments and ministerial labours' and setting out certain proposals for a compromise.[3] At the same time Conference renewed its efforts to avert further cases of this kind by passing the following minute:

Q. 24. What can be further done to secure our preaching-houses to the Connexion?

A. Let no house be built on any consideration, till the ground first be settled on the Conference plan.[4]

In September Coke issued his *Vindication of the Conduct of the Conference*. The crucial question, he says, is, 'Is it equitable, in this or any case of a judicial nature, that the same persons should be accusers, jury, judges, and executioners?' and he claims to have found no parallel to such 'barefaced tyranny and injustice' as was implied by the demands of the Dewsbury trustees, except in 'the histories of the Popish Inquisition'.[5] By now each side was stridently accusing the other of high-handed tyranny and the chances of mutual understanding and reconciliation rapidly dwindled.

As the Dewsbury trustees remained adamant, Wesley was left

[1] For the Dewsbury Chapel case, see: Tyerman, op. cit., iii. 551ff.; Wesley, *Works*, xiii. 245ff.; E. B. Perkins, op. cit., 53f.; Coke, *The State of the Dewsbury-house in Yorkshire*, 1788; and Mather's *Supplement* to this in the same year.

[2] *Letters of John Wesley*, viii. 77.

[3] Letter 'to the Trustees of the Preaching-House at Dewsbury', 6th August 1788 (Drew University).

[4] *Minutes*, i. 214f.

[5] Coke, op. cit., where he says that to submit to the trustees' demands 'would entirely cut the sinews of Christian discipline'.

with the alternatives of suing for possession of the chapel or building another. 'We prefer the latter,' he wrote, 'being the more friendly way'.[1] Methodism in Dewsbury was thus driven out of doors once more and forced for the time being to revert to its primitive simplicity. In July 1789, Wesley visited the town with Coke and both men preached in the open air.[2] Shortly after this, the Leeds Conference sanctioned the making of private and public collections throughout the Connexion towards the building of a new preaching-house,[3] Wesley and Coke leading the way with subscriptions of £50 each. For his part in the dispute, and in particular for his authorship of *The State of the Dewsbury House*, in which he vindicated the conduct of the Conference, Coke again drew upon himself much hostility and calumny, including the charge of inconsistency.[4]

The difficulties that arose at Birstall, Dewsbury and elsewhere were particular instances of a problem that was more than local. It was a problem that might have been averted, had Wesley had a little more foresight a few years earlier. In the Minutes for 1779, we find this item:

Q.22. Some Trustees may abuse their power after my death. What can be done now to prevent this?

A. It seems, we need take no thought for the morrow, God will provide when need shall be.[5]

The inadequacy of this admirable sentiment was fully exposed by the events of the next few years. Wesley's reluctance to act in the matter may have been due, in part, to an awareness that every step

---

[1] *Letters of John Wesley*, viii. 169; *Works*, xiii. 246.

[2] J. R. Robinson, *Early Methodism in Dewsbury*, p. 68.

[3] *Minutes*, i. 224. The same Conference ordered that no new preaching-houses were to be built that year, 'except one at Dewsbury, and those which have already been begun or set on foot'.

[4] *A Reply to what Dr Coke is pleased to call 'The State of the Dewsbury Chapel House'* appeared in 1788; Robinson also mentions *An Impartial statement of the known inconsistencies of the Rev. Dr Coke*, 1792. The trustees accused Coke of misrepresenting the facts and denied that Wesley had been rushed into signing the original agreement.

Another dispute of the same kind, in which Coke was involved on the part of the Conference, arose over the Milburn Place chapel at North Shields during the years 1786-8; this was complicated by rivalry between two neighbouring societies. See *W.H.S. Proc.* iv. 223ff., and references given there.

[5] *Minutes*, i. 136.

towards consolidating the Connexion hastened its formal separation from the Church of England. But in the end he was driven to recognize that nothing less than the future of the Connexion was at stake. Wesley himself was, by virtue of the course of events, the personal centre of unity for all those who were 'in connexion with' him. Inevitably, he was increasingly concerned about what might happen after his death, though disclaiming such concern as a principle by which to determine his present actions.[1] That there was reason for apprehension is demonstrated by the case of the New Room at Bristol. Before the 1783 Conference met in that city, and while the Birstall dispute was at its height, Wesley sent Coke to persuade the trustees of the New Room to alter the terms of their deed so as to secure to the Wesleys, and after them to the Conference, the right of appointing the preachers. The attempt failed, possibly through want of diplomacy on Coke's part. On the day the Conference opened, the trustees presented a protest to Wesley, rejecting the proposed alterations. 'They having maturely and seriously weighed the great Trust repos'd in them, namely for the use of the Methodist Church, in connexion with the Church of England, are of the opinion that they cannot conscientiously, legally, or justly, give up, or transfer the same, to any persons whatever.' At the same time, they added that 'the Trustees have no desire or wish but to act in concurrence with ye Conference as long as they continue to support Mr Wesley's Doctrines, and they hope the time will never come in which they shall be witnesses to the contrary'.[2] Superficially, this was reassuring, but the crux of the matter still lay in the fact that the Trustees retained the right to determine whether the Conference, or its appointed preachers, remained loyal to the doctrines and practice of Mr Wesley. Coke later asserted that the extreme disrespect which the Trustees showed to Wesley had been a major cause of the serious illness which overtook him during the Conference in Bristol and brought him to the brink of the grave. And when, a year later, they still remained adamant, he wrote to one of them, William Pine, that 'a Repetition of the same Behaviour

[1] E.g. in a letter to his brother Charles, 13th September 1785: 'I must and will save as many souls as I can while I live without being careful about what may *possibly* be when I die'. (*Letters of John Wesley*, vii. 289.) Cf. his letter to Thomas Taylor, February 1786 (ibid., vii. 316f.). Wesley was here reiterating a principle on which he had insisted ever since the first Conference in 1744 (*Minutes*, i. 6).

[2] Quoted in Simon, *The Last Phase*, p. 203.

will probably the sooner bring into your hand the *Power* you so much prize'—that of appointing the preachers after Wesley was dead.[1]

It is significant of the tangled skein of Coke's responsibilities during these years that up to the very eve of his sailing for America in 1784, he was involved in this far from edifying wrangle over the New Room deed. The fragment of his correspondence with William Pine which has survived illustrates the degree to which personalities as well as principles were involved in these chapel disputes, and enables us, for once, to glimpse something of the Trustees' side of the picture. Coke had been stung into making four charges against the Bristol trustees, some of which certainly appear rather rash and extravagant. Furthermore, he did not scruple to preach on the matter from the New Room pulpit, denouncing the opposing party vehemently as 'Achans in the camp' and 'wolves in sheep's clothing'. He accused them of dishonesty, and of being in fact enemies of the Church of England; for these charges there was little justification and he was forced, in part, to retract them. He accused them further of falsehood, on the grounds that they had eventually refused to sign an instrument of reconciliation, to the terms of which they had previously agreed. And, he said, they had insidiously sought to undermine the authority of Wesley and the Conference by enlisting the support of Charles Wesley, then in London, who had known nothing of the matter until informed of it by Durbin. 'Everyone that is intimately acquainted with Mr C. Wesley', wrote Coke, 'knows the deep Prejudices of his mind against us; I mean, the *Lay-Preachers*, who are *myself*, men who, I verily believe, are superior in every real Excellency necessary to qualify them for their Function, to any Body of Clergy, or Ministers, in the British Empire; at whose Feet I lie, and whose Servant in the Lord I delight to profess myself to be.' Pine's triple insertion of [!!!] in sending Charles Wesley a copy of Coke's letter eloquently expresses his opinion of this protestation.

One particularly interesting feature of this exchange is the attempt that was made to isolate Coke by driving a wedge between

[1] Letter to William Pine, 15th September 1784, transcribed by Pine in his letter to Charles Wesley, 23rd September 1784 (Archives Centre), from which the following quotations are taken. Pine had entered into correspondence with Coke on behalf of his friend Henry Durbin, one of the leading members of the New Room Trust, against whom in particular Coke's four charges had been made. The exchange was cut short by Coke's departure for America: 'The Dr sailed on Saturday last, the 18th, with general Concurrence, and not a Tear or Sigh followed him from hence.'

him and John Wesley. Coke had protested that he had been acting throughout 'in an official Character, for the good of the whole Body and by an express Order from Conference', and that his offending letter to Durbin had been read to Wesley, who fully approved it before it was sent. Pine professed to disbelieve this. 'Mr John Wesley I think could never *approve* of such a letter.—You must have read some-thing else to him or you must have read it in such a manner as he could not properly understand it.' As soon as Wesley returned to Bristol, Durbin sent him a copy of the letter, and asked whether it had his approval. 'To which he sent an Answer not a whit better than the Dr's—charging Mr. D. with an Intention of keeping the Premises for his own Family, and other Accusations equally *true*! By which he has thrown down the *Gauntlett*.—But we do not chuse to take it up, unless forced to it in our own Defence.' The trustees clearly believed themselves to be the injured party, and Durbin himself was genuinely hurt by what seemed to him Wesley's unkind treatment of him.

The combined efforts of Coke and Wesley had resulted in a break-down of relationships, and despite a further attempt in 1788,[1] there the matter rested until 1791. The result was that, in the struggle between the rival factions after Wesley's death to determine whether, or not Methodism should remain within the Church of England, matters in Bristol came to a head in the exclusion of Henry Moore from the New Room pulpit. Trustees and Conference thus met in head-on collision, and Wesley's worst fears were justified, for it was to avert just such a consequence that Coke had been employed in the petty squabbles over the chapels at Birstall, Dewsbury and else-where. It might appear from this survey of the administrative matters over which Coke busied himself during the 1780s, that Wesley, though concerned with vital connexional principle, was con-tent to deal with the problem piecemeal, as and when it arose in the local situation. Even the Conference directive in 1783, though it sent Coke scurrying around the Connexion, scarcely goes beyond this. In fact, however, while he was grappling with particular groups of stubborn, or misguided trustees, Wesley was also—and again, largely through Thomas Coke,—seeking a sounder basis for the whole Con-nexion and its itinerant system. He had read to the 1769 Conference a paper suggesting the most desirable steps to be taken following his death to secure the unity of the Connexion, and the continuing

[1] *Journal of John Wesley*, viii. 436 (20th September 1788).

authority of the Conference over the work which he had begun.[1] Benson Perkins is no doubt right that it was this which 'set in motion trains of thought which had ultimate issue . . . in the Deed of Declaration of 1784'.[2] Wesley's suggestions germinated in the minds of his preachers, so that in the measures he now took for the future of the Connexion he had their support and encouragement.

Ever since the first issue of the 'Large Minutes' in 1763, there had been available a Model Deed on which all new preaching-houses might be settled. This provided that after the death of the Wesleys and Grimshaw, only those preachers 'appointed at the yearly Conference of the people called Methodists' should occupy their pulpits. We have seen how much trouble ensued when chapels were settled on deeds which lacked such a clause. But there was a further difficulty in the inadequately defined term, 'the yearly Conference of the people called Methodists'. Was this specific enough in the eyes of the law? Many of the preachers in 1782 thought not, and their views, if not their consequent apprehensions, were clearly shared by some trustees, who openly declared that since the law would not recognize the authority of Conference, they would be free after Wesley's death to appoint preachers of their own choosing.[3] Consequently, there was general alarm among the preachers in Conference. 'Many', says Coke, 'expressed their fears that divisions would take place among us, after the death of Mr Wesley, on this account; and the whole body of preachers present seemed to wish, that some methods might be taken to remove this danger, which appeared to be pregnant with evils of the first magnitude.'[4]

Soon after the 1782 Conference, Coke took up the matter with Wesley's solicitor, William Clulow of Chancery Lane, whom Wesley describes (apparently in contrast to most of his profession) as 'a skilful and honest Attorney'.[5] Clulow drew up a statement of the case, which was presented to 'that very eminent counsellor Mr Maddox'[6] for his opinion. He was asked, in particular, whether the general description of the Conference in the Model Deed, supported by constant usage, was sufficient to identify it in the eyes of the law

[1] *Minutes*, i. 87f.   [2] E. B. Perkins, op. cit., pp. 42f.

[3] Moore, *John Wesley*, ii. 294f.

[4] *Address to the Methodist Society in Great Britain and Ireland, on the Settlement of the Preaching Houses.*

[5] Wesley, *Works*, xiii. 216.

[6] Coke's *Address*. John Maddocks or Maddox (both spellings occur in contemporary sources) had earlier been consulted on the Birstall Trust Deed.

and to enable it to maintain its authority over the appointment of the preachers and their right to use the chapels. Mr Maddocks considered that the position was not satisfactory, and advised that 'Mr John Wesley should prepare and subscribe a Declaration for that purpose, to be enrolled in the Court of Chancery for safe custody, naming the present members and prescribing the mode of election to fill vacancies . . .'[1] Coke reported this opinion to the following Conference, and says that 'the whole Conference seemed grateful to me for procuring the opinion, and expressed their wishes that such a deed might be drawn up, and executed by Mr Wesley, as should agree with the advice of that great lawyer, as soon as possible.'[2] The result was the famous Deed of Declaration, enrolled in Chancery on 9th March 1784, which gives definition to 'the Conference of the people called Methodists' and sets out the regulations governing its functioning.

The Deed was largely the work of Coke and Clulow, though Wesley, as we shall see, played a decisive part in one section of it. Coke immediately sent out copies to all the preachers, probably on his own initiative and without Wesley's knowledge. The Deed had been drawn up at their express request, but its first effect was to bring down a storm of furious protest, mainly on the head of the unsuspecting Coke. This was because at one point in the Deed Wesley had named one hundred preachers who were to constitute the legal nucleus of the Conference, though with no intention of excluding the rest from its deliberations and decisions. Most of the criticism and complaining naturally came from some of those left out of this list, especially certain senior preachers who were already inclined to jealousy over the confidence which Wesley placed in Coke. 'There were, indeed, some preachers,' says Crowther, 'particularly a few of considerable standing and respectability, who viewed Dr Coke with something of a jealous eye, from his first entering among them . . . Some of these were sometimes ready to ask, "Who made thee a prince and a judge over us?" '[3]

Feelings ran high among the preachers and John Hampson senior circulated an *Appeal* which summed up the dissatisfaction.

---

[1] Quoted in Simon, op. cit., p. 210. All printed references to this legal opinion give its date as 5th December 1783, although Coke states quite clearly that it was discussed during the 1783 Conference. It would appear that Maddocks was consulted twice on the matter.

[2] Coke's *Address*.   [3] Crowther, p. 122.

This together with the Deed itself was brought before the Conference when it met in Leeds. Wesley stood firm on his right to summon whom he would to confer with him, as had been his custom from the beginning. Benson, who was present, describes how he made a personal issue of it, insisting that the authors of the *Appeal* had betrayed him, had represented him falsely as 'unjust, oppressive, and tyrannical', and consequently had greatly harmed the Connexion. He insisted 'that they should acknowledge their fault, and be sorry for it, or he could have no further connexion with them'.[1] Before the Conference ended, the erring brethren capitulated in the face of this ultimatum, and were received back with the joy normally reserved for repentant sinners, thanks chiefly to an impassioned intervention by Fletcher. Though a few preachers resigned, peace was restored; yet some underlying resentment remained, chiefly against Coke for his supposed part in the preparation of the Deed. Those preachers whose names were missing from the 'Legal Hundred' were convinced that they detected his hand in the omission, and in their reconciliation with Wesley some at least of their resentment was transferred to Coke. The facts, nevertheless, are definite enough, and of Coke's innocence there can be no reasonable doubt. Coke himself, in an *Address to the Methodist Society . . . on the Settlement of the Preaching Houses*, which he circulated about 1790, categorically denied the charge. After describing his part in drawing up the Deed, he says:

There remained nothing now but to insert the names of those who were to constitute the Conference. Mr Wesley then declared that he would limit the number to one hundred. This was indeed contrary to my very humble opinion, which was, that every preacher in full connexion should be a member of the Conference . . . and I still believe it will be most for the glory of God, and the peace of our Zion, that the members of the Conference admit the other preachers who are in full connexion, and are present at the Conferences from time to time, to a full vote on all occasions. However, of course, I submitted to the superior judgement and authority of Mr Wesley. But I do publicly avow, that I was not concerned in the limitation of the number, or the selection of the hundred preachers who were nominated the members of the Conference.[2]

Wesley himself was not reluctant to accept responsibility for this controversial section of the Deed. His laconic reply to those who wished to saddle Coke with the responsibility for having selected the 'Hundred' was, *Non vult, non potuit*. In March 1785, while Coke was

[1] Macdonald, *Memoirs of Joseph Benson*, p. 160.
[2] Cf the statement in Coke and Moore, *John Wesley*, p. 358.

away in America, Wesley published his *Thoughts upon Some Late Occurrences*. He explained why he decided to limit the list to one hundred, and added 'In naming these Preachers, as I had no adviser, so I had no respect of persons; but I simply set down those that, according to the best of my judgement, were most proper . . . If I did wrong, it was not the error of my will, but of my judgment.'[1] Wesley's reasons are not our immediate concern,[2] but it is clear that Coke, though he acquiesced at the time, did not share them. The fairest summary is probably that of John Pawson, who wrote, 'I do not think that Mr Wesley had any improper design in this [the omission of some of the elder preachers] but that he did it without due consideration, not foreseeing the consequences which would follow. Dr Coke has been very unjustly blamed, as having selfish designs in procuring this Deed to be made, and influencing the mind of Mr Wesley in the choice of the preachers; but I am persuaded that, respecting both the one and the other, he was perfectly innocent.'[3]

There were occasions when Coke's diplomacy was brought into play in disputes of a more personal nature. Thomas Wride, appointed superintendent in Norwich in 1785, was soon at loggerheads with both his colleagues and many of the society. Wride's efforts to enforce some aspects of Methodist discipline that had fallen into neglect were not assisted by his eccentricities both in and out of the pulpit. His chief complaints against his fellow-preachers, McKersey and Byron, were that they allowed more than two hymns, and also the singing of anthems, in a service, refused to preach at 5 a.m., and neglected to meet the select band and the children.[4] Wesley visited the city in October to lay the dust of controversy, and seems to have taken the superintendent's side in the matter, telling his congregation, 'Of all the people I have seen in the kingdom, for between forty and fifty years, you have been the most fickle, and yet the most stubborn'.[5] On 14th December, he wrote to Wride, 'If they do not

[1] Wesley, *Works*, xiii. 216.
[2] At one extreme, Crowther allows that Wesley may have been moved by prejudice against those who were sufficiently independent of mind to have opposed him from time to time. (Op. cit., p. 121) Simon, on the other hand, in *W.H.S. Proc.* xii. 81ff., analyses the principles on which Wesley proceeded in his selection and concludes that he aimed at a balanced proportion of both old and young, so as to ensure 'a strong permanent element in the membership of the Conference'.
[3] *E.M.P.*, iv. 52f.   [4] *W.H.S. Proc.* i. 140ff.
[5] *Journal of John Wesley*, vii. 121 (22nd October 1785).

soon come to their senses at Norwich, I will remove you to Colchester',[1] and this step became necessary early in the new year. Whatever the justification for Wride's actions, he so offended an influential part of the society that it was in danger of being torn in pieces by the rancour and animosity engendered. It was scarcely diplomatic of Wesley to involve Coke in this fracas, since one of Wride's 'eccentricities' had been his opposition to the sale of Coke's Baltimore sermon on Ashbury's ordination on the grounds that it amounted to formal separation from the Church and would 'tear up Methodism by the roots'.[2] Coke, nevertheless, was sent and for once was instrumental in restoring good order and peace to the Norwich society.[3]

For his part in settling these disputes which troubled the Methodist Connexion in Wesley's closing years, Coke got little thanks, and perhaps experience taught him to expect none. In 1797, when it was learned that he intended to settle in America, the British Conference responded by electing him President, and requested the American Connexion to release him from his obligations to them, on the grounds that 'He has often been a peace-maker among us, and we have frequently experienced the salutary effects of his advice and exertions in behalf of this part of the Connexion'.[4] This official eulogy, however, did not represent the unanimous opinion of British Methodism. William Thompson reported to Joseph Benson that many were objecting to the description of Coke as a man of peace. 'They ask me, both preachers and people, what discord or division has been among the Methodists since he was admitted that he has not been at the bottom of it. They mention Birstall, Dewsbury, London, Bristol, Lichfield, and all the uneasiness about the Sacrament.'[5] So much for his readiness to be sent to the trouble-spots, and his attempts, however inept they may sometimes have appeared to the observer, to reconcile opposing parties in the interests of the Connexion as a whole.[6]

[1] *Letters of John Wesley*, vii. 305. Cf. his brusque letter to the other two preachers on the same date.

[2] Tyerman, op. cit., iii. 466.

[3] W. Lorkin, *Wesleyan Methodism in Norwich*, 1825, p. 27.

[4] *Minutes*, i. 400.

[5] Letter from Thompson to Benson, 20th January 1798, in *W.H.S. Proc.* viii. 197f.

[6] For Coke's own protestations concerning rival factions and schism, see his letters to Benson and Holder below, pp. 207, 209f.

For several years, Coke devoted himself to such uncongenial endeavours as have been described in this chapter. The extent to which in this and other ways he lightened the administrative burden on the ageing shoulders of Mr Wesley can scarcely be estimated. But to see all this activity in perspective we must bear in mind that, at the very time he was touring the Connexion endeavouring to get the preaching-houses settled on the Conference plan and helping to draft the Deed of Declaration, he was already looking further afield. At the end of 1783, he circulated his first 'Plan of the Society for the Establishment of Missions among the Heathens', an abortive but nonetheless prophetic move. And he was already preparing for a voyage across the Atlantic, to settle the Methodist Connexion in America on a more adequate basis, now that the War of Independence had run its course.

CHAPTER 5

THE EPISCOPAL PRESBYTER

The year 1784 was a momentous one for Methodism and for Thomas Coke. The enrolment in Chancery of the Deed of Declaration marked the coming-of-age of the Methodist movement, which, despite Wesley's expressed intentions, now had an independent existence. In the midst of this and other Conference affairs, Coke produced his first Plan for establishing foreign missions, a plan which was doomed to postponement only because still more momentous events were at hand. For at 4 a.m. on Thursday, 2nd September, in the house of Dr John Castleman of 6 Dighton Street, Bristol,[1] Wesley, by the imposition of his hands and by prayer, 'set apart' Thomas Coke as superintendent of the rapidly growing work in America. In this, as in the ordination of two preachers, Whatcoat and Vasey, he was assisted by the Rev. James Creighton whom Coke had brought down from London for the purpose and also, it would seem, by the two newly-ordained elders.[2] Coke, in his turn, was to lay his hands upon Francis Asbury as joint superintendent with him in the United States. Methodism on both sides of the Atlantic was poised on the threshold of adulthood.

Wesley's action, fraught as it was with so many implications and repercussions, was performed in such secrecy that it was known in advance to very few. It appears that Wesley had confided to the

---

[1] W.H.S. Proc. ii. 99ff. The house was badly damaged during the Second World War.

[2] Wesley's *Journal* is noticeably reticent about the ordinations, merely stating that on 31st August 'Dr Coke, Mr Whatcoat, and Mr Vasey came down from London in order to embark for America' and that next day Whatcoat and Vasey were appointed 'to go and serve the desolate sheep in America'. The entry for 2nd September, which is missing from some early editions (see W.H.S. Proc. vii. 9) reads cryptically, 'I added to them three more; which I verily believe will be much to the glory of God'. (Op. cit., vii. 15.) The Diary is more explicit: 'Thursday 2: 4 [a.m.] Prayed, ordained Dr Coke . . .' On the participation of Whatcoat and Vasey in the consecration, see E. W. Thompson, *Wesley, Apostolic Man*, pp. 8f.

68

Leeds Conference only his intention of sending Coke and others to America.[1] Of his plans to ordain them he said nothing, except to his 'select committee of consultation', which according to John Pawson unanimously opposed the idea.[2] Charles Wesley was in Bristol at the time, yet did not learn what had taken place until two months later, when he was not slow to condemn it as 'this infamous ordination',[3] by which, he declared, his brother had *realized the Nag's Head ordination*, and left an indelible blot on his name, as long as it shall be remembered'.[4] Neither John Wesley nor Coke was taken unawares by this reaction.

No other single act of John Wesley has been so strongly and widely criticized. He has been described as lapsing into Presbyterianism in the very act of aspiring to episcopal powers, and charged with a degree of inconsistency that can only be set down to senility, although all the evidence points to his having been still very much in possession of his mental and physical faculties at that date.[5] At the same time, efforts have frequently been made to exculpate Wesley by blaming Coke for taking the initiative in the matter and for seeking consecration for the most unworthy of motives.[6] Wesley's intentions and motives have already received the fullest attention elsewhere;[7]

[1] Coke and Moore, *John Wesley*, p. 458.

[2] Tyerman, *John Wesley*, iii. 428. A. Raymond George, in *L.Q.R.*, 1951, pp. 156ff., appears to have misunderstood this as referring to the full Conference.

[3] Letter to Henry Durbin, quoted in F. Baker, *Charles Wesley*, p. 135.

[4] Letter to Dr T. B. Chandler, 28th April 1785, quoted in Jackson, *Charles Wesley*, ii. 389ff.; *W.H.S. Proc.* ii. 102, etc. Charles told Chandler, 'I was then in Bristol, at his elbow; yet he never gave me the least hint of his intention'.

[5] See especially, E. W. Thompson, op. cit., pp. 12f., 'The truth is, that Wesley in his eighty-second year still was an extraordinarily fit and able man'.

[6] Notably Whitehead, *John Wesley*, ii. 413-8; Nightingale, *Portraiture of Methodism*, pp. 401, 405f. Alexander Knox, whose *Remarks* are printed as an appendix to Southey's *Life of Wesley* (Oxford Standard Authors, 1925), ii. 359, may be quoted as characteristic of this line of attack: 'That Dr C. urged Mr Wesley to this proceeding, I know with certainty from the doctor himself; and full acquaintance with this well-meaning but very inconsiderate man makes me feel that Mr Wesley could scarcely have had a more unfortunate adviser. The argument by which Mr Wesley brought himself to comply with Dr C.'s wish is itself an evidence that his reasoning faculty had greatly failed.' For a more sympathetic assessment of Coke's share of responsibility, see A. W. Harrison, *The Evangelical Revival and Christian Reunion*, pp. 145f.

[7] See especially the contributions of V. E. Vine and A. Raymond George and E. W. Thompson in *W.H.S. Proc.* xxx and xxxi; also A. B. Lawson, *John Wesley and the Christian Ministry*.

we are concerned with them here chiefly for their bearing on Coke's part in this sequence of events.

In laying hands on Coke and his companions, Wesley was far from acting with unpremeditated haste. He was responding to a situation which had been developing for many years and to a need of which he had long been aware; and he did so in the light of beliefs about the Church and ministry which he had held, though without acting upon them, since 1746.

Methodism in America had originated among Irish immigrants about the year 1766. The British Conference sent out its first group of preachers three years later, and among others who followed as the years passed was Francis Asbury in 1771. In 1773 Thomas Rankin was sent out to superintend the work and the first Conference of preachers was held, in Philadelphia. The work continued to grow rapidly, but meanwhile political trouble was brewing and with the outbreak of hostilities in 1775 several of the British preachers returned home. Rankin remained until 1778, but his indiscretions in public utterances brought suspicion on both himself and Methodism, while Wesley's widely-known views, especially as expressed in his *Calm Address to our American Colonies*, did nothing to help matters. Eventually, Asbury alone remained at his post, and even he was forced into retirement for a time when the war was at its height. The Annual Conference of 1779, held at Asbury's retreat, appointed him 'General Assistant in America', though his movements were still to some extent restricted and it was a troubled Connexion over which he was called to exercise authority. The withdrawal of all but a handful of the Anglican clergy meant that the Methodists were deprived of the sacraments, and pressure was growing, especially in the south, for administration by the preachers. Another Conference, held at Fluvanna, Virginia, in the same year, decided in Asbury's absence on a scheme of ordination, in order that the Methodist societies might receive the sacraments from their own preachers. A year later, however, Asbury successfully pleaded with them to abandon this innovation.[1] The tide was stemmed, but only for a short breathing-space.

Faced with this situation, Asbury wrote repeatedly to Wesley, appealing for help either from Wesley in person or from some other

[1] In the light of Wesley's eventual solution, it is interesting to find Asbury in 1775 expressing the conviction that presbyterian ordination was 'incompatible with Methodism' (*Journal*, i. 149).

ordained clergyman.[1] Wesley did what he could, though for the time being this was little enough. The Bishop of London had rejected his pleas to ordain one or more of the Methodist preachers for the American work. There were, it is true, technical difficulties in the way of providing episcopally ordained clergy for the newly independent States, since until a special Act was passed in 1784 they were still required to take the oath of allegiance, even though they might not be British citizens.[2] The need, nevertheless, remained, and Independence had merely increased its urgency. Wesley's letter to Bishop Lowth represents the American people as 'sheep scattered up and down'. 'Part of them have no shepherds at all, particularly in the northern colonies; and the case of the rest is little better, for their own shepherds pity them not. They cannot; for they have no pity on themselves. They take no thought or care about their own souls.' The effect of the war had varied from colony to colony, but nowhere were the remaining clergy numerically or spiritually adequate to meet the colonists' needs. Particularly hard hit was a state such as Virginia, where the Church of England, once established by law, now found itself disestablished and disendowed. 'At the outbreak of the war there were 95 parishes, 164 churches and chapels, and 91 episcopal clergymen. At the end of the struggle for independence 23 parishes were either extinct or abandoned. Thirty-four were without ministers, having no means of support. Some returned to England; others to secular pursuits.'[3]

This situation was felt especially keenly by the members of the Methodist societies, many of whom, as in England, looked upon themselves as loyal Anglicans and were accustomed to attend the parish churches particularly for the administration of the sacraments. Their plight was only partly mitigated by the efforts of an actively sympathetic clergyman like Devereux Jarratt, who for years travelled widely through Virginia and North Carolina to give the sacraments to the Methodist societies.

The only lasting solution lay in the provision of an American episcopate. This step had long been proposed, but was fraught with difficulties. In the 1760s the colonial clergy had renewed the

[1] Asbury, *Letters*, pp. 24ff.; *Journal*, i. 378.
[2] Statute 24 George III. c. 35, printed in A. L. Cross, *The Anglican Episcopate and the American Colonies*, pp. 346f.
[3] E. Clowes Chorley, *Men and Movements in the American Episcopal Church*, p. 27. Cf. the figures given by Jarratt (*Arminian Magazine*, 1786, pp. 397ff.).

campaign launched over a century before by Archbishop Laud, but the Declaration of Independence found the American Church still without a single bishop of its own. The reasons for this were two-fold. There was, on the one hand, the inflexibility of the Established Church, which, in its turn, aroused widespread opposition to any proposal for introducing into America bishops with temporal powers —the only kind of episcopacy to be found in, or envisaged by, the English Church of the day. Dissenters on both sides of the Atlantic, therefore, united with Whig politicians in greeting all such proposals with suspicion and hostility.[1] This was the context in which John Wesley, the high-church Tory, added his voice to the chorus demanding that an episcopally-ordained ministry be provided for the newly-independent American states.

What Wesley did on the morning of 2nd September 1784 arose from no unpremeditated impulse, but one which he had considered as a possibility long before events in America persuaded him to put theory into practice. Ever since reading Lord Peter King's *Account of the Primitive Church* in 1746, Wesley had been convinced of the original identity of episcopal and presbyterian orders and consequently of his right, as an ordained presbyter, to ordain others to the priesthood.[2] These views were further confirmed by his later reading of Stillingfleet's *Irenicon*, which demonstrated that the New Testament prescribed no one form of Church government, and gave him the Alexandrian precedent of which both he and Coke made so much use in justifying their actions in 1784.[3] Wesley was as much a high-churchman after his Aldersgate Street experience as before, but he was a high-churchman with a pragmatic approach to questions of church order. For him, the unity of the church was meaningless apart from its mission, and he was prepared in the last resort to sacrifice the one for the sake of the other. In June 1755, when the question of separation from the Church was very much in the air, he wrote, 'If we must either *dissent* or *be silent*, *actum est*.

---

[1] See W. W. Manross, *History of the American Episcopal Church*, pp. 154ff.

[2] *Journal of John Wesley*, iii. 232. After a lapse of nearly forty years, Wesley reverted to this moment of discovery in his letter to 'Our Brethren in America', (*Letters*, vii. 238).

[3] *Letters of John Wesley*, iii. 136, 182, vii. 21; E. W. Thompson, op. cit., pp. 31ff. Frederick Hunter has recently made the interesting suggestion that Wesley's appeal to the Alexandrian usage implies that 'originally he wanted Coke's ordination as Superintendent to take place in America'. (*John Wesley and the Coming Comprehensive Church*, 1968, p. 87.)

We have no time to trifle.'[1] To this man who, in all soberness, was convinced that he had been raised up to spread scriptural holiness, such externals as opinions about church government were always 'smaller matters than the love of God and mankind'.[2] In this respect, Wesley had a ready pupil in Thomas Coke.

As late as June 1780 Wesley was still protesting that, though the reading of Stillingfleet had convinced him of his right to ordain, yet, 'I see abundance of reasons why I should not use that right unless I was turned out of the Church'.[3] He was not turned out; yet little more than four years later we find him ordaining for America. What is the explanation? To hint at the onset of senility or at pressure brought to bear by the ambitious, self-seeking Coke, will not do. Wesley showed, by his subsequent words and actions, that he both knew what he was doing and did what he intended. He might cavil at the use of terms, when the American Methodists settled for the scriptural word 'bishop' instead of its anglicized form 'superintendent';[4] but, with or without the offending title, he still preferred the episcopal form of church government to any other, and his ordination of preachers went steadily on.

Wesley's own explanation is simply that the so-called 'logic of events', or the challenge presented by the desperate spiritual needs of the newly independent American states, led him eventually to put into use the power he had long believed to be his, along the lines foreshadowed in his letter to the Earl of Dartmouth as early as 1761.[5] This is made quite explicit both in the certificate of 'ordination' which he gave to Coke, and in his accompanying letter to 'our Brethren in North America'.[6] The former bears little resemblance to the normal form of an ordination certificate (which on other occasions it was Wesley's custom to copy) and was clearly composed for this very special occasion. Wesley speaks of those American Christians who had not abandoned the doctrine and discipline of the

[1] *Letters of John Wesley*, iii. 131. On the relationship of mission and union, see C. W. Williams, *John Wesley's Theology Today*, pp. 208ff.

[2] *Letters of John Wesley*, iii. 182.

[3] Ibid., vii. 21.   [4] See below, p. 118.

[5] *Letters of John Wesley*, iv. 146ff. The whole letter well illustrates Wesley's pragmatic approach to the question of Church Order in general.

[6] Coke's certificate is preserved in the M.M.S. Archives. See Appendix A. The certificate referred to in *W.H.S. Proc.* xii. 8off., appears to have been one of the many copies of the original document which once existed in Canada and America.

Church of England and who wished to remain under his care, and roundly asserts that he thinks himself 'to be providentially called at this time to set apart some persons for the work of the ministry in America'. In the letter he amplifies this. 'A very uncommon train of providences', he says, has set the American people free from the ecclesiastical authority of the English Church as well as from the civil authority of the Crown. Accordingly they have been left shepherdless, 'so that for some hundreds of miles together there is none either to baptize, or to administer the Lord's Supper'. Hitherto he has refused to exercise his right to ordain, 'not only for peace sake, but because I was determined as little as possible to violate the established order of the national Church to which I belonged'. But as things now stand in America, he has no further scruples over 'appointing and sending labourers into the harvest'. With the aid of scripture and reason, Wesley was prepared, like the prophets, to see the hand of God in the turn of current events; and though he would not carelessly or unnecessarily flout the traditions and practices of the Church, in the last resort the welfare of men's souls was the paramount consideration, and he was ready with the apostles to say, 'We ought to obey God rather than men'. It is easier to deride this as arrant enthusiasm, the exaltation of private judgement over the cumulative wisdom of the Church, than to suggest, as Wesley himself requests, 'a more rational and scriptural way of feeding and guiding these poor sheep in the wilderness'.[1]

A letter written by Wesley to Asbury while Coke was in mid-Atlantic sheds valuable light on what was in his mind at this time. Two things stand out. Firstly, Wesley was seeking for Methodism a middle course between Congregationalism and the confines of the Anglican parochial system, and was therefore chary of too close an association with the American Episcopalians. 'You are aware of the danger on either hand', he wrote, 'and I scarce know which is the greater? One or the other, so far as it takes place, will overturn Methodism from the foundation: Either our travelling Preachers turning Independents, & gathering Congregations each for himself: Or procuring Ordination in a *regular* way, & accepting Parochial Cures.'[2] Secondly, he had sufficient confidence in Coke's ability and

[1] *Letters of John Wesley*, vii. 237ff.; also Appendix A below. The letter was printed in the American *Minutes* for 1785, but with the odd omission of the sentence referring to Wesley's revised liturgy.
[2] *W.H.S. Proc.* xxxiii. 11.

integrity to leave Coke free to determine the best course to be taken after surveying the ground and consulting with Asbury.

It is difficult to be certain either how early Wesley first raised with Coke the possibility of his going to America, or at what stage in their discussions the question of Coke's 'ordination' was first mooted. Etheridge was content at this point to lean heavily on Drew's account; but though Drew may be substantially correct in his summary of what passed between Wesley and Coke in February 1784, he was certainly mistaken in thinking this to have been the first time the possibility of a visit to America was raised.[1] The account in Coke and Moore's *Life of Wesley*, which might have been invaluable in settling a number of disputable points, is unfortunately too vague and brief to be of much help here. It is nevertheless worth quoting as having Coke's sanction, if not originating from his pen. It states that Wesley, after considering Asbury's pleas for ordained clergy in America, 'informed Dr. *Coke* of his design of drawing up a plan of Church-government, and of establishing an Ordination for his *American* societies. But, cautious of entering on so new a plan, he afterwards suspended the execution of his purpose, and weighed the whole for upwards of a year.'[2] This suggests that the subject was first raised sometime in 1783, perhaps on one of the several occasions on which their paths crossed during that summer. (One of these, in August, was at Mr Castleman's in Bristol.)[3] In October of the same year, Coke informed Thomas Williams in a business letter, 'It is not very improbable but I may make a visit to our large Societies in America next Spring or Summer'.[4]

It seems likely that the question of Coke's ordination was deferred to a later stage in the discussions. Coke's letter to Wesley from Dublin on 17th April 1784, has been variously interpreted. Amid many uncertainties, two things at least seem clear: that the question of someone's going out to America had already been under discussion, partly by letter, for some considerable time; and further, that the ordination question, if it had been raised at all, was not yet in the forefront. Coke wrote:

[1] Etheridge, p. 100, quoting Drew, p. 62.
[2] Coke and Moore, op. cit., p. 458.
[3] *Journal of John Wesley*, vi. 441.
[4] Letter to Thomas Williams, 15th October 1783 (Wesley's Chapel, London). For Wesley's views at this time, see his letter to Edward Dromgoole, 17th September 1783 (*W.H.S. Proc.* xxvi. 27f.).

I intended to trouble You no more with anything about my going to *America*: but y^r. Observations concerning the Letter of Capt. *Webb's* Friend incline me to lay before You a few more Syllables on the Subject.

If some one in whom you could place the fullest Confidence & whom You think likely to have sufficient Influence & Prudence & Delicacy of Conduct for the Purpose, were to go over & return, You w^d. then have a Source of sufficient Information to determine on any Points or Propositions. You may, very probably, survive me many years: & I may also be destitute of the last-mentioned essential Qualification for the Business (to the former indeed I will beg claim without Reserve). Otherwise, the possibility of my surviving you w^d. render my taking such a Voyage expedient. Besides, (if we both live here below for many Years) 1st that You might have fuller Information concerning the State of the Country and the Societies, than Epistolary Correspondence can give you. 2dly That there may be a Cement of Union remaining after y^r. Death between the Societies of Preachers in the two Countries, & 3dly Because (if the awful Event of y^r. Death shd. happen, before my Removal to the World of Spirits) it is almost certain, for many reasons which might be given, that I shd. have Business enough of indispensable Importance on my hands in these Kingdoms.[1]

Since we know nothing of the course already taken by the discussion, it is hazardous, if not presumptuous, to interpret this passage, as some of Coke's critics have done, as indicating that the whole initiative in this American affair lay with the younger man, who was pressing Wesley in order to gratify his own ambition for honour and authority. The most that may be said is that he was aware of his unique position in relation to Wesley, and therefore to Methodism; and that he knew something of the dangers that the Connexion would—and, in fact, did—face when deprived of its founder.

By the end of May, Coke was writing that it was 'very probable' that he would be setting off for America in August or September and the matter was discussed, as we have seen, at the Conference, with the result that Whatcoat and Vasey volunteered to accompany him. A few days after the Conference had concluded, Coke wrote a further letter to Wesley, on the question of ordination, on which Wesley's mind was still not finally made up. Though he rejected the opinion of his brother and Lord Mansfield, that 'ordination is separation',[2] he was still reluctant to deviate unnecessarily from the prac-

---

[1] Letter to Wesley, from near Dublin, 17th April 1784 (Archives Centre).
[2] *Letters of John Wesley*, vii. 284f., 288.

tices of the national Church, and was, apparently, prepared to let Coke take upon himself the responsibility and the odium of ordaining for America. Since it has frequently been argued that for Wesley, a presbyter, to consecrate a bishop was either inconsistent or unnecessary, it is interesting to note that Coke's own arguments in favour of the laying on of hands are all purely practical ones. Already equal to Wesley *in ordine* he might be; but he was clearly far from being equal with him in the authority which the founder of Methodism wielded throughout his societies, even those across the Atlantic. Coke saw that the success of his mission might rest on his being accepted as Wesley's officially appointed delegate. Did this in Caesar seem ambitious? The answer depends on our interpretation of his motives, and of the purposes for which he sought a share of Wesley's influence. On the question of whether its writer was concerned for his own or the Connexion's advancement, Coke's 'somewhat dictatorial letter'[1] may be allowed to speak for itself.

9th August, 1784

Honoured and dear Sir,

The more maturely I consider the subject, the more expedient it seems to me that the power of ordaining others should be received by me from you, by the imposition of your hands; and that you should lay hands on Brother Whatcoat and Brother Vasey, for the following reasons:— 1. It seems to me the most scriptural way, and most agreeable to the practice of the primitive churches. 2. I may want all the influence in America which you can throw into my scale. Mr. Brackenbury informed me at Leeds that he saw a letter in London from Mr. Asbury, in which he observed 'that he should not receive any person deputed by you to take any part of the superintendency of the work invested in him,'—or words that implied so much. I do not find the least degree of prejudice in my mind against Mr. Asbury; on the contrary, a very great love and esteem; and I am determined not to stir a finger without his consent, unless sheer necessity obliges me; but rather to lie at his feet in all things. But as the journey is long, and you cannot spare me often, and it is well to provide against all events, and an authority *formally* received from you will be fully admitted by the people, and my exercising the office of ordination without that formal authority may be disputed, if there be any opposition on any other account; I could therefore earnestly wish you would exercise that power in this instance, which I have not the shadow of a doubt but God hath invested you with for the good of the Connexion. I think you have tried me too often to doubt whether I will in any degree use the power

[1] A. B. Lawson, op. cit., p. 142.

77

you are pleased to invest me with further than I believe absolutely necessary for the prosperity of the work . . . In short, it appears to me that
everything should be prepared, and everything proper to be done, that
can possibly be done, this side of the water . . . In respect to Brother
Rankin's argument, that you will escape a great deal of odium by omitting
this, it is nothing. Either it will be known, or not known. If not known,
then no odium will arise; but if known, you will be obliged to acknowledge that I acted under your direction, or suffer me to sink under the
weight of my enemies, with perhaps your brother at the head of them. I
shall entreat you to ponder these things.[1]

Wesley did ponder them, and on 2nd September, 'being now
clear in his own mind', he translated his thoughts into action.

[1] Moore, *John Wesley*, ii. 530ff. Etheridge gives the letter in abbreviated form.

CHAPTER 6

A CHURCH IS BORN

On the morning of Saturday 18th September, Coke set sail with his two companions on what was to be the first of eighteen voyages across the Atlantic. Fortunately, at this point he began to keep a journal of his travels, so that for most of his visits to America and the West Indies we are able to trace his movements in much greater detail than during the intervals he spent in England.[1]

Soon after they weighed anchor, a favourable wind sprang up, so that by Monday morning they had made about three hundred miles. They then found themselves driven back by violent storms; the decks were awash and the Methodist landlubbers were soon desperately seasick: or, as Coke put it, 'we were disabled from doing any thing but casting our care upon God'. He did not begin to recover until the Friday, when he normally fasted, but in his present weak state it seemed advisable to ignore his custom and he breakfasted on water gruel without bread. From then on things improved; the missionaries were able to take stock of their surroundings and to plan how they might improve the time. Coke soon learned to appropriate some corner of the ship as a study, and before long, as on his later voyages, was hard at work day by day. 'I enjoy one peculiar blessing,' he wrote, 'a place of retirement, a little secret corner in the ship; which I shall hereafter call my study. It is so small that I have hardly room to roll about, and there is a window in it which opens to the sea, and makes it the most delightful place under deck. Here, God willing, I shall spend the greatest part of my time.' His reading on board was quite varied. He found much pleasure in the Pastorals

[1] The Journal of this first American tour, published in 1789 in the *Arminian Magazine* (Philadelphia edition), vol. i, pp. 237ff., 286ff., 339ff., 391ff., was not printed in England until Coke included it in the collected reprint of his *Journals* in 1790. (But it was known to Wesley, presumably in MS form, as early as June 1785: see *Letters of John Wesley*, vii. 276.) The American edition, issued without Coke's immediate supervision, contains a number of variants and additions, some of which are noted below. Otherwise quotations are from the edition of 1816, pp. 37–75.

of Virgil, whose country scenes kindled his imagination and 'served now and then to unbend the powers of the mind'. St Augustine's *Confessions* were the staple of his devotional diet throughout the voyage, and the way in which his mind was moving on missionary matters is indicated by his reading the lives of Francis Xavier and of David Brainerd, the missionary to the North American Indians. Of Brainerd, while coveting 'his humility, his self-denial, his perseverance, and his flaming zeal for God', he was not uncritical in his admiration, commenting that in some respects 'he ran to great extremes'.[1]

On 18th October, with almost a sigh of relief, he notes the completion of another piece of substantial reading. 'I have waded through Bishop *Hoadley's* Treatises on Conformity and Episcopacy; five hundred and sixty-six pages octavo.' Reading Hoadley was clearly a formidable task, but also a necessary preparation for 'selling' Wesley's plan in America. Coke comments: 'He is a powerful reasoner, but is I believe wrong in his premises. However he is very candid.'

On Sundays the missionaries preached morning and afternoon on deck, and took the opportunity afforded by a sick sailor to visit the crew in the steerage. They also distributed copies of Wesley's tract, *A Word to a Sailor*, though sometimes Coke confessed himself 'ready to despair of doing them any essential good'. No one has recorded the reactions of the crew.

Once he had found his sea-legs, Coke always had an eye for natural beauty and noted any curious phenomena, such as his first sight of whales and porpoises. He was particularly moved by the beauty of dawn and sunset at sea. Shortly before they reached America he wrote, 'I never in my life saw so beautiful a mixture of colours, and so fine a fret-work. I do not wonder that the poor Heathen worship the sun.'

They landed in New York on 3rd November, after a 'very agreeable voyage' of six and a half weeks. Coke immediately sought out the Methodist preaching-house in John Street, where he lost no time in confiding to John Dickins, the preacher stationed in New York, the purpose for which Wesley had sent him over. 'He highly approves of it, says that all the Preachers most earnestly long for such a reformation,[2] and that Mr. *Asbury* he is sure will agree to it.' Dickins was

---

[1] Coke's *Journal*, American edition, p. 239.

[2] So the American edition p. 242; the English versions read 'regulation', probably a misprint.

strongly in favour of making Wesley's plan known without delay, but Coke does not seem to have taken the New York society into his confidence. He preached several times, and then, two days after landing, set off for Philadelphia to the south.

Nearly a week was spent in Philadelphia. On the Sunday Coke preached twice in St Paul's Church at the invitation of the minister, Dr Samuel Magaw, and again in the evening in the Methodist Chapel. Afterwards following Dickins's advice, he disclosed to the society 'our new plan of Church Government', to which there seemed to be a favourable response.[1] Next day Magaw called on him, together with Dr William White, who offered the use of his church the following Sunday. Magaw was on intimate terms with Asbury, but Coke studiously avoided any reference to Wesley's plans for American Methodism. Later he was to regret this, and in his approach to Bishop White in 1791 he apologized for having preached in their churches without confiding in them, a course which in retrospect appeared to him discourteous.

Before leaving Philadelphia, Coke was received by John Dickinson, the State Governor, 'a man of excellent sense and the utmost politeness', who was 'looked upon by many as the first literary character in *America*' and was personally acquainted with Wesley.[2] But his stay was not long enough for him to avail himself of White's offer. Moving into Delaware, he was entertained at Dover by a member of the state Executive Council and made the acquaintance of Freeborn Garrettson, one of the younger preachers who, he notes, had stoutly supported Asbury during the sacramental controversy.[3]

On Sunday 14th November, they went on to Barrett's Chapel, set 'in the midst of a forest' some miles from Dover. Coke preached to 'a noble congregation' on Christ as 'our wisdom, righteousness, sanctification and redemption', and immediately afterwards there occurred the most crucial meeting in the early history of American Methodism. 'After the sermon', wrote Coke, 'a plain, robust man came up to me in the pulpit, and kissed me: I thought it could be no other than Mr. *Asbury*, and I was not deceived.' We may set side

[1] Ibid. Wakeley's statement (*Lost Chapters Recovered*, p. 302) that Coke did not put Dickins's advice into execution until he had consulted Asbury is therefore untrue.

[2] Dickinson was a principal leader of the colonists and one of the architects of the new Constitution. Though not a Methodist, he had apparently met Wesley while in London between 1753 and 1755.

[3] Coke's *Journal*, American edition, p. 243.

by side with this the equally simple statement in Asbury's Journal: 'I came to Barratt's chapel: here, to my great joy, I met these dear men of God, Dr Coke and Richard Whatcoat, we were greatly comforted together.'[1]

The relationship between the two men who were thus brought together so many miles from their native land was immediately cordial, despite the fact that in almost every respect, except their devotion to Christ, they were contrasted personalities. Asbury had already been in America for thirteen years, and by courageous perseverance in the face of daunting odds had proved himself the natural leader of the American Methodists. Coke was an unknown newcomer, two years younger than Asbury and many years his junior in the itinerancy. Coke was short, with round, cherubic features often lit by a smile; neat, and even elegant, in dress and studiously courteous in bearing. His witty and informed conversation, though it made him acceptable in levels of society where Methodists were thin on the ground, aroused suspicion and even hostility among some of his fellow preachers. By comparison with this little Oxford doctor, the stalwart and forthright Asbury, for all his powers of natural leadership, might well seem uncultured. The fact that the newcomer was furnished with authority from Mr Wesley might have served only to underline the discrepancy, had Coke been tactless in his exercise of it. It says much for his handling of the situation, that the two men struck up a warm friendship, which survived, through many vicissitudes, to the end of their lives. Soon after their first meeting, Asbury wrote to his parents, 'I was made joyful above measure at the arrival of our British Brethren. We are greatly rejoiced if we are not worthy to have Mr. Wesley, . . . we are favoured with the man of his right hand, Dear Dr Coke, —if only for a few months.'[2] Coke, for his part, set down his first impression of Asbury thus: 'I exceedingly reverence Mr. *Asbury*; he has so much simplicity, like a child, so much wisdom and consideration, so much meekness and love; and under all this, though hardly to be perceived, so much command and authority, that he is exactly qualified for a primitive Bishop.'[3] Coke was, on the whole, a poor judge of character, but this was for once a very fair estimate of

[1] Asbury's *Journal*, i. 471. Cf Ezekiel Cooper's eye-witness account, in A. Stevens, *History of Methodist Episcopal Church*, ii. 172.

[2] Asbury's *Letters*, p. 39.

[3] Coke's *Journal*, American edition p. 244; several phrases are missing from the English editions.

the 'plain, robust man' whom he had just met for the first time. News of Coke's coming had been brought in advance by other visitors from England, so that he found himself generally expected as he went on from place to place. But nothing was known beforehand of Wesley's ordinations or of his plans for the American Connexion. Hence, as the administration of the sacrament followed the preaching service at Barrett's Chapel so closely that there was no immediate opportunity for the two men to converse, Asbury was startled to see Whatcoat assisting in the distribution of the elements. A lovefeast followed, and eventually the preachers dined at the home of Mrs Barrett, but lately widowed, about a mile from the chapel. In conversation with Asbury, Coke then revealed his purpose in coming to America. 'I privately opened our plan to Mr. Asbury. He expressed considerable doubt concerning it, which I rather applaud than otherwise.'[1] Asbury himself admits that he was shocked by the news, adding dubiously, 'it may be of God'. He insisted that the decision concerning his own appointment as superintendent should be left to the preachers.[2]

Knowing that Coke was in the neighbourhood, Asbury had summoned a number of the preachers to meet him at Barrett's, to welcome and consult with Coke. Wesley's plan for the organization of a Methodist Episcopal Church was made known to them, and after further discussion it was agreed that the whole matter should be referred to a general conference of the preachers. This was accordingly arranged for Baltimore at Christmas, and Freeborn Garrettson was sent off 'like an arrow, from North to South', to spread the news.

Asbury was eager that Coke should employ the interval before Christmas in travelling on southwards through Maryland and Virginia, following the route which he himself had just ridden. He procured him a horse and lent him his own negro servant, Harry Hosier. 'Black Harry', described by Booker T. Washington as the 'first American negro preacher of the United States',[3] quickly impressed Coke by his abilities. He proved himself acceptable to white congregations as well as to his fellow negroes. 'I really believe', Coke wrote, 'he is one of the best preachers in the world, there is such an amazing power attends his preaching, though he cannot read; and he is one of the humblest creatures I ever saw.'

[1] Ibid., p. 243.   [2] Asbury, *Journal*, i. 471.
[3] Quoted in *W.H.S. Proc.* ix. 16. See also Stevens, op. cit, ii. 174f.

Thus equipped, Coke set out on a route covering nearly a thousand miles, to explore for himself more of the country through which Asbury and his fellow pioneers were incessantly travelling to preach the gospel in scattered settlements and isolated farmsteads. The North American continent was still for the most part virgin land, unsettled and unexplored. By the Treaty of Paris (1763) the British had gained possession of all the territory east of the Mississippi; but the towns and plantations were all strung out along the Atlantic seaboard. When the thirteen colonies declared themselves to be independent of Great Britain, their total populations was well under three million. Philadelphia and New York were the largest towns, but most of the people were rural settlers. About a third of the population was composed of negro slaves or indentured servants whose condition differed very little from serfdom. The owners of the larger estates enjoyed considerable affluence; but for the small farmer and the lower orders, life was rough and elemental.

The country through which Coke now passed was one of great rivers and almost trackless forests; the hardships and dangers were considerable even for one accustomed to riding through the length of England and Scotland. In crossing the Cambridge ferry, they were in great danger of drowning when a violent wind got up; the boat would certainly have foundered if Harry had not persuaded Coke to leave their horses behind to be sent after them the next day. The parish churches were, for the most part, open to him, though there were exceptions. At Cambridge, for instance, a town notorious for its persecuting spirit, Coke writes, 'there arose a great dispute whether I should preach in the church or not. The ladies in general were for it, but the gentlemen against it, and the gentlemen prevailed. Accordingly the church door was locked, though they have had no service in it, I think for several years; and it has frequently been left open, I am informed, for cows, and dogs, and pigs. However, I read prayers and preached at the door of a cottage, to one of the largest congregations I have had in America.'[1] Preaching abroad was, in any case, no new hardship to him, and he frequently found himself taking his stand in an open space in the forest. 'It is quite romantic to see such

[1] He was similarly excluded at Kent Island, but at Churchill he preached at the invitation of the vestry 'in spite of the bigots'. The note of rivalry is unmistakable in the Journal for the following day, when, having preached at the door of the preaching-house in New Town because of the crowds, he records: 'The clergyman had but few I believe to hear in the church'.

numbers of horses fastened to the trees. Being engaged in the most solemn exercises of religion for three or four hours every day, and that in the middle of the day, I hardly know the day of the week: every one appearing to me like the Lord's-Day.'

The little 'English' doctor at first appeared in the pulpit attired in clerical gown and bands. But these were soon discarded as incongruous in the informal settings in which he preached and administered the sacraments, besides being too bulky for the circuit-rider's saddle-bags.[1] In other, more important ways, too, he began to show his readiness to learn from experience. He had at first expected to preach two or three times a day, but soon found that conditions did not allow this. 'I am convinced', he wrote, 'that the preachers cannot preach early in the mornings except in the Towns, which are very thinly scattered. Nay, they can seldom preach in the evenings. The middle of the day, even upon the weekdays, is their general time of preaching throughout the whole continent, except in the large towns.'[2]

He was not greatly impressed by what he saw of the work in Virginia, which he found to be 'a barren country for the gospel'. Methodism there was but newly planted, and there were as yet no preaching-houses.

One indication that the spiritual plight of the American settlers was no less grave than it had been represented lay in the numbers that flocked to receive the sacrament and to have their children baptized wherever he went. Before he left Barratt's Chapel Coke baptized thirty or forty children and seven adults, and by 6th December he estimated that already he had probably baptized more than he would have done in a lifetime in an English parish. Many outlying parishes were still without clergy, and those who were to be found did not impress him by their zeal. While in Virginia he wrote, 'The clergy in general in these parts, never stir out to church, even on a Sunday, if it rains'. And remembering the small congregation he had just had, he added, 'The people, I am told, expected me to be one of those lazy fellows'.[3]

On 14th December he crossed the Chesapeake Bay and rejoined Asbury, who had been travelling through the western parts of Maryland, where he found both preachers and people generally in favour of Wesley's plan, so that he himself was more disposed to think it

[1] *History of the Ecumenical Movement*, ed. Rouse and Neill, p. 223.
[2] Coke's *Journal*, American edition, p. 244.   [3] Ibid., p. 287.

'of the Lord'.[1] At Abingdon they inspected the site of the proposed college, for which they had already begun to collect funds, and on the 17th, went on together from Richard Dallam's to Perry Hall, a dozen miles north-east of Baltimore, the home of Henry Dorsey Gough, described by Coke as 'one of the most elegant in the thirteen States'.[2] Here for many years the Methodist itinerants found welcome. On this occasion, several other preachers besides Coke and Asbury were entertained before their Conference began. Despite this hospitality, Coke recorded his opinions of the family in his *Journal* with considerably more candour than tact. Of Mr Gough and his 'new mansion-house', he wrote, 'Alas, it has robbed him I am afraid of a considerable part of his religion . . . He intends to go to England next spring, to buy furniture for his house, which, I fear, will only still lower him in grace.'[3] The reason for this perhaps lies in the next sentence, for Coke's mind was at present preoccupied with the raising of money for the building of Cokesbury. 'On these accounts', he says, 'he will only give thirty guineas towards the college, and five guineas for tracts for the poor.'

The week spent at Perry Hall gave Coke and Asbury ample opportunity for deliberating on the momentous decisions to be taken at the forthcoming conference. Asbury, though still apparently with some reservations, was coming round to Coke's view, and wrote, 'I feel it necessary daily to give up my will'.

The Conference opened on Christmas Eve in the Lovely Lane Chapel. During its sessions there was a service at six each morning, an hour later than usual as a concession to the people—Coke's word for it is 'indulgence'—on account of the particularly severe weather. Coke himself preached at midday, except on the Sundays and ordination days, when the services began at ten. To accommodate the crowds, simultaneous evening services were held at Lovely Lane, at the Point chapel just outside the town, and in the Dutch Church of which Asbury's friend, the Rev. Philip Otterbein, was pastor.[4]

This Conference was to determine the future of a Connexion that was flourishing despite the hindrances and setbacks of the recent war

---

[1] Asbury, *Journal*, i. 472f.

[2] Coke's *Journal*, American edition, p. 290; cf. footnotes in Asbury's *Journal*, i. 180.

[3] Returning to Baltimore in February, Coke found that Gough had abandoned his plan, 'for which,' he says, 'I am not sorry'. (Ibid., p. 294.)

[4] Ibid., pp. 291f. Otterbein took part in Asbury's consecration.

years. Since Asbury's arrival, membership in America had grown from about five hundred to over fifteen thousand. There were eighty-one preachers in the itinerancy, and of these sixty were now present. It was a youthful gathering, half of those present having travelled three years or less, so that Asbury, at the age of 39 and with thirteen years' American service behind him, was 'quite a father among these striplings'.[1] Coke wrote of them, 'I admire the American preachers . . . They are indeed a body of devoted, disinterested men, but most of them young.' His admiration was perhaps a first-fruit of Asbury's shrewdness in sending him through the forests of Maryland and Virginia to learn for himself the conditions in which the American itinerants laboured.

Asbury's account of this Christmas Conference is succinct: 'It was agreed to form ourselves into an Episcopal Church, and to have superintendents, elders, and deacons. When the conference was seated, Dr. Coke and myself were unanimously elected to the super-intendency of the Church, and my ordination followed, . . . We spent the whole week in conference, debating freely, and determining all things by a majority of votes.'[2]

Asbury had insisted from the first that his superintendency should rest not merely on the authority of Wesley to appoint and of Coke to ordain him, but on the decision of his fellow-preachers. This was not in order to justify the appeal to the Alexandrian precedent, but for more immediate and practical reasons. Past experience had shown him that any attempt to assert authority from outside the Connexion, even on the part of the venerated Mr Wesley, was likely to arouse resentment; the case of Thomas Rankin was not yet forgotten. Asbury was quite prepared to rule, but preferred to do so by consent. Subsequent events amply proved his wisdom in this. Thanks to him, and to Coke's concurrence in the matter, the Methodist episcopacy was from the first a constitutional one, even though it vested in the bishops a degree of authority greater in some respects than that of the Anglican episcopacy. O'Kelly, with a peevishness that suggests a man who has attempted, but failed, to carry the Conference with him, later asserted that Coke and Asbury had not, in fact, been elected to the superintendency at all. 'Thomas and Francis were our superintendents as President elders, according to John's appointment, but

[1] Drinkhouse, *History of Methodist Reform*, i. 279; cf. Stevens, op. cit., ii. 187f.
[2] Asbury, *Journal*, i. 474–6.

they were not elected by the suffrage of Conference, although it is so written in the book of discipline.'[1] This runs counter not only to Asbury's explicit statements, but also to the account in Coke's *Journal*, which, although printed in the Philadelphia edition of the *Arminian Magazine*, does not appear to have been disputed by any other of the preachers present at the Conference. Speaking of their disinterested devotion Coke says, 'The spirit in which they conducted themselves in chusing the Elders, was most pleasing. I believe they acted without being at all influenced either by friendship, resentment, or prejudice, both in chusing and rejecting.'[2]

The climax of the conference was undoubtedly the ordination of Francis Asbury. He was ordained deacon and elder on 25th and 26th December respectively, and on the 27th was 'set apart for the office of a superintendent'.[3] Presumably the service followed the order provided by Wesley in the revised Prayer Book which he had provided for the American Methodists and commended to their use in the letter he sent them by Coke.[4] This in itself is an indication that he intended the act to be one of consecration to the episcopacy, in effect, even if not in name.[5]

Coke then preached a sermon on Revelation 3:7-11 in which he

[1] Quoted by Drinkhouse, op. cit., i. 284f.

[2] Coke's *Journal*, American edition, p. 291; English edition (1816), p. 52.

[3] Asbury's *Journal*, i. 474.

[4] The 1784 edition of the *Sunday Service of the Methodists* exists in two versions, one containing and one omitting certain elements in the services of Infant Baptism and the Lord's Supper. See articles by J. Hamby Barton and Wesley F. Swift in *W.H.S. Proc.* xxix. 12ff., xxxii. 97ff. Swift considers (chiefly on theological grounds) that Coke was responsible for omitting the manual acts in the Communion service and the Reception and signation in the Baptismal service; and that Wesley, discovering this, had them restored. (Wesley's letter to Churchey, *Letters*, viii. 144f., would appear to refer to this.) The omissions are certainly in line with Coke's current attitude towards the Church of England. On the other hand, Wesley entrusted to Coke the preparation of the edition of 1786, in which the manual acts reappear. (Letter from Coke to Mr Merryweather of Yarm, 5th October 1785 (Wesley's Chapel, London).)

[5] A. B. Lawson, *John Wesley and the Christian Ministry*, argues that Wesley did not intend any formal 'consecration' of Coke (and, through him, of Asbury) to the episcopacy, since he knew that he was not entitled to confer orders which he himself did not possess. He concludes from this that Coke wilfully misrepresented the act as one of 'consecration'. But this obscures the vital distinction in Wesley's mind between the office and the function of a bishop, and also ignores his provision of a separate order of service for the setting apart of a superintendent.

sought to vindicate the ordinations and 'to delineate the character of a Christian Bishop'. The separation of Methodism from the Anglican Church in America is treated as an accomplished fact, and one to be welcomed rather than lamented. 'The Church of England, of which the Society of Methodists, in general, have till lately professed themselves a part, did for many years groan in America under grievances of the heaviest kind.' It was 'subjected to a hierarchy which weighs everything in the scales of politics', so that one salutary effect of the Revolution was the virtual disestablishment of the Church and the expulsion of most of the 'hireling shepherds', whom Coke castigated in terms that were later to be condemned as unworthy of a fellow-clergyman.[1]

On the question of his right to ordain, Coke says he has 'the same right as most of the Reformed Churches in Christendom: Our Ordination, in its lowest view, being equal to any of the Presbyterian as originating with three Presbyters of the Church of England'.[2] Wesley, he says, was the spiritual father of the American Methodists and therefore, 'after long deliberation, saw it his duty to form his society in America into an Independent Church'. Most of the preachers would have separated earlier had they not submitted to the superior judgement of Mr Wesley who, 'till the Revolution, doubted the propriety of the step'. Like Wesley, Coke cites the church of Alexandria as the outstanding precedent, and on the question of apostolic succession, dismissed by Wesley as a fable, he appeals to Bishop Hoadley and Dr Calamy, besides Jerome and a variety of sub-apostolic authorities. In the last resort, however, it is practical considerations which determined the steps taken. For neither Wesley nor Coke, could matters of Church order be considered as involving more than the *bene esse* of the Church. 'Of all the forms of Church Government we think a moderate episcopacy the best. The executive power being lodged in the hands of one, or at least a few, vigour and activity are given to the resolves of the body, and those two essential requisites for any grand undertaking are sweetly united—calmness and wisdom in deliberating; and in the executive department, expedition and force.' Thus was the fable of an uninterrupted apostolic

---

[1] See below, pp. 102ff.

[2] He does not deal with the charge that, unlike Presbyterian ordinations, Wesley's were performed virtually in secret and without the consent of the Church. This criticism did not apply to the Baltimore ordinations, with which his sermon was concerned.

succession discarded, while a 'moderate episcopacy' was retained as the most effective form of Church government.

In expounding the ten 'grand characteristics of a Christian bishop' Coke, who was so often accused of worldly ambition, gives pride of place to humility as 'the guard of every other grace'. 'Let a man be ever so zealous, ever so laborious,' he states, 'yet if he wants humility, he will be only like Penelope with her web . . . undoing at one time what he does at another.' Meekness, too, is included, as a passive grace which is 'the sacred ballast of the soul', and impartiality, 'the rarest of all the virtues, and yet one of the most important for a ruler of the Church'. Every reader must determine for himself whether he detects in these words the accents of hypocrisy, or of a man blind to his own weakness.

By these steps was Mr Wesley's American Connexion transformed into the Methodist Episcopal Church, and the main part of Coke's mission completed. Not all the preachers were happy about the decisions taken. At least one, Thomas Haskins, would have preferred that any definite steps towards a formal separation should be delayed until there had been an opportunity to consult the Episcopalians. He saw little future for a Methodist Connexion severed from the parent body, and feared that dissensions would follow.[1] What Haskins did not know was that an informal consultation had already taken place, though without producing the result he hoped for. Either just before or during the early stages of the Christmas Conference,[2] two of the Maryland clergy, Dr John Andrews and the Rev. William West, hearing what was afoot, sought an interview with Asbury and Coke. Andrews described the result in a letter he wrote shortly afterwards. The Episcopalians explained that they had seen a copy of Wesley's letter to the American Methodists and enquired whether steps might not be taken to bring together the Methodist and the Protestant Episcopal Churches. As a basis for negotiation, William White's 1782 proposals were cited. 'The plan of church government which he had instituted in this state was very simple, and, as we trusted, a very rational plan; that it was to be

[1] W. W. Sweet, *Religion on the American Frontier*, iv. 22; *History of American Methodism*, i. 213.

[2] Manross, *History of American Episcopal Church*, p. 205, places it shortly *after* Asbury's ordination, and is followed in this by Sweet (op. cit., iv. 25); but on this point the evidence adduced by Drinkhouse seems for once to be more reliable.

exercised by a convention consisting of an equal number of laity and clergy, and having for their president a bishop, elected by the whole body of the clergy'. They suggested further that Coke (but not, it would seem, Asbury) might be consecrated as a bishop, as 'we could see no impropriety in having two bishops in one state, one of which might always be elected from among the people called Methodists, so long as that distinction should be kept up among them'. Coke's reply to these overtures was not encouraging: the most he could do, he said, would be to submit the proposal to Mr Wesley. The move therefore came to nothing, and Andrews ended his letter by drawing these conclusions: 'Thus ended our negotiations which served no other purpose than to discover to us that the *minds of these gentlemen are not wholly free from resentment*, and it is a point which among them is indispensably necessary, *that Mr. Wesley be the first link of the chain upon which their church is suspended*.'[1] It was perhaps this incident which prompted William White to seek an interview with Wesley while in England two years later.[2] Wesley's cool response to White in 1787 should be a warning against attempting to drive a wedge between Coke and the man he represented at the Christmas Conference.

Early in the New Year, Coke set out on a more extended tour which took him first to New York and then south again as far as North Carolina, where the work was still in its early stages. Again, he spent much of his time riding through extensive forests which were sometimes so transformed by frozen sleet that 'the trees seemed to be trees of ice'. And the sight of the Blue Ridge mountains away on the horizon, as he rode back through Virginia, was some compensation for the wolves that prowled menacingly about the fences of the homesteads at night and seized upon any straying sheep.

Crossing the great rivers of this country, especially in the winter months, was a serious hazard. One occasion, which he recorded in some detail, stayed vividly in his memory for years. He was travelling

[1] Letters from Andrews to Dr Smith, 31st December 1784 (Drinkhouse, op. cit., i. 267f.). Drinkhouse's theory is that the Methodists' hesitation was over the representation of the laity, for which neither Wesley, Coke nor Asbury was prepared.
[2] Wesley's comment on the recently consecrated Bishop Seabury is also illuminating: 'It may be a comfort to you that you have no need of him,' he wrote to Garrettson. 'You want nothing what he can give.' (*Letters of John Wesley*, vii. 276.)

south from Alexandria, through part of Virginia in which a number of rivers flow into Chesapeake Bay. A sudden thaw had made these very dangerous, and he was hampered by the absence of his usual guide. His worst moment came when crossing the Accotenk Creek.

I found that I had two streams to pass. The first I went over without much danger: but in crossing the second, which was very strong and very deep, I did not observe that a tree brought down by the flood, lay across the landing-place. I endeavoured, but in vain, to drive my horse against the stream, and go round the tree. I was afraid to turn my horse's head to the stream, and afraid to go back. In this dilemma I thought it most prudent for me to lay hold on the tree, and go over it, the water being shallow on the other side of the tree. But I did not advert to the danger of loosening the tree from its hold. For no sooner did I execute my purpose so far as to lay hold of the tree, (and that instant the horse was carried from under me,) but the motion that I gave it loosened it, and down the stream it instantly carried me. Some distance off, there grew a tree in the middle of the stream, the root of which had formed a little bank or island, and divided the stream; and here the tree which I held was stopped. Instantly there came down with the flood a large branch of a tree upon my back, which was so heavy, that I was afraid it would break my back. I was now jammed up for a considerable time (a few minutes appeared long at such a season) expecting that my strength would soon be exhausted, and I should drop between the tree and the branch . . . It was an awful time! However, through the blessing of my Almighty preserver, (to whom be all the glory,) I at last got my knee, which I long endeavoured at in vain, on the tree which I grasped, and then soon disengaged myself, and climbed up the little bank. Here I panted for breath for some time: and when I recovered, perceiving the water between the little island and the shore not to be very deep, or very strong, I ventured through it, and got to land. I was now obliged to walk about a mile, shivering, before I came to a house. The master and mistress were from home, and were not expected to return that night. But the principal negro lent me an old ragged shirt, coat, waistcoat, breeches, &c. and the negroes made a large fire, and hung my clothes up to dry all night. . . . At night I lay on a bed on the ground, and my strength having been so exhausted, slept soundly all the night. Thus was I wonderfully preserved, and I trust shall never forget so awful, but very instructive a scene.[1]

[1] Coke's *Journal*, pp. 55–7; cf p. 177. The road from Alexandria to Colchester crosses the Accotenk Creek at Pohick. The entire area is low and flat. In ordinary weather the creek would probably be fordable, but after heavy rain or spring freshet it would be far beyond its low banks and the crossing would be perilous.

It was in the same neighbourhood, on his return journey north-wards, that he encountered a series of similar hazards.

After the falling of heavy rains, I set off with one of the Preachers for Alexandria. This day I met with many difficulties. In crossing the water in one place, that I might reach the bridge under which the main stream ran, the water was above the top of my boot. In another place, where we endeavoured to drive our horses over the run, (the bridge being broke,) we were likely to lose our beasts, the stream being too strong for them, and carrying them down. At last we got them out, and with great labour and some danger, patched up the broken bridge with the loose boards, and got over with our horses safe. After riding about forty miles, it grew so dark, and our horses and selves were so fatigued, that we lay at an inn upon the road, though we were within five miles of our friend's house where we intended to lodge.

Two days after this, he confesses to the trepidation he felt in crossing a stream in full spate by means of a pine-tree which lay across it. Sometimes he rode through drenching rain, only to find the forest chapel for which he was making deserted. In New York, where he had anticipated the greatest opposition to the new plan, the Society proved unexpectedly in favour of it. 'They have already put up a reading Desk, and railed in a Communion table, also purchased a burial ground.'[1] Elsewhere, however, among the general public, he found rumour and misunderstanding at work. The landlord of a remote inn, who entertained him gratis when he lost his way in the forest, had heard something of the events at Baltimore, but seemed to associate them with the government, remarking to Coke, 'I suppose you are one of the bishops who go about under the authority of the congress to ordain'.[2]

Before his tour was completed Coke began to find his resources depleted. He had defrayed the passages of the preachers appointed to Nova Scotia and Antigua, but a gift of £60 from the societies in New York and Philadelphia went a long way to meeting this item. Nevertheless, he found the cost of travelling in America unexpectedly heavy, and in addition had to lay out considerable sums for the publication of the conference Minutes, and his two pastoral Sermons,[3] and for the binding of the revised prayer books he had

[1] Coke's *Journal*, American edition p. 293; cf Seaman, *Annals of New York Methodism*, pp. 84f.
[2] Coke's *Journal*, American edition, p. 295.
[3] Ibid., p. 297 under the date, 10th March. By the 15th he was down to his last

brought from England. By the middle of March he began to know, with the Apostle, 'how to want as well as how to abound,' and it was fortunate for him that he met with considerable hospitality on his way.

In spite of the transactions at Baltimore, Coke found most of the parish churches still open to him. In many places the Methodists had free use of these, if only because in the absence of a parish priest they would otherwise have been deserted.[1] His ecclesiastical sympathies, however, had widened immeasurably since the days of his curacy in South Petherton. In parts of Virginia, he came into frequent contact with Baptists, whom he found, almost to his surprise, to be a devout and kindly folk.[2] He made good friends, too, among the Presbyterians. There was Dr Smith, the Presbyterian minister of Princetown, New Jersey, 'a very candid, sensible and pious man', who entertained him and offered him his church.[3] And there was the Rev. Henry Patillo of the old Grassy Creek Church, North Carolina, a good friend of the Methodists, who lent his church for their quarterly meeting. Coke and Patillo shared the pulpit, and afterwards Coke's experience was once more enlarged. 'Our people in the neighbourhood, I found, (who had been brought up Presbyterians) had desired Mr. Patillo to administer the Sacrament to them, not knowing of my coming to see them; so, for the first time of my life, I partook of the Sacrament in the Presbyterian way.'[4]

The most important issue with which he was faced as he travelled through Virginia was that of slavery. The Conference of 1780 had passed a minute condemning slavery as contrary to the laws of God, man and nature, hurtful to society, and contrary to the dictates of conscience and pure religion. However, it was one thing to pass such a minute, but quite another to implement its practical consequences. With the extension of the work southwards into the Carolinas and eventually into Georgia, the issue inevitably became more acute; at

---

dollar. A little earlier he mentions publishing in New York his sermon on the Godhead of Christ 'at the desire of the Conference'. (*Journal*, p. 53.)

[1] Coke's *Journal*, pp. 59, 61 etc.

[2] Ibid., American edition, pp. 297, 339, 393. It is curious that none of his references to encounters with American Baptists has found its way into the English editions, perhaps because denominational feelings ran higher in England.

[3] Ibid., American edition, p. 293. He preached also in the Presbyterian Church at Alexandria.

[4] Ibid., p. 345. The English editions mention Patillo, but omit the passage quoted.

the same time attempts were made to exclude slave-holders from membership. These reached a climax in 1784 when the Christmas Conference at Coke's instigation threatened slave-owning members of societies with excommunication.[1] On the other hand, when he set out to visit the societies, Coke seems to have tackled the matter with a certain hesitation. On 1st April he 'began to venture to exhort our Societies to emancipate their slaves', and four days later bore his first public testimony against slavery at Colonel Bedford's in Charlotte County. Though he feared the effects, only one of his hearers was offended. On the 7th he spent several hours helping a dying man to make his will, in which he freed his slaves. But slaves were worth £30–£40 each, and emancipation could be a costly affair. Nevertheless, kindness was no substitute for freedom. One night he lodged with Captain Dillard, 'a most hospitable man, and as kind to his negroes as if they were white servants. It was quite pleasing to see them so decently and comfortably clothed. And yet I could not beat into the head of that poor man the evil of keeping them in slavery'.

It was not long, however, before his witness against slavery involved him in violent opposition, and he was threatened with a flogging.

A high-headed lady . . . told the rioters (as I was afterwards informed) that she would give fifty pounds, if they would give that little doctor one hundred lashes. When I came out, they surrounded me, but had only power to talk. Brother *Martin* is a justice of the peace, and seized one of them: and Colonel *Taylor*, a fine, strong man, who has lately joined us, but is only half-awakened, was setting himself in a posture of fighting. But God restrained the rage of the multitude. . . . Monday 11.—I preached at Brother *Baker's*. Here a mob came to meet me with staves and clubs. Their plan, I believe, was to fall upon me as soon as I touched on the subject of slavery. I knew nothing of it till I had done preaching; but not seeing it my duty to touch on the subject here, their scheme was defeated, and they suffered me to pass through them without molestation.

We cannot wonder that Coke found it a relief to cross the border into North Carolina, where, since the laws of the State forbade the emancipation of slaves, he had an excuse to abandon his campaign for the time being. He cont nted himself with raising the matter at the Conference held near Louisburg at the home of Major Green Hill, who was himself a well-to-do slave-holder. Asbury speaks of

[1] D. G. Mathews, *Slavery and Methodism*, 1965, pp. 10f.

95

the Conference being held 'in great peace';[1] and Coke says that they had 'a comfortable time' together. Neither even hints at the clash between Coke and Jesse Lee over the slavery issue. 'Calm, intelligent Jesse Lee, the anti-slavery son of a slave-holder, maintained that the new rule had been ill-timed and ill-advised, since it had excited "strong prejudices" against the preachers.'[2] By way of a compromise the Conference agreed to petition the General Assembly of North Carolina for an act authorizing any who wished it, to emancipate their slaves.

By the time he got back into Virginia, Coke had evolved a new approach to the matter, by which persecution was largely averted. 'Here I bore a public testimony against slavery, and have found out a method of delivering it without much offence, or at least without causing a tumult: and that is, by first addressing the negroes in a very pathetic manner on the duty of servants to masters; and then the whites will receive quietly what I have to say to them.' Nevertheless, there was at least one attempt on his life in Halifax County, and legal proceedings were begun against him.

The question of slavery was one cause of the estrangement between the Methodists and Devereux Jarratt, who had co-operated with them so fully for many years. He does not appear to have been apprised of their plans before the Christmas Conference, perhaps because both Coke and Asbury realized that he was unlikely to approve of the steps they took to establish the Methodist Episcopal Church.[3] On 30th March, Coke met him at Roanoak Chapel, and was nonplussed to find that Jarratt did not take him or his office with due seriousness. Jarratt was later stung by the publication of Coke's *Journal* into writing:

His little soul, I believe, was exasperated at me, for laughing at his epis-copal credentials, which he vainly drew out upon me, with Mr. Wesley's hand and seal annexed forsooth. The sight to me was truly farcical and ludicrous in the extreme—I could not forbear smiling—But my pleasantry, on viewing the parchment, was too serious a matter for the doctor . . . I freely forgive him, and pray God to forgive him, and cause him to know himself.[4]

[1] Asbury's *Journal*, i. 487.   [2] Mathews, op. cit., pp. 11f.
[3] For Jarratt's views, see *Life of Devereux Jarratt . . . Written by himself*, pp. 119f. It was natural and perhaps inevitable that Jarratt should see the actions of the Christmas Conference as an act of deliberate apostasy and, more personally, as a betrayal of his confidence.
[4] Ibid., p. 75. Cf. Asbury's *Letters*, p. 83.

Jarratt was reputed to own twenty-four slaves,[1] and for this reason, Coke believed, was not to be won over to the Methodist view. 'I am afraid', Coke wrote, 'he will do infinite hurt by his opposition to our Rules.' Jarratt received no invitation to the Virginia Conference at the beginning of May, and was convinced that he had been deliberately cold-shouldered. 'My not being at the Conference', he wrote to Edward Dromgoole, one of the preachers who had been present, 'was not owing to want of inclination, but not being invited by either of the Superintendents, I imagined my company was not desired; and since I have been more convinced of it, for I wrote to Dr Coke intreating him and Mr Asbury to pay me a visit before they left the State, to which the Doctor did not even vouchsafe a verbal answer, and Mr Asbury a very slight one.'[2] On his own confession, Coke had deliberately passed by Jarratt's house at the close of the Conference, and it is hardly surprising that Jarratt should resent the bitter terms in which he found himself condemned, in Coke's *Journal*, as 'that violent asserter of the propriety and justice of negro-slavery' and 'that fallen man' who was 'ruining our whole work in that neighbourhood'. Happily, this is not the end of the story, for Jarratt not only continued on friendly terms with Wesley, but was eventually reconciled to Coke, who in a calmer moment regretted the publication of these phrases and made an apology which was warmly accepted.[3]

In his passionate advocacy of emancipation Coke had moved too far ahead of public opinion. Before the end of the tour he realized that, however just his sentiments may have been on this subject, it was ill-judged of him to deliver them from the pulpit.[4] His public testimony had antagonized as many as it had converted to his cause. Nor was he able, as yet, to command the support of a majority

[1] But Jarratt himself denied this. 'God knows me better,' he wrote to John Coleman, 'and so do you'. And he asserted that Coke's *Journal* seriously misrepresented their conversation about slavery. (Asbury, *Letters*, p. 82.)

[2] Letter to Dromgoole, 31st May 1785, quoted in Sweet, op. cit., iv. 22f.

[3] Letter to Bishop White, 24th April 1791: 'Through great inadvertency (I suppose) [Asbury] suffered some reflections on the characters of [Jarratt and Pettigrew] to be inserted in the Magazine, for which I am very sorry: and probably shall not rest till I have made my acknowledgment more public; though Mr. Jarratt does not desire it.' (Asbury, *Letters*, p. 97.) It is only fair to Asbury to note that Coke allowed these offensive passages to stand in the English editions of his *Journals*. For Jarratt's reply to Coke, couched in most generous terms, see Sweet, *Virginian Methodism*, pp. 114f.

[4] Coke's *Journal*, p. 95.

among the Methodists. He had met with firm opposition at both the Carolina and the Virginia Conferences, and at the final Conference held in Baltimore on the eve of his sailing for home, prudence was allowed to prevail over principle. 'We thought it prudent to suspend the minute concerning slavery for one year, on account of the great opposition that has been given it, especially in the new circuits, our work being in too infantile a state to push things to extremity . . . But we agreed to present to the Assembly of Maryland, through our friends, a petition for a general emancipation, signed by as many electors as we can procure.'[1]

Here for the time being the matter was allowed to rest, and to this extent Coke was forced to concede victory to his opponents, in spite of the fact that his cause had recently gained a notable supporter. On 26th May Coke and Asbury dined with George Washington at Mount Vernon. They brought a letter of recommendation from General Roberdeau who had served under Washington during the war. Asbury dismisses the visit very briefly. 'We waited on General Washington, who received us very politely, and gave us his opinion against slavery.'[2] Coke allowed himself to expatiate on the visit.

The general's seat is very elegant, built upon the great river *Potomawk*; . . . He received us very politely, and was very open to access. He is quite the plain country gentleman and he is a *friend to mankind*. After dinner we desired a private interview, and opened to him the grand business on which we came, presenting to him our petition for the emancipation of the negroes, and intreating his signature, if the eminence of his station did not render it inexpedient for him to sign any petition. He informed us that he was of our sentiments, and had signified his thoughts on the subject to most of the great men of the State: that he did not see it proper to sign the petition, but if the Assembly took it into consideration, would signify his sentiments to the Assembly by a letter. He asked us to spend the evening and lodge at his house, but our engagement at *Annapolis* the following day, would not admit of it. I was loth to leave him, for I greatly love and esteem him and if there was no pride in it, would say that we are *kindred Spirits*, formed in the same mould. O that God would give him the witness of his Spirit![3]

Coke's original intention had been to visit both Nova Scotia and the West Indies before his return, but the demands of the American

[1] Ibid., American edition, pp. 397f.   [2] Asbury's *Journal*, i. 489.
[3] Both Drew and Crowther confuse this occasion with the presentation of the Loyal Address in 1789; see below, pp. 126f.

work soon forced him to abandon this part of his plan. The two preachers ordained for Nova Scotia were sent off without him. A passage was booked for Jeremiah Lambert to sail to Antigua, but he died of consumption before he could take up the work there. So John Baxter, shipwright and local preacher, who had gone out from Chatham in 1778 to work as storekeeper in the dockyard at English Harbour and had taken up the evangelical work begun by Nathaniel Gilbert, was left to labour on alone for a little longer. But one of Coke's last actions before sailing from Baltimore was to ordain Baxter, so that he returned to Antigua with the status and authority of an elder. Baxter is not listed among those chosen for ordination by the Christmas Conference, presumably because John Wesley had himself instructed Coke to ordain him, thus setting his seal upon the work begun unofficially by Gilbert and Baxter in the West Indies.[1]

Coke was soon to see something of that work for himself and to play a major part in its extension. But meanwhile he bade a moving farewell to his American friends and sailed for home. 'In my younger days', he wrote, 'one of the greatest afflictions in life to me during the time it lasted, was to be torn away from my friends whom I dearly loved. This through the extensiveness of my acquaintance, and the constant change of my place of abode, and partly perhaps, through the grace of God, has for late years considerably worn away. But I think for many years I have not felt myself so effeminate (shall I call it?) as I did on parting with my American brethren.'[2] A lasting partnership had been initiated.

[1] Coke's *Journal*, American edition, p. 398. Baxter's name appears among the *elders* in both the American and British *Minutes* of 1785, and in his *Address to the Pious and Benevolent*, 1786, p. 8, Coke speaks of Baxter as the only *minister* Methodism had in the West Indies. Most writers have wrongly assumed that Baxter was ordained by Coke during his first visit to Antigua in December, 1786.

[2] Coke's *Journal*, pp. 74f. Asbury's entry is more laconic: 'On *Thursday*, the Doctor took his leave of America for this visit. We parted with heavy hearts.' (Asbury, *Journal*, i. 490.) W. C. Barclay (*Early American Methodism*, i. 109), perhaps influenced by Drinkhouse, says that the question whether Wesley meant Coke to remain permanently in the United States and to devote himself exclusively to his duties as Superintendent there 'cannot be answered with certainty, but is an interesting query on which to speculate'. There is, however, ample evidence that both Wesley and Coke looked upon the visit from the outset as a temporary one. (See, e.g., Coke's letter to Wesley, 9th August 1784, quoted on pp. 77f. above; and *Letters of John Wesley*, vii. 261.)

CHAPTER 7

THE AFTERMATH

When he sailed for America, Coke had left behind a Connexion in which a storm was brewing. He arrived back just in time for the 1785 Conference, to find the storm at its height. Wesley's ordinations were now common knowledge; the Methodists were busy taking sides, and Coke's opponents, with Charles Wesley at their head, were out for his blood.

Coke returned from America strongly biased against the Anglicans. The pendulum had swung to the opposite extreme since the days of his bigoted churchmanship in South Petherton. We may gauge his present temper from a remark entered in his *Journal* during the outward voyage in the Autumn of 1784:

Tuesday, 5 [October]: I have just finished the Confessional, and believe the author does not speak without reason in his observations concerning national churches, that the *kingdom of Christ is not of this world*; that in proportion to the degrees of union which subsist between the church and state, religion is liable to be secularized, and made the tool of sinister and ambitious men.[1]

His experience in America had served only to strengthen these sentiments. In particular, he found the American clergy grievously wanting in every respect as leaders and pastors of their flock, and in his Baltimore sermon he virulently attacked them as 'the parasites and bottle-companions of the rich and great'.[2] In this anti-clerical mood he returned to the English Connexion; for the moment he was as ardent a Dissenter as he had formerly been a churchman, and was

---

[1] Coke's *Journal*, p. 40. In January 1786, Coke told Benjamin La Trobe that he considered all national Churches to be 'the invention of Satan and not of God'.

[2] *Sermon on the Ordination of Asbury*, p. 6. Some of the less charitable comments which he made on the American clergy in his *Journal* he was later to regret; e.g. his remark on the Rev. Charles Pettigrew of Edenton, North Carolina, a sturdy friend of the Methodists, that he 'does as much good in Edenton as a little chicken'. (*Journal*, American edition.) (Cf his letter to Bishop White, in Asbury, *Letters*, p. 97.)

fully prepared to see the Methodists follow the example of their American brethren and sever their remaining ties with the Established Church.

The fiercest hostility Coke had to face was from Charles Wesley, who had been the most outspoken of his brother's critics ever since the news of the Bristol ordinations leaked out. From the outset the relationship between Coke and Charles Wesley had been disturbed by strong cross-currents. Charles suspected Coke of championing the cause of the lay-preachers for his own ends. Coke, on his part, with the brash presumption of the newly-converted, doubted the spiritual integrity of the older man. A letter, written to John Wesley in December 1779, sets out his opinion of Charles with considerable frankness:

I was totally ignorant of your Brother's spirit till very lately. He appeared to me to be a *proud* man; but I am now satisfied that he is a man of *genuine humility*. I thought him an *enemy* to Methodism; but I now find him its *real friend*, as far as Methodism is a friend to the Church of England; and on *your* plan the Church of England never had so great a friend . . . I laboured during part of these last two years with some, who saw your Brother in the same light as I did; and no doubt, their prejudices served to heighten mine. Whilst I thus viewed everything, respecting him, with a jaundiced eye, it is no wonder that I interpreted all he said, that would bear a double meaning, in the very worst sense.[1]

When he heard of the ordinations at Bristol, Charles wrote a long letter to Dr Chandler, full of the pique of a slighted confidant. The event confirmed his suspicions that young Coke had ousted him from his brother's affections and trust; as he wrote to Henry Durbin, 'He thought he could do what he would with the Doctor; and the Doctor has done what he would with him'.[2]

He gave still more bitter expression to his feelings in a series of verses. One of the best known of these mocks at the illogicality of his brother's actions:

> So easily are Bishops made
> By man's or woman's whim?
> W—— his hands on C—— hath laid,
> But who laid hands on him?

[1] Letter to John Wesley, 15th December, 1779 (*Arminian Magazine*, 1790, pp. 50f.).

[2] Letter from Charles Wesley to Durbin, quoted in F. Baker, *Charles Wesley*, p. 135.

Hands on himself he laid, and took
An Apostolic Chair:
And then ordain'd his creature C——
His Heir and Successor . . .

In others the emphasis is on Coke's responsibility for leading Wesley astray in his dotage. The older man has been 'taught by Audacious Coke to slight the guilt'. Again:

W—— himself and friends betrays,
By his good sense forsook,
While suddenly his hands he lays
On the hot head of C——.[1]

Later, Charles was equally rude about Asbury's accepting ordination at Coke's hands:

A Roman emperor 'tis said,
His favourite horse a consul made;
But Coke brings greater things to pass,
He makes a bishop of an ass.[2]

And in 1787 he charged the City Road congregation never to receive the sacrament from 'these self-created bishops and self-made priests'.[3]

When copies of Coke's sermon on the ordination of Asbury reached England, Charles renewed his attack with the utmost vigour. Although positive proof is wanting, it is generally assumed that he was the author of the *Strictures* on Coke's ordination sermon. This pamphlet, issued anonymously in 1785, roundly asserted that, 'As an Englishman, he condemns the constitution of his country,—as a clergyman, he vilifies his brethren with the opprobrious names of hirelings and parasites;—as a Methodist preacher, he contradicts the uniform declarations of the Rev. John and Charles Wesley'.[4]

Coke's language in the sermon had certainly been unguarded, and he had failed to make any distinction between England and America.

---

[1] F. Baker, *Representative Verse of Charles Wesley*, pp. 367ff.

[2] Asbury, *Letters*, p. 65.

[3] Letter from John Pawson to Charles Atmore, 8th August 1787 (Archives Centre). Elsewhere Charles dismisses the American preachers ordained by Coke and Asbury as 'a troop of Jeroboam's priests'. (Baker, *Representative Verse*, p. 370).

[4] *Strictures*, p. 4. Quoted in Drew, p. 98, where a summary of Coke's reply is also given.

Not for the last time, he was the victim of the exacerbated feelings between the two countries resulting from the War of Independence, so that in parrying this anonymous attack he was concerned not so much to retract as to qualify what he had said in Baltimore. So far as his patriotic loyalty was concerned, his visit to the States had certainly increased his sympathy for the American cause and enabled him to appreciate their point of view. There had been a time, in the far-off days of his curacy, when he had put his signature to a commendatory preface to William Mason's tract, *The Absolute and Indispensable Duty of Christians*, and promoted its distribution in both English and Welsh. This pamphlet was written in 1775 to encourage Christians 'of all sects and parties' to honour, pray for and be subject to the King, as enjoined by Scripture, at a time of national disaffection. It called for a day of fasting and prayer in which the nation might seek 'some speedy method of abolishing the present unhappy divisions between us and our colonies'. Coke's preface breathed the same spirit and brushed aside all quibbling over 'taxation and representation' on the grounds that loyalty to the throne is a duty firmly grounded in the Bible.[1] Less then ten years later acquaintance with many of the citizens of the newly independent States caused him to modify these views. Before he had been long in America, he met a Mr Airey in Maryland, 'a most excellent man and our most valuable friend'. Concerning him, Coke wrote a passage which, understandably, appears only in the American version of his *Journal*: 'This man would no more have committed wilful rebellion than murder: and yet he was a friend to the revolution. He had no more idea than many others, that the English government, whenever distress came upon them like an armed man, had any right to throw their burden on this country.' Despite his dread of heresy, Coke was always ready to consider the views of others and to be persuaded by the truth; and here we catch him in the very act of modifying his opinion of the American 'Rebellion'. Not long after this, he delivered himself at Baltimore in words which found their way into the English edition of his ordination sermon only in very modified form: 'Blessed be *God*, and praised be his *holy Name*, that the memorable Revolution has struck off these intolerable fetters,

[1] This tract by William Mason of Rotherhythe, first issued in 1775, went through a number of editions. The 4th Edition, 1776, was the first to carry Coke's 'Recommendatory Preface', which is found also in the Welsh edition of the same year, printed by E. Evans, Brecon, presumably at Coke's instigation.

and broken the antichristian union which subsisted between Church and State. And had there been no other advantage arising from that glorious epoch, this itself, I believe, would have made ample compensation for all the calamities of the War.'[1] That Charles Wesley must have read these words in the American edition is indicated by this sarcastic attack on the ordination sermon:

> Happy America, whose ruinous wars,
> Direful calamities, & loss extreme,
> One single man, (above man's height) repairs,
> In rank sublime, in dignity supreme:
> To gain a C[oke] is 'ample Compensation
> For half a million slain, and general Desolation!'[2]

In his reply to the *Strictures*, Coke defends himself on this point by asserting that he was not condemning the British constitution as such, which he protests is 'superlatively excellent', but the effects and consequences of its abuse as felt in America.

As for the charge of having vilified his fellow clergymen, it is certainly true that Coke's language was pretty strong. Until the Revolution, he says, 'The Churches were in general filled with the parasites and bottle companions of the rich and great ... The drunkard, the fornicator, and the extortioner triumphed over bleeding Zion, because they were faithful abettors of the ruling powers.' The majority of both clergy and laity, he adds, either tacitly or explicitly deny such 'fundamental doctrines' as that of Justification by Faith. To the fervent evangelical, the religion of the majority must inevitably appear formal to the point of hypocrisy; how far Coke's condemnation would be echoed by present-day Methodism is more difficult to say. Some light is shed on what he meant by 'immoral clergy' by this passage from the sermon: 'We cannot be ignorant that they justify as innocent many of the criminal pleasures of the world—card-playing, dancing, theatrical amusements, &c.— pleasures utterly inconsistent with union and communion with God.'[3] Times and moral criteria have changed, with the result that most Methodists today would want to discriminate between different

[1] For details of the various editions of the sermon, see Bibliography.

[2] Baker, *Representative Verse*, where it is noted that the reference to 'dignity supreme' contains a satirical glance at Coke's description of the seriousness or dignity of a true bishop.

[3] Cf. Coke's letter to the Bishop of London in 1799 (pp. 202f. below).

forms of these 'criminal pleasures' before proceeding to judgement. We may recall, too, that from his South Petherton days Coke had been given to uttering words of stern rebuke when he felt them to be necessary. At the same time, it is only fair to add that in printing the sermon Coke added a footnote restricting this condemnation to a section of the clergy: 'There are many of them', he wrote, 'whose characters I greatly esteem, and at whose feet I should think it an honour to sit.'

The third charge against him in the *Strictures* is of special interest as one that has been often repeated. But Coke's assertion that he acted in all points on the delegated authority of John Wesley provoked no denial from Wesley himself; and this, in itself, is sufficient answer to most of the subsequent attempts to discredit him.

During the Conference that opened in London on 26th July 1785, Wesley followed up his Bristol ordinations by laying hands on three more preachers, who were thus authorized to administer the sacraments in the Scottish circuits to which they were appointed that year. Charles Wesley was now thoroughly alarmed at the trend of events and firmly believed that Coke's influence lay behind it. Coke, he was sure, had returned from his American mission not merely willing to see the separation of Methodism from the Church, but fully determined to bring about such a separation. It was Coke who was behind what Charles believed to be the growing clamour among the preachers for a formal separation,[1] and he did not hesitate to say to his brother, 'I told you so'. Writing on 14th August, soon after the Conference, he says:

When once you began ordaining in America, I knew, and you knew, that your Preachers here would never rest till you ordained them. You told me they would separate by and by. The Doctor tells us the same. His Methodist episcopal Church in Baltimore was intended to beget a Methodist episcopal Church here. You know he comes, armed with your authority, to make us all Dissenters. One of your sons assured me, that not a Preacher in London would refuse orders from the Doctor.[2]

John replied to this at some length on 19th August, asserting that though he had diverged from the Church in some points of doctrine and of discipline, he no more separated from it now than he did

[1] Probably because he was out of touch with the preachers, Charles Wesley almost certainly exaggerated the 'clamour' for ordination and separation. See Jackson, *Life of Charles Wesley*, ii. 403.

[2] Letter to his brother, quoted in Jackson, op. cit., ii. 394.

when he wrote his *Reasons against a Separation* in 1758.[1] He studiously avoided any reference to Coke, but Charles soon returned to the attack in a further letter, in which he left it in no doubt where he considered the blame to lie:

Do you not allow that the Doctor has separated? Do you not know and approve of his avowed design and resolution to get all the Methodists of the three kingdoms into a distinct, compact body? a new episcopal Church of his own? Have you seen his ordination sermon? Is the high-day of his blood over?[2] Does he do nothing rashly? Have you not made yourself the author of all his actions? I need not remind you, *qui facit per alium, facit per se.*[3]

I must not leave unanswered your surprising question, 'What then are you frighted at?' At the Doctor's rashness, and your supporting him in his ambitious pursuits; at an approaching schism, as causeless and unprovoked as the American rebellion; at your own eternal disgrace, and all those frightful evils which your 'Reasons' describe.[4]

John was stung into defending his lieutenant, who was too valuable to be used merely as a whipping-boy.

I believe Dr Coke is as free from ambition as from covetousness. He has done nothing rashly that I know; but he has spoken rashly, which he retracted the moment I spoke to him of it. To publish as his present thoughts what he had before retracted was not fair play. He is now such a right hand to me as Thomas Walsh was. If you will not or cannot help me yourself, do not hinder those that can and will. I must and will save as many souls as I can while I live without being careful about what may *possibly be* when I die.[5]

Charles Wesley was convinced that Coke's influence lay behind his brother's further ordinations at the 1785 Conference. So was Joseph Bradford, Wesley's travelling companion, who wrote, in a letter to Richard Rodda in 1794,

That he ever intended it [Methodist ordination] should take place in England I never did nor never can believe and, with respect to Scotland, he often declared to me and the congregation at Edinburgh so he were over

---

[1] *Letters of John Wesley*, vii. 284f.

[2] This is an allusion to John's remark, 'I do nothing rashly. It is not likely I should. The high-day of my blood is over'.

[3] 'He who acts through another acts himself.'

[4] Jackson, op. cit., ii. 397.

[5] *Letters of John Wesley*, vii. 288f. (13th September 1785). Charles brought the exchange to a close with a letter dated 19th September, in which he said, 'Of the second T. Walsh we had better talk than write'.

persuaded to it; and a few months before his death he was so much hurt by Dr. Coke's conduct in persuading the people to dissent from the original plan that he threatened him in a letter to have no more to do with him if he did not desist from so persuading the people.[1]

John Pawson, one of those ordained for Scotland, was of a different opinion. He came to the Conference without any expectation of being ordained.

I am well assured that this was a matter fully determined upon by Mr. Wesley himself, from the time that he ordained ministers for America; and although Dr. Coke might come into his views, believing that by these means the work of the Lord would prosper the more, yet I am satisfied that it was not through Dr. Coke's influence with Mr. Wesley that these steps were taken, but that the plan was wholly his own.[2]

This hardly accords with Bradford's words, but Pawson has an explanation of the discrepancy. Writing from Edinburgh in June 1786, he told Charles Atmore,

The truth is, the good old man has been so pestered with his brother & the High Church bigots on all sides that I really believe he does not know what to do. And you may add to this that Dr. Coke with his well-meant zeal drives quite too fast, & by that means defeats his own designs. When Mr. Wesley was here he told the whole Sunday night's Congregation that it never came into his head to separate from the Church of Scotland, but that Dr. Coke had entirely mistaken his meaning throughout the whole business. . . . So that it is quite evident that he has forgotten what he himself said on that subject last Conference. Poor dear soul, his memory fails him, therefore he speaks in a very unguarded manner sometimes'.[3]

The various pressures to which Wesley was at this time subjected were thus, in Pawson's view, a principal reason for those inconsistencies in his words and actions which have since taxed the ingenuity of his apologists.

Charles Wesley was so disturbed by the turn of events, and by his brother's replies to his protests, that he sought a *rapprochement* with the English Moravians, old friends from whom he and John Wesley had been estranged for many years. In the Autumn of 1785, he sought an interview with Benjamin La Trobe, a leading figure among the

[1] Letter to Rodda, 28th May 1794; copy in notebook belonging to James Everett (Archives Centre).

[2] *E.M.P.*, iv. 54.

[3] Letter from Pawson to Atmore, 2nd June 1786, in *W.H.S. Proc.* xii. 107ff. (Original at Archives Centre).

English Moravians, and showed him the correspondence that had passed between himself and his brother. 'Charles will not publicly oppose,' La Trobe reported to his superiors in Germany, 'but he declares he will oppose this new schism, which will end in a number of new sects; and now he wishes that *the Brethren might be of the use they were originally intended for, to nurse these souls* who are truly awakened and who adhere to the *Church of England*.'[1]

The Moravians still looked upon themselves as a leaven within the other Churches rather than as a separate body; so that La Trobe naturally found it easier to see things from Charles Wesley's point of view than from Coke's. Many of the phrases he uses reflect the influence of Charles. Coke he characterizes as 'a young clergyman who is very fiery' and who 'has lately got an ascendency over John Wesley and has been his chief counsellor. This young man [he continues] has at length persuaded him that he is as truly an apostolic bishop as any now living and he should use his authority.' Then, after an account of Coke's American mission, he concludes, 'Dr. Coke is returned and will not rest until he has formed a Methodist Episcopal Church in England.' The accent of Charles Wesley is here quite unmistakable.

Several further interviews followed during the autumn. La Trobe found Charles Wesley 'in deep affliction of mind and sickness of body' because his brother was being 'led away by young Coke'. The Moravians, he hoped, might be 'the means of preserving the true seed in the established church and of keeping the living souls among the methodists together'. On one thing, at any rate the two men were agreed—that the surest remedy lay with the Anglican bishops, who could readily prevent a separation if they chose. But even Charles had to confess that there was little to hope for from that quarter: 'I fear, betwixt you and me, their lordships care for none of these things'.[2]

Before the end of the year, La Trobe found himself in touch with Coke also. They were not strangers, having met two or three years earlier, when Coke had been contemplating a mission to the East

[1] La Trobe was President of the Moravian Society for the Furtherance of the Gospel. This correspondence between him and the Methodists is printed as Appendix E in W. G. Addison, *The Renewed Church of the United Brethren;* see also C. W. Towlson, *Moravian and Methodist*, pp. 157ff. Crowther (p. 199) says that he had seen a manuscript written by Coke at this time, but never published, in which he advocated separation from the Church.

[2] Letter from Charles Wesley to La Trobe, written during the 1786 Conference (Tyerman, *John Wesley*, iii. 479).

Indies and knew of and admired the Moravian missions among the West Indian negroes. Nevertheless, La Trobe was surprised to receive a letter from him, asking why, in view of the similarity of their doctrine and discipline, the United Brethren and the Methodists should not unite. La Trobe showed this to Charles Wesley at their next meeting, but Charles expressed the suspicion that Coke was acting at John Wesley's instigation and that they meant to 'spy out' the liberty of the English Moravians. However, Coke was invited to breakfast on 4th January and they talked through the morning. In his explanation of the steps by which Wesley was led to ordain men for America, Coke was at pains to stress that Wesley was seeking 'a church-constitution as near that of the Church of England as possible', but that this was intended only for America. He had not yet made up his mind about whether to form a 'Methodist Episcopal Church' in England. From this it would seem that, unless Coke wholly misunderstood his superior's mind on the matter, there was rather more substance in Charles Wesley's fears than his brother would have liked him to think.

The two parted on very friendly terms, Coke eager to follow up their preliminary discussion, La Trobe more cautious about the possibility of a union. The exchanges continued, but La Trobe remained wary of committing himself too far. Sceptical of effecting any union of the two bodies so long as John Wesley and Thomas Coke reigned, he wrote, 'As John is accustomed to be Pope (as his brother says) the old man will, without a particular work of God on his heart making him humble, hardly submit to it. Dr. Coke hopes to be his successor with full powers [Charles Wesley, it seems, had failed to acquaint La Trobe with the provisions of the Deed of Declaration]: this will make it hard for him to give the Brethren any power in his Societies though he now hopes for a Union.' Clearly La Trobe could foresee only disruption and disaster for the Methodist Connexion if Wesley, urged on by Coke, continued his present course, and he hoped for little more than the opportunity of picking up the pieces afterwards.

Coke and La Trobe continued their conversations into the new year. They went over some of the ground already covered, discussing national churches, the historical evidence for the Apostolic Succession and the validity of Wesley's ordinations. La Trobe asserted roundly that Wesley had gone the wrong way about it. 'If he had wanted to form a new church, he should have called an Assembly of the whole body . . . Wesley's method is neither episcopal nor independent and is likely to end in every man ordaining when he will.' Coke parried this with what was little more than an echo of Wesley's own argument: that those who had joined themselves to him freely were as free to leave him. To La Trobe, Wesley's insistence upon wielding such unlimited authority over his Connexion contrasted very unfavourably with the conduct of Count Zinzendorf.

In the course of their discussions, Coke more than once revealed that he was not averse to the setting up of an independent Methodist Church in England. Wesley had still not made up his mind, but 'the Doctor thought it might come to that either before or after Mr. W's death'. About this time La Trobe also had an interview with John Atlay, Wesley's Book-Steward, whom he found to be 'quite against their new scheme' and of the opinion that 'Dr. Coke, through inexperience and zeal without knowledge, if not stopped, will be the means of pulling down all that has been reared and built up by our Saviour among them'.

Throughout their discussions, it was Coke who had been eager to press forward to definite proposals for union, while La Trobe, the older and more cautious of the two, felt that the time was not yet ripe for these. Coke now produced a set of written proposals, outlining the preliminary steps which seemed advisable for effecting a union. Representatives of Wesley and of the United Brethren were to meet to consider a scheme of union, and Coke sketched its possible lines. But La Trobe seems to have suspected him of trying to utilize the Brethren in order to obtain a regular ministry for the Methodist Societies, and at the close of their interview the proposals were handed back.

Another conversation with Charles Wesley followed soon after this. Charles was able to convince La Trobe that his brother was being weaned from his intention of 'beginning a new church-system in England'; and this assurance encouraged La Trobe to seek the interview which Coke had been urging him to have with John Wesley. The opportunity, however, had passed. Both men were out of London for some time, Wesley on his northern tour, La Trobe on a visit to the Moravian settlement at Fairfield. Coke did his best; he wrote Wesley a full report of his conversations with La Trobe and advocated more formal negotiations with a view to some kind of union. In due course, Wesley agreed to a private conference with La Trobe, but there the matter seems to have rested. Within a few weeks of the close of the 1786 Conference, Coke was again crossing the Atlantic, and other affairs of importance, in both America and the West Indies, occupied his attention. Before he returned, La Trobe was dead, and the projected union died with him. Methodists and Moravians drifted apart again. Coke's personal relations with the Moravians remained cordial, since he found their simple piety and practical sympathy congenial. He was to encounter them several times in the West Indies and praised the missions they had established there.[1]

Though fruitless at the time, the exchanges offer us a valuable glimpse of the views and intentions of both the Wesley brothers and of Coke himself at this critical moment in their relationship. We are left with the impression that Charles Wesley now had little more confidence in his brother than he had in the Methodist preachers, whose integrity he had long suspected; while Coke emerges, in his view, as a sincere but headstrong young man—though now, indeed, nearing forty—who has not yet learned to make haste slowly.

Despite his ordinations for America and Scotland, John Wesley was telling the societies as he travelled up and down the country in 1786, 'The Methodists will not leave the Church, at least while I live'.[2] It is perhaps hardly surprising that he should be less ready to recognize the implications of what he had done than were younger men such as Coke and Pawson. At the Bristol Conference his voice prevailed, so far as the official records are concerned, but the unanimity was only superficial.[3] Some of the senior preachers, says Charles, came to Bristol with their minds so fully made up in favour of separation, that their only doubt was 'whether to be Independents or Presbyterians'.[4] Coke, among others, strongly advocated that at least in the larger towns Methodist services should be held in church hours, on the grounds that most of the converted clergy were Calvinists. On hearing this, Charles Wesley is said to have thundered out a violent 'No!' accompanied by such an angry stamp of the foot that Coke dropped into his chair as if shot, and did not utter a single further word on the matter. 'Mr. Mather, however, got up', says

[1] Coke's *Journal*, p. 210; *History of the West Indies*, ii. 131ff., 424ff.
[2] Letter from John Wesley to his brother Charles, 6th April, 1786 (*Letters of John Wesley*, vii. 324).
[3] *Journal of John Wesley*, vii. 192; *Minutes*, i. 191–3.
[4] Letter to La Trobe, quoted by Towlson, op. cit., pp. 163f., from the Moravian Archives, London.

Pawson, 'and confirmed what Dr. Coke had said, which we all knew to be a truth.'[1]

The Conference of 1787 was a hasty one to which only a selection of the preachers were summoned; it is ignored in Wesley's *Journal*, and the *Minutes* contain no reference to what had now become the burning issue of separation from the Church. The ambivalence of Wesley's position was never more clearly illustrated. On the one hand, he reiterated his determination to remain in the Church at every opportunity and 'in such a hot, fiery spirit', wrote Pawson, 'as I did not like to see'.[2] Pawson, despite his earlier ordination, now found himself required to give up his ministerial status on returning to an English Circuit. Yet he was able, on the other hand, to persuade Wesley, 'with much entreaty', to ordain two others for Scotland. Coke was not the only one to find himself perplexed and embarrassed by Wesley's stand.

In the spring of 1788, the question of Methodist services in church hours aroused fierce controversy in Dublin, and Coke found himself in the thick of it. One of his doughtiest opponents here was Edward Smythe, whose arrival in Bath had sparked off the heated dispute in 1779. 'Gentle Edward Smythe' was clearly a difficult and troublesome character, as Wesley himself had come to realize. 'I doubt Edward "needs a bridle",' he wrote in 1786, 'but who can put the bit into his mouth?'[3] Wesley was inclined to leave the attempt to Coke and showed a certain reluctance in coming to his rescue when the consequent storm broke. In the course of his Irish tour of 1788, Coke was too outspoken about his readiness to see Methodism separate from the Church.[4] The matter came to a head in Dublin, where the specific issue was the times of services in the Whitefriars Street Chapel. Finding that many members of the society were in the habit of attending dissenting chapels rather than the parish churches, Coke sanctioned the holding of Methodist services in 'Church hours'.[5] On hearing of this, Wesley at first firmly opposed the move, but then gave his approval on condition that the Methodists should receive the Sacrament once a month either in St

---

[1] Pawson's MS account, quoted by Tyerman, op. cit., iii. 478. Cf. *Wesleyan Methodist Magazine* 1860, p. 772. We may compare John Wesley's remarks in *Letters*, vii. 326, 327.

[2] Letter from Pawson to Charles Atmore, 8th August 1787 (Archives Centre) quoted in Tyerman, op. cit., iii. 497.

[3] *Letters of John Wesley*, vii. 324.   [4] Ibid., viii. 150.   [5] Ibid., viii. 58.

Patrick's Cathedral or in their own parish church.[1] This concession, intended to keep the Methodists from becoming open Dissenters, did nothing to lay the misgivings of Coke's opponents, and the controversy continued to rage for some time.

Returning from Dublin in time for the Conference, Coke again took the lead in proposing a formal separation on the grounds that to be associated with the Established Church was a hindrance to the work. He presented his case earnestly and with characteristic warmth; whereupon, says Adam Clarke, Wesley rose and answered him very calmly that, whereas Coke wished to tear all from top to bottom, he himself would not tear but unstitch.[2]

The Dublin fracas was but a local manifestation of a situation which was developing throughout the British Connexion, an unresolved tension which, after Wesley's death, led to the struggle between the two opposing parties, the 'Old' and 'New Planners'. Meanwhile, in the summer of 1789, John Wesley paid his last visit to the Methodist societies in Ireland. Though he conceded that Coke's words of the previous summer had been misrepresented by those who were opposed to his influence in the Connexion, Wesley was inclined, as he toured the Irish societies, to dissociate himself from what his lieutenant had said and done.[3] Indeed, he appeared more eager to protest his own loyalty to the Church than to vindicate Coke. The latter, however, was now far away from this particular battlefield, being once again engaged in the more important affairs of American Methodism.

[1] Ibid., viii. 59f. Duncan Wright describes how in earlier years the Methodists used to crowd into St Patrick's every Sabbath (*E.M.P.*, ii. 112).

[2] Letter from Adam Clarke to Humphrey Sandwith, 16th June 1829, quoted in *W.H.S. Proc.* xviii. 21ff. It was on this occasion that Wesley compared Coke and himself to a flea and a louse: see above, p. 46 note 7.

[3] Wesley's letter 'To Certain Persons in Dublin', 31st March, 1789 (*Letters of John Wesley*, viii. 126): 'At present I have nothing to do with Dr. Coke; but I answer for myself. I do not separate from the Church, nor have any intention so to do.' Cf. his letter to the Printer of the *Dublin Chronicle*, ibid., viii. 139ff.

CHAPTER 8

RETURN TO AMERICA

One result of his visit to America in 1784-5 was that Coke found his attention oscillating between the Old World and the New during the closing years of John Wesley's life. He had now contracted responsibilities to the Methodists on both sides of the Atlantic; his loyalties were similarly divided, and the resulting tensions were to complicate his life for many years to come. Since Wesley could not spare him permanently, for the time being his routine was to visit the States every two years, taking in the West Indies on the way. He spent the early months of 1787, 1789 and 1791 visiting the American societies and attending the several annual conferences as he went. Wesley's death shattered this orderly pattern, though it did not bring his American visits to an immediate end.

At the Conference of 1786 Wesley had ordained three more preachers. Two of these, William Warrener and William Hammet, were destined for the West Indies and Newfoundland respectively. These two, with John Clarke who was to be stationed with Hammet,[1] sailed with Coke on 24th September in a brig bound for Halifax, Nova Scotia.[2] The voyage was hindered by such prolonged and violent storms that the captain was eventually forced to make for the West Indies, with the result that Coke was again thwarted in his plans to visit the British territories in North America. After surveying the prospects for missionary activities in the Caribbean, he sailed for the American mainland on 10th February 1787 and reached Charleston on 1st March. Here he spent a month, being joined by Asbury on the 15th[3] for the first of three Conferences. At the beginning of April the two superintendents set out northwards together through the Carolinas and Virginia to Baltimore, where the final Conference opened on 30th April.

[1] *Minutes* i. 187. It is not clear whether Clarke was ordained with the others. See A. W. Harrison, *Separation of Methodism*, p. 18; *W.H.S. Proc.*, xxiv. 79f.
[2] This voyage and the subsequent tour of America are described in Coke's *Journal*, pp. 76-83, 92-99.
[3] Asbury, *Journal*, i. 535.

Though it was a month of unrelenting activity, Coke still found time, as they rode, to observe and record in his *Journal* both the progress of the work and the beauty of the country through which they passed. Methodism in Georgia and South Carolina was still in its infancy, but was already growing lustily, and Coke, remembering Wesley's visit to Georgia of sixty years before, was glad to have such a pleasing report to send him.[1] 'The preachers here ride about one hundred miles a week on an average; but the swamps and morasses they have to pass through in the winter, it is tremendous to relate! Though it is now in the month of April, I was above my knees in water on horseback, in passing through a deep morass, and that very late in the evening, when it was almost dark.'

While passing through Virginia, he was frequently on horseback until midnight after preaching at midday: Asbury, perhaps, was putting him to the test. 'Since I left *Charleston*,' he wrote, 'I have got into my old romantic way of life, of preaching in the midst of great forests, with scores and sometimes hundreds of horses tied to the trees, which adds much solemnity to the scene.' It was in Virginia that he had aroused the most heated opposition on his earlier tour by his open condemnation of slavery. Many thought he would not dare to show his face there again. 'However, when I came, they all received me with perfect peace and quietness.' He acknowledges that, however just his sentiments might be, he had been ill-advised in delivering them from the pulpit. The people of Richmond thought he would not venture among them again. 'But', he says, 'they did not know me; for I am a plain, blunt man, that goes directly on.' And instead of hostility, he was favoured with 'a very respectable and very attentive congregation' in the court-house.

If persecution languished, there were always the wags to whom the solemn extravagances of Methodism were an opportunity for hilarious leg-pulling. Fortunately Coke, though given at times to standing on ceremony, could both take and tell a joke against himself rather better than some of his fellow Methodists could. At an inn on the way to Alexandria, they fell in with 'a company of agreeable men, who were not unacquainted with God. These gentry', he says, 'laid a plot for us, I have reason to believe. For in our first dish of tea there was a little taste of rum; in our second a little more;

[1] Coke's *Journal*, p. 94. He speaks of Georgia as 'the residence and sphere of Mr Wesley's *usefulness* for some years', a description which perhaps neither the majority of the settlers nor Wesley himself would have echoed.

but the third was so strong, that on our complaining of a conspiracy, it seemed as if the rum had sprung into our tea of itself, for both company and waiters solemnly protested they were innocent.'[1]

Wesley had given Coke detailed instructions before he sailed, in a letter dated 6th September 1786: 'I desire that you would appoint a General Conference of all our preachers in the United States, to meet at Baltimore on 1st May 1787. And that Mr Richard Whatcoat may be appointed Superintendent with Mr Francis Asbury.'[2] In this, Wesley was not so much tactless as insensitive to the prevailing climate of opinion among the American Methodists. Coke had less reason to err through ignorance, and might perhaps have done more to persuade Wesley that the American preachers were unlikely to submit to any authority, even Wesley's, if it appeared to be arbitrarily imposed from without. Part of the trouble was that Coke's own schedule was too rigid. He was expected to take both Nova Scotia and the West Indies in his stride, and to be home in time to preside at the Irish Conference. To do so was incompatible with attendance at the several American conferences, if these were held on the dates originally fixed for them, and accordingly he consented to carry over Wesley's letter of instructions.

Asbury's resentment of this attempt by Wesley to keep the reins in his own hands was made clear as soon as he and Coke met in Charleston. 'Our interview', wrote Coke, 'at first was rather cool, but soon the spirit of power and love came upon us, and all jealousies were immediately removed.'

Asbury objected to Wesley's intervention through Coke on practical grounds as well as in principle. Wesley had not only miscalculated the sturdy independence of the American preachers, but scarcely appreciated the geographical difficulties under which they laboured. Asbury explained these in a letter to Jasper Winscom in the following year. To include all the preachers, he said, ten or a dozen conferences were now needed.

The arrangement of these conferences as to time and place to be fitted to the Doctor's movings was the only cause of the swelling of old Daddy

[1] Ibid., p.97. Methodists were not, of course, teetotallers at that time, but the sale and use of spirits were forbidden in the Societies. Coke himself had no conscientious scruples about rum while in the tropics; witness his *Journal* of a later visit to America (ibid., pp. 192f.).

[2] *Letters of John Wesley*, vii. 339. Stevens, *History of the Methodist Episcopal Church*, iii. 37f., points out that the Baltimore Conference of 1787 was not, in fact, a *General* Conference.

[Wesley] and me. I have been prevented from visiting some circuits that have been formed 3 or 4 years that have wanted my pastoral care: and as we are now fitted to meet the Doctor's coming I can only see these once in two years, whereas if I was wholly at my own disposal I should see them all in the space of 12 or 15 months.

Remote control of the American Connexion, moreover, was quite unthinkable. He says drily, 'I am sure that no man or number of men in England can direct either the head or the body here unless he or they should possess divine powers, be omnipotent, omniscient, and omnipresent . . . For our old, old Daddy to appoint conferences when and where he was pleased, to appoint a joint superintendent with me, were strokes of power we did not understand.'[1]

The altered dates of the Conferences were not the only cause of ill-feeling. The preachers themselves resented Wesley's appointment of Whatcoat to the superintendency and considered that any new superintendents should be elected by their brethren, as Coke and Asbury had been two years before. When the last of the Conferences met in Baltimore, there were 'some warm and close debates', as a result of which they not only refused to endorse Wesley's nomination of Whatcoat, but voiced their dissatisfaction by striking Wesley's own name from the list of superintendents. This was intended as a precaution against his exercising any 'uncontrollable and unlimited authority' over them, rather than as a personal affront, and by way of mitigating the blow they proceeded to write 'a long and loving letter', requesting Wesley himself to visit them as his 'spiritual children'.

It is hardly surprising, nevertheless, that Wesley did interpret their action as a personal rebuff, though his reaction was delayed. His letter to Asbury of 25th November 1787 gives no indication that he had yet seen the American Minutes or otherwise heard of the deletion of his name.[2] But a year later, on 20th September 1788, he wrote in a very different vein:

I am under God the father of the whole [Methodist] family. Therefore I naturally care for you all in a manner no other person can do. Therefore I in a measure provide for you all; for the supplies which Dr Coke provides for you, he could not provide were it not for me, were it not that I not only permit him to collect but also support him in so doing.[3]

[1] Letter from Asbury to Jasper Winscom, 15th August 1788 (Asbury, *Letters*, pp. 62f.).
[2] *Letters of John Wesley*, viii. 24f.   [3] Ibid., viii. 91.

'Old Daddy' was fighting a vigorous rear-guard action in defence of his sole authority over the Connexion. The paragraphs which follow in this same letter reveal what spark had set fire to the tinder. In the American *Minutes* of 1788, the term 'bishop' was for the first time substituted for Wesley's 'superintendent'.[1] According to Jesse Lee, this innovation was made by Asbury and Coke on their own initiative.

They changed the title themselves without the consent of the Conference; and then asked the preachers at the next Conference [1788] if the word 'bishop' might stand in the Minutes, seeing that it was a Scripture name, and the meaning of the word 'bishop' was the same with that of 'superintendent'. Some of the preachers opposed the alteration and wished to retain the former title, but a majority of the preachers agreed to let the word 'bishop' remain.[2]

Coke did not attend the 1788 Conferences, being out of America between June 1787 and February 1789; so that he can have been only indirectly involved in the adoption of the new title. Nevertheless, there is no reason to doubt his unqualified concurrence. Wesley, on the other hand, immediately scented danger, and bridled at what he supposed to be the implications of this change:

In one point, my dear brother, I am a little afraid both the Doctor and you differ from me. I study to be little: you study to be great. I creep: you strut along. I found a school: you, a college! nay, and call it after your own names! O beware, do not seek to be something! Let me be nothing, and 'Christ be all in all!'.

One instance of this, of your greatness, has given me great concern. How can you, how dare you suffer yourself to be called Bishop! For my sake, for God's sake, for Christ's sake, put a full end to this! Let the Presbyterians do what they please, but let the Methodists know their calling better.[3]

[1] Hitherto the question had been worded, 'Who are the Superintendents of our Church?' In 1788 this became, 'Who are the bishops of our Church for the United States?' The following Conference, in restoring Wesley's name, found a compromise solution, possibly at Coke's suggestion. The question was now divided into two, 'Who are the persons that exercise the Episcopal office in the Methodist Church in Europe and America?' and, 'Who have been elected by the unanimous suffrages of the General Conference to superintend the Methodist connexion in America?' (American *Minutes*, quoted by Candler, pp. 132f.). Coke's *Journal*, p. 129, speaks of Wesley's name being restored 'as the fountain of our Episcopal office'.

[2] Jesse Lee, *Short History of the Methodists in the United States*, p. 128.

[3] See p. 117, note 3. Asbury refers to receiving this 'bitter pill from one of my

When this is read in the light of what had happened at the Baltimore Conference the previous year, it seems little more than an
outburst of pique strengthened by his most cherished prejudices and
loyalties. Only by forgetting what provoked the outburst is it
possible to use this letter as evidence that Wesley had never intended
the establishment of the Methodist Episcopal Church. It was not for
exercising their superintendency that Wesley rebuked Asbury and
Coke, but for their use of the term 'bishop', which offended him
because of its overtones of 'worldly' pomp.[1] Only one blinded by resentment could seriously have accused the two bishops of seeking
power or 'greatness' for themselves. Their sin had been rather to
submit to constitutional checks on their episcopal authority:
Asbury had insisted on this from the outset, and Coke had quickly
realized the necessity and wisdom of it, though he now found himself in the unhappy position of a head boy, poised between the head-
master and the school and committed to carrying out the instructions
of the one without forfeiting the goodwill of the other. One anecdote
of the Baltimore Conference of 1787 is illuminating. It is said that at
one point Coke interrupted Nelson Reed, saying, 'You must think
you are my equals'; to which Reed retorted, 'Yes, sir, we do; and we
are not only the equals of Dr Coke but of Dr Coke's king'.[2] The
political factors in the situation of which this is a reminder, did not
make agreement and concord any easier to achieve.

So strong was the feeling among the American preachers, that
Coke himself was driven onto the defensive and agreed to sign an
instrument of partial abdication, accepting very definite limitations
to the exercise of his episcopal powers and acknowledging the ultimate authority of the American Conference in the event of Asbury's
death.

I do solemnly engage by this instrument, that I never will by virtue of
my office as Superintendent of the Methodist Church in the United
States of America exercise any government whatever in the said Methodist

---

greatest friends' at Charleston on 16th March 1789, soon after the beginning of
Coke's third American tour. (*Journal*, i. 594). If Coke was with him at the time,
it is interesting to speculate on his feelings about the letter.

[1] Cf. A. B. Lawson, *John Wesley and the Christian Ministry*, pp. 150f., citing
Watson and Moore. V. E. Vine, in *W.H.S. Proc.* xxx. 163, makes a strong case
for the view that Wesley had in mind the short-lived use of the title 'Bishop'
during the Scottish Reformation.

[2] Candler, pp. 121f. But Drinkhouse, i. 327, dates it in 1796.

Church during my absence from the United States. And I do also engage that I will exercise no privilege in the said church when present in the United States (except that of Ordaining according to the regulations and laws already existing or hereafter to be made in the said Church; and that of presiding in Conference). And lastly, that of travelling at large.

Given under my hand this second day of May in the year 1787.

Thomas Coke.

He further agreed, that, in the event of Asbury's death, his authority over the American Connexion should revert to the preachers in Conference.[1]

This document did no more than confirm that the American Conference stood on a similar footing to that of the British Conference since Wesley executed his Deed of Declaration. In so far as it reveals any hostility among the American preachers, it was as an alien and the instrument of Wesley's attempt to play the despot, rather than as an individual, that Coke was held in suspicion, and the two sides parted cordially enough. Coke interpreted the dissensions at Baltimore as the unsuccessful attempts of the devil to sow 'the seeds of schism and division' in a church which was growing and prospering to an unprecedented degree. 'Our painful contests, I trust, have produced the most indissoluble union between my brethren and me,' he wrote. 'We thoroughly perceived the mutual purity of each other's intentions in respect to the points in dispute. We mutually yielded and mutually submitted; and the silken cords of love and affection were tied to the horns of the altar for ever and ever.'[2] The story of their subsequent relationship hardly bears out this sanguine expectation, but Coke's words reflect very faithfully his impulsively affectionate nature which was far from harbouring resentment.

The building of 'a School or College on the plan of Kingswood-School' had been one of the first decisions taken jointly by Coke and Asbury in 1784. Coke lost no time in beginning to collect funds, and before the end of his first visit to America, the site had been purchased. It commanded wide views across Chesapeake Bay and seems to have pleased Coke more each time he visited it.[3] After the Baltimore Conference of 1787, the two Superintendents visited Abingdon to see

[1] See references in Asbury, *Journal*, i. 538, note 31.
[2] Coke's *Journal*, p. 97.
[3] See especially his *Journal* p. 133. Asbury (*Letters*, p. 253) says rather sullenly that Coke was 'much overseen' in the site.

how the work was progressing. Since the object was 'to serve our pious friends and our married preachers in the proper education of their sons', it is rather overstating the case to claim that, by choosing to establish a college rather than a school, Coke was a pioneer of higher education in America. It was, nevertheless, a far-sighted and worthy, though ill-fated, enterprise, in which Coke got little encouragement from Asbury, who had reservations about it from the outset. Devereux Jarratt was even more discouraging when Coke broached the scheme to him.[1] According to Emory the name was suggested by Coke as a compromise, when the Baltimore Conference in June 1785 failed to agree on other suggestions, including 'Coke College' and 'Asbury College'.[2] Undoubtedly a name such as 'Wesley College' or 'New Kingswood' would have been a more diplomatic choice, and Wesley might not then have dismissed the word 'college' as indicative of self-aggrandisement.[3]

Even before it was opened, shortage of funds caused the original plans to be modified. From then on, Asbury found its affairs a source of increasing embarrassment and worry; in Coke's frequent absences, responsibility for its finances fell on his shoulders, and he was inclined to blame Coke for having entered upon so ambitious a scheme too hastily.[4] Hearing of the fire which destroyed the building at the end of 1795, he wrote, 'The Lord called not Mr Whitefield, nor the Methodists to build colleges. I wished only for schools—Dr Coke wanted a college.'[5] Left to himself, Asbury would probably have accepted this severe set-back as an indication of divine displeasure at the scheme, but a group of prosperous well-wishers, supported by the generosity of the rest of the Baltimore society, made possible the refounding of the college in Baltimore itself. Early in 1797, however, a second fire destroyed the new college and the adjoining church. Asbury scarcely attempted to conceal his relief, and finally dismissed the whole project as having been 'all pain and no profit, but

[1] See *Life of Devereux Jarratt*, p. 181, quoted in Asbury, *Letters*, p. 138.
[2] Candler, pp. 99f., quoting Emory's *Defence of Our Fathers*. In 1789 it was agreed to build a college in Georgia, to be named 'Wesley College' (Coke's *Journal*, p. 129), but this was never built.
[3] Jarratt was of the same opinion; see Asbury, *Letters*, p. 138.
[4] Ibid., p. 144.
[5] Asbury, *Journal*, ii. 75. Asbury and others were perhaps a little unfair to Coke over the choice of the word 'college'. In a letter to Levi Heath, 23rd January 1786 (Methodist Historical Society, Baltimore) Coke referred to the word and said, 'We give high names to things in America'.

some expense and great labour'.[1] The financial loss was in fact estimated by Coke as about £10,000, and he was at last constrained to
agree with Asbury that 'the Methodists ought not to enter into such
expensive popular undertakings, but bend their whole force to the
salvation of souls'.[2] It was a natural conclusion, but one only partially endorsed by subsequent events. No doubt Coke had committed the infant Church to an enterprise beyond its resources, quite
apart from the repeated disaster. At the same time, the educational
enterprise of American Methodism since that day owes far more to
the inspiration of Coke than to Asbury's sceptical caution.

In tracing the chequered fortunes of Cokesbury, we have gone far
beyond Coke's second American tour and must now retrace our
steps. After the conference in Baltimore in May 1787, the two superintendents went on together as far as New York, where, Asbury
says, Coke preached each day 'with great energy and acceptance'.
Then, finding no suitable ship in the harbour, Coke returned to
Philadelphia, whence he sailed on 27th May in time to meet Wesley
in Dublin for the Irish Conference, at which he was able to give 'a
pleasing account of the work of God in America'.[3] He travelled back
with Wesley to the British Conference in Manchester,[4] and by 10th
August was at Southampton, waiting to sail with Wesley for the
Channel Islands. The Rev. Levi Heath was ready to embark with
his family, to take up his duties as the first principal of Cokesbury
College, so Coke seized the opportunity of sending a letter to
Asbury. Though the expense of the West Indian Mission was likely
to continue a heavy drain on his personal resources, he protested
nevertheless, 'Indeed, all I am and have is at the command of my
American Brethren & you as far as I can serve you.' His parting with
Asbury in New York had been more cordial than their meeting in
Charleston, but the very warmth of Coke's protestations betrays an
underlying tension in their relationship. Later in the same letter, he
writes, 'Will you believe me? You may command me; you may
confide in me with the fullest Confidence. You may depend upon
it (and may my repeated written Testimonies testify against me, if I

[1] Asbury, *Letters*, p. 171; cf pp. 62, 106f., 138.
[2] Coke's *Journal*, p. 246.   [3] *Journal of John Wesley*, vii. 294.
[4] See above p. 112. Significantly the 1787 Minutes are the last in which the
list of preachers 'on trial' and 'admitted to full connexion' are subdivided under
'Great Britain' and 'America'. After that, even Wesley gave up the pretence of
being able to regulate affairs in America from so great a distance.

ever prove false) that I am jealous of anything that may in any degree hurt your usefulness, because I believe God is & because I love you.' Then he turns to his plans for a further visit to America. 'I shall, if God will, be at Charleston next March twelvemonth, and will intreat the favour of having all the Conferences so fixed, that I may sail from New York on the 1st Thursday in June following. I'll also intreat the favour of you to draw up a Plan for me from Charleston, & to desire the Preachers to publish me accordingly.'[1] Little wonder that, as we have seen, Asbury should complain that accommodating this absentee bishop added to his already burdensome administrative problems.

*   *   *

Coke's third visit to America was undertaken as planned.[2] He landed in Charleston on 24th February 1789 and finding that Asbury had just left for the Georgia Conference, set off to overtake him. There is a hint of satisfaction in his tone as he records that he covered in two days as much ground as the veteran circuit-rider had done in three. 'The first day', he says, 'we rode forty-seven miles, for about two miles of which our horses were up to their bellies in water, with two great invisible ditches on the right and left.' From Georgia he rode northwards again, through country that was by now becoming familiar to him, attending the various Conferences on the way, and sailed from New York on 5th June. As before, he travelled much of the way in conditions of hazard and discomfort that were commonplace in the life of the American itinerants. Coming to the mainland straight from the Caribbean, he suffered especially from the intensely cold weather, from which not even swathes of flannel 'almost from top to toe' could protect him. Although the settlers had an abundance of the real necessities, life in the South was still quite primitive and there were few towns. Asbury was with him in Georgia yet they more than once missed their way.

In one instance we lost twenty-one miles. A great part of the way we had nothing in the houses of the planters but bacon and eggs and Indian corn bread. Mr. Asbury brought with him tea and sugar, without which we should have been badly off indeed. In several places we were obliged to lie on the floor, which, indeed, I regarded not, though my bones were a little sore in the morning.

[1] Letter to Asbury, 10th August 1787 (Drew University).
[2] For this third American visit, see Coke's *Journal*, pp. 127-37.

Again:

Frequently indeed we were obliged to lodge in houses built with round logs, and open to every blast of wind, and sometimes were under the necessity of sleeping three in a bed. Often we rode sixteen or eighteen miles without seeing a house, or human creature but ourselves, and often were obliged to ford very deep and dangerous rivers, or creeks (as they are here called). Many times we ate nothing from seven in the morning till six in the evening; though sometimes we carried refreshments with us, and partook of our temperate repast on stumps of trees in the woods near some spring or stream of water.[1]

These were travelling conditions of which, as Coke justly observes, the European itinerants had little knowledge; there was, indeed, nothing even in the indefatigable journeyings of Wesley, that could quite parallel them. His sharing of their rigorous life, if only for a few months at a time, won him the respect of the American preachers. 'The Americans', Asbury later wrote, 'knew his worth, and knew not only his labours and travels, but some of his sufferings, as he was often compelled by necessity to take up with very mean lodgings through some of the extreme parts of our country, and at a very early settlement; as Francis, who generally attended him, and many others can witness: add to this, that every visit, he had to cross and re-cross the Atlantic.'[2]

The natural beauty of this still virgin landscape offered some compensation for the hardships. An extensive vista between the lofty pines would unexpectedly enlarge his view; and sometimes the deer would trot out of the woods, only to disappear as suddenly at the riders' approach. In spring, the undergrowth was burned to enable the grass to grow, and at times they were so encircled by the fires that Coke was reminded of the nocturnal hunts of the French court. 'Sometimes the fire catches the oozing turpentine of the pine-trees and blazes to the very top. I have seen old, rotten pine-trees all on fire: the trunks, and the branches (which look like so many arms), were full of visible fire and made a most grotesque appearance.' By the time they reached Virginia, the peach orchards were a sea of blue, purple and violet blossom, and they rode with the Yeadkin sparkling in the sun at their feet and mountain ranges towering on either hand.

There were more lasting compensations. Each of the Conferences in turn 'cheerfully and unanimously' agreed to restore Wesley's

[1] Coke's *Journal*, pp. 128f.   [2] Asbury, *Letters*, pp. 552f.

name to the Minutes ('as the fountain of our Episcopal office') and to the form of discipline ('as the father of the whole work under the divine guidance'—a phrase echoing Wesley's own in his admonitory letter to Asbury).[1] Coke, on the other hand, was urged to relinquish his superintendency and to visit them in future as plain Doctor Coke, but, says Asbury, 'this was like death to him'.[2] Everywhere in the South, where there was no prevailing Calvinism to hinder it, the work prospered and large increases were reported. Cokesbury College was now open and under Dr Jacob Hall seemed to promise well. The way was opening for a mission among the Indian tribes, an enterprise to which Coke's heart readily warmed. At the North Carolina Conference there were preachers from Kentucky, 'the new Western World' across the Alleghenies. Further north, Jesse Lee and Freeborn Garrettson had been busy introducing Methodism into both New England and parts of New York State and there was an outbreak of spiritual fervour whose spontaneity took Coke by surprise. Compared with anything he had known hitherto, it seemed undisciplined, and he had to resist a natural inclination to condemn it. But he was soon convinced of its sincerity and worth.

At *Annapolis* in *Maryland* after my last prayer on Sunday the 3rd of May, the congregation began to pray and praise aloud in a most astonishing manner. At first I felt some reluctance to enter into the business; but soon the tears began to flow, and I think I have seldom found a more comforting or strengthening time. This praying and praising aloud is a common thing throughout *Virginia* and *Maryland*. What shall we say? Souls are awakened and converted by multitudes; and the work is surely a genuine work, if there be a genuine work of God upon earth. Whether there be wildfire in it or not, I do most ardently wish, that there was such a work at this present time in *England*.[3]

Similar scenes were witnessed during the Conference in Baltimore, where after one service between two and three hundred of the congregation burst out in prayer and praise and continued until the early hours.

This praying and praising aloud has been common in *Baltimore* for a considerable time: notwithstanding our congregation in this town was for many years before, one of the calmest and most critical upon the

---

[1] Coke's *Journal*, p. 129.
[2] Letter to Morrell, November 1789 (*World Parish*, April 1960, p. 22).
[3] Coke's *Journal*, p. 132.

Continent. Many also of our Elders who were the softest, most connected, and most sedate of our Preachers, have entered with all their hearts into this work.[1]

It was one of Coke's most likable traits that he was ever prepared for fresh experience to overturn or modify his prejudices; and on his return to England, he did not forget these manifestations of the Spirit, but saw in them an inclination that the Millenium was approaching.[2]

The year 1789 saw important constitutional changes in America. The original federation of states gave place to a more closely-knit union, with George Washington as the first President. At the New York Conference, Asbury put forward for consideration, 'Whether it would not be proper for us, as a church, to present a congratulatory address to General Washington, . . . in which should be embodied our approbation of the constitution, and professing our allegiance to the government'.[3] The Conference unanimously agreed that Coke and Asbury should draw up an Address, which they did the same day. Thomas Morrell, whose account is the most circumstantial, says, 'Brother Dickins and myself were delegated to wait on the president with a copy of the address, and request him to appoint a day and hour when he would receive the bishops, one of whom was to read it to him, and receive his answer.' Accordingly, on 29th May, the two Superintendents, with Morrell and Dickins, waited on the President. Coke himself would have presented the Address, had not Asbury persuaded him that so active a participation hardly accorded with his British citizenship.[4] Morrell continues, 'It was concluded that although Dr Coke was the senior bishop, yet not being an American citizen, there would be an impropriety in his presenting and reading the address; the duty devolved of course on Bishop Asbury.' There was, apparently, no suggestion of any impropriety in Coke's helping to draft the Address, or being present at its reception by Washington. Moreover his signature, as 'senior bishop', appears above that of Asbury on the document,

[1] Ibid., p. 133. There were further scenes during the Conferences at Chestertown and Philadelphia (ibid., p. 135).

[2] E.g. letter to Morrell, 23rd June 1790 (*World Parish* October 1961, pp. 29f.). For his millenarian interest, see below, pp. 330f.

[3] Letter of Thomas Morrell to Ezekiel Cooper, 26th August 1827 (Bangs, *History of Methodist Episcopal Church*, i. 279ff.).

[4] See Asbury's letter to Morrell, quoted on p. 129 below.

despite his British citizenship.[1] 'Mr Asbury, with great self-possession read the address in an impressive manner,' says Morrell. 'The president read his reply with fluency and animation. They interchanged their respective addresses; and, after sitting a few minutes, we departed.'

Of this notable occasion, for all his admiration for Washington on their earlier meeting, Coke's *Journal* says not a word. The reason is plain. The War of Independence was still uncomfortably recent history, and relations between the two countries were still such as to lead to inevitable conflicts of loyalty. As an American bishop who was also a British citizen, Coke was in as difficult a situation as the child of newly-divorced parents.

The rivals of Methodism were not slow to seize upon his British citizenship and point out the incongruities. The Address, published in the *Gazette of the United States* on 3rd June, and later in the *Arminian Magazine*, spoke of 'the glorious revolution' as the means whereby the civil and religious liberties of the nation had been providentially preserved, and of God as the 'source . . . of the most excellent constitution of these states, which is at present the admiration of the world'.[2] On 17th June, the *Daily Advertiser* carried the following letter 'to the Printer':

SIR: Observing the name of *Thomas Coke* to an address to the President assuming the title of *Bishop* of the Methodist *Episcopal* Church of America, I beg leave to inquire, through the medium of your paper, of some well-informed and patriotic member of that Church, whether *Bishop* Coke was the same man that was known in England by the name of *Doctor* Coke, and particularly during the war by the name of *little* Dr. Coke, and who was connected with and an assistant to Mr. *John Wesley*, both in the pulpit, pen, and press, when he preached and wrote most vehemently against *the Rebels*, as they then thought proper to term us? I am induced

---

[1] While no one would seriously contend that Coke's contribution to American Methodism was comparable with that of Asbury, this should not be allowed to confuse the question of seniority. In documents jointly signed by the two bishops, Coke invariably signed first, so that while Asbury undoubtedly wielded the greater authority on the strength of his American citizenship and closer acquaintance with his fellow-preachers, nevertheless it is clear that the seniority was definitely conceded to Coke as Wesley's delegate through whom Asbury received ordination. The title of 'first bishop of the American Methodist Church', so often conferred on Asbury, clearly belongs to Coke, since in any sense in which Asbury was a bishop, Coke was one before him. Morrell rightly terms him 'the senior bishop'.

[2] See Appendix B.

in this inquiry from a regard to consistency and the interests of religion. If the same *little Dr. Coke* I refer to has translated himself to the *Bishopric* of the Methodist *Episcopal* Church in America, he ought to give us full proof of his *political* conversion. *Doctor* Coke in *England* taught the highest *Tory* doctrine,—the king was the Lord's anointed, and our righteous resistance, although sanctioned by the wisest and best citizens of that country, was, in his opinion, *Rebellion.* He supported Mr. *John Wesley* in all that he chose to advance in support of *Lord North's* administration . . .

If *Bishop* Coke is this same *Doctor* Coke, no American, but a British subject, uniformly opposed to us in principle and conduct through the whole of the war, is it not the extreme of *hypocrisy* for such a man to take the lead of the *Episcopalians* in an address to the *President* of our republican Government? I am sir, AN INQUIRER.[1]

Coke was by now well on his way to England, while Asbury had also left the town. So it was left to Thomas Morrell to conduct the defence, which he did in a reply on 19th June, under the pseudonym of 'A Member of the Methodist Church'. In his later account of the incident, he wrote: 'The next week a number of questions were published in the public papers, concerning Dr Coke's signing the address . . . They affirmed he had written, during our revolutionary war, an inflammatory address to the people of Great Britain, condemning in bitter language, our efforts to obtain our independence.' Morrell says 'he applied to a gentleman who was in England at the time, to know the truth of the charge; he assured me the doctor had published no such sentiments in England during the revolutionary war, or at any other period, or he should have certainly had some knowledge of it. And this was the fact; for the doctor had written no such thing.'[2]

In answering the charges, Morrell admitted that 'Bishop Coke' and 'the little Doctor Coke', were identical. As evidence of Coke's present political sentiments he appealed both to the *Sunday Service of the Methodists* with its prayers for 'thy servants, the Supreme Rulers of these United States', and to Coke's own public utterances in prayers and sermons in New York. This was a fair comment on Coke's present sentiments, for, as we have seen, his first visit to America had convinced him of the righteousness of the colonists' cause. 'Inquirer', in a further letter on 24th June, was forced to admit the general loyalty of the American Methodists, and to shift his

[1] Seaman, *Annals of New York Methodism*, pp. 462–4.
[2] Letter to Ezekiel Cooper: see note 35 above.

ground by asking, somewhat belatedly, 'When, where and by whom Dr Coke and Mr Asbury received episcopal consecration'.[1]

Morrell was on less sure ground, however, when he denied that Coke had ever published anything against the Revolution while in England. It is true that he had never opposed it in print as violently as 'Inquirer' suggested, and the 'inflammatory address' to which the latter referred was possibly Wesley's famous *Address to our American Colonies*, wrongly attributed to Coke. The fact nevertheless remains that Coke was, by upbringing and inclination, a Tory loyalist, with little sympathy for either revolution or democracy.[2] Before joining the Methodists, he had printed a commendatory preface to William Mason's exhortation to honour and obey the King in times of civil dispute. This early excursion into print was no doubt little known and scarcely remembered, but Coke would hardly have welcomed its resurrection at this juncture.

When Asbury heard of this controversy in the New York press, his comment to Morrell was, 'I expected something of the kind would appear against us . . . It was with great difficulty and peculiar delicacy, that I prevented the doctor from presenting the address. The old church people mortally hate us, former friends, the great foes, the Presbyterians equally. We spoil the trade of the church, and their grand palladium, Calvinism. Each will watch an opportunity to wound us.'[3]

Coke returned home once again in time for the English Conference, only to find himself under further condemnation for his part in presenting the loyal Address. The criticism of his brethren was more bitter to him than any anonymous attack could be, and he sat in silence, with no attempt to parry the blows. The absence of his name from the *Minutes* of that year may have been deliberate omission, but was probably no more than accidental. The American stations were not included in the Minutes of 1789; and it is worth noting that Coke's name follows that of Wesley in the list of those approving the settling of the preaching-houses on the Methodist plan, as well as in the list of subscriptions towards a new house at Dewsbury.[4] After all, Wesley had himself spoken of the North American provinces gaining their independence by 'a very uncommon train of providences', and had declined to 'entangle' them again

---

[1] Seaman, op. cit., p. 464.   [2] See Chapter 14, below.
[3] Letter to Morrell, 9th September 1789 (*World Parish*, April 1960, pp. 21f.).
[4] *Minutes*, i. 224, 225.

with either the civil or the ecclesiastical authorities in England. If his own sentiments had altered so much between 1775 and 1785, it hardly befitted Wesley to chide Coke for having modified his views in the light of first-hand experience of the American scene.

In the letter to Morrell from which we have already quoted, Asbury gave his reasoned judgement on the struggle for power in the American Connexion. 'I am fully convinced', he wrote, 'it was not expedient for Mr Wesley or Dr Coke to claim the shadow of power, authority, names, or assignments of any kind. This subject, delicate as it is, I have told them too plainly for their feelings, and it has prevented that confidence and cordiality that would have otherwise subsisted.' Asbury had a sufficient grasp of the political realities of the situation to be aware that the most that either Wesley or Coke could command among the American Methodists was a 'shadow' of power or authority: to convince them of this was a different matter.

It is impossible for Mr Wesley ever to reconcile himself to this country, or for Dr Coke fully to satisfy the objections while he claims office here, while he continues to be a non-resident in this country. Nevertheless, I believe he is a real friend to this country, and all its rights and liberties, and that he would never do anything, great or small, without the consent of the residing bishop and conference; and that, according to the constitution of our Church, he cannot. But who of our enemies will believe this? If they do, they will speak otherwise.[1]

Writing of Wesley's hurt feelings, in another letter to Morrell, Asbury told him, 'He is now in a perfect good humour, and I would not wish to give him pain. Dear old man, he is near his journey's end, if not gone hence.'[2] Before Coke could complete another American tour, news of Wesley's death was to remove this particular source of embarrassment to Asbury's exercise of his episcopal responsibilities.

[1] See p. 129, note 3. Asbury was convinced that it was Thomas Rankin ('Diotrephes') whose influence led to the estrangement between Wesley and the American Methodists (Asbury, *Letters*, p. 546).

[2] Letter to Morrell: see p. 125, note 2.

CHAPTER 9

THE WORLD PARISH SURVEYED

The story goes that, after his expulsion from South Petherton, Coke went back to Wesley and asked what he was to do now that he had neither parish nor church; to which Wesley replied, taking Coke's hands in his, 'Why, go and preach the gospel to all the world'.[1] No words were ever taken more to heart. Wesley had refused to be confined to a single parish: Coke found even the nation too narrow a sphere. Despite his other multifarious activities, not least his important role in American Methodism, it is as founder of the overseas missions of British Methodism that Coke is chiefly remembered. Nor is this emphasis unjustified, for Coke so whole-heartedly took to himself Wesley's world parish that he must have overstepped more national barriers than any other man of his time.

Paradoxically, Wesley himself had been less concerned with the Church's mission to the heathen since his Aldersgate Street experience than he was before it. One of the unfulfilled intentions of his voyage to Georgia was that of preaching to the Indians. After 1738, he lowered his sights and, on the principle that he 'was not sent but unto the lost sheep of the house of Israel', bent all his energies to the spreading of scriptural holiness throughout his native land. For nearly half a century he did not again set foot outside the British Isles; and it is doubtful whether he gave serious consideration even to Asbury's pleas that he would pay a visit to his spiritual children in America. This concentration of purpose was a wise one: only thus could the Methodist societies be established and nurtured throughout England. Wesley had enough, and more than enough, on his hands for one man's lifetime.

By 1783, however, the situation was changing. The base had been established, and it was time for a fresh advance. Providentially, in the young and eager Thomas Coke, there was a man to match the hour.

Methodism had already begun to spread beyond the British Isles,

[1] See p. 33, note 1.

but in an unofficial and piecemeal fashion. In Antigua, Nathaniel Gilbert, returning from England in 1760, had begun preaching to his slaves and formed the earliest Methodist Society overseas. At his death, others took up the reins. In America, as we have seen, Methodism had been transplanted by Irish immigrants and matured by men like Captain Webb. From 1769 on, a steady flow of preachers went out to America, but the West Indies had to wait many years for similar help.

Meanwhile, in 1778 the shipwright John Baxter settled at English Harbour, and under him the work in Antigua went forward without the direct support of the British Conference. In the same year an opportunity of putting the foreign missions on an official footing was cast aside. Significantly it was Coke who, though still a newcomer to Methodism, seems to have been the prime mover. Two young princes from Calabar on the Guinea Coast, who had been sold into slavery in America, escaped and made their way to England. In Bristol they came under Methodist influence and, on returning to Africa, begged for missionaries to be sent out. Two German brothers belonging to the Bristol society responded to this call, but died on reaching the Coast. A further petition was received in 1778, in response to which Coke circulated to all the younger preachers an appeal for volunteers. One of those who offered was probably Duncan McAllum, to whom Wesley wrote just before the Conference, 'You have nothing to do at present in Africa. Convert the heathen in Scotland.'[1] It seems likely from this that Wesley's influence lay behind the decision of Conference to decline the call. Joseph Benson says that 'after the matter was seriously considered, it was concluded that the time had not arrived for sending missionaries to Africa.'[2] This was perhaps an early case of Coke's enthusiasm coming into conflict with Wesley's caution.

This neglected opportunity was not redeemed for some years; though Coke must have had it in mind when he planned his abortive Fula Mission in 1796. In the meantime, he did not abandon his dream of a mission to the heathen. Towards the end of 1783, he

[1] *Letters of John Wesley*, vi. 316.
[2] Macdonald, *Memoir of Benson*, p. 75; Tyerman, *John Wesley*, iii. 272f. Cf. John Prickard, in *E.M.P.* iv. 184ff. Prickard thought the Conference had been too cautious. 'I have always been of opinion that we ought to have gone; and if the Lord ever restores me to tolerable health, and it is judged right to send out a Mission into those dark regions, I hope I shall be as ready to go as ever.'

issued his *Plan of the Society for the Establishment of Missions among the Heathens*. At this time the Deed of Declaration was the outstanding, but by no means the only, administrative task assigned to him, and the plan for reconstituting American Methodism was already germinating in Wesley's mind, though he may not yet have discussed it with Coke. The latter was also actively involved in the revival which was then sweeping through Cornwall.[1] Amid these preoccupations, however, Coke had not relinquished his vision of a wider mission. The *Plan* was circulated without the explicit support—and possibly without the cognizance—of Wesley himself. It is worth noting the fact that this was eight years before William Carey's more widely known *Enquiry into the Obligations of Christians to use means for the Conversion of the Heathens* spurred the Baptists into missionary activity. Though the Wesleyan Methodist Missionary Society was not formally established until 1818, Methodists were committed to the support of overseas work long before by the enthusiasm of this young Welshman for whom the *Plan* of 1783 was but the first shot in a lifelong campaign on behalf of world Methodism.

The *Plan* was issued over the joint signatures of Coke and Thomas Parker, a barrister and able local preacher of York, in conversation with whom Coke had presumably conceived it.[2] Its circulation early in the New Year may have been a bid to by-pass the Conference. Coke still had reason to anticipate opposition from Wesley, but had learned the lesson of his previous failure. The appeal itself is addressed to 'all the real lovers of mankind', a phrase with a resoundingly Arminian ring to it, though coupled with a specific reference to Methodism.

To all the real lovers of mankind

The present institution is so agreeable to the finest feelings of piety and benevolence, that little need be added for its recommendation. The candid of every denomination, (even those who are entirely unconnected with the Methodists, and are determined to be so,) will acknowledge the amazing change which our preaching has wrought upon the ignorant and uncivilised at least, throughout these nations; and they will admit, that the spirit of a

[1] Coke's letter to Fletcher, written on the blank flyleaf of a copy of the *Plan*, 6th January 1784 (Drew University).

[2] Parker came from Shincliffe, near Durham, but little more seems to be known about him or his association with Coke. Oddly, his name is not on the list of subscribers printed in the *Plan*, although Coke's heads the list. Perhaps more significant is the absence of Wesley's name.

missionary must be of the most zealous, most devoted, and self-denying kind; nor is anything more required to constitute a missionary for the heathen nations, than good sense, integrity, great piety, and amazing zeal. Men, possessing all these qualifications in a high degree, we have among us; and we doubt not but some of these will accept of the arduous undertaking, not counting their lives dear, if they may but promote the kingdom of Christ, and the present and eternal welfare of their fellow creatures; and we trust nothing shall be wanting, as far as time, strength, and abilities will admit, to give the fullest and highest satisfaction to the promoters of the plan, on the part of your devoted servants,

THOMAS COKE,
THOMAS PARKER.

Those who are willing to promote the institution are desired to send their names, places of abode, and sums subscribed, to the Rev. Dr Coke, in London, or Thomas Parker, Esq., barrister at law, in York.

The main body of the *Plan* is practical and business-like. It proposes that everyone subscribing at least two guineas annually shall be a member of the society; that the first annual general meeting shall be held on Tuesday, 27th January 1784; and that a committee of seven shall conduct the affairs of the society between one general meeting and another. The rest of the proposals are concerned chiefly with the functions of this committee. It is worth noting that provision is made, *inter alia*, for the sending abroad both of missionaries and of others 'in civil employment'; and that there were plans 'to print the Scriptures, or so much thereof as the funds of the society may admit, for the use of any heathen country'. (The Bible Society was not founded for another twenty years.)

The initial list of subscriptions printed with the *Plan* totals £66 3s and Coke wrote to John Fletcher that he already had a further 20 guineas in hand. What final sum was received, and how it was disbursed, remain a mystery, though the money was still ear-marked for an Asian Mission in March 1786.[1] The first general meeting was presumably held as planned, at No. 11 West Street, Seven Dials, though from his *Diary* it would appear that Wesley did not attend.[2] The rest is silence; and all that can be said with any certainty is that

[1] See Coke's *Address to the Pious and Benevolent*. In 1794, he issued a detailed account of receipts and disbursements since the year 1787. The list of subscriptions for 1787, totalling £1167 12s 2d throws no light on what happened to the sum gathered in 1784.

[2] *Journal of John Wesley*, vi. 474, where the Diary fills in a gap in the *Journal*.

the Society did not survive Coke's absence in America. This was not for lack of interest on Coke's part, as the record of his reading on the outward voyage indicates. Concerning Francis Xavier, he wrote in his *Journal*, 'O for a soul like his! But, glory be to God, there is nothing impossible with him. I seem to want the wings of an eagle, and the voice of a trumpet, that I may proclaim the gospel through the East and the West, and the North and the South.'[1] The first apostle of World Methodism was already flexing his muscles.

The 1783 *Plan* nowhere specifies the countries, or even the continents, to which missionaries are to be sent. There is little doubt that the West Indies were already in Coke's mind, for he must have heard through Wesley of the work of Nathaniel Gilbert. But he was also looking to the East, and already contemplating that mission to India which was to occupy his thoughts for so long before it became the consummation of his life's work thirty years later. In the early part of 1784, Coke entered into a correspondence with Charles Grant, a merchant then serving with the East India Company near Calcutta.[2] (It may be an indication of the pressure under which Coke was then working that his first letter to Grant was apparently dated 'January–May 1784'.) He could not have chosen a better adviser, though the distance between England and India made their correspondence a very protracted affair.[3] The arrival of Coke's letter was recorded by Grant in his journal: 'Read two days ago a letter from Dr Coke, in connexion with Mr Wesley, with a scheme for a Mission in this country, and queries for information and assistance. A great project! May it be well influenced. May I answer rightly.'[4]

---

[1] Coke's *Journal*, p. 38.

[2] Charles Grant (1746–1823) first went out to India in 1767. On his second voyage out, he became acquainted with the Danish missionary, Christian Frederick Swartz. After his retirement, he was associated with the Clapham Sect, was a promoter of the Bible Society, the C.M.S. and other missionary undertakings. He was one of the first directors of the Sierra Leone Company. His *Observations on the State of Society among the Asiatic Subjects of Great Britain*, written in 1790 but not published until 1813, was a plea for missionary and educational work to be permitted in the East.

[3] Grant's reply, dated 19th February 1785, was acknowledged by Coke on 25th January 1786 (*Arminian Magazine*, 1792, pp. 83ff., 331ff.). At the end of his life Coke recalled this correspondence and referred to it in several of the letters he wrote during the voyage to India in 1814. He speaks of it as having taken place in 1794–5 and of its being printed in the *Magazine* for those years. But his memory was at fault here.

[4] F. Deaville Walker, *William Carey*, p. 137; cf. p. 102.

He replied in painstaking detail, welcoming the idea but realistically setting out the difficulties in its path.

By the time Coke found time to acknowledge Grant's advice, early in 1786, the tide of events was flowing fast in a different direction. He had just returned from surveying the missionary opportunities in the Channel Islands; towards the close of the previous year he had made a similar tour of the Scottish work. Nor had he forgotten the needs of the West Indies and the British territories in North America. His mind was busy with visions and schemes soon to crystallize in a new blue-print for Methodist missions both at home and abroad. 'At present', he told Grant, 'our openings in America, and the pressing invitations we have lately received from *Nova Scotia*, the *West Indies*, and the States, call for all the help we can possibly afford our brethren in that quarter of the world.' But the plans for a mission to Bengal were only shelved, and would be reviewed, he assured Grant, 'as soon as the present extraordinary calls from America are answered'. It was Wesley's opinion, he says, that when that time came 'not less than half a dozen should at first be sent on such a mission'. But the time did not, in fact, come until Wesley had been dead for over twenty years and Coke's own life's work was almost completed.

One interesting feature of Coke's second letter to Grant is the implication that Wesley was now prepared to consider such a mission and even to lend it his qualified support. He soon showed this by writing a commendatory letter to be prefaced to Coke's second missionary appeal issued in the spring of 1786.[1] In the two years since issuing his *Plan* Coke had learned the wisdom of gaining Wesley's approval, without which no project was likely to win general support in the Connexion. Wesley wrote from Bristol on 12th March 1786:

Dear Sir,
    I greatly approve of your proposal for raising a subscription in order to send missionaries to the Highlands of Scotland, the Islands of Jersey and Guernsey, the Leeward Islands, Quebec, Nova Scotia, and Newfoundland. It is not easy to conceive the extreme want there is, in all these places, of men that will not count their lives dear unto themselves, so that they may testify the gospel of the grace of God.[2]

[1] *An Address to the Pious and Benevolent*, now an extremely rare item. The M.M.S. have a photostat copy. The only other copy known to me is in the Library of Congress. See *W.H.S. Proc.* xx. 154ff.
[2] *Letters of John Wesley*, vii. 322.

The earlier *Plan* had in the main confined itself to practical, even business-like, arrangements for the organization of the proposed missionary society. Now Coke's approach was different: the *Address to the Pious and Benevolent* is at once more general and more specific. It leaves on one side questions of detailed administration; but on the other hand it takes the four areas named by Wesley as potential mission fields and considers the needs and opportunities of each in turn. The whole *Address* is couched in more personal terms, and begins with a final, half-regretful glance over the shoulder at the relegated mission to India:

Dearly beloved in the Lord,

Some time past I took the liberty of addressing you, in behalf of a mission intended to be established in the British dominions in *Asia*; and many of you were very generously entered into that important plan. We have not indeed lost sight of it at present; on the contrary, we have lately received a letter of encouragement from a principal gentleman in the province of *Bengal*, but the providence of God has lately opened to us so many doors nearer home, that Mr. Wesley thinks it imprudent to hazard at present the lives of any of our preachers, by sending them to so great a distance, and amidst so many uncertainties and difficulties; when so large a field of action is afforded us in countries to which we have so much easier admittance, and where the success, through the blessing of God, is more or less certain.

Here, certainly, are the accents of the prudent Wesley, not of the headstrong Coke. The *Address* then refers to the twofold need with which the present appeal is concerned.

We cannot but be sensible of the fallen state of Christendom, and the extensive room for labour which faithful ministers may find in every country therein. But some of the nations which are called Christian, are deeper sunk in ignorance and impiety than others; and even in the most enlightened, various parts are still buried in the grossest darkness.

An impassioned plea for missions to the heathen world ends with an appeal for Protestants to rival the missionary zeal of the Roman Catholics; after which he concludes:

Blessed be God! our spiritual resources are amazing. Numerous, I am fully persuaded, are the preachers among us, who, in the true spirit of apostles, count all things but dung, that they may win Christ, and win souls to him; who carry their lives in their hands, and long to spend and be spent in their Master's glorious cause. Let us therefore endeavour to draw forth these resources, and spread them out to the uttermost . . . And while we are unitedly watering the whole world around us, our own souls shall be watered again: the Methodist Connexion shall become a seminary to fill the vineyard of Christ with devoted labourers, and be made the most valuable, the most extensive blessing, not only to the present age, but to the generations that are yet to come.

Coke's language was extravagant, but the vision he expressed was less so. For the response which this appeal evoked from his fellow-Methodists goes a long way to justify the claim that it marks the birth of the Methodist Missionary Society some thirty years before it was formally constituted.

One of the fiercest attacks on Coke's passionate advocacy of overseas missions appeared in the *London Chronicle* in 1788, in the form of a letter addressed from 'Infidel corner in Drury Lane, 12th August 1788'.[1] It was clearly provoked by the very success of Coke's appeal, as well as by the extravagance of his pulpit manner, which it parodies:

We the heathens of London and Westminster, beg leave to address your honour in behalf of ourselves and our brothers—heathens of Great Britain and the Isles adjacent. Hoping that your bowels of compassion will yearn over us. As we hear you mean to do much for the heathens of Asia, Africa, and America, we humbly beg leave to remind you of the old proverb that Charity begins at home. Whilst then Ethiopia is stretching out her hands unto you for help [this was already Coke's favourite missionary text]; whilst the Hindoos, the Bramins, the Hottentots and various tribes of Negroes and Indians on the other side of the Atlantic are wishfully looking out for your Star to appear, Oh! let not these of your native land be beneath your notice. Pray send some Missionaries to instruct us, and it is but reasonable you shou'd pay them out of the large sums you collect here every year. You know we shou'd be just as well as merciful, therefore though we wish you good luck in propagating the Gospel over the whole Globe, yet we humbly presume that the greatest part of the money should be expended at home, and the surplus go abroad.

No missionary enthusiast ever deserved such an anonymous broadside less than Thomas Coke, for even a cursory reading of the *Address* of 1786 would have shown these 'infidels' of Drury Lane that

[1] A copy of this is found in the notebook of Francis Thursby (M.M.S. Archives). I have been unable to trace the letter in the files of the *London Chronicle* for 1788, but there seems no reason to doubt its authenticity.

he was not the man to promote the work overseas at the expense of needs nearer home. The juxtaposition in the *Address* of Scotland and the Channel Islands on the one hand and the West Indies and British North America on the other is a reminder that Home and Overseas Missions had not yet been sundered into separate departments. Certainly, in Coke's mind there was no such division. At a later date he was to initiate home mission stations in areas hitherto untouched by Methodism, for he recognized, that the world mission of the Church begins on its own doorstep.

Though it lies beyond our present purpose to consider in detail the origins of Methodism in the four areas designated in the *Address* as ripe for missionary activity, we may note something of the part played by Coke himself in each of them.

Coke had paid several visits to Scotland before 1786 and knew a good deal of the special difficulties of Methodism in a predominantly Presbyterian country. Many years later, in a letter to Walter Griffith, he spoke of it as 'miserable Scotland', and he was clearly convinced that its inhabitants needed the Methodist gospel, which might succeed where Presbyterianism with its Calvinistic theology had conspicuously failed, notably in the more remote parts of the country. His earliest visit to Scotland was probably in 1779. There is a fascinatingly cryptic letter from Joseph Pilmoor to Barnabas Thomas which, if it refers to Coke, indicates that he was touring the Scottish societies in September of that year. Pilmoor accuses 'the Reverend Priest', whom he later describes as 'the Doctor', of flagrant plagiarism.

The Reverent Priest has offered his sacrifice on the scotch Altars and is this morning gone off [from Edinburgh] for Dunbar. His Lecture on the Virgins did not succeed. On Sunday I received a letter from somebody giving me the hint that the Doctor was mistaken in the Scotch if he thought to 'repeat the Sermons of Old Bishop Leighton without being discovered', and assured me he could convince me he had done it almost Verbatim. On the Castle-Hill he scattered abundance of flowers, stolen from the fragrant beds of Fletcher's Garden, but left the Sage Scotsmen in possession of the field, for want of the Great Guns of Argumentation. On Sunday evening he read Isa. 60:1., told us the light and glory was Xt. divided it into 1st, 2nd, & 3rd, of which he 1st but two, so that the people seeing one, appeared tolerably satisfied. Monday night was appointed for the Conversion of the Arians to whom the Dr. promised to prove the Supreme Godhead of Christ. His method was to collect a great number of texts with Chapter and Verse by which he called together a cloud of witnesses and I believe gave pretty good satisfaction. Last night was taken up with descanting upon This is life eternal to know thee the only true God &C., but he seemed to be rather straitened and wanted the Prunella to keep him in countenance.[1]

There is little doubt that Coke was the preacher thus amusingly if spitefully caricatured, and a visit to Scotland in the early autumn of 1779 fits in with what little we know of his movements at that time.[2] He crossed the border again in 1782. An entry in the accounts of the Inverness society records a collection of 3s. 6d., taken when he was there in 1784; but it is difficult to find room for such a visit among all the other activities of that overcrowded year, and this entry should perhaps belong to 1785 when, after his return from America, we find him in Dundee and Edinburgh, administering the sacrament to the societies there.[3] As a direct result of this tour, Scotland was included in the missionary *Address* of the following spring.

'No kingdom under heaven', he wrote, 'has been more blessed with the light of the gospel than *North Britain*. Numerous have been the men of most eminent piety and abilities, whom God in his providence and grace has been pleased to raise among that people. And yet, in the *Highlands* and adjacent *Islands*, many scores, perhaps I may say hundreds of thousands, are little better than the rudest barbarians.' Providentially, to match this need, a young preacher had appeared who spoke Erse fluently and to whom Wesley had given 'an unlimited commission to visit the Highlands and adjacent Islands of Scotland'. Coke believed that, if the necessary resources were found, there would be other Gaelic-speaking volunteers for the

[1] Letter dated 22nd September 1779, in *W.H.S. Proc.* xxxi. 11f.
[2] In August 1779, Coke passed through Stafford on his way north, and in November returned via Sheffield and Nottingham to London. No other preacher with a doctorate was at large in the Methodist Connexion at that time, so that Coke was frequently referred to as 'the Doctor'. The celebration of the Lord's Supper was one of his chief activities as an ordained clergyman in visiting the societies on Wesley's behalf. The references to 'Fletcher's Garden' and to the refutation of Arianism in the sermon on the Supreme Godhead of Christ point in the same direction. The reference to 'the Prunella' is evidently intended as a pun. Prunella was a worsted material of which barristers' and clergymen's gowns were made; it was also the name of a throat disorder and its cure.
[3] Letter from Pawson to Charles Atmore, 8th October 1785 (Archives Centre; cf. *W.H.S. Proc.* xi. 50). In a letter to William Black, 5th January 1786, Coke spoke of his hopes for revival even in 'poor barren Scotland'. (M. Richey, *Memoir of William Black*, pp. 184-5.)

work, and this was therefore the first of the mission fields for which he made his appeal in 1786.

The young man to whom Coke refers was Duncan M'Allum, a native of Argyllshire, who in the stations for 1786 found himself set down for Ayr. Deaville Walker suggests that this was a first step to implement Coke's proposal for an Erse Mission, but that is hardly likely. Ayr in no sense belongs to the Highlands or islands envisaged by Coke as the scene of the mission, and it is doubtful whether Gaelic was still spoken anywhere in Ayr at that time.[1] This part of Coke's plan was never, in fact, put into effect. Scotland suffered a degree of neglect, perhaps because other fields always took priority over her. Quite apart from the growing demands of the overseas work, in due course there were the home mission stations in England and the vernacular missions in Wales and Ireland, all dear to Coke's heart. Not that he ever completely abandoned the idea. The account book of the Dundee society shows that he was in Scotland again in 1788, 1789 and 1790. After that, he does not appear to have returned until 1797, when on his way from America to Ireland. Meditating in his *Journal* on the 'miserable state of religion in Scotland', he put it down to the widespread antinomianism, 'that bane of inward holiness', and to the prevalence of speculative theology among the Scottish Presbyterians. The task of Methodism, as he saw it, was to 'preserve a seed of grace' until the day when God would be pleased again 'to visit Scotland with times of refreshing'.[2]

As late as 1808, he made a final attempt to establish an Erse mission. An appeal had recently come from Shetland, where a religious awakening led some to read Wesley's *Journals*. Perhaps because his hands were already so full, Coke was unable to help them, and Congregationalist preachers stepped in.[3] At the same time the proposal to station an Erse-speaking missionary in the Inverness

[1] *W.H.S. Proc.* xx. 15. Cf. W. F. Swift, *Methodism in Scotland*, pp. 41f.
[2] Coke's *Journal*, pp. 251f.
[3] James Catton, *History . . . of the Shetland Islands*, 1838, p. 122: 'They wrote to Dr Coke for help; but he being about to leave England on his mission, the request was not attended to, and they obtained help from Mr. Aldine'. James Haldane, who had visited the islands himself in 1799, sent over two representatives of the Society for the Promotion of the Gospel at Home, one of whom, George Reid, was ordained pastor of the Congregational Church, Lerwick, in 1808. The appeal to Coke must have been made not long before this, although the phrase 'being about to leave England on his mission' raises minor difficulties.

Circuit was revived. The name of Hugh M'Kay was brought before the Conference of 1808, on the joint recommendation of the Edinburgh and Glasgow superintendents, and M'Kay was accordingly set down for Inverness as an Erse Missionary. What followed can only be described as administrative chaos. One of the other preachers appointed to Inverness was withdrawn to fill a vacancy elsewhere, and M'Kay was put down to replace him, thus losing his missionary status. Coke, eager to salvage his scheme, hastily found a substitute among the preachers proposed for reception on trial, but this young man proved unwilling or unable to go out into circuit at such short notice. Coke could do little more, beyond referring the matter to the Committee in London, which eventually decided that M'Kay should remain in the Inverness Circuit, but shorn of his designation as 'Erse Missionary'. So this long-cherished scheme came to nothing after all, with Coke protesting that, though 'to make successful Gospel incursions among the Erse would be a great thing', the idea had never really been given a proper trial.[1]

* * *

The second field designated by Coke for missionary activity was the Channel Islands. In December 1783 Robert Carr Brackenbury had responded to an appeal for a bilingual preacher to go out to Jersey. He was to spend seven years in the islands, where he was joined later by the native preacher, Jean de Quetteville. The Conference of 1784 ratified Brackenbury's appointment, and in the Minutes of that year Jersey and America appear together, unnumbered, at the end of the English stations. Coke himself had not yet visited the islands, but was soon to do so. At Christmas 1785 he received a letter from Brackenbury telling of his recent visit to Guernsey and asking for another preacher to take advantage of the favourable opportunities there. Coke lost little time in setting out on a

---

[1] The Stations for 1808, as printed in the *Magazine*, p. 430, give M'Kay as stationed in the Inverness Circuit as 'Erse Missionary'; but this designation was deleted in the *Minutes* for that year. See Coke's letter to Joseph Benson, 20th September 1808 (Archives Centre). Coke was still hoping with the support of the President, James Wood, to persuade the Committee to change their minds, and even had in view an Irish preacher, James McQuigg, as a possible second missionary. But nothing came of this lobbying. M'Kay's name disappeared altogether from the 1809 Stations and McQuigg remained in Ireland. Probably the Committee saw in the turn events had taken a providential excuse for abandoning a project likely to overtax their all too slender resources.

personal tour of inspection.[1] During his stay in St Helier he preached not only in the meeting-room in Old Street but also, at the rector's invitation, in the Town Church. In the absence of a bilingual preacher for Guernsey, that 'very sensible and serious young man' de Quetteville agreed to go, and Coke spent a fortnight in that island, forming a small society and preparing the ground for the mission. He then returned to England via Jersey, convinced that a great work was now 'breaking forth' in the islands, and that Brackenbury should not be left to bear by himself both the financial and the administrative burden of this work. 'This is therefore our second view in the present institution,' he wrote in the *Address*, 'to nurse and carry on the work which is now breaking forth among the *French* Protestants in our islands of *Jersey* and *Guernsey*.'

As a result of Coke's recommendations to the Conference of 1786, de Quetteville was received on trial and Adam Clarke was sent out to Jersey as second preacher. Jersey and Guernsey now appeared as separate circuits, placed between the Scottish and Irish circuits in the list of Stations. Coke's personal survey of the opportunities and his subsequent recommendations in the *Address* thus bore immediate fruit in the Channel Islands, while proving barren in Scotland.

A year later, in 1787, Wesley himself was persuaded to visit this developing field, accompanied by Coke and Joseph Bradford. After a stormy and protracted passage, they reached Guernsey on 15th August, spending a night on Alderney *en route*. They found hospitality at the home of Henry de Jersey[2] and dined with the Governor[3]. Proceeding to Jersey, they stayed with Brackenbury. Both Wesley and Coke preached a number of times, despite the language difficulty, and Coke had a taste of the persecution which Adam Clarke had been facing in the island. The ringleader of the mob is said to have assaulted him 'in a most brutal and ignominious manner, almost lifting him from the ground by his ears'.[4] Their stay was

---

[1] Guiton, *Histoire du Méthodisme dans les Iles de la Manche*, pp. 52, 230f., (followed by later writers such as Lelievre, R. D. Moore and F. F. Bretherton) makes Coke arrive in Jersey before the end of the year. But not even Coke was quite so statesmanlike or so speedy. He left London on 17th January for Southampton, hoping to reach St Helier by the 21st. (Letter to Brackenbury, London, 17th January 1786, in *W.H.S. Proc.* viii. 163f.; also letter to Thomas Williams, same date [Wesley's Chapel, London]).

[2] See *Journal of John Wesley*, vii. 312, footnote.

[3] There is some doubt as to his identity; see *W.H.S. Proc.* iv. 21f., vii. 40ff.

[4] Drew, p. 191.

prolonged by the stormy weather, and they eventually returned via Guernsey. Wesley summed up his impressions thus: 'Here is an open door: high and low, rich and poor, receive the word gladly; so that I could not regret being detained by contrary winds longer than we intended.'[1]

The work had been established and was growing. By 1794 Coke was able to report that, although the islands were originally treated as a mission station, 'the Societies were formed with such rapidity, that they are now not only able to support the work themselves, but to send money to England to support the general work'.[2] A time of persecution lay ahead, in which Coke was to have further opportunities of serving the Methodists of these islands. But already it was clear that neither Brackenbury's pioneer labours nor Coke's far-sighted support had been in vain.

* * *

The third field of activity proposed by Coke in 1786, the West Indies, was the scene of so extensive a mission that it demands separate treatment, and will be dealt with in the next chapter. The fourth comprised the British territories in North America and the island of Newfoundland, where, says Coke, 'such an open door has not been known perhaps for many ages'. He reports:

We have lately sent a Missionary to *Harbour Grace* in *Newfoundland*, and his labours have been blessed; but his single endeavours are not likely to carry the work of God to that extent which every pious soul must wish for. In *Nova Scotia* we have about *three hundred* whites and *two hundred* blacks in society according to the last accounts, but have only three travelling preachers for the whole province; so that most of our congregations have preaching but once in a month. In the province of *Quebec* a few pious soldiers have formed societies at *Quebec* and *Montreal* on the Methodist plan, among whom we have reason to believe that our preachers would be gladly received.

How had these openings occurred?

The early history of Methodism in the British Provinces of North America, as in the colonies further south, is largely a story of sporadic and haphazard growth for which the initial credit is due to Methodist immigrants, especially from Ireland. Paul and Barbara Heck, who

[1] *Letters of John Wesley*, viii. 18; cf. ibid., p. 20. The visit is described by Lelièvre, *Histoire du Méthodisme*, pp. 248–67.
[2] *Statement of the Receipts and Disbursements. . . .* 1794, p. 19.

had been instrumental in bringing about the first preaching in New York, emigrated to Canada in 1774, carrying their Methodism with them to Montreal. The work in Quebec was begun by British soldiers about 1780. In Nova Scotia, too, the work began among emigrants from England, notably the Yorkshireman William Black, whose family had emigrated to the province in 1775, and who by over half a century of devoted ministry more than earned the title of 'Apostle of Methodism in Nova Scotia'. The War of Independence brought a flow of loyalist immigrants to Nova Scotia, including a number of Negroes for whom the settlement in Sierra Leone was later established. Two brothers from the New York society, John and James Mann, led a group of Methodists, as a class, to Nova Scotia in 1783.[1]

But Methodism in Newfoundland can claim to antedate that of these mainland provinces, since it took its origin from the ministry of Lawrence Coughlan, an Irish preacher who, though he went out in 1767 under the auspices of the S.P.G. after receiving episcopal ordination, never repudiated his debt to Methodism in word or deed. When ill-health forced Coughlan to return home in 1773, the work was sustained by laymen such as John Stretton and later by John Hoskin, for whom Wesley tried in vain to obtain episcopal ordination. Another Irish preacher, John M'Geary, was sent out in 1785, and it is of his labours at Harbour Grace that Coke speaks in his *Address to the Pious and Benevolent*.

Meanwhile reinforcements began to reach these British provinces via the newly formed Methodist Episcopal Church in America. The Christmas Conference of 1784, as we have seen, elected two preachers to be ordained as elders for the work in Nova Scotia; and the names of Freeborn Garrettson and James Cromwell appear alongside that of M'Geary in the Stations for 1785. Coke had intended to accompany these two preachers to Nova Scotia, to see for himself the state of the work there and assess the possibilities; and while he was touring the American Connexion, Wesley wrote to him asking him to visit Newfoundland and if possible to leave a preacher there too, before returning home.[2] It is more than likely that this letter never reached Coke, at any rate in time for him to carry out Wesley's request. Just as his intended visit to the West Indies was crowded out by the very full

[1] Drew, p. 119, confuses the Mann brothers with the two preachers sent to Nova Scotia by the Christmas Conference.
[2] *Letters of John Wesley*, vii. 260f.

itinerary he accepted on the mainland, so he was obliged to sail for home without seeing anything of the British provinces in the north. He had not, however, abandoned the Methodists there. As he toured the American societies after the Conference, he made collections on behalf of both Antigua and Nova Scotia;[1] and after returning to England, he continued to exert himself in begging for these missions wherever he went. Early in 1786, he was again planning to visit Nova Scotia in the autumn, on his way to the States; though as he did not expect to have time to call at Newfoundland, he arranged to meet Stretton and M'Geary in Halifax.[2]

Coke's proposals for reinforcing the work already begun in North America were accepted by the Conference of 1786. William Hammet and John Clarke, appointed to Newfoundland, and William War-rener, for Antigua, were ordained by Wesley and set out with Coke on 24th September. Battered by adverse winds, they were eventually driven south into the Caribbean, where they landed on the island of Antigua on Christmas morning, just three months after sailing from Gravesend. Coke's conviction that the hand of God was in the events of this fearful voyage made him all the readier to alter the original intention and leave both Hammet and Clarke in the West Indies. The Methodists of Newfoundland were therefore bereft of their missionaries, though other volunteers were found to go out in due course and the work went forward. It appears that Wesley was not well pleased that Coke should thus take the initiative in modifying the appointed stations. Moister prints a letter which escaped Tel-ford's net, in which Wesley told James Mann, 'When I consented to spare three of our Preachers for America, I supposed two of them would have been stationed in the Islands, and one in the North; but I suppose Dr Coke found so great a call for Preachers in the South that he believed it advisable to leave them all there.'[3]

When Wesley had first raised the question of his visiting Nova

[1] Coke's *Journal*, p. 52f.
[2] See his letter to Stretton, 26th February 1786, in *W.H.S. Proc.* xiv. 135.
[3] W. Moister, *History of Wesleyan Missions*, 1871, p. 95. Wesley's letter is dated 27th February 1789. (There is a slight discrepancy between Wesley's statement and the *Minutes* for 1786, which list *one* preacher for Antigua and *two* for Newfoundland.) The extracts of Coke's *Journals* describing this second visit to the New World were despatched to Wesley as reports of what he had seen and done, and a certain nervous apprehension is discernible here and there, lest he should have offended by taking too much upon himself or by modifying Wesley's instructions in the light of events.

Scotia, it is said that Coke was far from keen, replying that he did not think very highly of the place. 'That', said Wesley, 'is because you have never been there. When you are there you will think and feel for the people.'[1] In a man like William Black, Coke would certainly have found a kindred spirit; but in fact he never did visit the British Provinces. By the time his plans had twice been thwarted, the tide of events was flowing so swiftly that it swept him onward with little further opportunity of making a personal survey of the work there. His interest in it did not wane, however, and with his support, the work continued to advance steadily. Under his superintendency other missionaries went out from time to time. In 1788 he proposed to Joseph Sutcliffe, then in the St Ives (Cornwall) Circuit, that he should go out to Nova Scotia, and though Sutcliffe seems to have declined to offer himself and remained in English circuits, the letter Coke wrote him illustrates the care with which he sought to prepare and equip the missionaries, and his concern for their personal well-being.

Dublin, April 30, 1788.

My Very Dear Brother

I thank you for your kind letter; it breathes the true spirit of a Missionary. The part of the world, my dear Brother, I would wish you to go to is Nova Scotia. Our work in that province stands in much need of assistance. It is a cold Country, much colder than England; but by adding an extraordinary pair of stockings, flannel drawers, and a flannel waistcoat within the other you will bear the cold of winter with ease. Brother Ray writes me word that our Friends already raised in that Country supply the Preachers with everything they want after they have landed. If you be willing to go I will get Mr Wesley's permission for you to come to the Conference. If you have any books or anything you do not want at the Conference, you may pack them up that they may be ready to be sent on a day's warning to Falmouth, as you must sail immediately after the Conference if you go. The mode of your conveyance is out of the question. I cannot think of your sailing from London to Falmouth in the autumn; nor of trusting you to the westerly winds of the American coast at that time of the year in any other ship but the Packet. If Brother Button & you go together (as I wish to send two more to that Province) you will be a blessing, I trust, to each other as well as a blessing to the people of that land. You must be present at the Conference because you must be ordained. Clothes & books & everything you want shall be provided for you while you are in London. I don't mention these things as if they would be any Inducement

[1] Asbury, *Journal*, ii. 319.

to you to go. I know the contrary. I know nothing but the good of Souls & the Redeemer's glory influence you in the present instance. I only mention them that you may be fully informed concerning matters that so nearly relate to you.[1]

The West Indian mission always claimed first place in Coke's affection, but to the end he never lost sight of the needs of the Nova Scotia settlers. 'As to poor Nova Scotia', he wrote to the Missionary Committee in 1810, 'we really ought, as soon as the blacks are supplied with a proper complement of missionaries, to look out for two or three for that country.'[2] As he had written in his *Address* in 1786, 'Oceans are nothing to God, and they should be no obstruction to his people in respect to the love they should bear one towards another.'

[1] Copy supplied by Rev. R. Lee Cole.
[2] Letter to the Missionary Committee, 13th January 1810 (M.M.S. Archives).

CHAPTER 10

ISLANDS IN THE SUN

Of the four areas which Coke surveyed in his missionary *Address* of 1786, that which lay nearest to his heart and which was to engage his whole-hearted and most persistent attention was the West Indies. There is little doubt that, until the closing months of his life, not even India could oust the Caribbean from the first place in his affections. For thirty years he was to plan and beg and pray without respite for the mission to the slave population of these sun-drenched islands, though the four visits he paid to the Caribbean occupied less than seven months of his time. The name of Thomas Coke remains an inseparable part of the story of West Indian Methodism.

That story begins, as in the case of so much of the story of Methodism overseas, with the name of a layman. Nathaniel Gilbert, son of a wealthy planter and for six years Speaker of the Antiguan House of Assembly, had visited England in 1757 expressly to meet John Wesley. Returning to Antigua, he began to preach to the three hundred slaves belonging to the family estate which he inherited in 1761. The Religious Society which resulted from this had grown, by the time of his death in 1774, to 200 members. When John Baxter, the Methodist shipwright, took up his appointment at English Harbour in 1778, he found the remnant of this society being kept together by a Mulatto woman and a Negress, but under his leadership numbers once more began to increase. His appeals to Wesley for assistance had a twofold result which we have already noted. The Christmas Conference of 1784 appointed Jeremiah Lambert as a missionary to Antigua, and Baxter himself was ordained by Coke in Baltimore in the following summer. But Lambert died shortly afterwards, and Baxter had to wait another eighteen months before reinforcements arrived.

The needs of the Antiguan Methodists were not, however, forgotten, least of all by Coke. 'The third object we have in view', says the *Address*, 'is our West India islands, where a field is opened to us

149

among the negroes beyond anything that could have been expected.'
There were already 1,100 Negroes in society. Geographically, the
American Methodists were the most favourably placed to nurture
this growing work; but theirs was an infant Connexion whose resources were already taxed to the full by the speed of its own growth,
so that Lambert had no successor. Coke was not the man to neglect
so favourable an opening. 'The planters in general are constrained to
acknowledge, that the negroes who are united to *us* and the *Moravians*, are the most laborious and faithful servants they have: which
favourable sentiment, through the blessing of God, has laid open
the whole country to our labours among the blacks.' Though far
from unaware of the spiritual need of the European settlers, Coke's
chief concern from the outset was the plight of the black slaves in
their households and on their plantations—his 'poor blacks' in the
cause of whose spiritual and physical well-being he spent himself so
unstintingly. His appeal on their behalf in 1786 was on the grounds
of justice as well as compassion. There was a debt to be paid. 'These
islands seem to have a peculiar claim on the inhabitants of *Britain*.
Our country is enriched by the labours of the poor slaves who culti-
vate the soil, and surely the least compensation we can make them,
is to endeavour to enrich them in return with the riches of grace. But
the grand consideration to the children of God, is the value of the
souls of these negroes, a set of people utterly despised by all the
world, except the Methodists and Moravians.'[1]

The Conference of 1786 responded to Coke's appeal by appointing William Warrener to join Baxter in Antigua. At the same time,
because the needs of British North America were felt to be more
urgent, the similar opportunity in the island of St Christopher to
which Coke had also drawn attention had to be ignored for the time
being. Such was the decision of Mr Wesley and the British Conference, but in the providence of God events were to turn out quite
otherwise. Warrener and the two preachers appointed to Newfoundland set out, in company with Coke, on 24th September. Adverse
winds repeatedly drove them back; the ship was buffeted again and
again by tremendous storms, which seriously damaged her rigging
and left the sail in shreds. In mid-ocean she was found to have

[1] This statement overlooks the Quakers, but Coke's immediate concern was
with the West Indies, where the Moravians were the only other group actively
concerned with the Negro slaves. The anti-slavery movement associated with
the names of Wilberforce and Clarkson was still in the future.

sprung a leak, and by the beginning of December, after more than
two months at sea, she was oozing at every joint and scarcely more
than 'half a wreck'.[1] Under such conditions they made no more than
120 miles in three weeks, and at the height of the storm the captain
began to give way to superstition. While the missionaries were
fervently engaged in prayer in their cabin, he paced the deck, mutter-
ing to himself, 'We have a Jonah on board'. Eventually, rushing into
the cabin, he seized some of Coke's books and papers and flung
them overboard, threatening to do the same with their owner if he
persisted in prayer. But the captain's fury subsided and Coke escaped
with no more than a severe shaking.[2]

Convinced, however, of the impossibility of reaching the port of
Halifax, the captain now decided to run before the wind in the hope
of making one of the islands in the West Indies. In this way, after
three months at sea, they found themselves landing at St John's,
Antigua, early on Christmas morning. The whole voyage, graphically
described in Coke's *Journal*, is a reminder of the conditions in which
his task of establishing Methodist bases overseas was undertaken.
Nine successive voyages to America and back was no small feat in
the small sailing barques of that day.

The dramatic arrival of Coke and his companions in Antigua
early on that Christmas morning of 1786 has been frequently described. 'In going up the town of *St. John's*,' Coke wrote, 'we met
brother *Baxter* in his band,[3] going to perform divine service. After
a little refreshment I went to our chapel, and read prayers, preached,
and administered the sacrament. I had one of the cleanest audiences
I ever saw. All the negro women were dressed in white linen gowns,
petticoats, handkerchiefs and caps: and I did not see the least spot
on any of them. The men were also dressed as neatly. In the afternoon and evening I had very large congregations.'[4] If this shows a
rather ingenuous surprise at the degree of civilized decency attained
by the first non-Europeans he had encountered apart from the
slaves of the American planters, Coke was soon to have evidence of
the spiritual maturity of some of these West Indian Negroes and
their powers of endurance under the harshest persecution.

[1] Coke's *Journal*, pp. 76–83; cf. *Letters of John Wesley*, vii. 371.
[2] This anecdote is given by Drew, pp. 16off., but is not found in Coke's *Journal*.
[3] This refers not to Coke's companions, but to his clerical attire, a detail which underlines the fact that Baxter was already ordained.
[4] Coke's *Journal*, p. 83.

The slaves were not alone in rejoicing at the arrival of the missionaries, for they soon found a hospitable welcome among many of the Europeans on the island. The West Indies, like the American colonies, had suffered neglect in spiritual matters for many years.[1] Coke, as an ordained clergyman and an Oxford doctor into the bargain, found himself readily accepted in circles that had been closed to the ex-shipwright Baxter. He was offered a living on the island said to be worth £500 a year, but declined it with the comment, 'God be praised, five hundred thousand a year would be to me a feather when opposed to my usefulness in the Church of Christ.'[2] For the present, at least, his companions too were *personae gratae*. The chapel at St John's overflowed at the evening services, and so many of the gentry flocked to the preaching that the Negroes by whose sacrificial giving it had been built were in danger of being crowded out. Wherever they went on the island, the missionaries were entertained 'rather like princes than subjects'; and one day the Company of Merchants invited them to dine with Prince William Henry—later to become King William IV—whose fleet was then lying off the island. Coke wrote that he accepted the invitation more to avoid the appearance of disloyalty than out of any liking for such banquets; and, although he never disguised his gratification at finding himself so freely accepted in the higher circles of society, there is no reason to doubt the sincerity of this avowal. He was well enough aware of the besetting sins of wealth and social prestige, and could castigate them almost as severely as Wesley. (We may recall his unsparing comments on Mr Gough of Perry Hall during his first visit to America;[3] and a later occasion when, preaching in the Presbyterian meeting-house in Alexandria, Virginia, he wrote, 'Praised be God, I gave huge offence to the unregenerate rich, and great joy to the pious poor, by the testimony I then bore against sin.'[4] Though there was an element of schoolboyish devilment in his readiness to speak out in condemnation even at the cost of offending individuals or flouting social conventions, this did at least counterbalance the undue subservience toward those in authority which became more marked in his later years.)

[1] On St Vincent, only one of the five parishes had ever had a church building and even this had not been rebuilt since it was destroyed by a hurricane in 1780. The island's only clergyman officiated in the court-house at Kingston. (Coke's *History of the West Indies*, ii. 252)
[2] Coke's *Journal*, p. 84.   [3] See above, p. 86.   [4] Coke's *Journal*, p. 132.

On this occasion his acceptance by Antiguan society did not hinder him from pressing on with the organization of the mission to the Negro population of the West Indies. After holding an 'Infant-Conference', the first in the West Indies, he was soon on his way with John Baxter to visit other islands in the Leeward and Windward groups. Hammet and Clarke accompanied him; Warrener remained behind to begin his fruitful ministry in Antigua.

The first missionary tour lasted just over a month. First, in response to a 'pressing invitation', they sailed southward to St Vincent, putting in at Dominica on the way. Everywhere they found the kind of welcome and encouragement they had received in Antigua. A young Dominican planter named Burn, though roused from his bed by their calling on him, gave them every help that could be expected from an 'unawakened man' and promised both hospitality and support to any missionary who might be sent. In the capital, Roseau, a Mrs Webley, 'a mulatto gentlewoman of some property', received them 'with great joy and kindness' and threw open her house for the preaching. Returning to the island on their way back from St Vincent, they called on another planter, who had once belonged to the Dublin society, and were received by the Governor who gave his approval to their plans for a mission.

In St Vincent, they met a Mr Claxton, one of Nathaniel Gilbert's Antiguan converts, from whom no doubt the 'pressing invitation' had come. Several other planters and merchants also welcomed them and promised support for John Clarke, who was to be stationed there. Among these were Mr Steward, who had formerly belonged to the London society, and Mr Otley, a leading member of the legislative council. 'In short there is a little circuit opened to us already in this island.' Concerning the stationing of missionaries in Antigua and St Vincent, Coke wrote, 'All is as clear as if it was written with a sun-beam.' Wesley, as we have already noted,[1] was not so fully convinced.

Sailing northwards again to St Christopher, they found similar encouragement on every hand, as if to confirm the hopeful reference to the island in Coke's *Address*. Here William Hammet was to be stationed. They had crowded congregations in the Court House; but it was at this point that they began to encounter both indifference and opposition. A brief visit to the nearby island of Nevis 'proved to all appearance the most useless as well as the most expensive

[1] See above, p. 146.

153

journey' they had yet taken. They were received politely, perhaps on account of their letters of recommendation; but what mattered more to Coke was the fact that 'every door seemed shut against our ministry'.[1] Worse was to come. Away to the north of St Christopher lay the Dutch island of St Eustatius. Here they found their arrival expected by a group of free Negroes, by whom they were hospitably entertained. A Negro slave named Harry, formerly a member of society in America, had recently been constrained to preach and bear a public witness among his fellow slaves. The Governor at first gave his approval; but when his preaching began to arouse unusual and even alarming reactions among his hearers, he was forbidden to continue, under threat of severe penalties.

Being now under foreign rule, Coke was insistent that they should not preach in St Eustatius before they had waited on the Governor; but as the latter was indisposed, they met his deputies and were told to prepare their credentials and a doctrinal confession. These were duly presented to the court and appeared to meet with approval. The next day, a Sunday, Coke preached in private by invitation before members of the council; but as no permission for public preaching was yet forthcoming, he had to content himself with forming a number of classes. The gratitude of the Negroes for this brief, restricted ministry was overwhelming, and when he sailed for the mainland, they heaped gifts upon him to an almost embarrassing degree.[2]

During this first tour, Coke had visited six of the islands and left behind him missionaries in Antigua, St Vincent and St Christopher. He had been charmed by his first view of the tropical Caribbean landscape. 'The country is very romantic,' he wrote of Antigua. 'The cocoa tree is magnificent, and the milk which the nuts yield is most cooling and delicious. Everything is new, and therefore the more pleasing.'[3] More important, he had seen for himself how great was the opportunity and how eagerly the missionaries were received in one island after another. He returned home determined that this should be but the beginning.

Just under two years later, in the autumn of 1788, Coke set out once more for America, and paid his second visit to the Caribbean on the way. He landed in Barbados on 4th December, after a voyage

[1] Hammet later received invitations from Nevis, and on his second tour Coke was to find a more cordial welcome. (*Journal*, pp. 89f., 120f.)
[2] Ibid., pp. 90–2.   [3] Ibid., p. 84.

as pleasant as the previous one had been nerve-wracking. With him were three more missionaries, Matthew Lumb, Robert Gamble and Benjamin Pearce, appointed by the Conference to serve in the West Indies. Gamble and Lumb were despatched immediately to St Vincent, while the others were introduced by a group of Methodist soldiers from Ireland to a Mr Button who had provided one of his warehouses as a preaching-room. Mr Button turned out to be an old acquaintance who had heard Coke preach in Baltimore and who now welcomed Coke and his companion into his home. During the days that followed, the missionaries were warmly received by several other gentlemen of the island and encouraged to proceed with their plans. The island, unlike others in the Caribbean, was for the most part divided into small farmsteads, so that the European settlers were comparatively poor and industrious and there was less opportunity for the licentiousness which was all too prevalent in these tropical settlements. Pearce was left behind to develop the work, and Coke went on to St Vincent with the encouraging reflection that 'by a series of remarkable providences a wide door seems to be opened for us in Barbadoes'.[1]

The island of St Vincent, in which there had seemed so fair a prospect in 1787, was soon to become the scene of the first serious setback encountered by the West Indian missions. Coke arrived in the island on this second tour to find John Baxter waiting to welcome him. Baxter had come from Antigua to superintend the mission to the Caribs, a primitive people inhabiting the western part of the island. The two men lost no time in setting off to investigate the prospects for this Carib mission, in which Coke took a special interest. It was his first, and indeed his only, direct encounter with a people virtually untouched by either civilization or Christianity, and he took some pains to obtain trustworthy information about them. They took with them on their tour a Dr George Davidson who had lived for some time on the edge of the Carib territory and had already at Coke's request furnished a short account of the people and their way of life. This Coke had published the year before[2] as the basis of a special appeal for the Carib mission. In a prefatory section, obviously written by Coke himself, though in the third

155

person, he recounts how, during his first visit to St Vincent, 'the miserable and wretched state of the poor savage Caribbs, who are utterly destitute of every privilege enjoyed by civil society, affected him much; and, upon an application to the legislative body of the island, a grant was given of one hundred and fifty acres of valuable land on the borders of the *Caribb* country, for the purpose of raising a School-house, and a dwelling-house for the teacher or teachers, for the civilization and pious education of the children of the Caribbs'. This scheme was in line with the advice with which Davidson concluded his report, namely that 'the grand point at present to be aimed at is the civilization of them, and making them industrious, thereby rendering them first human beings before you attempt to make them Christians'.[1]

In reading Davidson's account of the primitive simplicity of their life, we must surely feel sympathy for these Carib people, who were about to be made partakers of the mixed blessings of Christian civilization. Nor does the sequel do much to allay misgivings. Coke, however, was well aware of the danger of the wrong kind of contact between Europeans and primitive peoples: the stimulus to materialism and the corruption of morals. In returning from the Caribbean in 1789, he found some observations on these dangers in an account of Captain Cook's voyages to the Pacific, and commented, 'What a pity it is, that the pure intentions of one of the best of sovereigns . . ., as well as all the expence of the different voyages should thus be unaccompanied with any beneficial effect. But if the salvation of many souls was to be the glorious consequence, his majesty and every person that loves our Redeemer, would have a compensation indeed.'[2] However naïvely expressed, this is at least a realistic appraisal of the dangers and benefits of contact with sophisticated Western culture, compared with which Rousseau's conception of the 'noble savage' and the anti-colonialism of our own time both appear sentimentally one-sided. In the case of the Caribs, any loss of primitive simplicity which might follow from their contact with European culture was offset by the possibility of improvement in their rudimentary standards of living. In social morality they had much to gain as well as to lose: the treatment of their womenfolk under a polygamous system, for example, fell far short of anything that could

[1] This passage was omitted when Davidson's account was reprinted in the *Journal*.
[2] Coke's *Journal*, p. 138.

be called either Christian or civilized. This side of the picture Coke was neither too sentimental nor too idealistic to ignore.

During his inspection of the work among the Caribs at the end of 1788, Coke was disappointed at the small amount of progress made so far by Mr Joyce, the schoolmaster sent out to work among them.[1] Baxter, however, was rapidly mastering their language and, though he had hoped to return to 'his beloved Antigua', immediately fell in with Coke's suggestion that he should spend a trial period of two years among the Caribs. Coke found himself charmed by these people as well as moved by pity for them. 'The sweet simplicity and cheerfulness they manifested on every side, soon wore off any unfavourable impression my mind had imbibed from the accounts I had received of their cruelties—cruelties originating probably with ourselves rather than with them. They are a handsomer people than the negroes, but have undoubtedly a warlike appearance, as their very women frequently carry cutlasses in their hands, and always knives by their naked sides.'[2]

Coke was convinced that these people, despite their warlike reputation, were 'more sinned against than sinning' and were now ripe to receive the gospel. But his hopes were to be disappointed. By the time he returned in 1790, the mission was already abandoned, and the Baxters had been forced to leave.[3] Political disaffection, fostered by the French who had formerly held the island, lay behind this failure. The rebellion was already brewing which led in 1796 to the deportation of the surviving Caribs to Honduras.[4] But a serious error of judgement by Coke himself, to which we shall have occasion to return, was another reason. Meanwhile, John Baxter returned to Antigua and the Carib mission, which had cost £2,000 to establish, had to be written off.[5]

We revert to the mission tour of 1788-9. Two of his companions were left in the eastern part of St Vincent, and Coke with Matthew Lumb and the Baxters took ship for Dominica to the north, where

[1] Ibid., p. 106; History of West Indies, ii. 264; Address to the Preachers, pp. 14ff. Joyce, a member of the Deptford society, had volunteered for the Carib mission.
[2] Coke's Journal, p. 107.
[3] Ibid., p. 143.
[4] History of West Indies, ii. 178ff.; Findlay & Holdsworth, ii. 49, 56.
[5] In his Address to the Preachers, 1793, Coke stated that £500 of this sum came from his own pocket, while the remainder was raised by subscriptions, mostly from non-Methodists.

they called once more on the Governor and formed a society of twenty-four members. Arriving in Antigua, Coke found that Warrener's labours had borne fruit. 'Surely', he wrote, 'this island is the favourite of Heaven,'[1] and as evidence of the influence of the Methodist and Moravian missions in the island he cites the fact that the practice of declaring martial law during the Christmas celebrations, which had hitherto been found necessary as a curb on the rioting, had now been abandoned.

After a brief stay in Montserrat, Coke went on to St Christopher, where Hammet was meeting with similar success. But in nearby St Eustatius the story was different. Since his earlier visit to this Dutch territory, bitter persecution had broken out, and Coke found the Methodists suffering under an infamous edict which, as he observes, was directed not against false religions or supposed heresy, as in the case of heathen or Roman Catholic persecutions of former times, but avowedly against religion itself and 'prayer, the great key to every blessing'. In support of this assertion he quotes the edict at length:

That if any white person should be found praying with his brethren—for the first offence he should be fined fifty pieces of eight: for the second, one hundred pieces: and for the third, he should be whipped, his goods confiscated, and he should then be banished the island. That if a coloured man should be found praying—for the first offence he should receive thirty-nine lashes; and for the second, if free, he should be whipped and banished; but if a slave, be whipped every time.[2]

Under this ban, the Negro preacher Harry had been banished from the island, but only after the harshest treatment had been meted out to him. 'When he stood before the Governor and Council, to answer for the unpardonable crime of praying with the people, one of the council observed to him, "*Harry* you must be flogged;" to which he calmly replied, "Christ was flogged, and why should not I?"' It did not improve matters that the man who carried out the flogging in a most unmerciful manner was Isaac de Lion, the very man who had previously welcomed Coke with so great a show of kindness. 'Such a picture of Satan for subtlety and barbarity', wrote the disillusioned doctor, 'never, I think, before did I behold.'[3] Even under such conditions, however, the society now numbered 258 and about 140 presented themselves for baptism.

[1] Coke's *Journal*, p. 116.   [2] Ibid., p. 118.   [3] Ibid.

Coke was preparing to hurry back to St Christopher after a single day on Dutch soil, when events took an unexpected turn. They had hardly set sail before they discovered that the sloop they had hired was manned by a drunken crew who soon brought it into collision with a larger vessel and seriously damaged some of the rigging. Before long they were in danger of drifting out to sea in an unseaworthy condition. The captain alone was still sober. Spurred on by a bribe and the desire to save his own skin, and with the unskilled assistance of the missionaries themselves, he at last succeeded in bringing the sloop round, so that, despite a further collision which seriously damaged rudder and stern, they eventually found themselves safely back in St Eustatius.

Seeing, as was his wont, the hand of God in this turn of events, Coke now prepared to redeem the opportunity thrust upon him. 'Lest any of our friends should suffer whipping, confiscation of goods, or banishment, by admitting me to preach in their houses, I hired a large room for a month, and the next day preached to a quiet and attentive congregation, and published myself for the Lord's-Day following.' The Governor was not long in taking action, threatening first their host, Mr Lindsey, and then the missionaries themselves. 'In the morning, while we were at breakfast, the marshal of the court entered with great form, and delivered us a message from the Governor and Fischal, which was, that they required us to promise, that we would not, publicly or privately, by day or by night, preach either to whites or to blacks during our stay in that island, under the penalty, on default, of prosecution, *arbitrary punishment*, (that was the very expression,) and banishment from the Island.' Faced with an impasse, and with so great a prospect of doing good in other islands, Coke eventually decided to withdraw, at least until a change of governor or the intervention of the Dutch authorities should create a more favourable situation. So, 'having nothing more at present to do in this place of tyranny, oppression and wrong, we returned to St *Kitt's*, blessing God for a British constitution and a British government.'[1]

A few days later they met with a very different reception on the small volcanic island of Saba, also under Dutch rule. The Governor, Council and people, who had been without a regular minister for seventeen years, were eager that one of the missionaries, William Brazier, who had been driven out of St Eustatius, should remain

[1] Ibid., p. 120.

among them. 'What could I do?' asked Coke. 'Mr *Brazier* was
appointed to labour under Mr *Hammet* at *Jamaica*: but I could not
bear that this delightful people should perish for lack of knowledge.
I therefore left Mr *Brazier* behind me, having spent two pleasing
days with these inhabitants of the rock. May they all be built on the
Rock of Ages!' Unfortunately, however, the Governor of St Eustatius was also Governor-General of all the Dutch West Indian possessions; and when he heard what had happened, he lost no time in
forcing the authorities in Saba to relinquish their minister, so that
this promising beginning came to nothing.[1]

From St Christopher, Coke also paid two visits to Nevis to the
south, and in due course went on to Tortola and Santa Cruz in the
Virgin Islands. The number and variety of the opportunities that
presented themselves were becoming a serious embarrassment to
the limited supply of missionaries. Hammet was now with Coke,
destined to begin a mission in Jamaica; but it was decided that for
the moment he should stay behind to take charge of the work in
Tortola and Santa Cruz. The latter was under Danish rule, and the
Governor-General welcomed them with promises of support and
protection.

So Coke sailed on alone and landed for the first time in Jamaica on
19th January 1789 with no missionary to station there. This was the
largest of the islands visited by Coke himself, and here, though there
were those who welcomed him as in other parts of the Caribbean, he
encountered also a measure of hostility and opposition. On the one
hand he was constrained to write that he had never received so many
civilities in any other place, either in Europe or in America, where
the gospel was not preached. On the other, his preaching was nowhere more frequently interrupted and his own person threatened
than in Jamaica. The European community here was more sophisticated than on the smaller islands, and in several of the towns there
were companies of young 'bucks and bloods' who welcomed the
sport of missionary-baiting as a change from their usual diversions.
They interrupted the preaching with rowdy behaviour or ridicule,
or clapped ironical encouragement. Sometimes they resorted to
direct threats. Coke's very first sermon on the island, at Port Royal,
was disturbed by a drunken group who began pressing towards the
preacher, bawling, 'Down with him, down with him!' and who withdrew, equally noisily, only when confronted by other members of

[1] Ibid., pp. 121-3.

the congregation. 'The spirits of the congregation', says Coke, 'were so deranged by this unhappy incident, that I gave out a hymn, and then chose a new text, and preached a sermon, with some degree of liberty, I bless God, to a serious, attentive audience.'[1]

This first visit to Jamaica early in 1789 was necessarily brief because of his commitments in America, but it sufficed to convince him 'that great good might be done in this island, if the gospel was regularly preached here with power'. He sailed for Charleston, determined that Hammet and others should go there as soon as it could be arranged. Meanwhile he could look back on a second tour in the course of which six new islands had been surveyed and opportunities noted on every side. Apart from the attitude of the Dutch authorities, there seemed to be no cloud in the Caribbean sky.

In the two years which elapsed before his third visit, the West Indies were seldom far from Coke's mind. He issued two appeals for support to the growing list of 'benevolent subscribers', by no means all of whom were members of the Methodist societies. When he sailed again for the New World in the autumn of 1790, he was accompanied by two further missionaries, Lyons and Worrell, the latter being destined for Jamaica. Again, their first port of call was Bridgetown, Barbados, where Pearce had successfully weathered an initial period of persecution. In St Vincent, the Carib mission was already seen to be a failure and was about to be abandoned. As some consolation for this, Coke found fresh encouragement in Grenada, the southernmost of the Windward Islands, which he now visited for the first time. This was, in fact, the last of the islands to be 'opened up' by Coke himself. Mr Dent, the minister at St George's, whom Coke had previously met as a curate in Barbados, had already proved himself a friend to the Methodists. He now welcomed the visitors with 'true Christian kindness'. Coke speaks of him as 'the only clergyman in these islands that has shewn any regard for the Methodists'; though on his second visit to Grenada he was to find another in the person of Mr Carew, the rector of Guave. Among the richer and more influential Europeans who gave every encouragement to the proposed mission was General Matthews, Governor of the island and Mr Dent's patron, at whose house Coke and Baxter dined in company with some of the leading inhabitants. Coke was constrained to promise them a missionary as soon as one could be found, and

[1] Ibid., pp. 125–6.

161

Baxter in his turn was moved to promise that he would himself return as their pastor if no one else was available.

Coke was greatly impressed by the beauty of this 'Island of Spices', and in visiting the lake cradled in the crater of the Grand Etang mountain he lapsed into one of his rare contemplative moods. In the midst of so active a life, he permitted himself for once to consider the pleasures of becoming a recluse. 'If I was to turn hermit', he mused, 'I think I should fix on this place, where I would make circular walks, and fix an observatory on one of the peaks, and spend my time in communion with God, and in the study of Astronomy and Botany.'[1] It was not often that the curtain was thus drawn aside, and the very next day Coke was embarking for St Vincent and Antigua, and then on to Montserrat, St Christopher and St Eustatius. Here a new Governor had just arrived from Holland, but any hopes this may have raised in Coke's mind were quickly dashed. He was received with such extreme rudeness that the only course seemed to be to leave the island as quietly as possible. The only encouraging feature was the reports they received that more than two hundred members were still meeting in class and were determined to keep in touch with the St Christopher missionary.

After a visit to Nevis, during which he found time to make a study of the process of sugar refining, Coke returned to St Christopher, where the missionaries gathered for a short conference. Time did not permit a visit to any of the Virgin Islands; so, before he sailed for the American mainland, he ended this third tour, like the previous one, with a visit to Jamaica. Here he preached a number of times in Kingston, Spanish Town, Montego Bay and Falmouth, besides returning to Port Royal. There were still wags ready to applaud the sermon with cries of 'Encore!' They followed him even when he hired a dingy building on the outskirts of Spanish Town in order to preach to the Negroes, who were eager to hear, without interruption. Sometimes he or one of his colleagues was threatened with violence. During Hammet's ministry in Kingston an outbreak of persecution endangered both the safety of the chapel and Hammet's own life. Only the intervention of the magistrates and the threat of legal action restrained the rioters. The newspapers continued to echo the conflict for some months. Hammet was maligned, and Coke was represented as a horse-thief who had fled to Jamaica to escape justice. During this second visit to the island, Coke preached in Kingston in the teeth of

[1] Ibid., p. 146.

this hostility, but encountered nothing worse than extreme rudeness. One of the most distressing features which he noted in his extensive tours of the island was the negligence and indifference of the parish clergy. One Sunday he went to the parish church in Montego Bay, only to find that because the rain had reduced the congregation to a mere half-dozen the minister walked out without even beginning his service. 'The Sunday before also there had been no service. In some of the parishes of this island there is no Church, nor any divine service performed, except the burial of the dead, and christenings and weddings in private houses, though the livings are very lucrative.' The situation was much the same, in fact, as Coke had found it to be in the American states. 'But I will write no more on this subject,' he concludes, 'lest I should grow indignant.'[1]

The extreme heat, the precipitous nature of the country and the emaciated horses which were all he could sometimes procure for his journeys, combined with the greater distances to make his travelling in Jamaica more trying than in any of the other islands. But as in America the great beauty of the landscape offered some compensation for this. The grandeur of the mountain scenery, with its ever-varying prospects and luxurious vegetation, was a source of constant delight. Indeed, their natural beauty was one of the things which fixed the West Indies firmly in his affections, and his *Journal* frequently recurs to the theme. Of all the smaller islands, he found St Vincent particularly delightful. 'The island of St Vincent's is romantic beyond any thing I ever saw before. The hanging rocks, sugar-canes, cotton and coffee plantations, &c. make such a beautifully-variegated scene, that I was delighted with it: but, I trust, did not lose sight of the great Author of the whole.'[2] This was written soon after his first arrival in the West Indies, but first impressions were strengthened by later visits. Some years afterwards he amplified his earlier description thus:

The country is very hilly, and singularly full of picturesque scenes. The steep mountains with their sharp peaks, the cocoa-trees and plantains, . . . the sugar-canes planted on the gentle declivities of the mountains, . . . the coffee and cotton plantations, the *Atlantic Ocean* constantly in view, the milk-white foam of the sea between the rocks and promontories, . . . and the burning sun exulting in his strength . . . form such scenes as persons unacquainted with the torrid zone have hardly any conception of.[3]

William Hammet had been labouring in Jamaica with remarkable

[1] Ibid., pp. 152f.   [2] Ibid., p. 88.   [3] Ibid., p. 142.

success, but the deterioration in his health was giving cause for serious concern and Coke decided to take him to America. Alas, this solicitude was to earn nothing but trouble, and Coke's high regard for Hammet was to prove sadly mistaken. But the sequel should not blind us to the outstanding contribution he had made to the establishment of Methodism in the West Indies. 'He has been employed', Coke wrote, 'in the most arduous undertakings during the time he has been in these Islands. The two most flourishing Societies in the West-Indies, (Antigua excepted)—those of St Kitt's and Tortola, were raised by the means of his indefatigable labours in the midst of much opposition: and there are but few in the world with whom I have been acquainted, that possess the proper apostolic spirit in an equal degree with him.'[1] The opportunities Hammet's ministry had created justified the leaving of two men, Worrell and Brazier, in his place.

It was this visit to the States that was cut short by the news of Wesley's death. Coke hastened back to England, but within eighteen months was again on his way to America and after a brief tour left New York for the West Indies, his fourth and last visit. With him was William Black, whom he intended to appoint as superintendent of the West Indian missions. They landed in St Eustatius on the last day of 1792, only to find that the previous governor had returned and persecution was at its height. During his short absence from office, though preaching was still forbidden, the society had been left in peace. Now, however, 'the flames of persecution were kindled afresh'. Coke relates the patient endurance of two Negro women, unmercifully whipped for the crime of attending a Methodist prayer-meeting, who, even as the lash furrowed their bleeding backs, 'gave such indubitable proofs of the genuine power of Religion, of patient suffering, and triumphant faith', that even some of the principal gentlemen of the island were moved to pity, though the Governor himself remained unmoved. 'The poor slaves, from one end of the Island to the other, who met together to sing and pray, and converse of the things of God, (the only method they had, in which to hold Divine worship) were cart-whipped, and many of them imprisoned. The consequence has been, that the precious Society we had here, is almost dispersed. About half a dozen little classes meet in corners: and, yet, there is not a single Minister of any kind in the Island!'[2] There was little that Coke could do for the victims of this vicious

[1] Ibid., p. 160.   [2] Ibid., p. 190.

164

régime beyond curtailing his stay and resolving to take up their cause with the Dutch authorities on his return to Europe.

On his previous visit to St Eustatius, Coke had returned to St Christopher 'blessing God for a British constitution and a British government'. On this occasion, however, he had hardly left Dutch soil before news reached him that persecution had broken out in St Vincent, where they had at first been received with so much kindness and there had seemed so fair a prospect. Now the missionary, Matthew Lumb, was reported to be imprisoned in the common gaol for the crime of preaching the gospel. Coke lost no time in taking a sloop from St Christopher, to come to Lumb's aid and enquire into the cause of 'this extraordinary event'. He found that a law had been passed, clearly aimed at the Methodist itinerant plan, forbidding any except the parish priests to preach without a licence and denying such a licence to anyone who had not resided on the island for twelve months. The penalty for the first offence was a fine of ten Johannes or between thirty and ninety days' imprisonment; for the second, corporal punishment followed by banishment on pain of death. There was reason to believe that this was the work of a minority of wealthy planters, perturbed by the success of the missionaries among their slaves, and that the majority of the European settlers still favoured the mission. The Act had been hurried through the Assembly at the close of a session, when very few members were present.

Lumb had unhesitatingly refused to be silenced by this law and preached as usual on the following Sunday. Within four days he was in gaol, where Coke found him sharing a cell with common criminals. 'Our kind friends supplied him with provisions sufficient for himself and his fellow-prisoners. Soldiers guarded him: and because he spoke of the things of God, through the grates to the poor negroes, who continually flocked around the prison, orders were given that he should be *closely* confined. However, the white people were suffered to visit him: but the guards took care that no coloured person should speak to him even through the grates. And the poor negroes would come up close to the grates, and while they stood silently glancing at him in the prison, the tears would trickle abundantly down their cheeks. And all this was done, because Mr. *Lumb* had preached the GOSPEL TO THE NEGROES IN OUR OWN CHAPEL, built with our own Money, on our own ground!'[1]

[1] Ibid., p. 193; *History of West Indies*, ii. 271ff.

Coke's hands were tied. The mission was for the present at a standstill, and there was little he could do either for Lumb or for his converts, many of whom were continuing to meet privately. He determined, however, to seek the annulment of this persecuting Act as soon as he returned to England.

Coke's theological reaction to this outbreak of bitter persecution is an interesting one. It would have been easy enough for him to give conventional expression in his Journal to a resignation which he was far from feeling. Instead, he gave way at this point to a series of utterances which have something in common with Jeremiah's complaints to God. There is a note of impatience, almost of indignant rebuke, in his summing up of the situation in St Eustatius. 'What a mystery! that the Great Governor of the Church should suffer it! my grieved, bleeding heart says (I fear with some reluctance) "thy will be done". But it also says, with all its powers, "How long, O Lord, holy and true, dost thou not avenge our blood!" '[1] And in considering the way in which the work in St Vincent was being disrupted, his prayer for the Methodists there was couched in similar terms: 'O God, upon my bended knees I pray thee, to remove the iron hand of persecution which now rests upon thy little flock. Can it be consistent with thine holy attributes, that *these* should perish through the malignity and wickedness of *thine* enemies? That be far from thee to do after this manner, to slay the righteous with the wicked: . . . shall not the judge of all the earth do right?'[2] For this once, at least, he permitted himself in public to rise above the pedestrian levels of conventional evangelical piety. There is no doubt of the sincerity that rings out clearly in his exclamation, 'O how difficult it is, and yet how comfortable, to believe that "all things work together for our good".'[3] For the rest, his distress at the plight of these victims of persecution quickened his interest in millenarianism and his conviction that the day of the last things was at hand.

Coke's time was running short and he was preparing to hurry on to Jamaica when the arrival of Abraham Bishop, one of the missionaries from Nova Scotia, persuaded him to turn south again and pay a short visit to Grenada. Bishop was a native of Jersey and his command of French was to prove useful in Grenada; but though his ministry promised fair, he quickly succumbed to fever and died before his work could bear fruit. Not long afterwards the climate of the island claimed another victim in Benjamin Pearce, and for many

[1] Coke's *Journal*, p. 190.   [2] Ibid., p. 204.   [3] Ibid., p. 207.

years the mission was retarded by the lack of suitable bilingual preachers. As so often in the early days of the West Indian missions, it was not the openings but the resources that were lacking, despite Coke's most strenuous and persistent efforts towards their support.

Grenada was not the only island to claim its victims. William McCornock had died at his post in Dominica and a replacement had still to be found. And when he reached Jamaica at the close of this tour, Coke learned that Worrell had died of fever and Brazier's health was so seriously affected that he was forced to retire. He nevertheless spent a busy fortnight touring the island and planning to extend the mission. His tour took him from Kingston to Montego Bay and back. On the way he enjoyed the warm-hearted hospitality of a Moravian settlement and delighted in the luxuriant beauty of the landscape with its hanging rocks and trees. At Montego Bay he was warned of a plot to blow up the assembly rooms where he was to preach, but refused to alter his plans and concluded the service unscathed. On occasions he was befriended by the most unlikely acquaintances; as when, discovering that his horse had been removed from the inn stable and its corn and fodder stolen, he was championed by a stalwart young drunkard who boasted rather pathetically of his former membership of the Countess of Huntingdon's Connexion. Coke imagined the Countess commenting, in the words of George Whitefield on a similar occasion, 'I see clearly you are one of my converts, and not a convert of Jesus Christ'.[1] Next day, he had a more amusing encounter with the curate at St Ann's Bay who claimed to be a fellow Oxford student. ' "Pray, Sir," said I, "of what House were you?" "House, Sir, house," said he. "Of what College, Sir," said I. "Oh Sir, of *Oxford* College, of *Oxford* College." He seemed a little confounded, apprehending he had made a small blunder; and quoted the first line of the Aeneid of *Virgil*, in Latin, and the first verse of the first chapter of St. *John's* Gospel in Greek, but in a most wretched manner. However, finding my mouth perfectly sealed, he and his companions, after a few more observations, were pleased to withdraw to my great joy.'[2]

This was to be Coke's last glimpse of the West Indies, though he was to continue to exercise supervision of the mission from a distance for many years to come.[3] His intention of appointing William

[1] Ibid., pp. 215f. [2] Ibid., p. 216.
[3] Some writers have spoken of a fifth, and even a sixth, visit to the West Indies, but this is an error. Coke's own *History of the West Indies* (1808–11)

Black as superintendent of the work throughout the islands was thwarted by the reluctance of the Methodists of Nova Scotia to relinquish him. Finding and equipping suitable missionaries was to remain a major preoccupation for the rest of Coke's life. 'The fields are ripe for harvest,' he wrote, 'but, alas! alas! there are none to reap it.' He had begotten a lusty child which was to make ever-increasing demands upon his energy and resources.

On his return to England in the summer of 1793, Coke lost no time in petitioning the Government on behalf of the Methodists of St Vincent. In this, as on later occasions, he had the advantage of personal acquaintance with those in high office. He approached the Privy Council and also individual members of the Government. The governors of the various West Indian islands under British rule were instructed to submit reports on the activities of the Methodist missionaries, and at the end of August the Home Secretary, Henry Dundas, informed Coke that, in the light of these, His Majesty in Council had been pleased to disannul the offending Act of the St Vincent Assembly.[1] This was the first of several such victories.

As soon as the affairs of the British Connexion would permit, Coke paid two successive visits to the Netherlands[2] in an attempt to gain similar redress for the Negroes of St Eustatius and Saba. In the early part of 1794 he spent some time in the Hague, awaiting a response to his memorial. He was able to produce a testimonial from Dundas which stated, 'I have lately had some communication with this society, who are members of the Church of England, and it is with great satisfaction I can bear testimony to the loyalty of their principles and conduct.'[3] But though he obtained an audience with the Stadt-holder, the Dutch authorities manifested no desire to emulate the enlightened colonial policy of the British Government, and Coke had

gives an account of only four visits. He planned to revisit the islands on his way to America in the autumn of 1799, but his departure from England was in fact delayed until February 1800 and he had to hurry to reach Baltimore in time for the General Conference on 6th May. (See *W.H.S. Proc.* xxxv. 43.) On his previous American visit, the ship on which he sailed was captured by a French privateer and taken to Puerto Rico; but Coke and his companions were allowed to board a brig bound for America.

[1] Drew, pp. 254–8.
[2] Letter sent to various American preachers, dated Bristol, 23rd July 1794 (copies at Garrett Theological Seminary and Baltimore Methodist Historical Society).
[3] Drew, pp. 260f.

to accept defeat.[1] There was to be no respite for the Methodists of St Eustatius until the death of Governor Rennolds in 1811, though contact with them was maintained through the missionaries stationed in St Christopher. Nor did Coke lose sight of the island or its people's needs, but was constantly on the watch for an opportunity of reviving the work there. Reviewing the missionary requirements of the West Indies in April 1810, he wrote that, when men were available, Bermuda, Trinidad and the Bahamas each needed a missionary, while 'Antigua must have three, or be ever low' and 'my beloved St Eustatius should have one as soon as possible'.[2]

* * *

The society which welcomed the Methodist missionaries in one West Indian island after another, like that of the American States, was based on a plentiful supply of slave labour. Indeed, for the most part the American settlers treated their slaves more humanely than did the West Indian planters. Yet Coke has sometimes been accused of showing a less outright opposition to West Indian slavery than he did in America, and there is some truth in this. Two examples will point the difference. In 1785 we found him deploring the attitude of one of his Virginian hosts, Captain Dillard, who, though he was 'as kind to his negroes as if they were white servants', yet could not be made to see 'the evil of keeping them in slavery'.[3] Eight years later, Coke's attitude had altered so radically that he could record his warm commendation of the humane treatment of the slaves of Grenada and the law passed for their protection as 'doing honour to the whole island'.[4] We must remember that his most violent diatribes against American slavery were uttered during his first visit to the country in 1784-5. We have already seen that he learned from experience the futility of such direct assaults from the pulpit and developed more

[1] During this period of enforced idleness, Coke was able to gather some of the material for his projected *Commentary*, and made the acquaintance of Dr Maclaine, and English minister in the Hague who gave him access to the expository notes of his father-in-law, a Dutch theologian (Candler, p. 273; letter to Maclaine in Drew, pp. 261ff; Etheridge, pp. 259f).

[2] Letter to Robert Johnson, 30th April 1810 (M.M.S. Archives). Though Drew states that the Governor was persuaded to show greater tolerance in 1804, there are no membership returns for the island in the *Minutes* between 1794 and 1811.

[3] Coke's *Journal*, p. 69.   [4] Ibid., p. 196.

subtle methods of opposing the evil.[1] Hence, by the time of his first visit to the Caribbean, he had learned to trim his sails enough at least to avoid being capsized by adverse gales. Slavery was so closely woven into the social and economic life of the West Indies, that an unqualified public opposition to it from the outset would certainly have alienated the majority of the Europeans, not least the upper classes on whose favour the prospects of the new mission greatly depended.

Another factor was the far greater proportion of slaves in the population of the West Indies. Candler states that, whereas in America there were four white settlers to every negro, in the West Indies the Negroes outnumbered the whites by seven to one.[2] Though it might not affect the moral principles involved, this discrepancy made emancipation as a practical issue much more difficult. During his last visit, in 1793, Coke heard accounts of the ruthless treatment of Europeans in Haiti by Negro rebels incited by the recent Revolution in France; and though he believed this to be a just retribution for the island's moral degradation, it was also a warning of what could result from the emancipation of slaves who were not in bondage to Christ.[3] Greatly as he detested the 'execrable villainy of slavery', in the last resort the eternal salvation of the slaves mattered to him more than their temporal emancipation; and he was not prepared to jeopardize the one to effect the other. This scale of values is nicely reflected in a letter to Ezekiel Cooper, one of the American preachers, in 1795:

My dear Brother, have great Compassion on the poor Negroes & do all you can to Convert them. If they have Religious Liberty, their Temporal Slavery will be comparatively but a small thing; but even in respect to this latter point, I do long for the time when the Lord will turn their Captivity like the Rivers of the South:[4] & he will appear for them: he is winding up the Sacred Ball.[5] He is sweeping off the Wicked with the Besom of destruction, with pestilence, famine & War; and will never

[1] See above, pp. 96ff.   [2] Candler, pp. 331f.
[3] Coke's *Journal*, pp. 207f; *History of West Indies*, iii. 438ff. Cf. Findlay & Holdsworth, ii, 257f.
[4] Psalm 126:5 (P.B.V.) (A.V.: 'as the streams in the south' i.e. the Negeb). In his *Commentary*, Coke interprets the phrase as referring to the river of Egypt (cf. Isaiah 27:12) and so symbolic of Africa.
[5] The Rev. George Lawton suggests that Coke may have in mind the expression 'to wind up your bottom' (=a ball of wool or thread), meaning 'to bring to a conclusion'.

withdraw his Hand until Civil & Religious Liberty be Established all over the Earth.[1]

On one occasion Coke certainly compromised too readily with the existing social order, but was quick to realize his error and to set matters right. One of the charges brought against him by William Hammet in 1792 was that, despite his avowed opposition to slavery, he had misused the funds raised for the mission among the Caribs of St Vincent by purchasing slaves for the cotton and coffee plantation presented to the Mission by the Legislature of the island. In his reply Coke admitted the fact and confessed that he had been in error. He explained:

My friends on all sides of me urged that the present might be an exempt case, that the gift of the land was undoubtedly *providential*, and that the slaves purchased for the cultivation of it would certainly be treated *by us* in the tenderest manner. These and other arguments prevailed, and I gave directions that a sufficient supply be procured for the cotton on the low land . . . I had hardly left the island when my established principles began to operate. I considered that no exempt case could justify the proceedings; that we are not to do evil that good may come. The wound continued to deepen in my mind for some months, till at last I wrote from Baltimore to inform our missionary (Mr Baxter) that I could not admit of any slaves upon the estate on any consideration . . . At the time I acted for the best, and *humanum est errare*.[2]

The dilemma was that of a Christian mission in a country whose economy depended upon a supply of African labour, but in which emancipation was not immediately practicable or acceptable to the ruling classes. Coke himself was the only one to lose financially in this instance by refunding out of his own pocket the sum that had been spent on slaves. He undoubtedly learned his lesson, and it was he who in 1807 persuaded the British Conference to forbid the preachers in the West Indies to marry anyone possessing slaves.[3]

It might fairly be said that in the interests of the mission to the Negroes of the West Indies Coke and his fellow-preachers came to terms with slavery as part of the established order. That is not to say that they gave it either their approval or their support. It is true,

[1] Letter to Ezekiel Cooper, 23rd April 1795 (Garrett Theological Seminary).
[2] *Address to the Preachers*, pp. 17–19. There is reason to think that Hammet himself became a slave-owner. See *W.H.S. Proc.* xxviii. 101, 124, and Coke's *Journal*, p. 247.
[3] *Minutes*, ii. 402; cf. Maldwyn L. Edwards, *After Wesley.* p. 70.

moreover, that, like St Paul in the Roman Empire, by their pro-
clamation of the Gospel they did a great deal to undermine the institution and to prepare the way for its abolition. To their owners the
slaves were often no more than semi-human cattle; to the missionaries they were children of God with immortal souls for whom
Christ had died. The revolutionary power of the Gospel of 'liberty
to the captive' was once again demonstrated in the social repercussions of the West Indian mission.[1]

* * *

When, on 9th February 1793, the preachers gathered in Antigua,
Coke seems almost to have known that this was to be the last Conference he was to preside over in the West Indies. 'We examined all
the important minutes of the preceding Conferences, and left nothing unconsidered, I think, which would be useful to each other, or to
the work in general. Our debates were free and full. All the preachers
seemed to speak their whole mind on every important subject; and I
believe, much profit will accrue to the work, from the regulations
which we then made.'[2] In less than nine years, Methodism in the
Caribbean had grown from the single society of nearly 2,000 which
Coke found in Antigua to a membership of 6,570. There were now
twelve missionaries working in ten of the islands. Some of Coke's
projects—a mission to the Bay of Honduras[3] and one to the Danish
island of Santa Cruz[4]—had come to nothing, though none was
abandoned lightly. For the rest of his life he was to continue to
supervise the work at a distance, but none the less with a fatherly concern for the well-being of every missionary equipped and sent out,
often at considerable expense to his own pocket. The seed sown by
Nathaniel Gilbert was growing apace. By 1814 there were twelve
circuits throughout the Caribbean, with a membership totalling
17,000. For this, the credit must go, not to Methodism as a whole,
but to Thomas Coke.

[1] Cf. Findlay & Holdsworth, ii. 26.   [2] Coke's *Journal*, p. 200.
[3] Letter to Joseph Sutcliffe, 16th January 1790 (Historical Society of
Pennsylvania). The *Minutes* of 1796 list William Fish as stationed at 'Honduras
Bay', but the appointment came to nothing and the present mission in Honduras
dates from the arrival of Thomas Wilkinson in 1825.
[4] In January 1789 Coke was cordially received by the Governor, who promised
protection and encouragement for the mission. But the Danish Government
intervened and twenty years were to pass before a fresh opportunity occurred.
Coke then seized it eagerly. (Letter to the Missionary Committee, 28th July
1809 (New Room, Bristol.)

CHAPTER 11

ICHABOD

For the many whose lives had been touched by his influence, the death of John Wesley in March 1791 meant that there had passed away a glory from the earth. Life for them would never again be quite the same. Thomas Coke was far away, on the other side of the Atlantic. His fourth tour of the American States had lasted barely two months when the news reached him, causing him to cut short his visit and hasten home.

The visit of 1791 was the last on which Coke was to enjoy the status of Wesley's personal representative among the American Methodists. As before, it followed a tour of the West Indies. A protracted voyage from Jamaica, during which the ship several times escaped danger from rocks and sandbanks, brought him ashore at Edisto Island, south of Charleston, on 21st February. Here he found warm hospitality among strangers, who helped him on his way to Charleston. Having spent a month, instead of the normal two weeks, at sea, he found that the South Carolina preachers had just concluded their Conference, but were waiting one day more in the hope of seeing him. So he was able to spend the day with them 'in many solemn and useful conversations'.[1]

Leaving Charleston, he made his way south for the Georgia Conference, then northwards, advancing with the spring through North Carolina into Virginia. As before, he found himself preaching daily to large congregations in the great forests, finding his way by means of the 'preacher's mark' of the split bush.[2] With Asbury, he paid a visit to the Catawba Indians, among whom there were hopes of establishing a mission school.[3]

Coke had found William Hammet debilitated by fever in Jamaica and had brought him to the mainland. Hammet was an able preacher, the fruits of whose work in several of the islands have already been noted. Coke's well-intentioned action, however, had unfortunate results, for Hammet quickly became a trouble-maker

[1] Coke's *Journal*, pp. 167f.   [2] Ibid., pp. 170, 175.
[3] Ibid., p. 172. Cf. Asbury, *Journal*, i. 670f.

and began to gather a faction about him in Charleston. Only a week after their arrival, Asbury wrote in his *Journal*: 'I am somewhat distressed at the uneasiness of our people, who claim a right to choose their own preachers; a thing quite new amongst Methodists. None but Mr Hammett will do for them. We shall see how it will end.'[1] The end was not yet in sight. Hammet later turned up in Philadelphia, armed with a petition from the society in Charleston. Perhaps out of deference to Coke, who had just left for home, Asbury agreed to Hammet's appointment, but Hammet was far from satisfied even by this concession. He clearly lacked the adaptability demanded of anyone who settled in post-colonial America. 'We are considered by him as seceders from Methodism', wrote Asbury, 'because we do not wear gowns and powder; and because we did not pay sufficient respect to Mr Wesley!'[2] In a letter to the British Conference he accused the two bishops of tyranny, Coke of murder, and the American Methodists of being in a state of schism. Against Coke personally he launched a broadside entitled, *An Impartial Statement of the known Inconsistencies of the Reverend Dr Coke, in his official station, as Superintendent of the Methodist Missionaries in the West Indies*, accusing him of inhuman and unchristian treatment of the missionaries and of having used the mission funds to buy slaves.[3] Coke's defence took the form of an *Address to the Preachers*, which he distributed in 1793 throughout the British Connexion in defence of both himself and the missions. Having divided the society at Charleston and built his own church, Hammet enjoyed a considerable following for a while; but later his popularity waned[4] and after his death in 1803 the breach was closed.

An issue which divided the two bishops at the outset of this fourth visit of Coke to America was the future of the 'Council'. In May 1789 the New York Conference had given somewhat hesitant approval to Asbury's scheme for a body to be composed of the bishops and presiding elders, to be convened as judged expedient by the bishops, which should have authority to determine matters concerning the worship, doctrine and discipline, abuses and disorders, and the

---

[1] Asbury, *Journal*, i. 668.   [2] Ibid., i. 706.

[3] *W.H.S. Proc.* xxviii. 99f. I have been unable to locate a copy of this pamphlet in England. For his accusation concerning slave-holding, see p. 171 above.

[4] Coke, *Journal*, pp. 247f. In his *Address to the Preachers*, pp. 20–22, Coke paid generous tribute to Hammet's work in the West Indies, but drew attention to some of the moral shortcomings of the members of his Charleston congregation.

general well-being of the Church. This was to replace the General Conference, and there were those, notably Jesse Lee and James O'Kelly, who feared that it gave undue power to the bishops. O'Kelly wrote to both Wesley and Coke, criticizing the Council, with the result that the latter returned to America in 1791, determined to lend his influence to the opposition. As on the occasion of Coke's second visit in 1787, relations between the two bishops were strained for a time. 'A few sharp words' passed between them on meeting,[1] but the tension was soon relieved and Asbury prepared to bow before the growing opposition to his scheme. He had written a little earlier to Thomas Morrell concerning his determination to oppose Coke when he arrived, adding, 'I wish to see the council empowered and consolidated, or the Methodists will be a confused, divided people, like some others'.[2] But in the event he found it wiser to yield. 'I found the Doctor's sentiments, with regard to the council quite changed,' he wrote. 'James O'Kelly's letters had reached London. I felt perfectly calm, and acceded to a general conference, for the sake of peace.'[3] And two months later he added, 'I hope to be enabled to give up all I dare for peace's sake; and to please all men for their good to edification.'[4]

It is probable that Wesley himself, rather than O'Kelly, was the influence behind Coke's *volte-face* concerning the Council. His relations with O'Kelly at this time were nevertheless extremely cordial, as is shown by a letter he wrote to him shortly before sailing for home:

You may depend on my being with you, God willing, at the General Conference. I think no step will be taken during my absence, to prevent the General Conference; it would be so gross an insult on truth, justice, mercy, and peace, that it will not be, I think, attempted. If it be, and successfully, we will call a Congress. I expect you to be faithful. But as Mordecai said to Esther, think not with thyself that thou shalt escape more than others; for if thou altogether holdest thy peace at this time, then shall there enlargement and deliverance arise to the Jews from another'

---

[1] Candler, p. 162, quoting Nicholas Snethen. But Asbury later denied this: 'There was no sharpness at all upon my side with Dr Coke at Charleston respecting the proposed general conference, which was afterwards held: I was fully convinced that nothing *else* would finish the unhappy business with O'Kelly: and that did finish it'. (*Journal*, i. 282.)

[2] Letter from Asbury to Morrell, 20th January, 1791 (*World Parish*, April 1960, p. 29).

[3] Asbury, *Journal*, i. 667f.   [4] Ibid., i. 672.

place; but thou and thy father's house shall be destroyed. Oh, be firm, be very firm, and very cautious, and very wise, and depend upon a faithful friend in
Thomas Coke.[1]

Coke's opposition was decisive and the Council was never again convened. But O'Kelly was soon to show his hand as a schismatic troublemaker, the Kilham of American Methodism; and Coke's association with him, like his championship of Hammet, scarcely enhances our opinion of him as a judge of his fellows.

* * *

The estrangement between Coke and Asbury was more than a mere clash of personalities. That their thoughts were at present moving in entirely different directions is clearly shown by Coke's exchange of views with Bishop White of Philadelphia. Since his first visit to America six years before, Coke's churchmanship had suffered a further sea-change: the pendulum had swung from profound antipathy towards the Church of England to a conviction that the widening rift between Methodism and the parent body must be bridged. What he felt at this point was expressed in a letter to Wilberforce in 1790:

There is one point I feel a desire of touching upon, assured that your candour will excuse my further intrusion on your patience. Some have said (from the steps I was unavoidably necessitated to take on the continent of America, or entirely abandon that work) that I would, if possible, separate the whole Methodist connexion in England and Ireland from the established church. I do assure you, Sir, upon the honour of a gentleman, and (which is in my view, and also I am confident in yours, abundantly greater) on the solemn word of a Christian, the assertion is utterly false. I not only wish for no such thing but would oppose a separation from the establishment with my utmost influence, even if that, or a division in the connexion, was the unavoidable alternative.[2]

Such was Coke's frame of mind when he arrived in America early in 1791. A little later in the same year, he recorded even more fully the chances and changes of his churchmanship in a letter to Bishop Seabury of Connecticut:

[1] Printed in Asbury, *Letters*, p. 99.
[2] Letter to Wilberforce, 24th August 1790 (*Correspondence of Wilberforce*, i. 73f.).

176

Being educated a Member of the Church of England from my earliest Infancy, being ordained of that Church, and having taken two degrees in Civil Law in the University of Oxford which is entirely under the Patronage of the Church of England, I was almost a Bigot in its favour when I first joined that great and good Man Mr John Wesley, which is fourteen years ago. For five or six years after my union with Mr Wesley I remained fixed in my attachments to the Church of England: but afterwards, for many reasons which it would be tedious and useless to mention, I changed my sentiments, and promoted a separation from it as far as my influence reached. Within these two years I am come back again: my Love for the Church of England has returned. I think I am attached to it on a ground much more rational, and consequently much less likely to be shaken, than formerly. I have many a time ran into error; but to be ashamed of confessing my error when convinced of it, has never been one of my defects. Therefore when I was fully convinced of my error in the steps I took to bring about a separation from the Church of England in Europe, I delivered before a Congregation of about 3,000 people in our largest Chapel in Dublin on a Sunday evening after preaching an exhortation, which in fact amounted to a recantation of my error. Sometime afterwards, I repeated the same in our largest Chapels in London, & in several other parts of England & Ireland: & I have reason to believe that my proceedings in this respect have given a death-blow to all the hopes of a separation, which may exist in the minds of any in those Kingdoms.[1]

This was certainly to over-estimate both the extent of his influence in the British Connexion and the permanence of his own present sentiments. But for the moment it faithfully reflected his frame of mind.

Whether or not the idea of reconciliation with the Anglicans originated with Wesley, or had at least been discussed with him, it is impossible to say. Drinkhouse argued strongly that Wesley must have been privy to Coke's proposals, and that their prime motive was to bring the headstrong Asbury back into subjection.[2] It would undoubtedly have strengthened Coke's hand in making overtures to the Episcopalians, had he been in a position to speak as Wesley's delegate in the matter. But while he certainly believed he was correctly

[1] Letter to Seabury, 14th May, 1791 (Facsimile in Bodleian Library, Oxford). Cf. Pawson's letter to Atmore, 14 September 1790 (Archives Centre): 'The Dr. told the Congregation at Leeds of his change of sentiment with regard to the Church. He said that he was now convinced that if we left the Church we should loose a great part of our Congregations. And that if the Preachers were to be Ordained they would be set up too high thereby.'

[2] Drinkhouse, i. 401.

interpreting the mind of Wesley in his discussions with Bishop White, he was in fact meticulously careful in his guarded references to Wesley not to claim the latter's authority for any of his proposals, beyond saying that he was certain Wesley would support any move towards a reunion. It seems probable that, though they may well have discussed the matter in general terms, Coke's detailed proposals to White, like his earlier scheme for union with the Moravians, were put forward on his own initiative. Certainly no hint of what he had in mind was given to Asbury, who, he was well aware, would not be favourably inclined towards the proposals set out in the following letter to the Bishop.

Right Reverend Sir,
Permit me to intrude a little on your time upon a subject of great importance.

You, I believe, are conscious that I was brought up in the Church of England, and have been ordained a Presbyter of that Church. For many years I was prejudiced even, I think, to bigotry in favour of it: but through a variety of causes or incidents, to mention which would be tedious and useless, my mind was so exceedingly *biassed* on the other side of the question. In consequence of this, I am not sure but I went further in the separation of our Church in America, than Mr Wesley, from whom I had received my commission, did intend. He did indeed solemnly invest me, as far as he had a right so to do, with Episcopal Authority, but did not intend, I think, that an entire separation should take place. He being pressed by our Friends on this side of the water for Ministers to adminster the Sacraments to them, (there being very few Clergy of the Church of England then in the States) he went farther, I am sure, than he would have gone, if he had foreseen some events which followed. And this I am certain of—that he is now sorry for the Separation.

But what can be done for a re-union, which I much wish for; and to accomplish which Mr Wesley, I have no doubt, would use his influence to the utmost? The affection of a very considerable number of the preachers & most of the people, is very strong towards him, notwithstanding the excessive ill-usage he received from a few. My interest also is not small; and both his and mine would readily and to the utmost be used to accomplish that (to us) very desirable object; if a readiness were shewn by the Bishops of the Protestant Episcopal Church to re-unite.

It is even *to your Church* an object of great importance. We have now about 60,000 adults in our Society in these States, & about 250 Travelling Ministers & Preachers; besides a great number of Local Preachers, very far exceeding the number of Travelling Preachers; and some of those Local Preachers are men of very considerable abilities . . .

178

The work now extends in length from Boston to the South of Georgia; & in breadth from the Atlantic to Lake Champlain, Vermont, Albany, Redstone, Holstein, Kentuke, Cumberland, &c. But there are many hindrances in the way. Can they be removed?

1. Our Ordained Ministers will not, ought not, to give up their right of administering the Sacraments. I don't think that the generality of them, perhaps none of them, would refuse to submit to a re-ordination, if other hindrances were removed out of the way. I must here observe that between 60 and 70 only out of the two hundred and fifty have been ordained Presbyters, and about 60 Deacons (only). The Presbyters are the choicest of the whole.

2. The other Preachers would hardly submit to a re-union, if the possibility of their rising up to Ordination depended on the present Bishops in America. Because tho' they are *all*, I think I may say, zealous, pious and very useful men, yet they are not acquainted with the learned languages. Besides, they would argue, if the present Bishops would waive the Article of the Learned Languages, yet their successors might not. My desire of a re-union is so sincere and earnest that these difficulties almost make me tremble; and yet something must be done before the death of Mr Wesley, otherwise I shall despair of success: for tho' my influence among the Methodists in these States as well as in Europe is, I doubt not, increasing, yet Mr Asbury, whose influence is very capital, will not easily comply: nay, I know he will be exceedingly averse to it.

In Europe, where some steps had been taken, tending to a Separation, all is at an end. Mr Wesley is a determined Enemy of it, and I have lately borne an open and successful testimony against it.

Shall I be favoured with a private interview with you in Philadelphia? I shall be there, God willing, on Tuesday the 27th of May. If this be agreeable . . . and I will wait upon you with my Friend Dr Magaw. He can then enlarge on these subjects.

I am conscious of it, that secrecy is of great importance in the present state of the business, till the minds of You, Your Brother-Bishops, and Mr Wesley be circumstantially known. I must therefore beg that these things be confined to Yourself and Dr Magaw, till I have the honour of seeing you.

Thus, you see, I have made a bold venture on Your Honour and Candour, and have opened my whole heart to you on the subject as far as the extent of a small letter will allow me. If You put equal confidence in me, You will find me candid and faithful . . .

I will intrude no longer at present. One thing only I will claim from Your Candour—that if You have no thoughts of improving this proposal, You will burn this letter, and take no more notice of it (for it would be a pity to have us entirely alienated from each other, if we cannot write in the manner my ardent wishes desire). But if you will further negotiate the business, I will explain my mind still more fully to You on the probabilities of success.[1]

Several features of this illuminating letter may be noted briefly. The deferential tone in which Coke addressed the Anglican leader is matched by the note of pride in the Methodist Church he represented. Some writers have seen this approach to the Anglicans as a panic measure inspired by the threatened splinter-movements led by Hammet and O'Kelly,[2] but this is a distortion of the facts. Coke was not negotiating from a position of weakness; American Methodism was flourishing and rapidly spreading into new areas as the settlers pushed westwards. Hammet was a thorn in the flesh to both Asbury and Coke personally, but hardly constituted a danger to the Church as a whole; while O'Kelly was, at this stage, enjoying Coke's confidence, and though already the leader of those opposed to Asbury's rule[3] had not yet shown his true colours.

Coke's eagerness to placate the Episcopalians led him not only to apologize for real or imagined slights in the past, but also, probably, to overstate the extent to which Wesley had come to regret his earlier actions. Though Wesley may have regretted the separation which resulted in America, as in England, from the course he took, there is little to suggest that in 1790 he would have chosen to act differently in the light of subsequent events in either country.[4] For that matter,

[1] Printed in Asbury, *Letters*, pp. 94ff. Facsimile in Bodleian Library, endorsed, 'The Original of a Letter to me from Dr Coke; afterwards Published in a Controversy which arose in Maryland. W.W.'.

[2] E.g. Bangs, *History of Methodist Episcopal Church*, ii. 225; Candler, p. 201.

[3] Writing to the General Conference in 1808, Coke asserted that a few months before his correspondence with Bishop White he had 'with great labour and fatigue . . . prevailed on James O'Kelly, and the thirty-six travelling preachers who had withdrawn with him from all connexion with Bishop Asbury, to submit to the decision of a General Conference'. (Asbury, *Letters*, p. 382). But Coke's memory was at fault here. Asbury's *Journal* and the annual Conference *Minutes* show clearly that no withdrawal took place prior to the 1792 Conference; nor, in the event, were anything like as many as thirty-six travelling preachers involved in the schism. It seems likely that Coke, remembering his own part in persuading Asbury to abandon the Council for a General Conference and the part subsequently played by that Conference in opposing O'Kelly's influence, subconsciously exaggerated his own role in preserving the unity of the American Connexion.

[4] Bangs, op. cit., ii. 223f, citing among other evidence Wesley's letter to Ezekiel Cooper, 1st February, 1791 (*Letters of John Wesley*, viii. 259f.).

Coke's subsequent actions in England showed that he too had not modified his views as much as this letter to White would suggest. His renewed attachment to the Church of England proved less enduring than he expected it to be. To accuse him of the inconsistency of a weathercock,[1] however, is to miss the point that his consistency lay in subordinating everything to the mission of the Church and the furtherance of the Kingdom. To this supreme end, all else was for him incidental.

Coke had no illusions about the formidable difficulties in the way of the re-union he so eagerly desired. He knew well enough that Asbury and other leading American Methodists had serious doubts about the advisability of entangling themselves again with a Church still hampered by its colonialist associations; hence his insistence on the need for secrecy in the initial stage of exploring the possibilities. A more open approach would certainly have diminished, if not destroyed, any chance of success the scheme might have had.

How far was reunion between the two bodies a practicable proposition at this stage? The separation was still recent, and given mutual good will a reconciliation might have been achieved. But, except in a few individuals on each side, the will to unite was lacking. The Methodist preachers, as Coke saw, would be hesitant about submitting to Anglican ordination; while the parochial system, as in England, was not sufficiently elastic to take into itself the Methodist itinerant principle. However, if the attempt was to be made, Coke had undoubtedly chosen the right man to approach. William White was of the same age as Coke, the son of a well-to-do citizen of Philadelphia. As rector of Christ Church, Philadelphia, during the War of Independence, he supported the revolution, but by his moderation and tolerance earned the respect of both parties in the post-war Church, of which he naturally became a leader. In 1782 he published *The Case of the Episcopal Churches in the United States Considered*, in which he expounded his solution of the problem facing the American Anglicans in the interval between the end of hostilities and the signing of a peace treaty. Though provisional only,

---

[1] Drinkhouse, i. 389, quotes Coke himself as saying, concerning his relationship with Asbury, Hammet and O'Kelly, 'You may say that I am a weathercock'. I know of no other authority for this, the nearest allusion being in Wesley's letter to Henry Moore, 25th April 1790, 'You keep your love and you keep your integrity even among weathercocks. But who was it that turned Dr Coke from east to west?' (*Letters of John Wesley*, viii. 215f.)

the measures he suggested are of great interest in showing the fluidity of Anglican thinking about the ministry and church order at that time. Like Wesley two years later, he was prepared to adopt a pragmatic solution to the problem. He proposed that, without abandoning the principle of episcopacy, the Church should resort to presbyterial ordination as a temporary expedient. Further, it should be organized into a federal system, with clerical and lay representatives elected to a general vestry or convention. In each district there was to be a permanent President who, with the assistance of other clergy, would be the instrument of ordination.[1] The parallel with John Wesley's views is illustrated by this passage from White's pamphlet: 'But it will be also said that the very name of "bishop" is offensive; if so, change it for another; let the superior clergyman be a president, a superintendent, or in plain English, and according to the literal translation of the original, an overseer.'[2]

The unexpectedly early signing of a peace treaty made most of White's proposals obsolete. Towards the end of 1784, Samuel Seabury having been unsuccessful in England was consecrated for Connecticut by three Scottish bishops. Three years later, White and Samuel Provoost were also consecrated, and in 1789 a new constitution was adopted, together with a revised Prayer Book. While he was in England in 1787, White tried to obtain an interview with Wesley to discuss the newly-formed Methodist Episcopal Church, but the latter was too fully engaged to see him immediately. 'If you stay a week or two longer in town,' he wrote, 'to have an hour's conversation with you will be a great pleasure.' White interpreted this as 'a civil evasion', and amid the pressure of his own affairs did not renew his efforts.[3] The broken threads were not taken up until Coke's approach to the Bishop in 1791.

As might be expected from one of the more liberal of the American clergy, White's reply to Coke's letter was prompt and encouraging:

Rev. Sir,
My friend, Dr. Magaw, has this day put into my hands your letter of the 24th of April, which I trust, I received with a sense of the importance of the subject, and of the answer I am to give to God for the improvement of every opportunity of building up his Church. Accordingly, I cannot but make choice of the earliest of the two ways you point out, to

[1] White, op. cit.; W. W. Manross, op. cit., pp. 188ff.
[2] Op. cit., p. 17, quoted in Emory, *Defence of 'Our Fathers'*.
[3] *Letters of John Wesley*, vii. 366.

inform you, that I shall be very happy in the opportunity of conversing with you at the time proposed.

You mention two difficulties in the way of the proposed union. And there are further difficulties which suggest themselves to my mind. But I can say of the one and of the other, that I do not think them insuperable, provided there be a conciliatory disposition on both sides. So far as I am concerned, I think that such a disposition exists . . .

Therefore, with assurance of the desired secrecy, and with requesting you to accept a like promise of candor to that which I credit from you, I conclude myself at present

Your brother in Christ, and very humble servant,

William White[1]

Before this reply could reach Coke, the news of Wesley's death caused him to make drastic alterations to his plans in order to hasten home. However, a severe attack of sciatica prevented his reaching New York in time for the British Packet. As a result, he was able to spend over a week in Philadelphia before sailing from Newcastle, Delaware, and had three interviews with Bishop White and Dr Magaw.[2] Their attitude to his proposals was more encouraging than he had dared to hope. They assured him 'that every concession would be made on their parts that was consistent with what they believed to be essentials, in order to accomplish so desirable an End as a Re-union of the two Churches'. The status of the two Methodist bishops was considered, and Coke reported that 'they went so far as to intimate, that the Leading Men in their Church, they had reason to believe, would even consent that the Bishops should consecrate Mr Asbury & me, & that we should still act in the most independent manner as to all our spiritual concerns, if we would only acknowledge practically their Episcopal Succession, use their Common Prayer-Book on the Lord's Day, & look upon ourselves as the same political body with them'.[3]

White's account of the interviews is essentially the same:

The general outlines of Dr. Coke's plans were a Re-ordination of the Methodist Ministers, and then continuing under the Superintendence

---

[1] Bangs, op. cit., ii. 204f., from White, *Memoirs of Protestant Episc. Church*, 1830, p. 343.

[2] Magaw was Vice-President of the University of Philadelphia, and a close friend of Asbury—see his letter to the latter, *Arminian Magazine* (American edition), 1790, pp. 611ff.

[3] Letter to Joseph Benson, 15th July 1791 (Archives Centre).

183

then existing and in the Practice of their peculiar Institutions. There was also suggested by him a Propriety, but not a Condition made, of admitting to the Episcopacy himself and the Gentleman associated with him in the Superintendence of the Methodist Societies . . . It was understood between Dr. Coke and me that the Proposal should be communicated to the Bishops of the Episcopal Church, at the next Convention, which was to be in Sept. 1792 in New York. This was accordingly done, after which I perceived no Use of further Communication on the Subject. And I have not since seen Dr. Coke nor heard from him, nor written to him.[1]

Following these conversations, Coke wrote a hasty letter to Asbury, asking him to meet him at Newcastle, before he embarked for England. Meanwhile, however, Asbury had come to hear of Coke's proposals. It appears that White had directed his reply to Baltimore, where it was opened by Asbury in the absence of Coke, who was on his way to New York in the hope of catching the British Packet.[2] As Coke had anticipated, Asbury proved to be 'decidedly against the re-union at that time', but agreed that the matter should be referred to the next General Conference, at the end of 1792.[3] With John Wesley dead and Asbury firmly opposed to the scheme, the prospect for reunion was certainly not bright.

Before he sailed for home, Coke wrote at considerable length to Samuel Seabury, Bishop of Connecticut, telling him of his conversations with White and setting forth his proposals with considerable candour. 'How great would be the strength of *our* Church, (will you give me leave to call it so? I mean, the Protestant Episcopal) if the

[1] Letter from Bishop White to Simon Wilmer of Chester Town, Md., 30th July 1804 (Copy at Emory University).

[2] In his letter to Simon Wilmer (see note 1 above) White states that he had heard that his reply to Coke had been opened by Asbury in Coke's absence, 'such a Freedom being understood, as I supposed, to arise out of the Connexion between the two Gentlemen. But for this part of the Statement', he adds, 'I cannot vouch.' If this did happen, it must have been during the Conference in Baltimore, 5th–7th May, which Coke did not attend, because he was on his way to New York to catch the British Packet.

[3] Letter to Benson, 15th July 1791 (Archives Centre). In his letter to the 1808 General Conference (Asbury, *Letters*, pp. 382ff.), Coke reiterated his statement that he had confided in Asbury at Newcastle before sailing, but played down Asbury's reaction: 'With that caution which peculiarly characterized him, he gave me no decisive opinion on the subject.' Drinkhouse, on the other hand, quotes this fragment from a letter written by Asbury in the summer of 1791: 'I cannot confide in ecclesiastics passing through the degrees and intrigues of a university as I trust to a ploughman.' (Drinkhouse, op. cit., i. 259, quoted in Asbury, *Letters*, p. 101.)

two Sticks were made one?' he asked. But the will to union must be matched by a readiness to face the very real difficulties in its path, and to these, in the light of his conversations in Philadelphia, Coke then turned:

The magnitude of the Object would justify *considerable Sacrifices*. A solemn engagement to use *your* Prayer book in all our places of worship on the Lord's Day would of course be a *sine qua non*, a concession we should be obliged to make on our parts (if it may be called a concession): and there would be, I doubt not, other concessions to be made by us. But what concessions would it be necessary for You to make? For the opening of this subject with all possible candour, it will be necessary to take a view of the present state of the Ministry in the Methodist Church in these States.

He then gave a detailed account of the threefold ministry and of the arrangements for ordination in the Methodist Episcopal Church, and explained, as he had done to White, the grounds on which the Methodist preachers were likely to have misgivings about submitting to reordination. The objection that reordination would imply that their previous ordination was invalid does not seem to have occurred to him; he himself was quite prepared to be reconsecrated without repudiating the authorization he had received from Wesley. But the Methodist preachers, under their present superintendents, had the assurance that the higher offices in the Church would go to those who merited them; rightly or wrongly, they could not be sure of this if they submitted to reordination in a united Church. What was to be done about it? Coke wrote:

I will answer this important question with all simplicity, and plainness, and boldness: and the more so, because, . . . I think I am not in danger from your charitable spirit, to be suspected in the present instance of pressing after worldly honour: as it is probably I shall be elected President of the European Methodists, and shall not, I believe, receive greater marks of respect from the Methodists in these States, supposing I ever be a Bishop of the Protestant Episcopal Church, than they are at present so kind as to shew me.

Mr Asbury, our Resident Superintendent, is a great and good man. He possesses, and justly, the esteem of most of the Preachers & most of the People. Now, if the General Convention of the Clergy consented that he should be consecrated a Bishop of the Protestant Episcopal Church on the supposition of a Re-union, a very capital hindrance would be removed out of the way.

Again, I love the Methodists in America, and could not think of leaving them entirely, whatever might happen to me in Europe. The Preachers and People also love me. Many of them have a peculiar regard for me. But I could not *with propriety* visit the American Methodists possessing in our Church on this side of the water an Office inferiour to that of Mr Asbury.

But if the two Houses of the Convention of the Clergy would consent to yr Consecration of Mr Asbury and me as Bishops of the Methodist Society in the Protestant Episcopal Church in these United States (or by any other title; if that be not proper) on the supposition of the Re-union of the two churches under proper mutual stipulations: and engage that the Methodist Society shall have a regular supply on the death of their Bishops, and so *ad perpetuum*, the grand difficulty in respect to the Preachers would be removed—they would have the same men to confide in, whom they have at present, & all other mutual stipulations would soon be settled.

I said *in respect to the Preachers*, for I do not fully know Mr Asbury's mind on the subject. I have my fears in respect to his sentiments: and if he do not accede to the Union, it will not take place so completely as I could wish. I wish you could see my sinful heart, but that is impossible.[1]

Few other words ever penned by Coke laid him open so fully to the charge of self-seeking ambition. His enemies, who made so much of other indiscretions in his correspondence, would certainly have seized eagerly upon so frank an unveiling of his hopes and intentions. The most that can be said in its favour is that Coke was so concerned to convince Seabury of his disinterestedness that he succeeded in giving exactly the opposite impression.

So far as is known, Coke received no reply to this letter. Seabury was a High-Churchman in a state which was a stronghold of High Church principles, and was far less likely than White to favour any concessions to the Methodists. His *Address to Ministers and Congregations of the Presbyterian and Independent Persuasions* in 1790 showed an essentially Romanist approach to the question of reunion, inviting the schismatics to return to the true fold and denying the validity of their orders and sacraments.[2] Nevertheless, Coke returned to England convinced that the Episcopalians as a whole were genuinely willing to unite on any reasonable terms, and though for the most part he kept his own counsel, he did confide to Joseph

[1] Letter to Seabury, 14th May 1791 (Bodleian Library, Oxford).

[2] J. T. Addison, *Episcopal Church in the United States, 1789–1931*, 1951, pp. 84f.

Benson his hopes that neither in America nor in England was the breach between Methodism and the Church of England as yet impossible to bridge.[1]

At the General Convention of the Protestant Episcopal Church in the following year, the question of reunion with the Methodists was raised as White had promised. A resolution of Bishop Madison in favour of closer relations was adopted by the House of Bishops, but was then withdrawn in the face of strong opposition in the lower House.[2] Clearly the rank and file of the Church, both Anglican and Methodist, were not yet ready to follow the lead offered by Coke and White. The proposals were dropped; the General Conference of the Methodist preachers later in the same year was told nothing of them, and only those immediately involved knew that the exchange of views had taken place. The dawn of a more ecumenical spirit was thus indefinitely postponed.[3]

Having failed to reconcile the two Churches, Coke would no doubt have been happy enough to hear no more of the matter; but some years later the correspondence was brought into the limelight in the course of a controversy which broke out in Maryland. In response to enquiries from both an Anglican and a Methodist correspondent,[4] Bishop White outlined the proposals Coke had made and their subsequent fate. Later on, he gave a copy of Coke's letter to a Dr Kemp, who published it, probably without White's cognizance.[5] This provoked an outcry against Coke among the Methodist preachers in America. They saw his approach to the Anglican bishops as a betrayal of their liberty and a denial of their ministerial orders, and demanded an explanation of what seemed an act of treachery. Coke was driven onto the defensive. In a long letter to the General Conference that was due to meet in 1808, he confessed that he no longer believed that a reunion would have strengthened the hand of the American Methodists. Nevertheless, he claimed, his proposals had been made as a sincere attempt to remedy the constitutional

[1] Letter to Benson 15th July 1791 (Archives Centre).
[2] Coke believed this was due to a misunderstanding of the intention behind the proposal. The Rev. Uzel Ogden of New Jersey told him that 'it was thrown out because they did not understand the full meaning of it'. (Letter to the General Conference, 29th January 1808, printed in Asbury, *Letters*, p. 382.)
[3] J. T. Addison, op. cit., pp. 86f.
[4] The Rev. Simon Wilmer and the Rev. John McKlaskey (see White's letter to Wilmer, 30th July 1804, quoted above).
[5] Bangs, op. cit., ii. 205f; Drinkhouse, op. cit., i. 405.

weaknesses which had been exposed by the controversy over the short-lived Council. He wrote:

There are very few of you who can possibly recollect any thing of what I am next going to add. Many of you were then only little children. We had at that time no regular General Conferences. One only had been held in the year 1784 . . . . Previous to the holding of [the General Conference of 1792], there were only small district meetings, excepting the council which was held at Cokesbury College, either in 1791 or 1792. Except the union which most justly subsisted between Bishop Asbury on the one hand, and the preachers and people on the other, the Society, as such, taken as an aggregate, was almost like a rope of sand. I longed to see matters on a footing likely to be permanent. Bishop Asbury did the same; and it was that view of things, I doubt not, which led Bishop Asbury, the year before, to call, and to endeavour to establish, a regular council, who were to meet him annually at Cokesbury. In this point I differed in sentiment from my venerable brother. But I saw the danger of our situation, though I well knew that God was sufficient for all things. I did verily believe then that under God the Connection would be more likely to be saved from convulsions by a union with the old Episcopal Church than any other way—not by a dereliction of ordination, sacraments, and the Methodist discipline, but by a junction on proper terms.[1]

It has been argued that from the Anglican point of view Coke's proposals were so 'sadly defective' that they had no chance of success—though they were not rejected immediately by White on such grounds. 'They amounted', says one writer, 'neither to federation nor to organic union. Methodism was to receive episcopal orders but otherwise was apparently to continue its independent career.'[2] But this very defect appeared to Coke himself one of the merits of his scheme considered in retrospect. 'I had provided in the fullest manner, in my indispensably necessary conditions, for the security, and I may say for the independence, of our discipline and places of worship. But I thought (perhaps erroneously, and *I believe so now*) that our field of action would have been exceedingly enlarged by that junction, and that myriads would have attended our ministry in consequence of it who were at that time prejudiced against us.'

[1] Letter to the General American Conference, 29th January 1808 (Asbury, *Letters*, pp. 382ff.). Coke wrote a similar letter to Asbury himself on 3rd February (Paine, *Life of McKendree*, i. 237ff.). Coke's expressed concern for the unity of the American Connexion explains, though it scarcely justifies, the references to his proposals for reunion as a 'panic measure'.

[2] J. T. Addison, op. cit., p. 85.

There were two further grounds on which Coke's procedure was criticized by the American preachers: his failure to consult Asbury before approaching the Episcopalians, and the implied repudiation of his own episcopal office. In replying to the first that to consult Asbury was impossible on geographical grounds, Coke was being less than candid. The scheme for reunion was certainly not hatched fully-fledged overnight; it must have been incubating during the earlier part of his visit, when there had been ample opportunity for con-fiding in his fellow-bishop. Moreover, on 24th April, the very day on which Coke wrote to White, Asbury met him at Colonel Clayton's, near Richmond, and they were together for the rest of the month. Nor does the fact that Coke laid the matter before Asbury on the eve of embarking for home mitigate the force of this criticism. Asbury, as we have seen, almost certainly had learned of the proposals al-ready, and Coke probably knew this. The truth is that, as his letters to both White and Seabury demonstrate, Coke's secrecy was in-spired by his awareness that Asbury's initial reaction to the plan would be unfavourable, if not hostile. His feelings about the Epis-copalians in 1797—and equally, no doubt, in 1791—was that they were a 'settled, man-made, worldly ministry under no discipline', who 'if they have the doctrine, . . . do not preach it at all'.[1] Coke knew, therefore, that he must rally as widespread a support as possible and show that his scheme was well received by the Anglicans, if he was to have any hope of carrying the majority of the American Methodists with him in spite of Asbury's influence among them.

The further objection, that his proposals implied the invalidity of Methodist ordination, and of his own 'consecration' by Wesley, has a fresh relevance to our current discussions on the reunion of episcopal and non-episcopal Churches. To the questions, 'If you did not think that the episcopal ordination of Mr Asbury was valid, why did you ordain him? Was there not duplicity in this business?', he replied:

1. I never, since I could reason on those things, considered the doctrine of the *uninterrupted apostolic succession of bishops* as at all valid or true.
2. I am of our late venerable father Mr. Wesley's opinion—that the order of bishops and presbyters is one and the same.
3. I believe that the episcopal form of Church-government is the best in the world, when the episcopal power is under due regulations and responsibility.

[1] Asbury, *Letters*, p. 160.

4. I believe that it is well to follow the example of the primitive Church as exemplified in the word of God, by setting apart persons for great ministerial purposes by the imposition of hands, but especially those who are appointed for offices of the first rank in the Church.

Coke was here very close to the position of his 'late venerable father' to whose opinion he appealed. Matters of Church government were not among the essentials; episcopacy could never be more than a means to an end for the Church which existed as the vehicle of the Gospel. 'From all I have advanced you may easily perceive, my dear brethren, that I do not consider the imposition of hands, on the one hand, as essentially necessary for any office in the Church; nor do I, on the other hand, think that the repetition of the imposition of hands for the same office, when important circumstances require it, is at all improper.' These words demonstrate how great was the gulf between Coke's thinking and that of High Churchmen like Bishop Seabury. Their ideas were not so much in collision as moving on different planes. They also bring into focus the dilemma of the Free Churchman for whom matters of Church order are never more than a means to an end and the Church itself is subordinate to the kingdom whose furtherance it seeks. Coke had no scruples about accepting reordination in the interests of so great a purpose.

If it be granted that my plan of union with the old Episcopal Church was desirable . . . [and] if the plan could not have been accomplished without a repetition of the imposition of hands for the same office, I did believe, and do now believe, and have no doubt, that the repetition of the imposition of hands would have been perfectly justifiable for the enlargement of the field of action, etc., and would not, by any means, have invalidated the former consecration or imposition of hands. Therefore, I have no doubt but my consecration of Bishop Asbury was perfectly valid, and would have been so even if he had been reconsecrated . . . I should have had no scruple then, nor should I now *if the junction were desirable*, to have submitted to, or to submit to, a reimposition of hands in order to accomplish a great object.[1]

The ecumenical conversation has moved so far in the last century and a half that there is little now to be learned from the details of Coke's scheme. The spirit in which he approached the issue and his

[1] Cf. his letter to Ezekiel Cooper, 1st March 1808 (Garrett Theological Seminary): 'As to the repetition of the imposition of hands, I considered it then, as I do now, as a perfectly unessential point. I acted for the best; but with no intention of taking any actual step but by the consent of a *General Conference*.'

190

insistence on the primacy of the Church's mission are, however, a different matter. He belonged more to our day than to his own in his conviction that the Church was seriously hampered in its witness to the gospel of Jesus Christ so long as it remained divided. This same concern for the Church's mission to the world was to inspire a similar attempt in 1799 to heal the breach between British Methodism and the Church of England.[1] In the meanwhile, as the *William Penn* sailed from Newcastle, Delaware, on 16th May 1791, Thomas Coke was heading back to an orphaned Connexion in which he would find enough urgent problems to occupy his mind for the foreseeable future.

[1] See below, pp. 202ff.

CHAPTER 12

THE MANTLE OF ELIJAH

Before he sailed for home in May 1791, Coke preached at memorial services for John Wesley in Baltimore and Philadelphia. His text was 2 Kings 2:12, from the account of the passing of Elijah. The sermon was published and caused many tongues to wag. It was widely surmised that in comparing his own relationship to Wesley with that of Elisha to Elijah he was staking his claim to be Wesley's successor.[1] Nor was this very wide of the mark. On his own confession in the letter to Bishop Seabury, he did expect to be elected 'President of the European Methodists', and this was one motive for his precipitate return to England. After an uneventful voyage he came ashore in a Cornish fishing boat and hastened overland to London. Accompanying him as far as Truro, Jonathan Crowther gave him the latest news of connexional affairs.[2] In particular, he learned that a number of the senior preachers had met in Halifax and elaborated a plan with the avowed aim of preventing the appointment of any successor to Wesley.

'There appears to us but two ways,' they wrote, 'either to appoint another King in Israel; or to be governed by the Conference Plan by forming ourselves into Committees. If you adopt the first, who is the Man? What power is he to be invested with? and what revenue is he to be allowed?—But this is incompatible with the Conference Deed.' They then suggested, as an alternative, that vacancies in the Legal Hundred should be filled according to seniority in the work; that the President and other officers should be elected for one year only; and that continuity between conferences should be maintained by dividing the Connexion into districts, each with its own Committee and 'president' or chairman.[3] The Conference later in the summer

---

[1] Coke was aware of this; in a letter to Asbury dated 23rd September 1791, he mentions 'the imprudence I was led into in preaching Mr Wesley's funeral sermon'. (Asbury, *Letters*, pp. 101f.)

[2] Crowther, p. 296.

[3] Smith, *History of Wesleyan Methodism*, ii. 688f.

adopted much of this scheme, and William Thompson, who was foremost among its promoters, became the first to occupy the presidential chair after Wesley's death.

If all this was a mortal blow to Coke's hopes and ambitions, he did not show it. The degree of confidence Wesley had placed in him and the number of important commissions entrusted to him inevitably disposed him to expect that he would continue to occupy a key position. But for positive evidence that his expectations went beyond this, that he was consumed by a worldly ambition for personal glory and authority, we are dependent on those whose suspicions were whetted by envy and malice. So far as his actions may witness, no one behaved at this or any other time less like a frustrated, ambitious or self-seeking man.

Against the advice of his friends, who feared he might suffer a rebuff, Coke first hurried off to attend the Irish Conference. Although he had several times presided on Wesley's behalf, no provision had been made for a delegate to attend that year. Therefore, the preachers who assembled in Dublin on 1st July formed themselves into a committee and elected one of their own number as chairman, 'in order', says Crookshank, 'to give Dr Coke a plain intimation, once for all, that however highly they esteemed and loved him, they could not accept any minister as occupying the exalted position long sustained by the venerated Wesley'.[1] This did not prevent his being appointed to preside over the Irish Conference every year almost without exception during the remainder of his life. The loyalty and zeal with which he served the Irish Methodists, and which endeared him to them, were not born of disgruntled pride.

A similar fate awaited him at the Manchester Conference shortly afterwards. Thompson was elected President, with Coke as secretary, an office he continued to fill for many years. That this fell short of his expectations is obvious; but the extent of the rebuff has frequently been exaggerated. In the first place, he could hardly have been expecting as much as his critics have made out. As the authors of the Halifax Circular pointed out, it was incompatible with the provisions of the Deed of Declaration that the personal authority of Mr Wesley should be inherited by any one of his sons, since that was vested in the legal Conference; and Coke, as one closely concerned in drawing up the Deed, was perfectly aware of this. Nor have we any evidence that he disapproved of or opposed the Halifax proposals,

[1] C. H. Crookshank, *History of Methodism in Ireland*, ii. 38.

his only recorded reaction being the cryptic comment, 'That is a weight too great to attempt to wield.'[1] Furthermore, while Coke undoubtedly had enemies, the extent to which his exclusion from the presidency was a personal rebuff may easily be exaggerated. He was still relatively new to the Methodist itinerancy; those who preceded him in the presidential chair were all many years his senior,[2] and there was no president junior to him until Henry Moore, in the year before Coke took office for the second time. Whatever his expectations, to have elected him to the chair in 1791 would have been a singular honour even for one so unusually favoured by Wesley.

Nevertheless, Wesley's death meant an inevitable loss of status for one who had been so closely associated with him; and it soon became clear that Coke's authority in the Connexion had been largely derivative. The spirit in which he accepted this change is reflected in a letter he wrote at the time to William Black:

Our Conference ended in great peace and unanimity. There were innumerable heart-burnings at first: and I saw no way of preserving the unity of the body, but by sacrificing all my little honours which I held in Europe. I accordingly resigned the power with which Mr Wesley invested me, and also a few of my most chosen friends, in the management of Mr Wesley's books, copyrights, &c., and resigned my right to nominate the preachers for the new chapel in London, and some other privileges. Satan said—'Divide'—but the Spirit of God said—'Unite'. I obeyed the latter, and fell that Christ might rise. The Conference then elected Mr Thompson President for one year, and me Secretary. They gave me leave to visit all the societies in England, appointed me to hold the Conference in Ireland; and authorized me to raise whatever money I might judge necessary for the carrying on of the work in the West Indies, appointing me their Delegate for the West India Islands.[3]

Coke was, in fact, not the only one who anticipated election to the presidency in 1791, and the general determination that no single person should step into Mr Wesley's shoes was probably directed quite as much against Alexander Mather as it was against Coke. If a permanent successor were to be considered, Mather was the only other serious contender, and though lacking Anglican orders, in other

[1] Crowther, p. 297.

[2] With one exception, Coke's predecessors had all entered the ministry between 1754 and 1762; the exception was Joseph Bradford, who was only four years his senior.

[3] Letter to William Black, 7th September 1791 (M. Richey, *Memoir of William Black*, pp. 283–4).

respects he had the stronger claim. He had been in the ministry since 1757 and enjoyed Wesley's confidence to an unusual degree. He was one of those ordained by Wesley in 1788 for English circuits; according to John Pawson, Wesley's intention was that, like Coke, he should be set apart as a Superintendent, or Bishop, with power to ordain others.[1] He came to the 1791 Conference expecting to be made president, and was 'deeply wounded' by the preachers' determination to choose William Thompson. 'He therefore printed a small handbill, and distributed rather privately among the preachers . . . But his friends, wise and wary men, got round him, and said that as the preachers could not recede from their word to put Mr. Thompson in the chair, he had better look it over, and rest assured that he would be righted the second year. A wise man knows how to desist from strife. We heard no more of the handbill.'[2] This little-known bid for the Presidency is in marked contrast to Coke's reaction. Though undoubtedly disappointed, Coke neither expressed chagrin nor attempted to win supporters, but accepted the secretaryship of the Conference, as he was to do in many future years, and gave himself to the tasks that lay nearest to hand.

* * *

In the years immediately following Wesley's death, the British Connexion had to settle a number of vital issues, most of which centred upon its relationship to the Church of England. Though theoretically in communion with the parent body, the Methodists were in fact often driven out of the parish churches and debarred from the sacrament; while the Anglican clergy for their part showed little inclination to welcome these strange sheep into the flock. Wesley's reluctance to admit that separation was the inevitable outcome of his own actions prevented him from making more detailed provision for the Connexion after his death. The Deed of Declaration had established its legal position, but left the practical issues undetermined. The consequent dilemma in which the Connexion found itself in 1791 is reflected in the decision of the Conference, 'to follow strictly the plan which Mr Wesley left us at his death',[3] a resolution so ambiguous as to settle nothing.

[1] Letter from John Pawson to Charles Atmore, 13th December 1793 (Archives Centre).

[2] Joseph Sutcliffe, MS *History of Methodism*, vol. iv. p. 21 (Archives Centre).

[3] *Minutes*, i. 254.

The more vocal part of the Connexion, both ministerial and lay, was divided into two camps. The 'Old Planners' included a number of trustees and other wealthier members, who were strongly opposed to any formal separation from the Church. The 'New Planners', on the other hand, were ready to acknowledge the degree of separation that already existed and to accept among its implications services in church-hours, an ordained ministry and the administration of the sacraments by their own ministers. The one party could claim the support of Wesley's words, the other of his actions; so little meaning was there in the resolution to 'follow the plan which Mr Wesley left us'.

We have seen that Coke returned from America in 1791 disposed to work for the strengthening of ties with the Anglicans on both sides of the Atlantic. For Methodism to sever her relations with the Established Church now seemed to him a step fraught with the gravest political as well as theological dangers. Shortly before the Conference he expressed his fears in forceful terms to Joseph Benson. Both men were opposed to any plans for a 'gradual, imperceptible separation', but Coke could not deny that Wesley's own actions towards the close of his life had tended in that direction. He wrote to Benson:

I have no doubt but the Ordinations which our dear, honoured deceased Father in the Gospel, & myself, were concerned in, sprung from *great imprudence*, & will be very prejudicial unless—(what shall I say?)—God intended by suffering us to run into the error, to bring about a sifting time. I see a Separation from the Established Church, whether gradual or immediate, pregnant with all the evils you mention. It would probably drive away from us and from God thousands of our People. We should lose our grand field of action. When once the Members of the Established Church had embraced a confirmed Idea that we were a *proper Dissenting Body*, they would pass by the Doors of our *Meeting-houses* with the same unconcern, with which they pass by the doors of the Presbyterian Meeting-houses.

These considerations had prompted his overtures to White and Seabury in America. But his next words reveal a further reason for his concern, and one which would have evoked little response among the American Methodists.

More than this, we should soon imbibe the Political Spirit of the Dissenters: nor should I be much surprized, if in a few years some of our people, warmest in politics, and coolest in religion, would toast (as

196

I am informed a famous Society did lately in the short hours of the night) *a bloody Summer and a headless King*. Is not this, think you, what Dr Priestly aims at? Nay, the Dr perhaps might even be more victorious still. When he had got us so very near him, he might take the Crown off the head of the Great Messiah by pouring into our ears and eyes all the poison of Socinianism.[1]

This inclination to scurry from the threat of radicalism and dissent back to the bosom of the Establishment soon passed, however. Perhaps the mood of the Conference made him realize how meagre were the chances that Methodism, deprived of its founder, would remain a leaven within the national Church, even if it were welcome there. The tide was flowing against reunion, and those who would have been his allies in keeping Methodism faithful to the 'Old Plan' were chiefly men with whom he had most often crossed swords in the past. When it came to the point, he took sides with those who were ready to accept the separate existence of Methodism and to make the adjustments and innovations demanded by the new situation. Before long he was advocating the 'New Plan' so openly as to forfeit the goodwill of some of the wealthier subscribers to the missions.[2]

One important facet of the controversy was the question of ordination, and in this respect neither faction was eager to follow Wesley's lead. Mather failed to carry the 1791 Conference when he asserted that, in ordaining him as 'superintendent' Wesley had intended him in his turn to ordain others for England as Coke had done for America and the mission field.[3] The following spring, some of the preachers took matters into their own hands and several unofficial 'ordinations' took place. Clearly this state of affairs would quickly lead to chaos. The 1792 Conference, in deciding by lot that the Lord's Supper should not be administered in any of the chapels outside London during the ensuing year, also resolved that no ordinations should take place without prior consent of the Conference, and that 'If any brother shall break the above-mentioned rule, by ordaining or being ordained . . . he does thereby exclude himself'.[4]

[1] Letter to Joseph Benson, 15th July 1791 (Archives Centre). Cf. his letter to William Black, quoted above: 'A very powerful party were for immediate separation from the Church of England: I was against it for reasons too long to mention here. In this I prevailed.'
[2] Crowther, p. 317; Drew, p. 258.
[3] Letter of John Pawson to Charles Atmore (see p. 195, note 1).
[4] *Minutes*, i. 270.

A year later, and in response to increasing pressure from the societies, limited permission was granted for the administration of the sacrament. At the same time, the ban on ordination was confirmed by a minute abandoning the distinction between ordained and unordained preachers and the use of the title 'Reverend'.[1] The resulting ecclesiastical hotchpotch was unlikely to satisfy either faction. John Pawson, who was the President that year, complained that 'At present we really have no government', and was in favour of an episcopal form as being nearer to Wesley's intentions, though no more scriptural than Presbyterianism. Wesley, he wrote,

foresaw that the Methodists would, after his death, soon become a distinct people . . . In order, therefore, to preserve all that was valuable in the Church of England among the Methodists, he ordained Mr Mather and Dr Coke bishops. These he undoubtedly designed should ordain others. Mr Mather told us so at the Manchester Conference; but we did not then understand him . . . I sincerely wish that Dr Coke and Mr Mather may be allowed to be what they are, bishops; that they ordain two others chosen by the Conference; that these four have the government of the Connexion placed in their hands for one year, each superintending his respective District, being stationed in London, Bristol, Leeds, and Newcastle. We can give what degree of power we please; but I would not cramp them. If any should abuse the power given, woe be to them! They would not be entrusted with it again! . . . We must have ordination among us at any rate.[2]

Pawson's scheme would have had the effect of bringing into existence a Methodist Episcopal Church similar in all essentials to that in America. Others were thinking along the same lines, including Coke who felt very strongly that Conference had been wrong to abandon so apostolic a form of ordination as the laying on of hands. Though tradition might not be allowed to shackle the Church, it had its value as a guide to present conduct. 'Without a debate', he complained to William Thompson, 'we laid aside a mode prescribed by the oracles of God and practised by the universal Church. It is with us a point that cannot *on any terms possible* be dispensed with. We will not run counter to the Oracles of God, and the universal practice of the Christian Church, even to prevent a division. Don't be rash, you cannot plead conscience in the present case, but we do most sincerely and feelingly. It will not do to tell us that the inward

[1] Ibid., i. 290. This was reiterated in 1794 (ibid., p. 314).
[2] Letter from John Pawson to Charles Atmore (see p. 195, note 1).

Kingdom is all in all. For we pay deep regard to modes prescribed by the Oracles of God and the Universal practice of the Christian Church.'[1]

The witness of Scripture and universal custom were reinforced for Coke by his experiences in America, which convinced him that a three-fold hierarchy of superintendents, elders and deacons would bring a much-needed stability to the British connexion. He circulated proposals for such a scheme among a few of the senior preachers, and took the initiative in calling them to a confidential meeting in April, 1794.[2] The rendezvous, Lichfield, was chosen in the hope that their meeting would pass unnoticed in a town where there was as yet no Methodist society. Coke proposed that, in order to bring the connexion into line with the American Church, he himself in his capacity of superintendent (and apparently without the participation of Alexander Mather) should ordain those present who were not already ordained and so enable them to administer the sacraments among the societies. This met with general approval, but Henry Moore with Mather's support argued strongly that no such step might be taken without first consulting the Conference. Consequently it was agreed to submit their proposals to the preachers later that year. These provided for an order of superintendents, appointed by the Conference and subject to annual reappointment. The connexion was to be organized in eight divisions, each under a superintendent who 'shall have authority to execute, or see executed, all the branches of Methodist discipline . . .' Further, there was to be an ordained ministry of deacons and elders. The choice of preachers to receive further ordination as elders was to be in the hands of the Conference.[3]

This whole scheme was duly recommended to the Conference as 'a thing greatly wanted, and likely to be of much advantage to the work of God'. But long before Conference began, the opposition was mobilizing. The day after he left Lichfield, Coke broached the matter to two of the Birmingham preachers, who both opposed it, as did Alexander Kilham when it was brought to his notice.[4] The

[1] Letter to William Thompson, 21st April, 1794 (copy in M.M.S. Archives).
[2] Those attending were Coke, Mather, Thomas Taylor, Pawson, Bradburn, James Rogers, Moore and Clarke.
[3] Smith, op. cit., ii. 691. See also letters of John Pawson to Charles Atmore, 21st March and 8th April 1794 (Archives Centre).
[4] Jonathan Edmondson, in *Wesleyan Methodist Magazine*, 1850, p. 9. The Superintendent of the Birmingham Circuit, James Rogers, was one of those present at the Lichfield meeting.

Conference of that year was beset by problems and under a variety of pressures. A deputation of Trustees presented an address demanding adherence to the 'Old Plan'; at the same time, Kilham was making his voice heard in support of a more democratic form of government, including lay representation in Conference. The general desire among the preachers to set their house in order was tempered by a fear of acting too precipitately, with the result that they were in the mood for patching rather than rebuilding. The Lichfield scheme was too comprehensive and far-reaching to commend itself at this juncture and was firmly rejected 'as tending to create invidious and unhallowed distinctions among brethren'.[1] It was no doubt a tactical error which contributed to this rejection, that the Lichfield meeting had gone so far as to nominate eight preachers for the proposed superintendency, all but one of whom were chosen from their own ranks.

Coke's attempt to bring the British Methodists into line with their American brethren had failed, and not until 1836 was the practice of receiving preachers into full connexion by the imposition of hands reintroduced. But the matter did not rest there so far as Coke was concerned; the superintendency invested in him by Wesley involved the power to ordain others, and this, as his letter to William Thompson shows, was a privilege and responsibility he could not relinquish lightly. While Wesley was alive, Coke had exercised this power not only in America and the West Indies, but also at home—and with Wesley's approval. On 24th October 1785, he ordained Robert Johnson, then stationed in Edinburgh, as a deacon; and Wesley gave his sanction to this by ordaining him elder in the following year.[2] In 1790 he administered a form of ordination in Wesley's presence to a dozen of the younger preachers. Joseph Sutcliffe, who was one of the ordinands, later described this impressive scene at the close of Wesley's last Conference. After each had spoken briefly of his experience and call to preach, 'Dr. Coke came on the fore-bench with the Large Minutes on his left arm and delivered a copy to each, putting his right hand on each of our heads. This was ordination in every view.'[3] It is possible to interpret this as no more than a com-

[1] Smith, op. cit., ii. 104.
[2] W.H.S. Proc. xxiv. 77, 79. The certificate which Coke gave Johnson is at the Methodist Archives Centre.
[3] MS History of Methodism (Archives Centre), quoted in W.H.S. Proc. xv. 57ff.

mission to preach the Gospel. But in that case would Wesley, who so meticulously distinguished between the offices of priest and preacher in his sermon on the Ministerial Office,[1] have permitted Coke to lay his hands upon them in a way that might so easily be misunderstood? Sutcliffe for one had no doubt that, however defective the act might be in Anglican eyes, it was in intention no less than full ordination. 'I am told it followed the Scottish ordinations, and though it was not called ordination, what else could it be? Mr. Wesley took no part in those proceedings; he kept his seat, but saw the Doctor deliver the Minutes to the twelve, laying his right hand in silence on the head of each. His presence sanctioned the whole . . .'

After Wesley's death Coke continued to exercise his superintendency in this as in other ways. In the autumn of 1791 he ordained Jean de Quetteville and William Mahy, in preparation for the mission to France. The Conference prohibition of 1793, with which he so profoundly disagreed, did not put a halt to his practice of ordaining those who went out to the West Indian mission. On 6th October, 1793 he ordained Francis Thursby and Thomas Dobson at Liverpool,[2] and did the same to James Alexander on 15th April in the following year.[3] After that there is a gap of eight years in the evidence, but there seems no reason to doubt that these missionary ordinations continued unbroken, despite the abandoning of the primitive practice in the connexion at home. The ordination certificates that have survived show that his custom was to ordain in his capacity as 'Bishop of the Methodist Episcopal Church', which he no doubt considered as enabling him to act independently of the British Conference. From 1802 the evidence that Coke continued to ordain for the mission field again becomes a steady flow.[4] These later missionary ordinations were certainly performed with the approval and

[1] Sermon cxv (text: Hebrews 5:4), dated 'Cork, May 4, 1789', but apparently preached during the 1788 Conference (Diary entry for 31st July 1788, *Journal of John Wesley*, vii. 421; cf. Whitehead, *John Wesley*, ii. 498ff.). Wesley clung to his distinction with a certain doggedness (Moore, *John Wesley*, ii. 339f.).

[2] Letter from John Pawson to Charles Atmore, 9th October 1793 (Archives Centre). Copy of Thursby's ordination certificate in M.M.S. Archives.

[3] Certificate at Wesley's Chapel, London, dated, 15th April 1794.

[4] See list in Appendix C. The earliest known example after 1794 is that of Edward Thompson, ordained elder for the work in St Christopher, and referred to in a letter from Coke to John Brownell of Basseterre, 27th September 1802 (Original in possession of Miss O. Austen of Brede, Sussex). This evidence disposes of the usual assumption that these missionary ordinations did not begin until about 1816. See further, *W.H.S. Proc.* xxxvi. 36ff., 111ff.

sanction of the Missionary Committee and, *ipso facto*, of the Conference which had appointed it to work with Coke.[1] The case of John Ogilvie in August 1808 is of particular interest, since there seems to have been no question of his going overseas: he had just been appointed superintendent of the Chester Circuit.[2] This leaves open the possibility that other ordinations for the English work may have taken place during these years, despite the Conference ruling.

* * *

Although Coke was prominent among those who helped Methodism to cast off her moorings, he did not turn his back upon the home port entirely without regret. To the end, like Wesley, he was bound by strong ties to the Church of his childhood and early ministry. In 1799, perhaps in reaction to the excesses of the Kilhamites, he turned back once more to the hope that Methodism might yet remain what her founder had intended, a leaven within the Established Church. His approach to the Anglicans, as in 1791, was entirely personal, though in this case it was made only after private consultation with other leading figures in the Connexion. On 29th March, 1799, he wrote to the Bishop of London on the possibility of 'securing the great body of Methodists to the church of England'.

The Methodist people, he says, are still 'friends of the liturgy of the church of England, and of its Episcopacy', but many of them have scruples about receiving the sacrament from clergy whom they consider immoral. 'I have found it in vain to urge to them that the validity of the ordinance does not depend upon the piety or even the morality of the minister.' As a result, since Wesley's death an increasing number of societies had requested and been granted the administration of the sacrament in their own chapels, 'so that now a considerable number of our body have deviated in this instance from the Established Church, and I plainly perceive, that this deviation, unless prevented, will, in time, bring about an universal separation from the Establishment'.

Coke's words in this letter show how gradual and piecemeal was the process which led to the final separation; even in 1799 he was hopeful of putting it in reverse. The remedy he proposed was that a

[1] See, e.g., letter from William Myles to William Jenkins, 14th November, 1807 (M.S.S. Archives).

[2] Ordination Certificate at Wesley College, Bristol, dated 10th August 1808. (*W.H.S. Proc.* xxvi. 30.)

number of the leading Methodist preachers should receive Anglican orders and be allowed to travel through the Connexion, administering the Sacrament wherever desired. He was sanguine about the chances of this scheme succeeding. 'I have no doubt,' he wrote, 'that the people would be universally satisfied. The men of greatest influence in the connexion would, I am sure, unite with me; and every deviation from the Church of England would be done away.' But a more hesitant note creeps into a later paragraph of the letter: 'I could wish that something might be done as soon as convenient, as some of my most intimate friends, to whom I have ventured to disclose this plan, are far advanced in years. These are men of long standing, and of great influence in our connexion. The plan meets their decided approbation and cordial wishes for success.' Enthusiastic support was less likely, it would seem, from the younger generation who had grown up in a Methodism already largely estranged from the Established Church.[1]

It is some indication of the extent to which the ecumenical climate has changed, that every one of Coke's earlier biographers was faced with the alternative either of ignoring his efforts to restore Anglican-Methodist relationships or of apologizing for them as misguided though well-intentioned aberrations. His chances of success were admittedly very slight: events were moving in a different direction and there were few who shared his concern for the closing of the Christian ranks. What might have been the reaction of the rank and file of Methodism to these proposals in 1799 is impossible to say, beyond the certainty of a cleavage of opinion such as Coke himself envisaged in his letter. His suggestion was, in fact, never submitted to them for judgement, since it met with a decidedly cold reception by the Archbishop of Canterbury, to whom Coke's letter was passed. Bishop Porteus had gone so far as to concede that a healing of the breach was a 'very desirable' object, though doubting the practicability of the means suggested; but the Archbishop, who spoke for the rest of the bishops, was less compromising. He firmly rejected both the charge of immorality among the 'regularly ordained clergy' and Coke's suggestion that 'the bishops should . . . ordain a number of persons upon the recommendation of [the] Conference, without any other enquiry as to their fitness, and without any title or appointment to any place where they might legally exercise their

[1] The letter is printed in Drew, pp. 288ff., and Etheridge, pp. 301ff.

functions.'[1] To this rebuff was added the displeasure of Coke's fellow-preachers when the Conference of 1802 censured him for making these unofficial overtures.[2]

The century which saw the rise of Methodism thus ended with a determined refusal on the part of the Church of England to take any measures to draw back into the fold those who had been allowed to stray through intransigence and lethargy in the Establishment. Though Coke's proposals may have been defective, they might have been met by more adequate alternatives offered in the same spirit. But it would be difficult to find many among his contemporaries in either camp who were as deeply concerned as Thomas Coke that the mission of the Church was being rendered ineffective by the lack of unity among Christians.

[1] Ibid. Coke concedes that for the Methodists clerical 'Immorality' is a term of wide reference, including theatre-going and other fashionable entertainments.

[2] Journal of Richard Treffry, 26th July 1802 (M.S. in possession of Mr F. L. Harris of Redruth).

CHAPTER 13

THE DIVIDED INHERITANCE

The unity of 'the people called Methodists' had been so closely bound up with their common loyalty to John Wesley that his death inevitably heralded a period in which underlying tensions became open conflicts and unresolved issues had to be faced. Coke had been Wesley's chief assistant in the attempt to ensure the proper settlement of Methodist property on the 'Model Deed', securing the right of the Conference to determine the appointment of preachers throughout the Connexion; and the same problem continued to engage much of his time and attention after 1791. But now there was no longer any doubt that the conflict between Conference and local trustees was a symptom of a fundamental cleavage, involving the sacramental issue and the relationship of Methodism to the Church of England.

In 1793 the trustees of the Newcastle Orphan House drew up a statement of their objections to the allowing of Methodist services in Church hours or the administration of the sacraments by the Methodist preachers. Once again, it was Coke who was appointed by Conference to visit Newcastle and 'to adjust, as far as was practicable, the points in dispute'. He achieved a compromise, in which the trustees, in return for official recognition, conceded the right of the Conference to appoint the preachers; while it was agreed that there should be no services in Church hours and no administration of the sacraments without their unanimous consent.[1]

Such a compromise, however, was wholly inadequate as a basis for a permanent settlement of such a far-reaching issue as confronted the Connexion. The Bristol Conference of 1794 had scarcely ended when the smouldering fires of dispute burst into flame there; the advocates of the 'old' and 'new' plans found themselves in open conflict and there was bitter feeling on both sides. There is every indication that both factions looked upon this as a test-case which might determine the balance of power in the Connexion. Coke, who had not yet left the city, was fully involved and was accused by some of

[1] W. W. Stamp, *The Orphan House of Wesley*, pp. 173ff.

205

being the chief trouble-maker. It would be patently unfair to make his presence the sole cause of the trouble: the tinder was dry and so many sparks were flying about that an outbreak sooner or later was probably inevitable.[1] But he was not given to sitting on fences; his liberal views were widely known, not least in Bristol, and the passion with which he was accustomed to advocate his cause served to fan the flames.

Personalities apart, the responsibility for having created an explosive situation lay with the Conference itself, which had replaced its directive of the previous year with this more cautious, negative instruction: 'As the Lord's Supper has not been administered, except where the Society has been unanimous for it, and would not have been contented without it, it is now agreed that the Lord's Supper shall not be administered in future, when the union and concord of the Society can be preserved without it.'[2] This, like the decision in 1791 to follow 'Mr. Wesley's plan', was open to so wide an interpretation that trouble was certain to result. It is a matter for debate whether the trustees of the New Room or Coke and Henry Moore were the first to begin it. Both sides appear to have been ready for a show-down, and the actions of each were calculated to provoke the other.

Moore was one of the preachers appointed to the Bristol Circuit for the coming year. On the day after the Conference ended he and Thomas Taylor assisted Coke in administering the Sacrament in Portland Chapel. This the New Room trustees interpreted as a deliberately provocative action: a sacramental service was quite unnecessary so soon after the one held there during the recent conference, and Coke had ignored the presence of an ordained minister, Thomas Vasey, who could have assisted. He had, moreover, been repeatedly warned of the probable consequences, but had chosen to proceed with the service. This was, the trustees claimed, a concerted effort 'to force the Ordination Scheme upon the People, without their general Concurrence'.[3]

[1] The altercation between Wesley and the New Room trustees in 1784–8, in which Coke had incurred local disfavour, was still remembered. The building of Portland Chapel soon after Wesley's death was taken by some as a move to by-pass the opposition of the 'Old Planners' to such innovations as services in Church hours and the administration of the Sacrament by Methodist preachers.

[2] *Minutes*, i. 314.

[3] Letter from the Bristol trustees to the Preachers in the Methodist Connexion, dated 30th August 1794, and issued in pamphlet form.

Shortly afterwards, Moore was served with legal notice that the trustees were not prepared to allow him to preach in the New Room, since he had not been appointed by them. Encouraged by support among the members and leaders of the Society, he nevertheless went to the Room at the time of his next service there, but was barred from the pulpit by the trustees. He therefore retired to Portland Chapel, accompanied by the larger part of the congregation. Thus the issue over the power to appoint and dismiss the preachers was brought to a head in a most personal way. The lines of battle were drawn and everyone hastened to take sides.

The preacher appointed as superintendent of the Bristol Circuit that year was Joseph Benson, who was known to be a staunch supporter of the 'old Plan'. Coke feared that his arrival in the city would only serve to fan the flames, and therefore sent him a blunt appeal to keep out of the controversy. He wrote:

I cannot satisfy my conscience, if I do not write a few words to *you*. You seem now placed in a very awful situation. Your very considerable abilities make the circumstances of your case, peculiarly important. You have been a very useful man in your time: but it is perhaps in your power now to do more harm, than ever you did or will do good. The great employment of Christ is to reconcile God to Man, and man to man. The great employment of Satan is to separate God from Man, and man from man. Let there be no deductions from the good you have done, or may do. The best of us all does so little good, that it will not bear substraction. Let not the remainder of your life be, to support a party. Keep among the great Body of the Methodists. I see clearly that the moment you make yourself a party man in Bristol, the scabbard of that Sword which has been already drawn, will be thrown away. You will be the Head of a party. You will perhaps be more honourable than ever with a few worldly men. You certainly will be peculiarly honoured by your own party. But what is all this to your (I know) disinterested mind. Alas! the Glory will de departed. Your genuine usefulness will be over. Your remaining Life will be spent in what is infinitely worse than nothing. You were faithful to me when you apprehended I was going to make a division—rather than which I do declare I would rather die ten thousand deaths, almighty Grace assisting me. Now permit me to turn the tables. Don't labour to divide us. Labour for the Union. Sooner die than divide such a Body as ours. You may in the violence of party-debate and party-spirit, root up some tares: but think you that you will tear up none of the wheat?[1]

Three days after this, Coke was joined by three other preachers in

[1] Letter to Benson, 14th August, 1794 (Archives Centre).

a further appeal to Benson to stay in Manchester, unless he was prepared to side with the Conference party in Bristol. 'We now beg leave to inform you, that things have been carried to so great a length by the Trustees, that there is not the most distant probability of a reconciliation. Yea, the people are irritated to that degree, that we are persuaded that they would not now submit to a reconciliation, if Mr. Moore were ever so desirous of it.' Their only justification for this attempt to supersede the stations authorized by Conference was the conviction that the trustees, by their rejection of Henry Moore, had themselves abrogated the authority of Conference and were acting in a manner subversive of the stability of the entire Connexion.[1]

Benson set out from Manchester undeterred by these appeals. When he got as far as Gloucester, he received a further letter, signed by Coke and other preachers, containing an ultimatum to the effect that 'unless he unequivocally assured the Trustees of Portland Chapel that he would not preach at the Room or at Guinea-Street Chapel, they could not admit him into their's . . .'[2] He nevertheless continued his journey, convinced that 'if Dr. C and the Preachers who had signed the above mentioned Letter had been in their own proper places, minding their own business, and had not meddled with the affairs of others, either the breach would never have happened, or it would soon have been healed'.[3]

Benson's arrival in Bristol did not contribute to a healing of the breach, since, as Coke had feared, he ranged himself alongside the trustees. At a specially convened District Meeting, on the other hand, the majority of the preachers gave their support to Moore. Among the more unseemly incidents all too indicative of the spirit in which the wrangling went on, was the occasion on which Richard Rodda was

[1] Unaddressed letter, clearly written to Benson, 17th August 1794 (Archives Centre).

[2] Quoted in a letter from Benson, Rodda and Vasey to the preachers, dated 26th September 1794 and issued in pamphlet form. Cf. Coke's letter to Benson, 1st September 1794 (Archives Centre).

[3] In the same pamphlet, pp. 14f.: 'If Dr. Coke had taken the advice repeatedly given him, and in the most earnest and solemn manner urged upon him by Mr. Gifford on the Sunday morning; and either had omitted administering the Sacrament at Portland Chapel, (where it had been administered the fortnight before) or had declined asking Mr. Moore and Mr. Tho. Taylor's assistance, of which there certainly was not the least need, as Mr. Vasey was there and was appointed by Conference to administer it, what occurred next evening at the Room would not have taken place.'

forcibly prevented by Moore's supporters from preaching at Kingswood, while Coke was carried in triumph to occupy his place.[1]

Coke's language was always inclined to become emotional and extravagant under the stress of controversy. The Bristol trustees, like those at Dewsbury, were castigated as being worse than the Roman Inquisition. 'God is with us', he wrote, '& the People are with us, & every Preacher who regards the right of the Conference to station the Preachers, will surely be with us also. Such an attack *on that right*—on Liberty of Conscience—& on Justice, has not, we think, been known before in the Annals of Methodism. The Popish Inquisition first receives an accusation, & then examines the accused: but here was *no Process at all*! Oh fie, Old England, that such an instance of tyranny should ever be known in thee! But blessed be God, Trustee-tyranny is now at an end in Bristol! The People would not submit themselves to these Men, if we would.'[2]

Coke seems to have despaired at an early stage in the dispute of effecting any permanent reconciliation of the conflicting parties, and pinned his hopes on a policy of disengagement.[3] If the Trustees were determined to wield this power over the preachers, and so undermine the connexional principle, then the only response was to withdraw from the New Room and build another chapel which could be settled unequivocally on the Model Deed. While claiming to have at heart the peace and unity of the Connexion, Coke considered there was a limit to the price that should be paid to gain even these desirable ends. Before the Conference in the following year he wrote to George Holder, 'O my Brother, why do you talk of a division? I would not have a hand in it for ten thousand worlds. It was not the old or the new Plan which influenced me to take Mr. Moore's part; it was the Trustees exercising the power, *alone*, of expelling a preacher.' And he added, 'If you are for God, come to the Conference, determined to promote peace. This & the last year have been the best ever known in the annals of Methodism for the conversion of souls. What else is worth thinking of? Give me & the other lovers

[1] Ibid., p. 17. Cf. letter from Mrs Fletcher to Mrs Sarah Crosby, 13th October 1794 (Archives Centre), expressing her determination to 'stand to the old plan': 'How shocking their dragging Mr Rodda out of the pulpit, & turning him out for the "old Serpent", while they carried Dr Coke about to put him into the pulpit for "their little angel".'

[2] Letter to John King, 25th August 1794 (Archives Centre).

[3] Letter to Bogie, Cummins and Eversfield of the Edinburgh Circuit, 19th September 1794 (Archives Centre).

of peace, on both sides, yr hand & yr heart, & God will bless you with the blessings of a Peace-maker.'[1]

The fracas at Bristol sent ripples of renewed controversy through the whole Connexion and made more urgent a proper settlement of the sacramental issue. The opening of the new King Street chapel, very near the New Room, was the least important result of the dispute. It solved the difficulty only by dodging it and could not serve as a precedent throughout the Connexion. The year that followed was filled with discussion and much lobbying on both sides, in which Coke had his share.

At the end of March 1795 he met Pawson and Mather in Liverpool. One result of this was his *Address to the Preachers*, prefixed to Pawson's *Chronological Catalogue of all the Travelling Preachers*[2] and containing this impassioned plea for unity:

O Brethren, shall our bright candle be extinguished, and leave a noisome smell behind it? Shall we set district against district, circuit against circuit, society against society, husbands against their wives, children against their parents, and be the authors of innumerable other evils, which would necessarily follow a division? God forbid! Come, then, let us join our hands and hearts together in the great cause of the conversion of a world. Let us agree to disagree in every immaterial circumstance, and lend our whole strength to bring immortal souls to our adorable Redeemer. Then shall we be the people whom he will delight to honour. He will dwell in us and among us; he will make us terrible like an army with banners; and jointly with his people who serve him zealously under other denominations, and perhaps more extensively than them all, will make us chief instruments in hastening and completing his universal reign. Even so, Lord Jesus. Amen.

A further result of this meeting was a set of proposals, designed to promote peace and prevent a division in the Connexion. These were in all essentials the proposals subsequently adopted by the Conference in the form of the Plan of Pacification. Coke was their principal author, and they were circulated privately among some of the other preachers,[3] who were invited to submit their comments.

[1] Letter to George Holder, 3rd July 1795 (M.M.S. Archives).

[2] Pawson's *Chronological Catalogue*, a precursor of 'Hill's Arrangement', was published in 1795. Coke's *Address* is dated 'Liverpool, 30th March'.

[3] E.g. A copy of the proposals was sent to John King at Gainsborough, with a covering letter from Coke, dated 17th April 1795 and beginning: 'Above you have some proposals for peace, drawn up by Messrs Pawson, Mather & myself, when we met about 3 weeks ago in Liverpool, in order humbly to draw up some-

One who did so was George Holder in the Isle of Man, to whom Coke sent the following reply:

I am very much obliged to you for your many excellent remarks. The propositions were drawn up in haste, but, I trust, from the purest motives to prevent a division. But as they were only written in the way of private letters, and contained no engagement, I think myself at full liberty to retract any of them I choose. If they prove the means of stirring up any to seek for peace in a better way, they will then have their uses.[1]

When the Conference assembled in Manchester, therefore, much of the spade-work had already been done. There was little doubt in the minds of the preachers that the issue must now be faced and settled without further procrastination. Accordingly, after a day had been spent in fasting and prayer, a committee of nine was chosen by ballot to draw up proposals for settling the differences that threatened to tear the Connexion apart. This committee was representative of all the rival view points and included Benson, Moore and Mather, as well as Coke himself. Without the intensive lobbying of the preceding months, their deliberations might have been protracted and indecisive. Instead, they quickly resulted in the Plan of Pacification, which was subsequently approved by both the preachers in Conference and the assembled representatives of the trustees. Thus was provided a basis for the future stability of the Connexion. The appointment of preachers remained with the Conference, with provision for the examination of any accused of immorality or other short-comings. The Lord's Supper was to be administered where a majority of the stewards, leaders, and trustees were in favour of it and the consent of Conference had been obtained, but not in Church hours or on any Sunday when it was administered in the parish church. In this way a further milestone was passed on the long road by which Methodism emerged as a Church with its own ministry and sacraments.

* * *

The strongest cross-current in the troubled waters through which Methodism had to pass during this decade was the agitation for the

---

thing of the kind, being in each other's neighbourhood, & exceedingly desirous to prevent a division. If you have a leisure half [hour] & favour me with a few lines . . . I shall be glad to hear from you.' (Original in possession of Dr Frank Baker.)

[1] Letter to George Holder (see p. 210, note 1).

admission of lay representatives to the Conference and the District Meetings which led to the expulsion of Alexander Kilham and the formation of the Methodist New Connexion in 1797. Both as an outstanding figure in the Connexion and as Secretary of the Conference during these years, Coke was at the centre of the storm.

As early as 1791, Kilham had issued an anonymous pamphlet strongly advocating separation from the Established Church. There were many preachers, including Coke, who, without carrying their arguments or their invective to the same extremes, shared Kilham's views on this; so that, when he was taken to task by the 1792 Conference, it was for nothing more serious than having 'acted imprudently', and his appointment as superintendent of the Aberdeen Circuit was interpreted in some quarters as a vindication of his cause. Under Presbyterian influence, he now began to agitate for a more democratic form of church government and for lay representation at every level. This he continued to advocate in opposition to the various proposals for creating a constitutional episcopacy in British Methodism, until his expulsion by the Conference of 1796.

Coke had been Kilham's main accuser at the Conference of 1792, chiefly on the grounds of his presumption in criticizing Mr Wesley. As Kilham's views became more dangerously radical, so Coke's hostility grew. Under the impact of the American revolution, Coke had at one time gone a long way towards becoming himself a republican, but subsequent events brought about a reaction in his political outlook. Those were hazardous times for either an individual or a church to hold radical sympathies. Ever since the days of the Young Pretender, the Methodists had insisted, against the repeated insinuations of their enemies, that they were a loyal people. In the years following Wesley's death, amid revolutions abroad and unrest at home, the Conference repeatedly affirmed its loyalty.[1] The radicalism of young Kilham seemed dangerously subversive of political as well as ecclesiastical good order, and must therefore be curbed.

Wherever his political sympathies might lie in America, at home Coke was uncompromising and vocal in his loyalty to the throne. His fear of 'the Political Spirit of the Dissenters' epitomized in Dr Joseph Priestley had inspired in 1791 a temporary reaction in favour

---

[1] See R. F. Wearmouth, *Methodism and the Common People of the Eighteenth Century*, 248ff.; *Methodism and Working-Class Movements of England 1800–1850*, pp. 37ff.; E. R. Taylor, *Methodism and Politics*, pp. 24ff.; W. J. Warner, *The Wesleyan Movement in the Industrial Revolution*, pp. 127ff.

of the Church of England. The reaction passed, but the fear of radicalism remained, strengthened by what he saw of the secular spirit of revolutionary France during his abortive mission to Paris at the end of that same year. What he heard of the by-product of the French Revolution in Haiti, inspired in him a healthy dread of anarchy. Elsewhere in the West Indies the painful contrast between the attitudes of the Dutch and of the British authorities made him grateful for the British constitution as a bulwark against tyranny. This was at the root of his opposition to Kilham.

At one stage, Coke, Pawson and some of the other leading preachers considerably modified their attitude to Kilham and went some way towards accepting his demands for a more representative form of church government. This was in 1794, at the time when the trustees were pressing most strongly for adherence to the 'old Plan' and the authority of the Conference seemed in danger of being seriously curtailed. Perhaps to their embarrassment, Kilham lent his support to the 'Conference Party' against Benson and the New Room trustees in the Bristol dispute. Coke wrote him a letter at the time in which he gave his qualified approval to the idea of lay representation.

Religious liberty requires that the people or their representatives should have some negative in respect to their ministers. Hitherto, we have been, since the death of Mr Wesley, the most perfect aristocracy, perhaps, existing on the face of the earth. The people have had *no* power: we, the *whole*, in the fullest sense that can be conceived. If there be a change in favour of religious liberty, the people certainly should have some power. Less than what is offered them in this article [a clause enabling the trustees, stewards and leaders to summon a special disciplinary meeting to deal with accusations against a preacher], it appears to me they cannot have. And indeed, what preacher would wish, or at least ought to wish, to labour in a circuit, where the majority of the trustees, leaders, and stewards, disapproved of him? The little power given in this instance to the trustees, is, I think, no more than they have a claim to; as we cannot do without men who will be responsible for our debts, and we are very much obliged to them for becoming responsible: and their votes, when united to the stewards and leaders of the whole circuit, becomes (of consequence) of small weight in so numerous an assembly.[1]

This concession was in due course incorporated in the Plan of Pacification. Kilham was present in Conference and accepted the Plan, although it fell so far short of his own proposals. The 1795

[1] Letter to Kilham, quoted in *Life of Kilham* [by J. Blackwell], 1838, pp. 202f.

Conference was scarcely over, however, before he was preparing a fresh campaign. His most important publication, *The Progress of Liberty among the People called Methodists*, attacked the Plan as not going far enough in conceding power to the laity. This aroused an uproar of protest. A letter to the Chairman of the Newcastle District, of which Coke was one of the ten signatories, condemned the pamphlet as the worst to be published since the Methodist revival began. Kilham in turn was stung into replying in his *Candid Examination of the London Methodistical Bull*. Quoting the letters he had received from Coke and Pawson, whom he considered to be chiefly responsible for the 'Bull', he asserted that he had been betrayed by those who had given him reason to expect their support. Coke's letter he said, represented the Methodist preachers as 'the most perfect aristocracy in the world'. 'Have I declared anything equal to this in my pamphlet? He represents the Methodists as in a state of slavery . . . I have endeavoured to shew what liberty they expect to have, and have pressed on my brethren to grant it without hesitation. This good man comes forward with all the zeal of a cardinal in the tenth century, to persecute me for speaking out to the people, what he had declared to me in secret. Is it right for us to hold *the whole* power, and our people *none*? . . . I hope the good man will learn in heaven to be consistent with himself, if he cannot learn this useful lesson on earth!'[1] Clearly there was misunderstanding on both sides. Coke had expected Kilham to accept the very limited measure of democratization embodied in the Plan of Pacification; Kilham, for his part, had hoped that the pressure exerted by the trustees would force the preachers to make more radical concessions to the rank and file members whom he claimed to represent. Disappointment led him to accusations of betrayal; but it is very doubtful whether either Coke or any of the other leading preachers ever seriously considered giving more support to Kilham's programme of reform than was embodied in the Plan.

It is important in this respect to realize that both Coke and Kilham were, each in his own way, children of their age. Kilham belonged to that growing minority who were eager to welcome the dawn of a new day in the name of liberty and equality. We have seen so many revolutions since then that his proposals strike us as no more than reasonable and just. It is not easy to put back the clock so as to view things as they appeared before the days of universal political franchise, when men had not yet come to believe in the infallibility of the majority.

[1] Kilham, *Candid examination*, p. 25.

The fact that the past two centuries have witnessed the victory of demagogy should not blind us to the fact that in an age of revolution and violence there was a case for making haste slowly. To reasonable and moderate men the case seemed a strong one, and Coke's experience, especially in Paris at the height of the revolution, disposed him to accept it. In common with many of his contemporaries, he dreaded Jacobinism as an organized attempt to overthrow both civil rule and the Christian religion; there could be no question of either compromise or co-existence with so diabolical a system.[1]

* * *

The secession which followed Kilham's expulsion was one of the reasons why Coke changed his mind about settling in America. On the fleeting visit which he paid to the States in the autumn of 1797, he carried with him an appeal from the British Conference that he should be released from his obligations in America, as the schism in British Methodism made his return essential. Coke himself was certain that, for the time being, his rightful place was in England, not so much because of the loss of several thousand members as because of the effect of the schism on the mission fund, which was threatened with a fatal loss of support from the home Church. 'The schism . . . has so alarmed the Preachers', he wrote, 'that the great work in the West Indies seemed to be almost forgot; and I do believe would soon have dropped to the ground, if I had not returned.'[2] Towards the end of 1798, viewing the secession in retrospect, his chief concern was again for the missions: ·

We lost so many Chapels, just at first, by the Division which took place, that great exertions have been made this year for the building of new ones. Owing to this, there has been no public Collection for the Work in the West Indies, and the whole lies upon me. We have sent some able Missionaries over to those Islands this year, and are going to send three more immediately. Three of them have Families: so that the West India work will cost this year upward of Two thousand pounds Sterling: all of which I either have raised or must raise or that work would be essentially injured.[3]

---

[1] See especially his account of, and comments on, the French Revolution in *The Recent Occurrences of Europe Considered* (first printed as an appendix to his Commentary), sections iv and v.

[2] Letter to Ezekiel Cooper, 21st April 1798 (Garrett Theological Seminary).

[3] Letter to Cooper, 18th December 1798 (Garrett Theological Seminary).

Early in the new year he reported, almost casually, to Cooper the news of Kilham's sudden death;[1] but the mutton bone which thus ended a stormy career did not put an end to the disputes between Wesleyans and Kilhamites, and as late as 1810 we find Coke engaged in unedifying correspondence over disputed chapels.[2]

* * *

Hardly more than a decade after the foundation of the New Connexion, Hugh Bourne was expelled by the Burslem Quarterly Meeting for absenting himself from his class in order to attend Camp-meetings. But Bourne was no second Kilham, and history refrained from repeating itself. Primitive Methodists have always insisted that their branch of Methodism originated not in a secession but in a fresh outpouring of evangelistic fervour which the old wine-skins of Wesleyanism were unable to contain; unlike the Kilhamites, they took with them no chapels and very few members. This is reflected in the complete absence of any reference either to Bourne and Clowes or to the new movement of the Spirit in the correspondence of Thomas Coke. Kilham's voluble agitation had been concerned with matters of ecclesiastical politics and ended by dividing the Connexion; whether he liked it or not, Coke had been in the thick of the conflict and Kilham's name recurs in his correspondence of that period. So far as such evidence goes, he might, on the other hand, have been entirely oblivious of what was happening in the neighbourhood of Burslem during the years 1807–10. The nearest he and Bourne came to meeting each other was probably in March 1803, when Bourne went to Congleton to hear him preach. 'He showed much of the nature of Love,' Bourne reported. 'We had a lively time. He afterwards spoke about the missions, and made a collection for the same. He told us of the success of the missionaries, and said there had been one soul converted for every guinea and half that had been collected: that the greatest part of the places were now able to support themselves, but Wales, Ireland and the West Indies we had still to support.'[3]

Another copy, to an unknown recipient, is in the possession of the Baltimore Historical Society.

[1] Letter to Cooper, 12th January 1799 (Garrett Theological Seminary).
[2] Cf. letter to John Ridgeway, 30th April 1810 (Archives Centre).
[3] Bourne's *Journal* (MS at Hartley Victoria College, Manchester).

Coke was present at the Conference of 1807 which condemned the English Camp-meetings as 'highly improper and likely to be of considerable mischief', but in the absence of direct evidence we can do little more than guess how far he endorsed this official view. It is possible that his experience of similar occurrences in America[1] disposed him to be more sympathetic and open-minded than most of the elder brethren at the Conference; the series of eye-witness accounts of the American Camp-meetings which appeared in the *Methodist Magazine* during the early years of the century had been communicated through him. On the other hand, he was not the man to condone wilful irregularities or the defiance of Methodist discipline. At the Irish Conference of 1800 he took the lead in refusing formal recognition to the work of the American evangelist Lorenzo Dow unless he submitted to the authority of the Conference;[2] and the fact that two years later Dow was the man responsible for bringing the Camp-meeting to England would not dispose Coke to hail the new movement with enthusiasm. 'If we do not stand firm to our Rules,' he once wrote, 'we may as well break up Methodism and go to our tents.'[3]

[1] See above, pp. 125f.
[2] Crookshank, *Methodism in Ireland*, ii. 192. Coke's offer to send Dow as a missionary to Halifax or Quebec was refused.
[3] Letter to Benson, Lomas and Entwisle, 27th August 1805 (M.M.S. Archives). Cf. his letter to Ezekiel Cooper, 23rd April 1795 (Garrett Theological Seminary): 'We should, my dear Brother, be exceedingly jealous for the preservation of the parts of our Discipline: all that is Carnal militates against it; but it is the [blessed?] Hedge which in the Hand of God is the means of preserving the Divine [?] among us.'

CHAPTER 14

THE LOYALIST

First impressions of post-Revolutionary America in 1784 had gone a long way to turn Coke into a republican, but the transformation was neither deep nor lasting. Whatever sympathy he may have retained for the cause of the Colonists, whenever he was in England his loyalty to the Crown was never in doubt. We have seen that political motives prompted his determined opposition to Kilham in 1796, a fact which is demonstrated by his correspondence with Joseph Benson at that time. The two letters which have survived refer to arrangements for a Loyal Address from the Methodist societies, which Coke had proposed as a demonstration of their loyalty in the face of growing threats from radical elements both within the nation and on the Continent. He was at this time busy in London with plans for a mission to Sierra Leone, which brought him into contact with influential members of the Clapham Sect and enabled him to learn what was being said in official circles. 'In an interview which I lately had with a Gentleman of rank', he told Benson, 'I was informed by him (whose information, I am certain, is authentic) that the Government has received very unfavourable impressions concerning the Loyalty of many of the Methodists; and that nothing can remove that Jealousy but an Address to his Majesty, assuring him of our Loyalty. Indeed, unless this step be taken, I have reason to believe, that the Government will soon think it necessary to take some steps to check our (in that case) alarming growth. I have reason to believe that they will not only be jealous of, but put a stop to our *Conference*.' This situation, he says, calls for urgent action; to wait until Conference met in the following summer might well prove a fatal delay. 'We are commanded of God to honour the King: & if the King be jealous of our Loyalty, the best we can do is to inform him of his mistake. It is not necessary for us to enter into any one political discussion, but to keep to the point, *Loyalty to the King*. Mr Pawson thinks it necessary to address the King as soon as possible; and has desired me to draw up an Address.'

After giving a copy of the Address he has drafted, in which he asserts unequivocally that the Methodists are 'determined Friends of Monarchy, of the illustrious House of Hanover, and of the British Constitution', he continues:

We here keep only one object in view, *Loyalty*. If this be proposed to our Congregations, we shall have tens of thousands to sign: and it's not Aleck Kilham & a few more can prevent its taking due effect . . . Let us go on, fearing God, honouring the King, & preaching the Gospel in its power, & nothing will stand before us: but don't let us presume upon our God, by neglecting the evident, necessary means for the preservation of the peace of our Zion.[1]

Coke was clearly disturbed at the possibility that Kilham's views and activities might discredit the Connexion in the eyes of a Government that was very sensitive to any hint of disaffection. If the authorities were once convinced that the Methodist societies were hot-beds of radicalism and sedition, they would not hesitate to take suppressive measures and the work of many years might be undone. He accordingly lost no time, in conjunction with Pawson, in sending out letters to the circuit superintendents asking them to obtain as many signatures as possible for the Address, with the minimum of delay.[2]

A few weeks later, at the beginning of February 1796, he wrote once more to Benson, to report progress. Several of the leading preachers were whole-heartedly behind the proposed Address, but Alexander Mather had suggested that it should first be referred to the District Meetings in May. Coke, however, was convinced that, as things stood, this might do untold harm: 'I am sure', he wrote, 'it will only turn them all into disputing Clubs.' Rather, let the senior preachers be united in commending the loyal address and the majority of the Methodist people would follow their lead. 'If Mr Mather, Pawson, yourself, Hanby, Bradford, Bradburn & myself join, it will be sufficient. It will so turn the scale, that the cause of Loyalty,

---

[1] Letter to Benson, 21st December 1795 (Archives Centre).

[2] A letter to Thomas Hanby, superintendent of the Nottingham Circuit, dated 9th January 1796 (Emory University) says, 'We . . . beg the favour of you to proceed in the business with all expedition. You have the Address in our last. We are quite satisfied that application should be made on the Lord's Day, as well as other days. The Bible commands us to Honour the King: & as the present step is necessary to give evidence at this time, of our compliance with this Divine command, it will be no breach of the Sabbath to urge this matter, & to sign on that day; & dispatch absolutely requires it . . .' He adds in a postscript, 'The London-Society enter into the business with amazing spirit. There is no time to be lost.'

meekness, & God, will prevail. But if we give up the point, the cause of Democracy (which I look upon as the cause of Anarchy & Terrorism) will gain treble strength by the steps we have taken. Whereas, if but three fourths of our Congregations be properly applied to, and their Signatures be presented, it will give a fatal Blow to Methodist Jacobinism.' He feared that if, having gone so far, they were now to draw back, they would have done 'infinite mischief, instead of infinite good'. So it was doubly important to have the Address ready to present by the time Conference met. 'The Neck of Jacobinism may thus be broke: but by turning our District-meetings or Conferences into disputing Clubs, it will be strengthened, & Methodism ruined.'[1]

There is no more eloquent witness to the gulf between Thomas Coke's world and our own than the change in the meaning and overtones of a word such as 'democracy'. As this letter to Benson aptly illustrates, 'democracy' was at that time a 'dirty' word, to be used, rather like the word 'Communist' in our present Western society, only as a jibe or insult flung in the teeth of an enemy. Coke clearly was unable to dissociate the government of the people from the ideas of mob-rule, sedition and atheism. A further example of this occurs in a series of letters which he wrote in the spring of 1801 to the Duke of Portland, the Home Secretary, at a time when the Government was apprehensive of a French invasion and therefore eyed with suspicion every sign of disaffection among the working classes. Coke was on a tour of the northern counties, begging for the missions, and sent a number of reports concerning suspicious activities which came to his notice. Yorkshire and Lancashire were buzzing with rumours of a grand Association similar to the one that had been formed during the recent Irish rebellion. Considerable numbers were gathering for secret nocturnal meetings, and there were reports that a seditious oath, based on a text from Ezekiel, was being administered. Further south, Birmingham was said to be deeply affected with the same rebellious spirit. 'That there is a Conspiracy against the State now on foot, I have no doubt,' Coke wrote; 'and I am sure that the utmost watchfulness of Government is necessary.'[2] Again, 'I do not apprehend any danger from these things, if our implacable enemies the French be not suffered by Providence to evade the bravery and watchfulness of our Navy, and land on our Coasts: but if that was

[1] Letter to Benson, 6th February 1796 (Archives Centre).
[2] Letter to Duke of Portland, 7th April 1801 (Public Record Office, H.O. 42/61 f. 474). Cf. Wearmouth, *Methodism and the Common People*, p. 262.

the case, I am greatly afraid that the People who now assemble in these parties would become very dangerous indeed, by diverting our forces.'[1] A postscript to one of the letters in this correspondence aptly illustrates the attitude of contemporary Wesleyanism to the growing democratic spirit of the times: 'I was not a little alarmed two or three days ago', he wrote, 'in hearing that three Methodists were taken up on suspicion or proof of being engaged in this rebellious business. But on the strictest scrutiny and fullest satisfaction, I was happy enough to find that these three men had been expelled the late Mr Wesley's Society about five years ago [i.e. at the time of Kilham's expulsion], solely for their democratic sentiments, and that since that time they had had no connexion with that religious Society, not even so much as by attending Divine Service in their Congregations.'[2] Coke was convinced that at such times as these it was the duty of the Wesleyan Connexion to gather her skirts about her and protect her children, as far as she might, from contamination by the secular spirit of radicalism. It was left to the Kilhamites, and later to the Primitive Methodists, to demonstrate that the Church is not always on the side of reaction and against the struggle of the 'lower orders' for political and economic advancement.

It would be unfair, however, to Thomas Coke to suggest that his attitude towards the masses was entirely negative and antipathetic. There are indications of a more liberal attitude alongside his inevitable dread of the rule of King Mob. At the Leeds Conference of 1797, it was he who, from the presidential chair, moved that the Circuit Stewards be allowed to attend the District Meeting, hitherto composed entirely of the Preachers. Mather, Bradford and Moore were all opposed to this and the motion was defeated by 77 to 55.[3] This suggests that Coke's qualified approval of Kilham's proposals for reform in 1794 was motivated by more than either apprehension or hypocrisy. Again, his compassion was not directed exclusively to his 'poor Blacks' in the West Indies; in 1801, he was fully aware that the social unrest had economic as well as political roots. Throughout the country, the labouring classes were crying out for bread to feed their starving families. The problem was one of human destitution and misery, for which Coke had a solution to propound. 'Would it not be best, my Lord,' he wrote at the close of one letter to

[1] Letter to Duke of Portland, 19th August 1801 (P.R.O.; H.O. 42/62 f. 408).
[2] Ibid., 4th April 1801 (P.R.O.; H.O. 42/61 f. 432).
[3] *Wesleyan Methodist Magazine*, 1845, pp. 435ff.

the Home Secretary, 'for public Granaries for Corn to be erected in every County and great City, built by Taxes raised as those for Churches, &c. are? There is no reason to believe, that the price of labour will be equal to the price of provisions [i.e. that wages will overtake the cost of subsisting] for many years to come. I think therefore that the Plan just suggested is expedient in order to balance in some degree the spirit and practice of monopoly, without injuring the necessary freedom of trade and commerce; not that I join in opinion with those who are vehemently crying out against Monopolists. I think, my Lord, that a million of money (if not less) expended annually, for some years to come, with wisdom and economy on this Plan, would exceedingly ingratiate the Government into the favour of the lower orders of the People.'[1] His emphasis on political expediency is an indication not of insincerity in Coke's concern for the plight of the poorer classes, but rather of his shrewdness in pressing on the Government a proposal likely to run counter to influential economic interests. There is undoubtedly a place for idealism, but your practical politician, then as now, was inclined to keep it firmly in its place unless it happened to have desirable economic or social consequences.

* * *

The loyalty of the Methodist people was a valuable weapon in Coke's armoury whenever he found himself defending them against successive waves of persecution. Prior to the formation of the Committee of Privileges in 1803, he held the pass almost single-handed, aided by his personal association with those in high places. His freedom of access to men like Lord Eldon, Lord Bathurst, Lord Liverpool, Henry Dundas and William Wilberforce,[2] proved a great asset in this, and he did not scruple to use such influence as he had in the defence of the persecuted.

One such occasion occurred in the Channel Islands, which were in the front line of battle throughout the French wars of this period.

[1] See p. 221, note 1.
[2] See his letter to Wilberforce, p. 343 below. John Scott, 1st Earl of Eldon, one of his contemporaries at Oxford, became Attorney-General in 1793 and Lord Chancellor in 1801. Henry, 3rd Earl Bathurst (1762–1834), was President of the Board of Trade under the Duke of Portland. Charles Jenkinson, 1st Earl of Liverpool, was Chancellor of the Duchy of Lancaster from 1786. Henry Dundas, 1st Viscount Melville, served under Lord North and the Younger Pitt; was Home Secretary, 1791, and Secretary of State for War, 1794.

It was the practice for military exercises to be held on Sundays, a custom acceptable to the greater part of the population and even sanctioned by the Church. The Methodists were prominent among the minority who objected on conscientious grounds to this profanation of the Sabbath and suffered the jeers and hostility of their fellows. In 1796, the appointment of Sir Hugh Dalrymple as lieutenant-governor, ended the persecutions in Guernsey; but in Jersey, several members of the society were imprisoned or threatened with banishment between 1794 and 1798.[1] Coke gave an account of the matter in writing to some of the American preachers. The Methodists of Jersey, he said, 'were willing to exercise on two common days in every week, to pay all the extraordinary Expences, to keep guard in their turn on the Lord's Day, & to take up arms & fight for the defence of the Island on that or any day, but all this would not do. The Government of the Island fined our Friends time after time, till many in affluent circumstances were reduced to poverty: after this they imprisoned them in small dark solitary Cells of about seven feet square, for three days, then for a week, then for a fortnight, a month & six weeks together; till the health of many of them was irretrievably injured.'[2]

The persecution came to a head in October 1798, when a new law was passed imposing banishment on any who refused to exercise on Sundays. Faced with this further threat, the Methodists of Jersey sent MM. Philippe Vivian and Pierre Le Sueur to London to plead their cause. Coke hurried back from Manchester and, accompanied by Mather, Pawson and Le Sueur, went to consult Wilberforce, who promised his support and advised Coke to write individually to the members of the Privy Council. This he did, explaining the grounds of their objections to the persecuting law and strongly emphasizing the loyalty of the Methodists both in the British Isles and in the West Indies.[3] To Dundas he wrote: 'The Law is made expressly . . . to punish those who will not perform the manual exercise on the Sabbath-day. Now, Sir, I should be exceedingly sorry, if any

[1] Guiton, *Histoire du Méthodisme*, pp. 77ff.

[2] Letter of 18th December 1798, sent to several of the American preachers. (Copies at Garrett Theological Seminary and in the possession of the Baltimore Methodist Historical Society). Cf. his letter to General Don in 1806 (Archives Centre).

[3] Guiton, op. cit., pp. 100ff; Lelièvre, op. cit., pp. 349ff. There is a letter to Coke from Fr. Le Breton, dated 12th November 1798 (original at Archives Centre), reporting on the passing of the law.

Law was to pass in the British Empire, which should authorize, under the severest penalty next to death, or even seem to authorize, a breach of the Sabbath; when the greatest Enemies of Christianity and Civil Society that ever existed, endeavour to stab Christianity through the sides of the Sabbath.'

He went on to warn Dundas of the probable effect of the persecution on the loyalty of the British Methodists: 'I have more especially since the death of my honoured Friend Mr Wesley, laid myself out to inspire into our People the spirit of Loyalty: and when a considerable number of Democrats had crept in among us, to the number of about 5000, I was a principal means of their being entirely excluded from our Society. But the Bill in question is so entirely repugnant to every idea I have given our People, and justly given them, of our Government, that if it receive the Royal Assent . . . I declare I know not what I can possibly say in vindication of it. And it will afford our Enemies whom we have excluded and who are as great enemies to Government as to us, the greatest triumph.'

Later in the letter there occurs an appeal against the persecution on the grounds of both humanity and expediency, a familiar combination: 'Even supposing that they carry their regard for the Sabbath to a little extreme, should a company of loyal men for this be persecuted to imprisonment, banishment, and ruin at any time, but especially when there are so many enemies in the bowels of the Empire, longing to destroy it?' Then follows a disavowal of pacifism which again reminds us of the gulf between Coke's world and our own:

The preamble of the Law, I think, says that some have refused to bear arms at all. I have heard of only one in Jersey, who answered this description; and he has been already banished from the Island. We plead not for such. We look upon them at best to be only poor Fanatics or arrant Cowards, and have no objection to their Banishment. They have no right to the protection of the Laws, who will not themselves be ready to protect those laws when in danger.

He concludes with a protestation of his own loyalty in the strongest terms: 'I can truly say, Sir, that though I very much love our Society, I love my King and Country better.'[1]

[1] Letter to Henry Dundas, 8th November 1798 (Southern Methodist University).

Coke's energetic lobbying of various members of the Government, including the Earl of Liverpool and the Duke of Portland[1] soon bore fruit. Coke, Pawson, Mather and Le Sueur were summoned to give evidence to the Privy Council on 7th December[2] and he was soon able to report joyfully that they had decided to annul the Bill.[3] It was a happy ending to weeks of anxiety. 'Our People in Britain,' he wrote, 'are certainly unspeakably obliged to their Government for the pains it has taken in consequence of our appeal. But this business, which lay *entirely* upon me, has engrossed my time almost night and day for about ten weeks.'[4] For a brief interval, even his begging for the missions had been laid aside.

Early in the New Year Coke set out in person to carry the good news to the Methodists of the Channel Islands. It says much for his standing in government circles that the official despatches from the Privy Council were entrusted to him. The Governor of Jersey, General Gordon, received him rather coolly and did not hesitate to express his misgivings about the action taken by the Privy Council.[5] But Colonel Messervy, who commanded the islands forces, had a high opinion of the loyalty of the Methodists and showed his sympathy for their cause. 'He spoke very highly of the excellent discipline of our Friends, who are in his regiment; and observed, that there can be no reason against the indulgence they desire, as there are Men continually exercised in the Drill on the common Week-days.'[6]

The Methodists of Jersey were thus rescued from further persecution, and for the time being a more tolerant attitude prevailed towards those with conscientious scruples concerning the Sunday exercises. For some years the Methodists were left in comparative peace. Then, in 1806, the arrival of a new Governor brought a fresh outbreak of the same trouble. The Committee of Privileges wisely referred the matter to Coke, who lost no time in taking it up once more with the authorities in London and with the

[1] Letter to Earl of Liverpool, 24th November 1798 (British Museum, Add. Mss 38463f. 250).

[2] Lelièvre, *Histoire du Méthodisme*, p. 373, gives the date of this meeting as 12th December; but it is clear from Coke's letters that this should be 7th December.

[3] E.g. Letter to Moore and Palmer, 8th December 1798 (Archives Centre).

[4] Letter to Cooper and others: see p. 223, note 2.

[5] Letter to Dundas, 9th January 1799 (Archives Centre).

[6] Ibid.

Governor himself.[1] Even supposing their conscientious scruples to be misguided, he wrote, 'the question is, Whether we shall please or displease God, or whether we shall obey God or man?'[2] His intervention was again successful and the persecution ceased.

* * *

While he was championing the civil rights of Methodists in the Channel Islands, Coke was fighting a similar battle in Ireland. In 1798, the United Irishmen with active support from the French broke into open rebellion. The country was thrown into confusion. The atrocities committed by the rebels were matched only by the brutality of the counter-measures. The Methodist itinerants found their labours seriously hindered and their freedom to gather in Conference threatened. Once again Coke's association with those in influential circles was pressed into service, and again the success of his efforts depended in large measure upon the demonstrable loyalty of the Irish Methodists. In a letter to Dundas already quoted, he says, 'We have never, Sir, had the opportunity, since the rebellion of 1745, to show our loyalty by fighting in England . . . But, in Ireland, some of the most faithful and useful Yeomen in the Kingdom are members of our Society.'[3] In the evidence he gives in support of this claim, Coke was writing from first-hand knowledge of the Rebellion, since he was himself in Ireland at the height of it. Despite the considerable danger, he spent much of 1798 in the country and but for his intervention no Irish Conference would have been possible that year. The whole country was under martial law, but a close friend, Alexander Knox, had just been appointed Under-Secretary of State. 'With his assistance I obtained an order from the Lord Lieutenant of Ireland, allowing us to hold our Conference without molestation, and assuring the Preachers full Protection both in coming to & returning from the Conference.'[4] Had the loyalty of the Methodists been in any doubt, not even this

[1] Letters to William Jenkins, 15th September, and 1st October, 1806 (M.M.S. Archives).
[2] Letter to Joseph Butterworth, 19th October 1806, enclosing copies of his letters to General Don and Lord Spencer (Archives Centre).
[3] Letter to Dundas, 8th November, 1798 (see p. 224, note 1).
[4] Letter to Ezekiel Cooper, 18th December 1798 (Garrett Theological Seminary); Cf his letter to Cooper, 12th January, 1799 (also at Garrett). See also Crookshank, *Methodism in Ireland*, ii. 144ff.

influential acquaintance would have enabled Coke to win this official protection for the Methodist preachers.

* * *

Inevitably, when the Committee of Privileges was formed in 1803, the name of Thomas Coke headed the list of those appointed to it. His past record made any other choice unthinkable. The task assigned to the Committee—that of 'guarding our religious privileges in these critical times'—was, after all, one which he had undertaken single-handed for many years. His acquaintance with members of the government continued to prove an invaluable asset during the closing years of his life. Whenever a serious threat to religious liberties arose, either at home or in the West Indies, it was to Coke that the rest of the Committee looked for a lead. During the opening years of the new century, repeated attempts were made in Jamaica to cripple the work of the Methodist missionaries on the plantations by enacting a law, as in Bermuda, which would restrict all forms of religious instruction among the slaves to the Anglican clergy. Renewed efforts in the autumn of 1807 led to a law which, though it ostensibly encouraged slave-owners to see that their slaves were instructed in the principles of Christianity, was specifically directed against the 'Methodist missionary, or other sectary, or preacher'. The missionaries, not to be silenced so easily, soon found themselves committed to prison, but lost no time in reporting these developments to Coke. He was at Harrogate when the news reached him, devoting himself to the completion of his *History of the West Indies*, a task which he was quick to lay aside. 'By this day's post', he wrote on 7th February 1808, 'I received intelligence that the Government of Jamaica is determined to crush our work entirely . . . I have written to the Committee in London, to inform them of these particulars; & have promised that, if they judge it expedient, I will hasten on to London as fast as we can.'[1] The next few days were a period of unavoidable inactivity, which to Coke was more galling than the most feverish bustle. 'Tho' I bless God, I enjoy constant peace in him, and under his sweet peace with the precious partner of my life, this business is continually as it were, before me. I would not, for the world and all that is in it, that our work in Jamaica, which makes half our field of action in the West Indies, should be

[1] Letter to R. C. Brackenbury, 7th February 1808 (Wesley's Chapel, London).

entirely shut up. I think I should not forgive myself for life, if anything was undone that might prevent the success of that business, which I could possibly do by night or by day.'[1]

By the end of February he was back in London. Petitions were quickly prepared and presented to the Privy Council, reinforced by the usual lobbying of influential persons.[2] Official action was considerably delayed by the fact that the government was not notified of the new act by the Jamaican authorities until the last possible moment. However, in the spring of the following year, redress was at last obtained, and Coke sent out a circular letter to the preachers in the British Connexion, giving them the news. 'I have the pleasure of informing you,' he wrote, 'that on last Wednesday His Majesty in Council, was graciously pleased to disavow (or repeal) the dreadful persecuting Law, passed in Jamaica last December twelvemonth. By that Law about four or five hundred thousand of the human race were debarred from all means of instruction; among whom were about thirteen or fourteen hundred of our own Society. This fresh instance of the liberal and tolerating Spirit of our Government should, *if it be possible*, still more attach us to our good King and his Government.'[3]

The preachers in Jamaica were thus afforded the protection of the Toleration Act; but before the full benefit of this victory could be felt, further trouble was caused by the ill-advised action of two of the missionaries there. Although they had been licensed before leaving England, they applied for licences to the hostile Jamaican magistrates and were persuaded to subscribe to a document which, by implication, condemned the actions of their predecessors. Coke was deeply disturbed, but for once his concern was less for the preachers involved than for the half-million West Indian Negroes whose spiritual welfare he considered to be jeopardized by their folly.[4]

* * *

[1] Letter to Robert Lomas, 10th February 1808 (M.M.S. Archives).
[2] See letter to Thomas Allen, solicitor to the Committee of Privileges, 22nd April 1808 (Archives Centre).
[3] Printed letter of 28th April 1809 (Copy in W.H.S. Library).
[4] See letters to Robert Johnson and the Missionary Committee, 29th and 30th November 1809 (M.M.S. Archives). The two offending missionaries were George Johnston and John Wiggins. Coke pleaded for Isaac Bradnock to be sent in their place as 'a man of solid sense' and 'greatly esteemed by the magistrates of Jamaica'.

In March 1808, at the height of the trouble in Jamaica, Coke wrote in a letter to Ezekiel Cooper, 'O what a blessing it is to be in a country where there is no danger of persecution'.[1] But only three years later, such a danger materialized in England itself in the shape of a bill introduced into the Lords by Lord Sidmouth with the intention of clarifying and amending the Toleration Act, upon whose protection the Methodists, had come to rely. This was the most serious threat to their religious liberties that the Methodists had encountered, and the Committee of Privileges was quickly alerted.

There was, however, a division of opinion within the Committee, and the initiative in opposing the Bill came, in this case, not from Coke but from its two most prominent lay members, Thomas Allan and Joseph Butterworth.[2] Lord Sidmouth had taken the precaution of granting an interview to Coke and Adam Clarke, in which he succeeded in convincing them that he had the good of the Methodists at heart.[3] Their suspicions were allayed by his claim to have the support of none other than Wilberforce himself. Wilberforce later protested against this false claim and complained at the readiness of the Methodists to credit it, despite his championship of their cause on similar occasions in the past.[4] Coke was certainly disposed to accept the fact of Wilberforce's complicity. 'From accounts sent to Suffolk and Norfolk by the Dissenting Committee in London,' he wrote, 'there is reason to fear *that Mr. Wilberforce has been much more active in Lord Sidmouth's business* than *we* imagined. He has used us *exceedingly* ill, you may depend upon it.'[5]

As soon as Sidmouth's real intentions became apparent to him, Coke threw himself without further hesitation into the opposition; the Methodist petition to the House of Commons bears unmistakable traces of his hand.[6] Public opinion among the Dissenters

[1] Letter to Ezekiel Cooper, 1st March 1808 (Garrett Theological Seminary).
[2] Maldwyn Edwards, *After Wesley*, pp. 77f.
[3] T. P. Bunting, *Life of Jabez Bunting*, 1887, p. 342.
[4] *Life of Wilberforce* by his sons, ii. 507ff. Wilberforce refers to Pitt's attempt in 1800 to limit the privileges of Dissenters by means of a bill which foreshadowed Lord Sidmouth's. On that occasion, too, Coke had been alerted (see his letter to Dundas, 10th February 1800 [Archives Centre]).
[5] Letter to George Highfield, 20th June 1811 (M.M.S. Archives).
[6] A draft of the petition, now in the Archives Centre, is in Coke's hand, and his influence is particularly clear in the passage pointing out that the Act would lead to widespread disaffection among otherwise loyal Protestants at a time of national danger.

generally had by now been mobilized so successfully that on 11th May, after its second reading, the Bill was dropped. This was not, however, quite the end of the story. The very strength and success of the dissenting opposition alarmed many friends of the Establishment, and an attempt was now made to effect through the magistrates' courts what had failed to pass through the legislature.

By means of a new interpretation of the Toleration Act, coupled with the revival of such obsolete penal legislation as the Conventicle Act, the Quarter Sessions began to refuse licences to any Methodist preacher who could not prove himself to be the pastor of one particular congregation. Coke was in the West Country in the early part of 1812, but kept in close touch with these developments, especially since they threatened to jeopardize the work he was initiating among the French prisoners-of-war.[1] He seems, at the same time, to have retained some impressions of Lord Sidmouth's good intentions towards the Methodists. 'I shall not be surprised', he wrote on February 13th, 'if Lord Sidmouth bring in another Bill. I am sure that his Lordship is sincerely afraid of being the cause of putting down the itinerancy. If you could assure yourselves that he had any such intention, perhaps you would do well to employ Dr Clarke to negotiate with Lord Sidmouth. I know that the Dr has the confidence of his Lordship. We cannot be worse off than we are at present. Parliament alone can relieve us, and if we thoroughly rouse the whole Church, we are undone.'[2] Thomas Coke was more easily convinced than most of his Methodist contemporaries of the sincerity and goodwill of the Government towards them; but then, he was able to move with comparative freedom in official circles to which they were strangers. At any rate, he was right about the possible means of redress for the Methodists in this instance, since it was through legislation securing the religious freedom of all Dissenters that the matter was finally settled in July 1812, early in the premiership of the Earl of Liverpool.

[1] Letter to George Highfield, 28th January 1812 (M.M.S. Archives).
[2] Letter to Highfield, 13th February 1812 (M.M.S. Archives).

CHAPTER 15

DIVIDED LOYALTIES

The chief problem in dealing adequately with Coke's life arises from the growing complexity of his activities. During the last decade of the century, he was busy in at least four different ways, and to consider each in turn is a necessary over-simplification of a tangled web of commitments. His part in the affairs of the British Connexion following Wesley's death has already been considered. But to ensure a true perspective, we must realize that he was simultaneously concerned with important developments in American Methodism, that he continued to sustain the overseas missionary work with very little assistance from others, and that he found time also to begin several important literary projects, including his commentary on the Bible. To each of these activities we must now turn.

When he took stock of the situation in British Methodism in the summer of 1791, Coke seriously thought of devoting the remainder of his life to America. Disappointment at the relatively minor role allotted to him in the refashioned Connexion may have played a part in this impulse. However, before the end of the year, he was clear in his own mind that for the present his place was still in Europe. 'I had some design of going over to you for good and all, as the German proverb is,' he told Ezekiel Cooper; 'but I now feel such a desire of being the happy instrument of spreading the Gospel in France, that I believe I shall never give up my labours there entirely to others.' In the same letter he speaks of the opportunities not only in France, but also in Sierra Leone and Nova Scotia; and always there were his responsibilities for the West Indian missions. So, although he planned to return to America for the next General Conference in the following year, Coke's prospect was already broadening and America could not yet hope to claim him.[1]

His fifth visit to the States, in the autumn of 1792, was a particularly short one. The voyage out was a pleasant respite from

[1] Letter to Ezekiel Cooper, 21st November 1791 (Garrett Theological Seminary).

the problems which engaged his attention at home. The company was agreeable and his quarters were unusually convenient, so that he was able to make full use of his enforced leisure. 'I find a ship a most convenient place for study: though it is sometimes great exercise to my feet, legs and arms, to keep myself steady to write. From the time I rise till bed-time, except during meals, I have the cabin-table to myself, and work at it incessantly. I never was accustomed to dream much till now; but I seem to be at my pleasing work even whilst I sleep.'[1]

He reached Baltimore just in time to snatch a few hours sleep before the Conference opened. This was the first of the regular quadrennial conferences; it lasted fifteen days and its main task was to deal with O'Kelly's challenge to Asbury's authority, particularly in stationing the preachers. Asbury was unwell and, as a party in the dispute, was glad to leave the chair to Coke. The latter had at an earlier stage shown some sympathy towards O'Kelly, perhaps because he too resented Asbury's monopoly of the stationing. But he now realized that O'Kelly was a serious threat to the unity of the Methodist Church. He says nothing of this urgent issue in his *Journal*, contenting himself with a general account of the spirit in which the sessions were held and praising the American preachers for their piety and zeal.[2]

Coke preached a Conference sermon on the Witness of the Spirit, which was afterwards published. During a visit to Philadephia, he found time to prepare a new edition of the *Discipline*. But his other commitments were already calling him away, and on 12th December he embarked at New York on a brig bound for the West Indies.

Coke was too busy elsewhere to return to America until the next General Conference in 1796, and the idea of settling there was for the time being crowded out. But in the autumn of 1796 he was again crossing the Atlantic, accompanied by a refugee from Revolutionary France, Pierre de Pontavice.[3] The voyage was probably the most wretched Coke ever experienced, largely as a result of the churlish attitude of the captain. By the time they made landfall, Coke was

---

[1] Coke's *Journal*, p. 182.   [2] Ibid., p. 186.

[3] Pontavice, a convert from Catholicism, was a native of Brittany. He was converted in Guernsey. References to him are sparse, but he probably continued to travel with Coke until he entered the itinerancy in 1800. (Letters to unknown recipient, 6th March 1796 (Emory University), to George Morley, 31st July 1798 (Wesley College, Bristol); Coke's *Journal*, pp. 248f; W. Toase, *Wesleyan Mission in France*, pp. 21-4; and obituary in 1811 *Minutes*).

growing anxious about his chances of reaching Baltimore in time for the Conference, but the captain placed every possible obstacle in his way, and it was with undisguised relief that he finally reached land. As he hastened on to Baltimore, the beauty of the autumn woods was a balm to his wounded spirits after nine weeks aboard ship, and he arrived with just two days to spare.

The important business which engaged the attention of this Conference included the organization of the Methodist Episcopal Church into six districts, each under the jurisdiction of an Annual Conference. It was also decided to produce an annotated edition of the *Discipline*, a task in which Coke and Asbury shared.[1] Coke's account of the Conference again concentrates on the spirit of the Conference, to the exclusion of any reference to specific issues:

On the 20th [October] our Conference commenced, which sat for a fortnight. All, was unity and love. There was not a jarring string among us. For two or three years past we have had a sifting time, after the great revivals with which we were so long and so wonderfully blessed. But in all I saw the hand of Providence. The preachers now seem to have a full view of the Scylla and Charybdis, the rocks and whirlpools, which lie on either hand; and are determined to avoid them. They are like the heart of one man. Surely this sweet and entire concord must be very pleasing to the Prince of Peace.[2]

The most urgent of all the matters that concerned this Conference was the need to strengthen the episcopacy, the burden of which was placing an increasing strain upon Asbury. A committee appointed to deal with this question was disbanded before it could produce any proposals. When the matter was debated in the open Conference, Coke was in the chair, but his opinion does not seem to have been sought, perhaps because it was felt that he still belonged more to the British than to the American Connexion. Asbury was asked to nominate a new bishop, but hesitated to make a choice, whereupon Coke requested that the business might be held over until the afternoon. He then produced this formal offer to devote himself to the American Connexion for what remained of his life:

I offer myself to my American brethren entirely to their service, all I am and have, with my talents and labours in every respect, without any mental reservation whatsoever, to labour among them and to assist Bishop Asbury; not to station the preachers at any time when he is present, but

[1] Candler, pp. 171f. Cf. Coke's *Journal*, p. 249.　　[2] Coke's *Journal*, p. 232.

to exercise all episcopal duties when I hold a Conference, in his absence and by his consent, and to visit the West Indies and France when there is an opening, and I can be spared.[1]

This offer was received with mixed feelings among his American brethren. A number of the preachers, notably Jesse Lee, opposed its acceptance on the grounds that Coke's loyalties and commitments lay in Europe rather than America, while there were several candidates among the American preachers. Asbury, however, intervened decisively in Coke's favour, arguing that to reject his offer would undermine his standing among the British Methodists; and after a two-day debate it was eventually accepted by all but a handful of the hundred preachers.[2] A memorable scene ensued. 'The Reverend Superintendent Asbury then reached out his hand in a pathetic speech, the purport of which was, "Our enemies said we were divided, but all past grievances were buried, and friends at first are friends at last, and I hope never to be divided". The Doctor took his right hand in token of submission, while many present were in tears of joy to see the happy union in the heads of department, and from a prospect of the Wesleyan episcopacy being likely to continue in regular succession.'[3] No other nomination was now considered necessary, and the Conference proceeded to draft a reply to the greetings which Coke had brought from the British Conference of that year.

Relations between the two bishops were not, however, so happy as the affecting scene just described would suggest; there were qualifications and misgivings on both sides. Shortly afterwards Asbury suggested a 'plan of operations' whereby they should divide the Connexion between them. Coke's domain was to be Albany, Vermont and New England, together with Philadelphia and New York. Coke wrote in retrospect:

I was astonished. I did not see in this plan anything which related in the least degree to my being a Coadjutor in the Episcopacy, or serving to strengthen it; though it was for that purpose, as the primary point, that it was thought eligible by the General Conference that I should reside for

[1] Minute book of the Baltimore Conference; copy entered under the date 1808.

[2] Candler, pp. 172ff., quoting an eye-witness account. Cf. Asbury's *Journal*, ii. 103.

[3] *Memoirs of Bishop Whatcoat*, by William Phoebus, quoted in Candler, pp. 175f.

life in America. Bishop Asbury was to hold the three Southern Conferences entirely by himself; & I was to spend my whole time *merely* as a
Preacher; & on a plan, upon which I should spend the chief part of my
time in preaching to very few. The Northern States would be covered
with snow. I should have Mountains of Snow to ride over, only to preach
in general (a few Towns excepted) to the Family where I was, and a few
of their neighbours. When Bishop Asbury retired, I fell on my face before
God, & said, 'O my God, what have I done?'[1]

Coke was nevertheless determined to stand by his undertaking,
but when the British Minutes arrived and it was learned that he
was appointed to preside once more over the Irish Conference, there
was general agreement that he should return to Europe to fulfil his
engagements and wind up his personal affairs. Coke proposed that
he should accompany Asbury to the three Southern Conferences,
before sailing for home. 'We accordingly went together; but to my
astonishment I was not consulted in the least degree imaginable concerning the station of a single Preacher. I did not expect or wish to
be anything more than a Chamber-Council, the ultimate decision in
everything still to remain with Bishop Asbury. In short, I neither
said nor did any thing during the whole tour which had any usefulness attending it, as far as I can judge, but preach.'[2] This resentment
at what seemed a deliberate attempt to circumscribe his episcopal
functions smouldered for some years.

While in Baltimore, Coke heard of the phoenix-like rise of
Cokesbury from the flames which had destroyed the original build-
ings. He and Asbury then set out on a tour which eventually
brought them to Charleston. The experience of preaching in one
village where there had been no public worship for twelve years was
a reminder of how inadequate were the provisions made for the
spiritual needs of the American people. From Charleston he sailed
for home on 6th February 1797. At the close of this sixth tour of
the States, he summed up his impressions thus: 'From all the
observations I have been able to make, I can perceive that the
inhabitants of the United States are verging rapidly into two grand
parties—real Christians and open Infidels. I confess, I have my
doubts, whether religion has gained ground or not on this Continent,
since my last visit. But of one thing I have no doubt—that *O'Kelly*

[1] Letter to the New York Annual Conference, 6th January 1806 (Drew
University).
[2] Ibid.

and his schismatic party have done unspeakable injury to the cause of God.'[1] Of his abhorrence of the very spirit of schism as a device of Satan he speaks more than once in the Journal of this tour,[2] though his mind may well have been dwelling on the English rebel, Kilham, as much as on his American counterpart.

Asbury seems to have had doubts about Coke's determination to settle in America, and therefore gave him this reminder on the eve of his departure:

When I consider the solemn offer you made of yourself to the General Conference, and their free and deliberate acceptance of you as their Episcopos, I must view you as most assuredly bound to this branch of the Methodist Episcopal Church in the United States of America. You cannot, you dare not but consider yourself as a servant of the church and a citizen of the continent of America. And although you may be called to Europe, to fulfill some prior engagements, and wind up your temporal affairs, nothing ought to prevent your hasty return to the continent, to live and die in America. I shall look upon you as violating your most solemn obligations if you delay your return.

If you are a man of a large mind, you will give up a few islands for a vast continent, not less that 1400 miles in length and 1000 miles in breadth. We have sixteen United States for ingress and regress, rising not like little settlements, but like large nations and kingdoms. I conclude, that I consider you are no longer a citizen of Wales or England, but of the United States of America.[3]

At the same time, Asbury still had misgivings about Coke's British citizenship, and later in the same year, aware of the frailty of his own health, wrote, 'I am sensibly assured the Americans ought to act as if they expected to lose me every day, and had no dependence upon Doctor Coke; taking prudent care not to place themselves at all under the controlling influence of British Methodists.'[4]

Coke's homeward voyage was very much more pleasant than the outward one had been, though they were threatened by a privateer as they neared the Irish Channel. When almost in sight of harbour, a prolonged calm brought out a strain of superstition in the captain. 'I was reading with deep attention', wrote Coke, 'a Folio-book on

[1] Coke's *Journal*, p. 249.   [2] E.g., Coke's *Journal*, pp. 239, 248, 249.

[3] Letter to Coke, 8th February 1797 (Asbury, *Letters*, pp. 157f.).

[4] Asbury, *Journal*, ii. 133 (23rd September 1797). The earlier part of the letter shows that Asbury had serious doubts whether Coke would return to America at all before the next General Conference.

the Bible. Frequently during the calms the Captain cried out, "I wish that book was finished." At last he burst forth, "We shall never have a wind, till that book is finished." I then told him, that I would lay the book aside. "No," said he, "that will not be sufficient. It must be finished, or we shall have no wind." I doubt not but he was in some measure confirmed in his opinion; for just as I had finished the book, the wind sprung up and in six and thirty hours brought us into harbour.'[1]

He landed at Greenock on 22nd March, 1797 and immediately set off on a short tour of Scottish Methodism. The religious condition of Scotland seemed to him deplorable, and he set it down to a combination of barren orthodoxy and Antinomianism, 'that bane of inward holiness'.

There was a time, when *Scotland* was the glory of all the Churches; but that time is passed. Speculative knowledge is the all in all among the generality of the Professors; whilst the Infidels who compose a very considerable part of the nation, beholding nothing in religion but a bare profession—nothing of that image of God, which is the only desirable thing in the universe—fly naturally to Deism for a refuge from hypocrisy. And who can be surprised? For what sensible man in the world can believe, that God would give his only-begotten Son to die upon a Cross, in order to make us *orthodox*?[2]

At the end of March he crossed from Port Patrick to Ireland which he found on the brink of further revolution.[3] Though still in the prime of life, at the age of 49, his youthful figure had given way to corpulence, so that he began to be aware of his years. Taken to Downpatrick by friends, he was persuaded to climb the tower of the newly-rebuilt cathedral. Though he enjoyed the view, it taught him a lesson. 'I felt that old age was creeping on me apace; for my limbs were so fatigued, as to feel the effects of it for several days.'[4]

Though fully aware of the many problems and difficulties which beset the European Connexion, Coke's thoughts were more with the American Methodists. As he toured the Irish societies, he took a solemn leave of each in turn, and of the preachers in their Conference. He was already making his arrangements to settle his practical

[1] Coke's *Journal*, p. 250. [2] Ibid., p. 251.
[3] Coke's *Journal*, p. 261. This is the only one of his many Irish tours of which any detailed account has survived.
[4] Ibid., p. 254. A few days later, remembering this experience, he refrained from climbing the tower at Armagh (Ibid., p. 258).

affairs. On 5th April, he wrote from Downpatrick to Thomas
Williams:

I have found it indispensably necessary to bring my long voyages across
the Atlantic to a conclusion, and for that purpose to determine on
which side of the Ocean to spend the remainder of my days. I have therefore after most mature consideration resolved in favour of the States of
America. It will therefore be necessary for me to settle my little affairs in
Europe as soon as possible, . . . Now I am going to take my leave of
Europe, I will inform you of my temporal circumstances: by the considerable sums which I have myself given from time to time in my zeal
for the preaching of the Gospel in the different parts of the world, I shall
not have now more of my fortune remaining, after settling all my affairs,
than the Coity Mortgage, if you except my library, which may be worth
two or three hundred pounds. You see therefore the necessity I am under
of taking that small sum over with me, notwithstanding I am conscious of
it that I shall have my travelling expenses borne in America. I might
according to the judgment of the world have done better in more respects
than one, but I have long consecrated all I am and have to God, and the
many thousands of poor heathens I have been the instrument of bringing
to Christ, infinitely more than compensate for all my losses and sufferings,
nor has the Lord left my ministry without success among professors of
Christianity in different parts of the world.[1]

'My engagements to our American Connexion', he added, 'are
irrevocable.'

Clearly, at this point Coke's mind was made up; but it was to be
remade for him over and over again in the next few years, during
which he experienced a kind of shuttlecock existence, striving in
vain to fulfil his obligations on both sides of the Atlantic. The
English Conference of 1797, meeting in Leeds, received the official
letter from the American General Conference and the news of Coke's
intentions with something approaching dismay, and perhaps a
measure of self-reproach. They hastened—belatedly as it has seemed
to some—to elect Coke to the Presidential Chair and addressed a
reply to their American brethren, begging that he be released from
his obligations, since the 'violent convulsions' which had disturbed
the British Connexion were still too recent for them to dispense with
his aid.

It is on this ground, that we much request the return of our friend and
brother, the Reverend Doctor Coke. He has often been a peace-maker

[1] Letter to Thomas Williams, 5th April 1797 (M.M.S. Archives).

amongst us, and we have frequently experienced the salutary effects of his advice and exertions in behalf of this part of the Connection. He has informed us of the engagements he has made to you. But you must spare him to us for a time, at least while these convulsions continue in our Societies, and the sooner you permit him to return, the greater will be the favour. In this we address you, as your elder brethren; and therefore we had almost said, we will not be denied: and if, when our affairs are in a settled state, he must return to you, to devote the remainder of his days to the work of God upon your continent, he shall return with our blessing and thanks. And at all events he shall visit you, if God preserve his life, at your next General Conference.[1]

We have already noted that this official eulogy of Coke as 'a man of peace' was not the unanimous view of the preachers. In fact, he was elected to the Presidency by one vote only, despite the fact that Samuel Bradburn, his chief rival, was also one of his strongest supporters. Bradburn found himself accused of seeking to raise himself on the shoulders of Coke. As Secretary of Conference for that year, he had drafted the official reply to the American Methodists. To those who later criticized its wording he replied that since it was printed in the *Minutes* exactly as read out in Conference, the accusations and insinuations were directed not at him personally so much as at the whole body. 'It is true', he told John Pritchard, 'I did what I could fairly to get the Doctor to be President, because I believed he deserved it, as a small reward for his labours and spending his money for the Missionaries; and because I believed he was well qualified for the office. And when I found that *my vote alone* had decided in his favour *against myself*, I was exceedingly pleased. But I verily believe the Dr intends to return to America, and has not a thought of being anything more among us after next Conference, at least I know and expect nothing else! . . . I confess I would rather he remained among us now, as I think he may be very useful. But which of you all ever talked to him as I did in times past? Not one soul of you! When I thought him wrong, I *told him so*. Now I think him right, *I love him* . . .'[2]

Asbury had not anticipated seeing Coke again before the spring of 1798, if at all before the next General Conference. But not long

[1] *Minutes*, i. 400f.; cf. *W.H.S. Proc.* x. 131. Coke told the New York Annual Conference in 1806 that the matter was raised four times before he could be prevailed upon to take over the letter.

[2] Letter from Bradburn to Pritchard, 17th March 1798 (*W.H.S. Proc.* x. 130ff.).

after the British Conference of 1797 was over Coke was once more on his way to America, bearing the official letter which requested that he be released from his American obligations. His arrival was delayed because the ship in which he sailed was captured by a French privateer; he and his fellow passengers lost all their possessions, and it was only by a stroke of good fortune that he was permitted to board another vessel bound for America, instead of being taken to Puerto Rico.[1]

The official letter of the British Conference was duly delivered at the Virginia Annual Conference towards the end of November, and an interim reply was formulated and signed by Asbury, who clearly suspected that his English brethren underestimated the urgent need for leaders of Coke's calibre in America. 'With respect to the Doctor's returning to us, I leave your enlarged understandings and good sense to judge. You will see the number of souls upon our Annual Minutes; and, as men of reading, you may judge over what a vast continent these Societies are scattered . . . The ordaining and stationing of the Preachers can only be performed by myself, in the Doctor's absence.'[2]

What Coke privately thought about this last sentence may be judged by his later protestation that he was still 'not consulted in the least degree whatever either in public or in private concerning the station of a single preacher, & had nothing . . . peculiarly useful to do, but to preach'. Nor was this all. 'What astonished me, I think I may say, almost above expression, was the following mysterious circumstance—Bishop Asbury was at that time so weak in body, that he could not reach Charleston in time to attend the Southern Conference, & therefore did not go. I offered my service, as it would have been equally the same for me to have sailed from Charleston as from New York. But he refused me, & appointed Brother Jackson to station the Preachers & Brother Jesse Lee to sit as Moderator in the Conference.'[3] Asbury seemed determined to make Coke's Superintendency a nominal one. It is little wonder that Coke should have had second thoughts about settling in America

---

[1] An extract from Coke's Journal, describing this voyage, was printed in the *Methodist Magazine*, 1814, pp. 125ff. The rest of his Journal of this visit is not extant, and little more is known of it. Extant correspondence shows that he was in New York by 6th December, and back in London by 26th February, 1798.

[2] *Minutes*, i. 429ff.

[3] Letter to the New York Conference: see p. 235, note 1.

and was hard pressed to reconcile Asbury's behaviour with what had transpired at the General Conference.

With the consent of the Virginia Conference, Coke returned home and during the next three years again busied himself with the affairs of the British Connexion and the missions. But he was still bound by his obligations to America, and in 1799 the British Conference once again urged 'that the work of God, and the good of the Church, considered at large, call for his continuance in Europe'. His responsibility for the West Indian and Irish missions was specifically mentioned in their letter to the American Conference which was once again delivered personally by Coke, during his eighth visit to America in 1800.[1]

The exchange of official courtesies had reached a point at which neither side was quite certain who was lending to whom. The reply of the General Conference in 1800, after referring to 'the critical state of Bishop Asbury's health, the extensions of our new work, our affection for and approbation of the Doctor, and his probable usefulness,' goes on to say, 'We have, therefore, in compliance with your request, *lent* the Doctor to you for a season, to return to us as soon as he conveniently can; but at farthest, by the meeting of our next General Conference'.[2] The same Conference, however, took another step which made Coke's residence in America rather less urgent a necessity. In view of Asbury's ill-health, it was decided that the time had come at last to appoint a third bishop, and after three ballots, Richard Whatcoat was elected. Though himself in poor health, Whatcoat was able to relieve Asbury of some of his burden during the next few years.

Coke's own feelings during this period are difficult to summarize. Even his solemn engagement could not reconcile him to the more restricted sphere of usefulness which Asbury appeared to have in mind for him. He was bound, moreover, by strong ties of affection to the Methodist preachers and people on both sides of the Atlantic, as well as to his 'poor blacks' of the West Indies. It is hardly

[1] Coke published no journal of this visit, so that we are dependent on incidental references in his correspondence etc. for information about it. Drew, p. 305 (cf. Asbury, *Letters*, p. 185 note), says that Coke sailed in 1799, but the headings of his letters at this period indicate that he embarked at Falmouth early in February 1800. (See especially his letter to Henry Dundas, from Falmouth Roads, 10th February 1800 [Archives Centre].) Nor did he, as stated by Etheridge, pp. 308, 310, visit the West Indies on the way.

[2] *Minutes*, ii. 197f.; Asbury, *Letters*, pp. 185ff.

surprising that he should vacillate in his loyalties and that he found it difficult to give himself exclusively to any one section of the widening field in which he laboured. His perplexity is reflected in a letter he wrote to Ezekiel Cooper in April 1798, soon after returning from America. 'Unless I am particularly wanted in America, I believe I shall spend the next winter in England, God willing, which will enable me to settle all my little affairs in this Country in the compleatest manner, so as to be ready to devote myself to the Service of my American Brethren: not but I shall be at any time ready at the call of those whose Servant for Jesu's sake I now particularly consider myself; I mean the Methodist Societies on your Continent.' Despite the solemn engagement into which he had entered at Baltimore two years before, he could not easily abandon the missions he had sponsored: 'In one respect it certainly was peculiarly providential that I returned to Europe; the Schism which has taken place, has so alarmed the Preachers, that the great work in the West Indies seemed to be almost forgot . . . But I am now endeavouring to set that whole Business on a solid basis, and if I can but succeed in this, my heart will be light indeed and truly joyful.'[1]

The Irish Methodists, too, had strong claims on his affections. 'I do love Ireland above all other places,' he wrote in 1800, 'and my Brethren the Irish Preachers especially . . . I sacrificed my important position in America for your sakes, and there is nothing gives me equal delight (Communion with God excepted) as serving my Irish Brethren.'[2]

After the turn of the century, his time and attention were taken up more and more with his Commentary; yet, at the same time, his thoughts were once more turning to America. 'I am yours,' became almost a refrain, as in one letter after another to his friends among the American preachers, he reiterated the idea of eventually settling among them. 'In America only I consider myself at home. I have been kept abroad [i.e. from the United States] for several years past by the will of God. However, I shall endeavour to wind every thing round, so that, if the Lord will but suffer me, I may close my Career among you. Hitherto I have been kept from residing among you, I doubt not, by the will of Heaven. But I do assure you, it

[1] Letter to Cooper, 21st April 1798 (Garrett Theological Seminary).
[2] Letter to Thomas Barber, 7th August 1800 (*W.H.S. Proc.* ii. 205f.; the original at Wesley College, Bristol).

would be my supreme earthly delight, if I know my own heart, to hide myself in your woods and labour and dwell among you.'[1] Again, 'I . . . consider my solemn offer of myself to you at the General Conference before the last, to be as binding on me now as when first made; and nothing shall keep me from a final residence with you, . . . but such an interference of Divine Providence as does not at present exist, and such as shall convince the General Conference, that I ought to tear myself from you.'[2]

Coke was aware that America was a country of potential greatness and, as he contemplated its future, did not doubt the importance of the Christian gospel to its growing population. In subsequent letters to several of the Annual Conferences, he wrote: 'I love the cause in America. I saw how wonderfully God owned the work under the present form of things. I considered your continent as making about a third part of the globe; that in time, under the Blessing of God, it will be fully peopled, and with people chiefly speaking the English Language.'[3]

Asbury's attitude to Coke's superintendency was certainly equivocal. The sincerity of their mutual affection and admiration is not in question. But for Asbury, who had identified himself so unreservedly with the American people, the ties which still bound his fellow-bishop to Europe were a real stumbling-block to their full co-operation. Quite apart from the political factors involved, Asbury felt towards the American Connexion as paternally posses-sive as did Coke towards the West Indian missions. In 1804 he wrote to George Roberts, 'I am deeply sensible that neither Dr Coke nor any other person can render me any essential services in the Annual Conferences, . . . unless they will take the whole work out of my hands.'[4] He could not lightly relinquish an authority which he

[1] Letter sent to George Roberts, James Moore and probably other American preachers, 28th February 1801 (Drew University).

[2] Letter sent to a number of the American preachers and variously dated 25th and 26th February, and 6th March 1802 (copies at Boston and Drew Universities, Garrett Theological Seminary, the Pennsylvania Historical Society and Baltimore Historical Society).

[3] Letter to the Baltimore and Philadelphia Annual Conferences, 6th January 1807 (Garrett Theological Seminary and Old St George's Church, Philadelphia). The text of these letters is substantially identical with the letter to the New York Conference (see p. 235, note 1), the chief variants, of which this is one, occurring at the end.

[4] Asbury, *Letters*, p. 274. A letter to Alexander M'Caine later in 1804, after Coke had sailed for home, strongly suggests that Asbury suspected Coke of

exercised in so personal a manner to one who was by comparison a bird of passage and a stranger in their midst, although an honoured one. Admitting that Coke was 'better fitted for the whirl of public life than to be hidden in our woods', he told Daniel Hitt, 'If I must bear the burden now laid upon me, I can call forth men of our own to help me, in or out of conference, men that know men and things by long experience.'[1] As the years passed, Coke inevitably became aware of the attempt to clip his wings. During his brief visits to the States he had no opportunity of effectively exercising his episcopal authority; he was still a figure-head, and a valued link between the two Connexions, but if he was to devote himself entirely to the American work, this was not enough. When matters finally came to a head, after his ninth and last visit in 1804, his pent-up resentment and frustration could no longer be contained.

Before he set sail in the autumn of 1803, the British Conference again reiterated its request for Coke's return, because of 'the state of our several Missions, and various other very forcible reasons that might be mentioned'.[2] Coke had warned the Conference that, in view of his American engagement, they might well never see him again, and he wrote shortly afterwards to Ezekiel Cooper, 'The Lord has opened my way wonderfully & clearly (I was going to say, that he has written it on my mind as with a Sunbeam) to be wholly yours.' The main obstacle to his settling in America seemed at last to have been removed: 'He has endued the British Conference with the true Missionary Spirit: & they can & will support the West India Missions, God willing, with ease. I am now going to spend the remainder of my days with you.'[3] On reaching Virginia, he wrote in similar vein to Bishop Whatcoat, adding, 'Every shackle, every engagement, every obligation, in Europe, has been loosed or discharged'.[4]

---

wanting to oust him from his unique position in the American Church: 'I should not wonder if he should be upon the continent in less than a year. And I know not how soon death may put me out of his way. Some are bold to say, I am the only person in his way.' (Ibid., p. 301.) Was Asbury perhaps recalling Coke's approach to the Episcopalians in 1791?

[1] Letter from Asbury to Daniel Hitt, 21st January 1804 (Asbury, *Letters*, p. 276).
[2] *Minutes*, ii. 198f.
[3] Letter to Ezekiel Cooper, 29th August 1803 (Garrett Theological Seminary).
[4] Letter to Bishop Whatcoat, from Petersburg, 2nd November 1803 (Historical Society of Pennsylvania).

Nevertheless, the ambiguity of Asbury's intentions continued to exercise Coke's mind, and another letter written just before he set sail, reveals that he still had reservations about devoting himself entirely to America. By reaching the States in the autumn, he said, he would have five or six months in which to visit the principal societies and so determine whether or not it was God's will that he should settle there. 'I am persuaded that God will make my way plain before me: and I consider my engagement to my brethren at the late Manchester Conference binding—that nothing but an indubitable assurance that the will of God requires me to continue there [in America] shall prevent my return.'[1] It is difficult to reconcile the various statements made in these letters. Clearly, his mind was still far from made up, and the conflict of loyalties remained unresolved when he sailed for America.

We know very little of this last American visit, since no detailed journal has survived. He embarked at Gravesend about 21st September[2] and landed in Norfolk, Virginia at the end of October, 'after an agreeable passage from land to land of 29 days'.[3] Quite apart from the impending General Conference, his arrival was opportune. The work was developing in Canada and spreading into the new state of Ohio. But Whatcoat was ill, and Asbury himself could sometimes scarcely mount his horse because of his rheumatism. His fellow-bishop was therefore agreeably surprised at Coke's speedy arrival in the States, and wrote proposing to him a tour of nearly 5,000 miles, which would have occupied him for about nine months. This did not chime with Coke's own intentions. He had plans for a short northern tour, but hoped first to put the finishing touches to the Commentary on which he had so long been working. However, he had a sudden conviction that he ought to go south to meet Asbury at the Georgia Conference. 'The impression made on my mind by this thought', he wrote, 'completely robbed me of a night's rest', and he accordingly set out. The sequel, as he related it in 1806 in his letter to the New York Conference, was an unhappy

[1] Letter to Francis Wrigley, September 1803 (Archives Centre). Cf. letter to Alex. Sturgeon, one of the Irish preachers, written at the same time and now in the possession of the Irish Branch of the W.H.S.

[2] Letter of Jabez Bunting, 19th October 1803 (W.H.S. Irish Branch). Cf. note dated 29th October 1803 on the letter of Coke to Wrigley in note 1 above.

[3] Letter from Petersburg (recipient unknown), 14th November 1803 (Baltimore Methodist Historical Society). Cf. letter to Whatcoat (p. 244, note 4).

one; his work as a bishop was again so grievously hampered that it seemed pointless for him to be in America at all.

So far from my having any opportunity of strengthening the Episcopacy, . . . I was not to be consulted on the station of a single Preacher: nay, when I asked for a copy of the Stations of the Preachers at the close of the Georgia Conference, which was granted to every Travelling Preacher present, I was refused. I then saw the will of God concerning me—that I ought not to labour in America, unless the General Conference would consent to comply in some degree with its engagements. I did not want to station the Preachers as Bishop Asbury does. Nothing should be done to grieve that venerable Man . . . But every Bishop ought to have a right of giving his judgment on every point, or he is but the shadow of a Bishop.[1]

Later he and Asbury had a frank exchange, in which Coke reminded the other of his extensive responsibilities in the European Connexion. Besides these, he added, 'In Europe, I have incomparably more time for literary matters, than I could have in the United States. In respect to Preaching, I can preach in the year to three or four times the number of People I could preach to in the United States . . .' In view of this, he was reluctant to remain in America as 'a *mere* Preacher'.[2]

Though it was agreed between them that Coke should after all return to England, at Asbury's request he did set out on a tour of New England, though regretting that this would prevent his attending the Virginia and Alexandria Conferences.[3] His route cannot be reconstructed in detail, but it is clear that he worked his way north from Charleston at least as far as Boston.[4] While in New England, he visited Rhode Island, preaching among other places in Providence and Bristol.[5] A more important occasion was undoubtedly that on which he preached before the Congress in Washington on 'the wisdom, dignity, and importance of the gospel, as contrasted with the spirit of the world,'[6]—a worthy climax to his long series of American visits. The possibility of a mission to France was still in his mind, and the Vice President offered to provide him with letters

[1] Letter to the New York Conference (see p. 235, note 1); cf. Asbury, *Journal*, ii. 418, 421.

[2] Ibid.   [3] Ibid.

[4] Asbury, *Letters*, pp. 273f., 276f., 282; also *Journal*, ii. 421, *Methodist Magazine*, 1804, pp. 330ff.

[5] Asbury, *Journal*, i. 681, ii. 347.   [6] Drew, p. 316.

of commendation to the French government, including one from President Jefferson to Napoleon himself.[1] But this offer does not seem to have been taken up.

The General Conference, meeting at Baltimore in May, once again agreed that Coke should return to England, so long as he undertook to respond to the call of three of the Annual Conferences, or to return in 1808 for the next General Conference. He played a leading part in revising the Book of Discipline clause by clause, and at his suggestion it was separated into two parts dealing with doctrine and 'discipline' respectively. Soon afterwards he left the New World for the ninth and last time, protesting that he found himself 'perfectly attached' to America and 'weaned from every other', and proposing to return in three years' time.[2] But by now it was clear that Asbury was not prepared to relinquish to the little Welshman any of his episcopal authority over the American Methodists; and in the light of that, Coke could not reconcile himself to the prospect of abandoning his 'usefulness' in Europe to become a 'mere preacher' in the American backwoods. The prospect of ever settling in America was fading from his mind, though he could not foresee the turn of events which would finally settle the matter for him.

[1] Letter from Zachary Myles to his brother, 29th March 1804 (*Methodist Magazine*, 1804, pp. 331f.).

[2] Letters to the Rev. Mr Kibby of Boston, 28th and 30th May 1804 (New England Methodist Historical Society).

CHAPTER 16

THE MARRIAGE OF TRUE MINDS

Less than twelve months after the close of his ninth American tour, Thomas Coke took a step which was to prevent him from paying any further visit in the last few years of his life. In the spring of 1805, a bachelor of 57, he married Miss Penelope Goulding Smith of Bradford-on-Avon. This step did not lead to any settled domesticity, but it did set limits on his wanderings.

Of a naturally sociable disposition, Coke had remained so long a bachelor not by conviction but by force of circumstances. His peripatetic existence ever since he left South Petherton left little room for the virtues and comforts of home life. Had he married earlier, the course of his career in the service of Methodism must inevitably have been drastically modified. One tantalizing allusion in a letter from John to Charles Wesley in 1783 suggests that a suitable match was then in the air. 'I am in hope T.M. will satisfy Dr Coke,' Wesley wrote. 'I suppose she loses her annuity if she owns her marriage.'[1] But no marriage took place; and both the identity of 'T.M.' and the reasons for her failure to 'satisfy' Dr Coke remain a mystery.

So Coke went on his way unfettered; but Asbury rightly divined that, despite the long years of celibacy to which his itinerant ministry had condemned him, Coke was 'the marrying sort'. And when marriage did come, Asbury claimed to have had some premonition of it. 'I told Brother Whatcoat at the General Conference 1800 the Doctor I thought would marry. I have told him since I expect to hear he was married.'[2] One difference between the two bishops was in their attitude towards a married ministry. Coke deplored as much as Asbury the constant loss to the American itinerancy of preachers forced to 'locate' because of their family responsibilities. But whereas Asbury advocated a celibate ministry, Coke's solution was more adequate provision for preachers' families.

[1] *Letters of John Wesley*, vii. 177.   [2] Asbury, *Letters*, pp. 322f.

248

The problem had especially exercised his mind during his visit in 1797, when he wrote in his *Journal*, 'It is most lamentable to see so many of our able married preachers . . . become located merely for want of support for their families . . . I am truly astonished, that the work has risen to its present height on this continent, when so much of the spirit of prophecy, of the gifts of preaching . . . should thus miserably be thrown away.'[1] He was not, however, content to deplore the situation, but himself took a first tentative step towards its solution, by offering to find £60 a year to support the families of three of the married preachers, in the hope that the General Conference might be persuaded to take more effective steps to deal with the problem.[2] 'I continually bemoan that great deficiency among you—*the want of support for a Married Ministry,*' he wrote. 'I have known America for fourteen years, and when I consider what a number of holy, experienced, zealous, able Men have been cast aside, & rendered comparatively useless through this great Evil, I am sometimes grieved above measure.'[3]

Penelope Goulding Smith was the daughter of a well-to-do solicitor from whom she had inherited a substantial fortune.

They met in the autumn of 1804 in Bristol, where Coke was, as usual, busily soliciting support for the missions. When he called on her in Bradford shortly afterwards, he found her promised subscription doubled, an indication perhaps that the lady was not loth to be wooed. The strength of Coke's own feelings may be gauged by the very reticence of his earliest allusions to her; writing to the Missionary Committee on 1st November, he told them that 'a lady, whose name, I think, I am not at liberty to mention just at present at least . . . has promised me *one hundred guineas* for the missions, to be paid in a fortnight or three weeks' time'.[4] On 3rd December, she is still no more than 'the generous individual who promised me [a hundred guineas] for the Missions';[5] and not until he forwarded the

[1] Coke, *Journal*, p. 242; cf pp. 244, 246.
[2] Letters to Ezekiel Cooper, 6th December 1797, 18th December 1798, and 12th January 1799 (Garrett Theological Seminary). Coke made similar provision for married preachers in the British provinces. (Letter to Joshua Marsden, 31st August 1804 (M.M.S. Archives): 'I informed Brother [William] Black that I would allow you £15 pr. ann. if you married, & wanted it . . .')
[3] Letter to Cooper, 12th January, 1799 (Garrett Theological Seminary).
[4] Letter to Entwisle and the Missionary Committee, 1st November 1804 (M.M.S. Archives).
[5] Letter to Robert Lomas, 3rd December 1804 (M.M.S. Archives).

second hundred guineas on 16th January did he reveal her identity.[1] Of the strength of his passionate attachment to the lady, however, there can be no doubt. His affectionate nature, so long inhibited by the circumstances of his itinerant life, suddenly flowered in a belated but exuberant spring. Mercifully, only one fragment of their correspondence during the few months of their courtship has survived, in which, addressing his 'Most dear of all created Beings', he writes, 'O my love, I do love you with an ardent increasing unabated and never diminishing love, and it is a great addition to my happiness that I am fully assured that we shall be with each other and love each other to all eternity. [2]

Coke appears to have said nothing of his intention to marry in his correspondence with the Committee during the early weeks of 1805, beyond an almost curt denial of the rumour that he was already married.[3] But on 5th April, four days after the wedding, he wrote from Ashburton to Charles Atmore:

My very dear Friend,
I have the pleasure of informing my highly esteemed Friend Atmore, who I know will rejoice at any addition to my felicity, that last Monday I was married to my most beloved Penelope Smith, of Bradford, Wilts; passing through perhaps 1500 spectators, who in spite of the Sexton broke into the Church like a Torrent. Mr Thos. Roberts gave her to me according to ye ceremony. On our Wedding-day we set off on *her* first pilgrimage, to Plymouth Dock: the second will be, God willing, Bristol: the third, London: the fourth, Dublin: the fifth, Sheffield. My dear Atmore, I am almost too happy in the possession of my God & my Penelope.[4]

In similar vein he wrote to Jabez Bunting: 'We love each other as much as I think two created Beings ought—I was almost going to

[1] Letter to Lomas, 16th January 1805 (M.M.S. Archives).

[2] Undated letter to Miss Penelope Smith (Archives Centre). Those with a taste for indulging in romantic passion at second-hand are referred to another letter, written two years after their marriage, the original of which is in the possession of the Baltimore Methodist Historical Society.

[3] Letter to Lomas, 12th February 1805 (M.M.S. Archives). In letters to Lomas and Entwisle on 2nd March, he studiously avoided the subject of his matrimonial intentions.

[4] Letter to Charles Atmore, 5th April 1805 (Garrett Theological Seminary). Thomas Roberts was a close friend of Coke's. He left an account of his tour with Coke through the West Country in the early part of 1805. (Buckley, *Memoir of Thomas Roberts*, pp. 53f., 73ff.) He was one of Coke's executors and published a memorial sermon on his death.

say *can*.'[1] Next day he sent the news to his old friends at Raithby Hall, requesting that Mrs Brackenbury should write to 'his Penelope', and adding, 'She is really all the world to me. But it is almost impossible to be with her, and not to be more holy, & more zealous for God'.[2]

Penelope Coke fully reciprocated these elevated sentiments, and recorded their marriage in her diary in these terms: '*Monday, 1st April*, 1805. My most beloved brother in Christ, Dr Coke, and myself, being clearly and fully convinced, it was our gracious God's holy will and pleasure, for us to be united; and being fully and entirely satisfied, that we could lay ourselves out much more for the glory of God, and live in a greater degree of devotedness to him in the married than in the single state; . . . we presented ourselves before him, made a solemn surrender of ourselves before him, and under him to each other, and were solemnly married in the Lord this morning: our God condescended to be very graciously present with us . . .'[3]

John Pawson, who had first introduced the happy couple to each other at Clifton, described the bride as 'a deeply pious, simple-hearted woman' who dressed 'quite plain'. 'They made a great show at the wedding,' he told Atmore. 'There were five chariots all the way to the Church. They then came to Bath and dined at an inn. After dinner the doctor and his dearly beloved Penelopy went to an Inn called the Old Down and lodged there; and the next day set forward for Plymouth Dock.'[4] Such was the nature of their 'honeymoon': their travels began on the very day of their marriage and in the first six weeks of married life they covered 400 miles.[5] Rather than be parted for long periods, she undertook to accompany him on his extensive tours, even to Ireland; for though she was far from robust, it was agreed between them from the outset that their marriage should not hinder Coke's work. Pawson reported, 'She intends to travel with him everywhere, even to America. But what will Bishop Asbury say to the doctor now? I doubt the union will be dissolved. I think the doctor has lived so long single that he will feel himself in an odd situation, having a wife by his side. But as Mr

[1] Letter to Samuel Bradburn, 5th April, 1805 (copy at Archives Centre).

[2] Letter to Robert Carr Brackenbury, 6th April 1805 (Wesley's Chapel, London).

[3] Quoted by Drew, pp. 319f.

[4] Letter from Pawson to Charles Atmore, 3rd April 1805 (Archives Centre).

[5] Printed letter to the American preachers, 1st June 1805 (Asbury, *Letters*, pp. 318ff.).

Wesley used pleasantly to say, "We need not wonder at anything of this kind, for it is what we must all come to, as the old woman said." '[1]

Two or three years after their marriage, Coke told Asbury that they were 'continually on the wing' and had 'no home but God';[2] and he was able to claim, 'We are always . . . travelling, and I annually visit and preach at more places than I did for many years before my marriage.'[3] Coke was tireless in his solicitude for her well-being, but could do no more than mitigate the considerable hardship and discomfort of travel at that time. His earliest biographer has given an engaging picture of their domestic economy:

The Doctor now bought a plain carriage, in which they took their routes; but he did not encumber himself with either horses or servants.— He hired post-horses and drivers at the different stages. There was something singularly striking in the appearance of this couple when together.— She was remarkably fond of the Doctor, and constantly manifested this; while he did everything in his power to accommodate and serve her . . . They did not, indeed, appear to have the most convenient method of packing up their luggage. A great deal of this was tied up in separate handkerchiefs; and the vast quantities of these little packages would sometimes occasion an innocent smile, and a pleasant remark by the spectators, at the times of loading and unloading. Sometimes a considerable pile of these things was with them in the carriage. This, however, did not prevent them from labouring to do good even while the carriage was in motion. Quantities of religious pamphlets came flying out of the windows of their chariot, on the roads and in the streets, when they saw persons who were likely to gather them up and read them.[4]

In such a fashion did the Cokes travel throughout the British Connexion during the next five years, almost as ceaselessly and extensively as Coke himself had done while a bachelor. We may smile at the quaintness of Crowther's picture, but it should not blind us to the heroic devotion which lay behind Penelope Coke's acceptance of such a vagrant life. Although in her middle forties and in

[1] See p. 251 note 4.
[2] Letter to Asbury, 3rd February 1808 (Paine, *Life of McKendree*, i. 237ff.).
[3] Letter to the General American Conference, 16th November 1807 (Asbury, *Letters*, pp. 374ff.).
[4] Crowther, p. 491. In a letter to Lomas, 13th October 1806, Coke confirms one detail of this account: 'My dearest wife . . . is leavening me the land with practical tracts. Hardly a man or woman, on the roads or in the streets, is suffered to pass without a tract, except it rains.' (M.M.S. Archives).

indifferent health, she wholeheartedly threw in her lot with her husband. The home at Bradford was soon sold up, a large portion of the proceeds going to support the missions; and henceforth she too became a sojourner and pilgrim, with no abiding place other than the carriage in which they travelled and the homes in which they were entertained. Not even Coke's vigilant concern for his wife's well-being could prevent its being an existence fraught with insecurity. In October 1806 they arrived unheralded in Taunton at the time of the Quarter Sessions, intending to stay over the weekend. 'We went from inn to inn (it was dark) but no inn could supply us even with a chamber, they were so full. I had received letters from Mr Wilshaw and Mr Lackington, but no one said in them, or when we were last in Taunton, we have a bed or lodging at your service, and my dearest wife can on no account get over her delicate feelings to go to a private House at once, where there has been no invitation given even directly—unless I had been published [to preach]; then she would have consented to my rummaging about among the private houses. So we set off another stage in a pitch dark night without lighted lamps.'[1] To her unfailing cheerfulness in affliction, Coke himself bore witness. A particularly stormy crossing of the Irish Sea in 1809 brought on a prolonged fever, from which she never fully recovered. Towards the end of 1810, the symptoms of dropsy were added to her other ailments, and she became almost incapable of walking, even with assistance. Her death on 25th January 1811, after a sudden relapse, ended their brief but happy partnership in a cause to which they were equally devoted.[2]

His marriage inevitably modified Coke's plans for further visits to America. Not that he immediately abandoned the possibility of another voyage across the Atlantic; but he realized that, for the sake of his wife's health, if they came at all, it must be for life. That is the gist of what he wrote to Bishops Asbury and Whatcoat in telling them his news. His letter to Whatcoat reads:

Very dear Friend,
        Before you receive this Letter, you will probably hear of my marriage, & will naturally say 'We shall never see him more in this world'. I'll tell you my heart. I consider my engagements in respect to the *American Episcopacy* as binding as ever. But I believe I shall make you no

[1] Letter to Lomas, 13th October 1806 (M.M.S. Archives).
[2] Coke's memoir of his first wife was published in the *Methodist Magazine*, 1812, pp. 120ff, 211ff. Cf. Stevenson, *City Road Chapel*, pp. 178f.

more *transitory* visits. If I come at all, it will be for my life. My most beloved Penelope (that is my Wife's Christian name) is as much a Pilgrim, & breathes as much of the spirit of a genuine Christian Pilgrim, as myself. I may take my flight to Heaven before either you or Bishop Asbury. If Bishop Asbury were to die before me, I should think it an unanswerable call to leave Europe. But I have not a wish to divide or limit his labours. However, if I cross the Atlantic during his Life, it will be necessary for the plan of our Episcopal labours to be fixed *on a most permanent & unalterable basis*. I bless God, I am better in soul, body & spirit than I was before my marriage. If ever we come to the United States, we shall be no burden to the Societies. Pray for me & my blessed Companion.[1]

The news provoked Asbury's famous comment on the married state: 'Marriage is honourable in all—but to me it is a ceremony awful as death'.[2]

Two months after his marriage, Coke sent a printed circular letter to each of the preachers in the American Connexion, setting out his intentions in fuller detail. His 'solemn engagement' of 1796 he still considered binding upon him: its fulfilment had merely been delayed by a series of unforeseen circumstances. He and his wife were of one mind in this matter; she would go with him anywhere, even through fire and water, to do the will of God. 'She is indeed a twin soul to myself. Never, I think, was there a more perfect congeniality between two human beings, than between us.' But out of consideration for her health and feelings, another transitory visit to the States was out of the question; and if they were to come for life, it must be 'under the most express, permanent and unalterable conditions'. Coke had learned from his experience, and was no longer willing to sacrifice his position in British Methodism in order to exercise limited or ill-defined functions in America. In the case of Asbury's death, he considered it would be his duty to sail without delay, in order to maintain the episcopacy. Otherwise, he would settle among them only if Asbury were no longer able to attend all the annual conferences in person, and then 'on the express condition that the seven Conferences should be divided betwixt us, three and four, and four and three, each of us changing our division annually'. On these terms, he undertook that he would immediately set out in answer to their summons. 'Nothing in that case shall detain me in

[1] Letter to Whatcoat, 1st May 1805 (Garrett Theological Seminary). The letter to Asbury was similar in contents, as may be inferred from references in his *Journal*, ii. 474 and *Letters*, p. 322.
[2] Asbury's *Journal*, ii. 474.

Europe for a moment after I have settled my affairs, but such an illness of my wife's or my own part, as will absolutely incapacitate her
or me from going on ship-board: for I can be no means leave her
behind me.'[1]

A reply to this letter was sent by the preachers of the New York
Conference, rejecting the conditions with which Coke now sought to
hedge the offer of himself to America. This in its turn produced from
Coke early in 1806 a lengthy exercise in self-defence from which we
have already quoted extensively. He was constrained to withdraw his
circular letter, since the conditions he had laid down in it had been
no part of their previous agreement. (It should be remembered, however, that the idea of dividing the Connexion between them had
originated with Asbury, in 1796.) But he was now more adamant than
ever that he was under no obligation to settle among them as 'a mere
preacher'. 'Am I to come to you in any sense as a Bishop, & in what
sense? I don't wish to act, if I come, but in perfect subordination to
the General Conference, but yet still as a Bishop, & having a right to
give my judgment in all Episcopal matters, unless I render myself
unworthy of the office.'[2]

During the spring and summer of 1806, each of the annual conferences in turn followed the lead of the Maryland Conference in
answering Coke's letter by a firm refusal to summon him back to
America on the terms he demanded.[3] Asbury's influence had triumphed. 'Dr Coke has made proposals', he wrote, 'to serve the connexion on a *different ground*, the conferences, all that have heard,
have rejected the Doctor's letter, . . . Nothing is hidden.'[4] But in
the very moment of triumph, to soften the blow, he wrote an affectionate letter reminding Coke of their long-standing comradeship
and the hardships they had endured together. 'Ah my brother, the
deep rivers, creeks, swamps and deserts we have travelled together,
and glad to find a light to hear the voice of human, or domestick

[1] See p. 251, note 5.
[2] Letter to the New York Conference, 6th January 1806 (Drew University).
In expanded form the letter was sent to the Baltimore and Philadelphia Conferences (Garrett Theological Seminary and Old St George's Church, Philadelphia)
in January 1807. Cf. also his letter to Alexander M'Caine, 8th February 1807
(Asbury, *Letters*, pp. 361f.).
[3] Asbury, *Journal*, ii. 498, 535. Paine, *Life of McKendree*, i. 242f. describes the
reply of the Baltimore Conference as 'unnecessarily and unjustly severe' in tone
and that of the Philadelphia Conference as much more mild and respectful.
[4] Asbury, *Letters*, p. 347; italics mine.

creature; the mountain rains, and chilling colds or burning heats, to say nothing of the perils of the deep. How often you have stemmed the flood, the vast Atlantic with Columbian courage . . . You have never', he concluded, 'had more undissembled friendship shown to you than in America.'[1]

A stalemate had now been reached in this exchange, and though the correspondence continued during the two years which remained before the General Conference of 1808, neither side had anything significant to add. Whatcoat's death in the summer of 1806 made very little difference, since he had for some time been too frail to take any real share of the episcopal burden. In November 1807 Coke wrote to the General Conference, explaining his absence and reiterating his position. He is still prepared, he says, to relinquish his situation in the European Connexion, though he prizes it highly; but he will do so only if they guarantee that he will be free to exercise his superintendency among them. 'I want no new condition. I only want to be perfectly ascertained, that if I reside with you, I shall be authorized by you to fulfil my office . . . without which our reciprocal engagements would be a perfect nullity . . . I want nothing but a full explanation, and a part of that liberty which I have in the European connexion.' Failing this, he is content to be set down in their Minutes in whatever way they think best, 'or if this be not agreeable', he concludes, 'you must expel me (for dropping me out of your public minutes will be to all intents and purposes an expulsion,) and leave what I have done for your connexion to God alone: and though you forget me, God will not forget me'.[2]

He wrote also to Ezekiel Cooper, charging him in the name of their long-standing friendship, to speak on his behalf at the Conference. 'I do not wish any arbitrary power, any individual decisive voice. I would not use it, if my Brethren gave it to me. On this ground I stand; & I am sure it is the will of God . . . I do not deserve to be treated severely by any of my American Brethren. But if instead of calling me in such a manner as will *enable* me to fulfil my engagements to them, they blot my name out of their printed minutes, it will not be blotted out of the Lamb's Book of Life.'[3] Coke had not forgotten the treatment meted out to Wesley years before.

The response of the General Conference to this cap-in-hand

[1] Letter to Coke, 7th May, 1806 (Asbury, *Letters*, pp. 342ff.).
[2] Letter to the General Conference (see p. 252, note 3.)
[3] Letter to Ezekiel Cooper, 1st March 1808 (Garrett Theological Seminary).

approach was to elect William McKendree to the episcopacy and to accede to the appeal from the British Conference that their 'worthy secretary' should be permitted to remain in Europe despite his American commitments. Two further resolutions were recorded: 'That we retain a grateful remembrance of the services and labors of Dr Coke among us . . .' and, 'That the Doctor's name, agreeably to his request, be retained in our minutes; but as he continues in Europe, his name shall stand last in the list of bishops, with a "N.B.—Doctor Coke resides in Europe, at the request of the British Conference, till he be called to the United States by the General Conference or by the Annual Conferences." During his residence there he shall exercise no episcopal authority whatever in the United States among us . . .'[1]

This firm, though courteous, refusal to have Coke on his own terms virtually severed his official connexion with American Methodism. The final separation was no less painful for having been long awaited. Soon after receiving the news, Coke wrote once more to Ezekiel Cooper:

I am fully satisfied with the determinations of the General Conference. Even the only paragraph which a little affected me at first reading, I fully approved of on cool reflection—that Dr Coke shall not superintend in these States, unless first called upon, &c. Tho' abstractedly considered, it was not necessary, as I never interfered in the smallest degree with the affairs of the American Connexion, when absent; yet it might be, & I believe it was, very expedient to mention it, lest it should be imagined for a moment by the American Government, that I interfered in any thing relating to your Country, while I was in a foreign Country.

I am fully determined to keep up a correspondence with several of my most beloved Brethren (tho' I do love them all, & almost daily pray for them all) in America.

Not even now, however, was he fully resigned to the idea of abandoning the superintendency bestowed upon him by Wesley. 'I will tell you my whole heart. The Lord does wonderfully preserve my most precious Wife & myself. We are always travelling. The Lord has been pleased to give us a competency; but we have no house which we can command. Now, if judged expedient by the General Conference, or by all the Annual Conferences, we will come over to you

---

[1] Baltimore Conference Minute Book; Candler, pp. 199ff. The same Conference also considered Coke's approach to Bishop White in 1791.

either for Life, or to make you a transitory visit.[1] The man who could continue to pocket his pride in this way was not motivated by personal ambition or self-seeking.

Coke did not again visit the States, though he maintained a friendly correspondence during the last five years of his life with Asbury and others among the American preachers. When the news of his death was received, Asbury wrote and spoke of him as 'the greatest man of all the Oxonian Methodists',[2] and even 'the greatest man in the last century',[3] terms so extravagantly eulogistic as to suggest that his conscience may have been troubling him. The course of their long friendship had been far from smooth. Asbury guarded too jealously his authority among the American Methodists whom he knew and served so well; and he undoubtedly had misgivings about Coke's British citizenship and continuing ties with the British Connexion. Coke, for his part, came to resent the curtailment of his superintendency (though he disclaimed any desire to exercise it independently of the Conferences), and he was inclined to be jealous of Asbury's unique influence and popularity. Each at times acted in such a way as to strain the relationship between them. 'At times Coke must have found Asbury almost unendurable. Perhaps the feeling, intermittently, was mutual.'[4] Yet the significant fact is that their friendship survived the stresses to which it was subjected; and there was never any serious question of their personal differences leading to factions within the Church.

In the quarter century between the Christmas Conference of 1784 and the General Conference of 1808, membership of the Methodist Episcopal Church increased tenfold from 15,000 to over 150,000, and the number of itinerant preachers rose from 83 to 540. As Candler justly observes, 'Coke contributed no little to this great achievement.'[5] Of course, he was dwarfed by the figure of Asbury, the lone giant of the American Methodist scene. But Asbury gave

[1] Letter to Ezekiel Cooper, 8th September 1808 (Garrett Theological Seminary). Cf. his graciously-worded letter to McKendree, 5th October, 1808 (Paine, op. cit., i. 203f.).
[2] Letter from Asbury to Thomas L. Douglass, 21st May 1815 (*Methodist History*, i. 55).
[3] Asbury, *Journal*, ii. 780.
[4] *History of American Methodism*, i. 464. The same writer says (ibid., p. 463), 'Asbury suffered much from a martyr complex and also took great pleasure in it . . . This type of personality was bound to clash with more urbane spirits'.
[5] Candler, p. 203.

himself utterly and exclusively to America for over forty years; whereas Coke came and went, and had many commitments elsewhere. Comparatively little of his time—rather less than three years in all—was spent on the American continent. But his influence on American Methodism during this formative period was out of all proportion to the time he spent there. Despite his attempts at different times to bring about a reconciliation between Methodism and the parent Church on both sides of the Atlantic, there is no evidence that he ever regretted his key role in the establishing an independent Methodist Church in America. Writing to the Bishop of London in 1799, he confessed that for a time he had been 'warped' from his attachment to the Church of England. His old affection and loyalty had now returned. 'But', he added, 'I return with a full conviction that our numerous societies in America would have been a regular presbyterian church, if Mr Wesley and myself had not taken the steps which we judged it necessary to adopt.'[1]

In the years following the Christmas Conference, Coke played a continuing part in guiding the infant Church through its early vicissitudes, and in shaping its constitution and discipline. His was the decisive influence which defeated Asbury's plan for a permanent Council and determined the system of annual and quadrennial General Conferences by which the Church has been governed ever since. He himself attended every General Conference, and many of the annual ones, up to 1804, and it was Asbury's custom to vacate the chair whenever he was present. He was, too, a pioneer in the Church's educational activities, for Cokesbury College, despite its brief existence, was destined to set an example to later generations. In a similar way, the social witness of the Church, and notably the campaign against slavery, derives from the stand he himself took at a time when the social conscience of a majority of Christians was scarcely beginning to awaken to the need for uncompromising opposition to that great evil. Finally, though the links between Coke's American ministry and the later missionary activity of the Methodist Episcopal Church are tenuous,[2] it is undoubtedly true that he widened the

[1] Letter to Bishop of London, 29th March 1799 (Etheridge, pp. 302f.).

[2] I can find little evidence to support Barclay's sweeping claim that it was Coke who 'launched early American Methodism on its foreign missionary course' and who was 'the herald and apostle' of American, as of British, Methodist missions (*Early American Methodism*, i. 104). Coke's influence in this respect was more indirect and diffused than such expressions would suggest.

horizons of the American Methodists. Not least important is the fact that, in his own person, he provided a link between the American and the British Methodists at a time of strained relations between the two nations, a link which was virtually severed by his death and which has been laboriously reforged only in recent days by the formation of the World Methodist Council.

CHAPTER 17

DRUDGERY DIVINE

The picture of Thomas Coke as first and last an enthusiast for overseas missions, though it does far less than justice to his many-sided career, is not altogether unfair to him. Through all else that he undertook, this concern for world mission runs like an unbroken thread which he never let slip from his fingers, even at the busiest of times. In 1794, we find him apologizing to his friends among the American preachers that they have not heard from him for so long. 'When I inform you of the crowd of important business on my hands, I think you will excuse me. Since my return from the West Indies, I have twice visited Holland, Ireland once, and the principal societies in England twice. Besides, I am now devoting much of my time in order to make myself a perfect of the French language, that we may exert our utmost efforts for the saving of souls in France, when in the Providence of God peace is established. Added to all this, the raising the necessary fund for our Missions in the West Indies, entirely lies upon me; and that great work now costs us about 1200£ Sterling a year.'[1]

From 1798 on, he is regularly set down in the *Minutes* as superintendent of the Missions, a growing responsibility which absorbed more and more of his time and concern. Other matters were rarely allowed to take precedence. When he realized that his participation in the controversies of 1791–7 had made him a number of enemies among the wealthier members, and that the West Indian missions were in danger of losing their financial support, he determined as far as possible to avoid such controversies in the future. To the end, it was the needs of a world living in the darkness of paganism which most deeply moved him both to compassion and to action. The very mention of the missions would instantly dispel his weariness, so that an acquaintance once remarked that if, after his death, someone were to whisper the words 'mission' or 'missionary' in his ear, it might well bring him back to life![2]

[1] Letter to various preachers, 23rd July 1794 (MS copies at Garrett Theological Seminary and Baltimore Methodist Historical Society).
[2] Crowther, p. 200.

261

For many years the cost of the expanding missions was to be met by the fruits of Coke's begging tours, supplemented by his own substantial giving. From time to time he circulated printed appeals, the earlier of which have already been noted. In 1787 he pleaded specifically for the Carib mission in St Vincent; in 1789 and 1790 he addressed his 'benevolent subscribers' in more general terms. But the promise made in the 1786 *Address*, that he would print an annual statement of accounts, was not immediately fulfilled, partly because of his other commitments and partly because of the confusion into which the Connexion was thrown by Wesley's death. When he was not busy on the other side of the Atlantic, Coke was usually touring the British Isles in search of subscribers and preaching the world-mission of the Church from every pulpit he occupied. It is no coincidence that his first detailed statement of accounts was prepared during a rare period of enforced idleness, while waiting upon the Dutch authorities in The Hague.

Begging from door to door was a necessary drudgery which Coke accepted only with reluctance. But again and again he was able to carry the Conference with him in his proposals for extending the missions only by promises that he would make himself responsible for raising all the money needed. And year by year he pressed on in a task that was never congenial and often very distasteful to his natural inclinations. His 'cheerful and confiding manner' in soliciting subscriptions, and 'the satisfaction he evidently felt when the coin was deposited in his trusty purse' were long remembered by those whom he persuaded to accompany him on these begging tours.[1] His custom in London was to travel around in a hackney-coach, engagingly described by one writer in 1850 as 'a slow and ponderous affair, as compared with the fleetness of a modern cabriolet'.[2] Coke was at pains to assure those from whom he obtained a subscription that this conveyance was paid for not from the mission funds, but out of his own pocket.[3] However, he did not always indulge in this luxury. One of the Sunderland Methodists who sometimes accompanied him and recalled his meekness and patience in the face of the occasional haughty refusal, wrote that he must have walked thousand of miles to beg from door to door, and was sometimes on his feet, with scarcely a break, from morning till evening

[1] *Wesleyan Methodist Magazine*, 1850, p. 1038.
[2] Ibid.   [3] T. Jackson, *Life of Robert Newton*, p. 78.

and at considerable risk to his health.[1] In October 1809, he reported
to the Committee from Liverpool, 'I have received upwards of
£180 here for the missions in private, but I begin to fear I shall not
be able to make it up to £200. How tired my feet are with walking!'[2]

Both persuasive eloquence and the most forcefully expressed
moral indignation had their places in his armoury. The captain of a
man-o'-war at Plymouth, from whom he received a larger subscription than perhaps either of them had expected, afterwards
called on a friend whose Methodist sympathies were familiar to
him. ' "Pray, Sir," said the Captain, "do you know anything of a
little fellow who calls himself Dr Coke, and who goes about begging
money for missionaries to be sent among the slaves? . . . He seems
to be a heavenly-minded little devil. He coaxed me out of two
guineas this morning." '[3]

On another occasion, when begging in the City, he met with no
more than 'stern looks and flat denials' from one of the West India
Merchants to whom he applied. His companion vividly remembered
Coke's outburst of indignation on behalf of the negro slaves, whose
plight always aroused his deepest feelings. 'He gave the gentleman
such a specimen of Welsh scolding, "that the missionaries took
their lives in their hands, crossed the seas, and encountered climates
to do good to the most abject of the human kind, dragged away in
chains, & often with bloodshed, to augment the wealth of the planters and merchants, who refused them even the consolations of
religion." ' The merchant so enjoyed this demonstration of Welsh
eloquence that he subscribed five guineas on the spot.[4]

But even the persuasiveness of this 'heavenly-minded' little
Welshman did not always succeed, and sometimes he met not only
with refusal, but with abuse and even violence. One extreme case
has been recorded in picturesque, almost Dickensian detail. Coke
had called, accompanied as usual by a friend, on a London business-
man who, as soon as he learned the purpose of their visit, 'fell into
a most violent passion, called the worthy Doctor by the most
opprobrious names, and insisted in the most haughty and insulting
language, that he should instantly quit the place; at the same time

[1] G. Marsden of Sunderland, in *Methodist Magazine*, 1815, p. 100.
[2] Letter to Robert Johnson, 3rd October 1809 (M.M.S. Archives).
[3] Drew, p. 388.
[4] Joseph Sutcliffe's MS *History of Methodism*, Vol. iv, pp. 25f. (Archives
Centre).

observing, that he never suffered beggars upon his premises. The Doctor and his friend immediately withdrew; but the gentleman, not satisfied with this outrage upon decency and politeness, called to a large yard-dog, and encouraged him to seize upon them; but providentially they both escaped unhurt. On reaching the street, the Doctor took his handkerchief from his pocket, and having carefully wiped the dust from his shoes, he turned round and shook his handkerchief, with this observation, "Naughty man, I leave this dust as a testimony against you!"' The *Methodist Magazine*, in giving this anecdote to its readers, added a delightfully edifying postscript to the effect that 'within a few years, this same gentleman, who then was in high repute, became somewhat embarrassed in his circumstances, and shortly after died of a broken heart'.[1]

Not surprisingly, Coke's fellow-preachers showed a certain reluctance to shoulder part of this burden for him. In March 1805, he wrote to Joseph Entwisle, suggesting that the Committee might make up for his prolonged absence from London by themselves undertaking the drudgery of begging for the missions. He outlines the necessary procedure. They are to go in pairs—either two preachers or preacher and layman—and call upon the previous year's subscribers. 'I write with the utmost confidence of a heart full of esteem for you all. Never fear. God will find friends for the missions. If you lose anything in London by my absence, I will make up for it, and more than make up for it, in the country.'[2] But little was ever done in his absence, and four years later he was still exhorting and rebuking them: 'Indeed, my beloved Brethren, you ought to be more zealous than most of you have been, in applying in private for the missions in London—*you*, the members of the Committee, above all other circuit preachers.'[3] Samuel Bradburn no doubt spoke for all when he wrote of Coke's visit to Bristol in 1812, 'Dr Coke relieved me from the task of begging for the Missions, for which I feel truly thankful. The Lord bless him!'[4]

In this respect, Coke provides unexpected support for Walpole's

[1] *Methodist Magazine*, 1819, p. 210 (from an eye-witness account). For a similar incident in Lancashire, see article by William Lancaster, in *Methodist Recorder*, Winter Number, 1898.

[2] Letter to Joseph Entwisle, Bodmin, 2nd March, 1805 (M.M.S. Archives).

[3] Letter to Robert Johnson, 2nd October, 1809 (M.M.S. Archives).

[4] Bradburn's Memorandum Book, 20–25th April 1812 (Archives Centre). For a different reaction to Coke's begging, see a letter of Zechariah Yewdall to Robert Dall, 12th March 1790 (*W.H.S. Proc.* xxi. 72).

maxim that 'All men have their price'. During one of his Cornish tours, he declined an invitation to preach at Mevagissey because it would involve modifying his subsequent arrangements. Samuel Drew was then deputed to offer him the promise of a good missionary collection as a bribe. Coke was amused that they should have hit upon his price so exactly, and eventually agreed to go.[1]

'I would sacrifice everything and myself to the Missions', he wrote in 1804, 'but I judge that, except in a case of urgent necessity, I ought to give a very little of every day even now to my Commentary.'[2] But he was always reluctant to allow circumstances or less vital issues to impede this all-important work which supplied the life-blood of the missions. This was one recurring cause of tension between him and the missionary Committee in London with whom he shared his responsibility after 1804. Sometimes the need for keeping closely in touch with them over all the decisions to be made seemed to clog the wheels and provide insufferable hindrances to his progress in begging. At the end of one long letter in 1811, in which he gave detailed replies to a number of issues they had raised, he wrote:

I hardly know what to do for you to satisfy you. I must not *now* melt away all my fortune. You, yourselves, my good dear brethren, have been the sole cause of my doing so little as I have done. I told you that *every* Friday morning you kept me among you, we lost £20. You with very great energy pressed me unanimously to draw up a statement of facts concerning the West India Work, of about 300 pages octavo. In this, I have made considerable progress, and if it be not drawn up in a very elegant style and with great judgment, it will not be received by those for whom it was principally intended. If you do not call me to London, I shall be brought into perfect subordination to begging, and I shall do *much more* even this year (before Conference) than I ever did in any year before in my life. You desired me, or at least approved of, my making the selection of hymns. Even this letter, will rob me of three hours of my begging time. I don't mean I have been three hours writing it, but for the ease of my mind I put off my begging work this morning till 12 o'clock, that I might write to you. It is well that I have a most precious wife to comfort me.

Then, with more than a touch of exasperation, he adds,

And don't write to me letters which require such long answers. Let me

---

[1] Drew, pp. 388f. Drew adds that Coke himself was fond of quoting Walpole's maxim.

[2] Letter to Entwisle or Lomas, 2nd October 1804 (M.M.S. Archives).

go on begging in good earnest, and you shall before the Conference see that I shall do more than you expect.[1]

When in 1794, at the request of Conference, Coke eventually drew up a detailed *Statement of Receipts and Disbursements*, it revealed that a considerable deficit had already accumulated. The report includes detailed yearly accounts from 1787, the list of subscribers for each year being followed by a statement of expenditure. Among the subscribers appear several notable names. The Rev. Thomas Haweis contributed on a generous though diminishing scale, beginning with £20 in 1788–9. Wilberforce, another member of the Clapham Sect, gave in all a total of £80 10s. during the six years under review; and in the final year's accounts appears a subscription of five guineas from the Earl of Belvidere. The funds were certainly in need of as many such noble and generous friends as Coke could muster. In those years when Coke had been free to go begging, the subscriptions averaged about £1,200; but in his absence they slumped to a fraction of this and the deficit soared accordingly. Only in the first year was there a credit balance of £120; thereafter the deficit mounted steadily from a mere £63 in 1788–9 to £2,167 17s. 2½d. in 1792–3.[2]

Coke's efforts in begging for the missions had clearly failed to keep pace with their rate of expansion. But where his personal efforts fell short, his personal liberality stepped in and wrote off the debt. Addressing the subscribers at the outset of the report, he says, 'The large balance which you will find due to me, will never again be brought into account. It is my Subscription for this great work.' The extent of this open-hearted gesture has sometimes, quite needlessly,

[1] Letter to the Missionary Committee, via George Highfield, 26th December 1811 (M.M.S. Archives).

[2] The yearly totals may be summarized as follows:

	Subscriptions			Expenditure			Balance			Deficit		
1787–8	£1167.	12.	2	£1027.	12.	8	£119.	19.	6	—		
1788–9	£1409.	0.	1	£1472.	7.	0	—			£63.	6.	11
1789–90	£1424.	14.	2	£1971.	15.	3½	—			£547.	1.	1½
1790–91	£339.	15.	0	£1544.	3.	11	—			£1204.	8.	11
1791–2	£1052.	19.	6	£2816.	2.	9½	—			£1763.	3.	3½
1792–3	£620.	15.	6	£2788.	12.	8½	—			£2167.	17.	2½

These figures speak for themselves. Coke's explanatory note on the leanest of the years reads complainingly, 'The smallness of the sum subscribed this year, arose from my having so little time to apply to the pious and benevolent, there being nothing done during my absence'.

been exaggerated. Of the enormous deficit shown, over half was accounted for by mortgages on various chapels towards which Coke had himself advanced sums totalling £1,250; most, if not all, of this would in due course be repaid. It was the remaining £917 17s. 2½d. which Coke wrote off as his own subscription to the work. In addition, he had paid most of his own travelling expenses both in crossing the Atlantic and in touring the British Connexion. Little wonder that he sometimes found himself short of ready cash[1] and much of his correspondence with Thomas Williams was concerned with realizing more of his assets in order to devote them to this cause, as the following letter illustrates:

My dear Sir,
      I find it expedient to make up the sum of one hundred pounds before I sail for the West Indies & America, which will be the beginning of October, if it please Divine Providence. I therefore beg the favour of you to transfer the inclosed Turnpike-Bonds in the best manner you can, and also the Turnpike writings which you have now in your hands. I'll also beg of you to send me the year's Interest of the mortgage. And I'll intreat you to oblige the landlord of the Shoulder of Mutton, Howell (by kind means if these will do, otherwise by other proper means) to pay me through you the Interest now due to me. Be pleased to send me the money in the course of next Month, & favour me with a Line by the return of the Post. Deduct whatever will be due to you for your trouble. If the Bonds cannot be transferred without some loss, I will consent to it.[2]

This letter demonstrates how ruthless Coke could be with his creditors when the needs of the mission fund were involved; but it shows, too, that he was prepared for personal loss in order to realize his assets quickly, in the same cause.[3] The substantial fortune which he had inherited from his father[4] was steadily whittled away as the needs of the missions increased. In April 1797, when he was

[1] On a number of entries referring to minor travelling expenses in the West Country in 1788, he comments, 'N.b. I must have been very low indeed in respect to ready cash, when I made this and the following charges'. The items total less than £5.
[2] Letter to Thomas Williams, 30th August 1790 (in possession of the Historical Society of Pennsylvania).
[3] See my article in *Brycheiniog*, 1964, pp. 1ff., reprinted in *Methodist History*, January 1966.
[4] Bartholomew Coke's will cannot be traced at present, but the figure of £3,000 given by Crowther, p. 489, is probably correct.

settling his temporal affairs with a view to spending the rest of his life in America, little enough remained in his possession.[1] This remnant of his fortune continued to dwindle until by 1804 virtually nothing was left to him. He was constrained to propose to the newly-formed Missionary Committee that for the future his postage on official correspondence should be charged to the mission fund, though such a step went against the grain. 'I have never been a debtor to the Missions', he wrote, 'and no one shall take from me this glory.'[2] However,

> In man's most dark extremity
> Oft succour dawns from Heaven;

and in 1804 the solution to his problems was nearer than he realized. His marriage to Penelope Smith rescued the mission fund from the threat of bankruptcy, for his wife devoted herself and her wealth to that cause as wholeheartedly as he had done. Her ample fortune, as Coke himself put it, was 'vastly unequal to her liberality, and even this fell short of her ardent desire to do good'.[3] As a result, much of her estate followed his into the fund, and a mere twelve months after their marriage we find him writing to Lomas, 'We are not overcharged with money, I do assure you. Our expenses and *benefactions* the last year considerably exceeded our income, but I don't intend it shall be so in future (at least soon) except to save the missions from material injury. In that case we would become poor. We pray *ardently* for the missions twice a day frequently and have them most deeply at heart.' In a later letter he elaborated on this:

The produce of the sale of the house and gardens my dearest wife lived in, &c., in Bradford, is gone except some dividends we funded in the Stocks, which do not amount to above a third part of what we sold. However, we have an ample sufficiency with prudence and also ability to do some good in the way of beneficence from time to time without going at all beyond bounds in future.[4]

During the five years of his marriage, Coke's begging tours continued almost without a break, though the delicate state of his wife's health frequently caused anxiety and sometimes forced him to modify his plans. Towards the end of 1807, for example, concern for her health caused him to go straight on to York instead of begging,

[1] See letter to Williams, 5th April 1797, quoted p. 427 above.
[2] Letter to Lomas, c. 22nd October 1804 (M.M.S. Archives).
[3] Memorial tablet, now in the Coke Memorial Church, Brecon.
[4] Letters to Lomas, 2nd and 25th April 1806 (M.M.S. Archives).

as he usually did, in Hull. He explained to the Committee:

Some of our leading friends, urged my dearest wife and me not to go to Hull (that is, I ought not to take her to Hull) in the winter time on account of the fogs and damps of Hull. They instanced in examples of asthmatic persons who were essentially injured by going there in the winter . . . I could make allowances for the great esteem they evidently felt for my good wife, who needs only to be known, to be loved and esteemed. However, their arguments were urged with such kind ardour, that it appeared to me, that I ought not to take her there at present. I love Hull very much. I have been remarkably blessed there. And it was with concern of mind that I gave up going there at present. But the health of my precious wife rises above every other consideration.[1]

It was a strong consideration that could induce Thomas Coke to neglect any opportunity of furthering the missionary cause. Though he was much more ready than the Committee to live by faith rather than by thrift, the news of a serious deficit in the mission funds was calculated always to galvanize him into yet more frantic efforts. Even the overwhelming shock of his first wife's death did not prevent his responding to this stimulus: it was, indeed, a solace to have so urgent and practical a task to engage his attention at such a time. His old friends the Brackenburys wrote inviting him to Raithby Hall, but he knew that this was not for him the way out of the valley of the shadow.

My very dear Friends, [he wrote]
                            I am very much distressed in mind. Thanks to you for yr. kind letter. I am quite shaken from every thing terrestrial. If God's will & Missions were out of the question, I should long to drop my Body, & be with my dear, dear, dear Penelope. I do compose myself, & repose myself in God in some measure, glory to his name.
    I have been in Brecon, So: Wales, to deposit the dear remains of my precious Jewel in the Priory Church in that Town. I thank you for yr. kind invitation but yr. sweet groves wd. too much feed my melancholy, in spite of yr. valuable company & conversation. I was on the point of setting off for So: Wales since my return from Wales, & to make my & Yr. common Friend Mr Robert's house a kind of central place. But I cannot satisfy myself without plunging into active life whether I sink or not: I am therefore going into Cornwall both to preach & to beg for the Missions which are now 1,400£ in debt, & will be soon £1,700.[2]

    [1] Letter to the Missionary Committee, 5th December 1807 (M.M.S. Archives).
    [2] Letter to Mr and Mrs Brackenbury, 16th February 1811 (Wesley's Chapel, London).

Despite his renewed efforts and the official backing given to them by Conference, this debt continued to grow. Early in 1812 Coke abandoned himself entirely to rescuing the foundering vessel. Even the limited time reserved for the literary tasks he had in hand was now sacrificed. He wrote:

Nothing shall interrupt my labours in begging. When I received Mr Blanchard's letter, informing me that the Fund was above £4,000 in debt, it robbed me of my rest for two nights. And I could not pacify myself, till I had resolved to sacrifice all my literary labours and to be nothing but a preacher and a beggar, and to beg morning and afternoon. I felt the sacrifice very great, because I am so foolish as to think that I could do some good through the Press. But all is over. The History of the Bible is over. I must return the money back to the subscribers for about half a quarto volume. The 3rd. Vol. of the West Indies must remain over. I will never rest, till I have liquidated all your debt. Begging morning and afternoon is hard work.[1]

It was becoming increasingly clear as the years passed that the basic weakness in the organization of Methodism's work overseas was that too much of the responsibility had been concentrated into one man's hands. The burden was too heavy for one man's shoulders. How far this fault may be blamed on Coke himself, and how far on the reluctance of the Methodist people as a whole to undertake the task, is a question for separate consideration.

[1] Letter to George Highfield, 28th January 1812 (M.M.S. Archives).

CHAPTER 18

FATHER OF THE MISSIONS

Methodism was one of the first of the Protestant denominations to undertake overseas missions and one of the last to establish a missionary society. The interval was filled largely by the exertions of one man. The first tentative step towards replacing Coke's one-man-band by a more adequate organization was taken as early as 1790. The last Conference attended by John Wesley appointed a committee 'for the management of our affairs in the West Indies', with Coke at its head. Three of the members were missionaries in the field and can have participated only by correspondence; the rest were leading preachers at home, stationed as far afield as Bristol, Wakefield, and Dublin. It seems doubtful if this committee ever met, except possibly during the Conference; and if it did so, it left no minutes of its activities. The following year a similar committee was nominated to examine 'accounts, letters and Missionaries that are to be sent to the Islands'. But Coke was still appointed the official delegate to the West Indies: no doubt the Conference realized that as yet no one else had either the knowledge or the resources to supervise the work overseas.[1]

Perhaps because of the ferment in the church at home, the missions received no further official notice in the *Minutes* until 1793, when the Conference was persuaded, undoubtedly by Coke, to authorize a general collection for the work in the West Indies because the fund was 'exhausted, yea considerably in debt'.[2] But the burden of responsibility still rested on Coke's shoulders alone. The title, 'Father of the Methodist Missions', so often conferred on him, was fully deserved. Unlike most of the preachers at home, he knew the difficulties under which the missionaries worked. He had a paternal concern for those he had chosen and sent out, and nothing would persuade him to sink to false economies in equipping them. In the financial *Statement* which he drew up in 1794 at the request of the Conference, we find such annotations as this:

[1] *Minutes*, i. 240, 256; cf *W.H.S. Proc.* xxx. 27.   [2] *Minutes*, i. 290f.

When the Missionaries sailed from England in the winter-time, I generally sent them by the packet from Falmouth, though the expence of the passage was five guineas more, besides the journey from London to Falmouth. I thought that the life of a Missionary was so precious, that he ought not to be obliged to run the hazard of coasting England from London to Land's End in the winter time [a hazard Coke knew well enough from his own experience] for the sake of saving about ten guineas. The hazards of the Torrid Zone were quite sufficient for those valuable men.

On the cost of an umbrella for the same missionary, Coke commented, 'Umbrellas may be esteemed as luxurious in this country, but are highly necessary for Europeans under the torrid zone. We should not study the health of the Missionaries, if we did not allow each of them an umbrella.'

He proposed, in future, to print biennial accounts, in order to avoid the expense of employing a secretary in the years when he was abroad. But if such accounts were ever issued, they have disappeared. The Conference of 1797 resolved on a collection to be made in every congregation throughout the country and instructed superintendents to look out for suitable young missionary candidates. But in the following year, the Church was in such financial straits that Coke was instructed to seek private subscriptions in place of the public collection. Wherever he was unable to visit personally, the preachers were to do all they could instead. The treadmill of begging to which this resolution condemned him has already been described.

Meanwhile, in the spring of 1798, a Committee of Finance for the support of the West Indian missions was set up in London. The inaugural meeting, with Coke in the chair, appointed a secretary and carried certain resolutions. The president and vice-president appear to have been Coke and the superintendent of the London Circuit respectively; and the rest of the committee was composed of eighteen prominent London laymen. The intention was to relieve Coke of the task of begging in London by dividing the city into a number of areas, in each of which members of the committee would collect subscriptions. Whether this machinery ever functioned is hard to say. The absence of any further minutes suggests that it broke down at an early stage and that yet another attempt to assist Coke in financing the missions creaked to a standstill.[1]

[1] The Minutes of this Committee are in the M.M.S. Archives. The last of the resolutions passed at their first meeting reads, '8th. The reasons for forming the Committee'; but the rest of the page and its reverse are left blank. Then follow the first minutes of the 1804 Committee.

In 1799, however, Conference made a more decisive move to take the missions under its care, with Coke as its agent. The general collection now became an annual one, and Coke was asked 'to draw up a statement of the work of God in the West Indies, with a short address to the people; and to send printed copies of it to all the Superintendents'.[1]

Throughout this period, the administration of the missions was complicated by Coke's repeated visits to America. He was so fully responsible for the missions that in his absence little could be done and very little seems, in fact, to have been attempted. His final visit to America, in 1803, took him out of England for over nine months, and this prolonged absence appears to have brought matters to a head. The arrangements Coke had made before sailing proved so inadequate that the preachers in the London Circuit took matters into their own hands. Early in 1804 a circular letter was sent out to all missionaries and subsequently published in the *Magazine*. It explained the measures that had been taken. 'Since the departure of our esteemed Friend and Brother Dr Coke, for America, we have been much concerned for the prosperity of the Methodist Missions. Feeling their great importance . . . we have been very desirous of placing them upon some regular establishment, so that, under the Divine Blessing, we might reasonably expect a continuance of their success.' Coke had left the general supervision of the missions in the hands of Joseph Benson, with George Whitfield, the Book-Steward, in charge of the funds. But Benson's other responsibilities left him little time for the missions and Whitfield was ill. There was a danger that some of the bills that were coming in might remain unpaid. So an emergency committee was formed of the London preachers and the laymen recently appointed to the Committee of Privileges. Benson was made president, and the secretary and treasurer were prominent London Methodists who already held those offices in the Preachers' Friendly Society.[2]

Though they disclaimed any intention of challenging Coke's superintendency, one of the first decisions of this committee implied a pointed criticism of his handling of the missionary finances. 'It was found to be the general desire of the People', they wrote, 'to have some Accounts of the Missions regularly published, with a full detail of receipts and expenditure. The Committee feel very desirous to

[1] *Minutes*, ii. 27. For the resulting circular, see Appendix E, item 42.
[2] *Methodist Magazine*, 1804, pp. 332ff. Cf. pp. 376ff.

comply with the wishes of the numerous Subscribers, and to render every satisfaction in their power.' The missionary accounts were, in fact, in a chaotic state. T. P. Bunting tells how his father, then a junior minister just appointed to the London Circuit, found himself tackling the formidable task of reducing things to order.[1] Neither Coke nor Whitfield can be held solely responsible for this lamentable state of affairs. Coke was more competent in keeping his accounts than has sometimes been suggested, but his itinerant life complicated his management of the missions and made it difficult for anyone else to take up the reins. Whitfield, for his part, clearly had little ability and less experience in financial matters, and certainly contributed his share to any confusion that already existed by failing to differentiate between the mission account and that for Coke's Commentary on the Bible.[2]

Among other provisions for the future the new committee instructed every missionary to keep a journal and submit it twice a year for publication. Superintendents were again asked to look out for 'proper persons to be sent out as missionaries', and to report the result to the next Conference.

'The step', says Bunting, 'was carefully taken. Dr Coke's authorized superintendence was left undisturbed; but he was not in England to do his work.' Nevertheless, when Coke returned to find all this machinery in motion, he took it as an attempt to usurp his authority, and deeply resented it as a reflection on his ability to sustain the work. He feared, too, that their circular must be harmful to the cause because it gave too pessimistic an impression of the financial state of the missions and so discouraged their supporters.[3] As late as March in the following year his resentment still smouldered and occasionally burst into flame, as when, in stirring up the London preachers to call on the subscribers in his absence, he added, 'But don't take with you on any account one of the last Committee, altho' I greatly respect and esteem them. If you be so rash as to do that, you will grieve me almost to death.'[4]

Coke's resentment was focused on the lay members of Benson's committee, who seem to have been determined to wrest his authority

[1] T. P. Bunting, *Life of Jabez Bunting*, 1887 edition, pp. 205ff.

[2] See Coke's letter to Joseph Taylor, 31st August 1804 (M.M.S. Archives).

[3] Letter to the Committee, sent from Bristol some time in November 1804 (M.M.S. Archives).

[4] Letter to Entwisle, 2nd March 1805 (M.M.S. Archives).

from him, under the conviction that the missions were growing too rapidly to remain in the hands of an absentee superintendent. When it was proposed that Benson's committee should be given Conference recognition, Coke objected to the inclusion of these lay members on three grounds:

1st. Because those gentlemen, with all that honour and candour which they truly possessed, informed me that if they were a Committee at all, *all official* correspondence must come to them solely through their Secretary.

2ndly. That every thing, at all times, should be *finally* determined by a vote of the Committee.

3rdly. Because that in this case, I should of course be laid aside as the Superintendent of the Missions. That the word Superintendent would be a *mere delusive* name, and that God himself had made me the instrumental Father of these Missions, and that I could not give them up, unless removed from them by death or otherwise in the Providence of God, or compelled to give them up by the Conference. That in the last case I should consider myself as having nothing more to do in England: that I had no other name or appointment in the Minutes, respecting England, but that of General Superintendent of the Missions.[1]

Conference dealt with this delicate situation by means of a compromise. The missions still depended so much upon the dedicated zeal of one man that it was hardly practicable to oust Coke entirely from his superintendency. At the same time, some restraint upon this exuberant little Welshman was clearly desirable, and 'dear Mr Benson's committee', though it may have been set up a little hastily and tactlessly, was nevertheless a step towards continuity of administration. On a motion of Benson's, Coke was re-appointed to the office of General Superintendent, and a new Committee of Finance and Advice was set up. This consisted of the London preachers, with Coke as its president, Joseph Entwisle as Secretary and Robert Lomas, the new Book-Steward, as treasurer. To emphasize that it had no connexion with the earlier committee, and as a concession to Coke's feelings, there were no lay members. Coke accepted this new committee in the confidence that it was to act in a financial and advisory capacity, and was not 'a Committee of control and superintendency'.[2]

The Conference regulation made it clear that the aim was to establish a balance of power, though the final decision in the intervals between conferences was left with Coke:

[1] Letter to the Committee, 9th September 1804 (M.M.S. Archives).
[2] Ibid.

275

4. All official Letters & communications whatever from the Mission-aries should be laid, from time to time, before the Committee, & their advice taken upon the same.

5. If any difference of opinion should arise between the General Superintendent & the majority of the Committee concerning any important measure, both parties shall have the privilege of appealing to the Con-ference, but if, in such case, an immediate decision be necessary, the right thereof must of course remain with the General Superintendent till the ensuing Conference.

For the rest, arrangements were made for a public collection 'after the manner of the Kingswood collection', and for a regular annual financial report to be issued; while Coke was to draw up 'an account of the Spiritual State of the Missions' to be published after approval by the Committee.[1]

It was hardly to be expected that these arrangements would immediately begin to work without friction. Coke had been running the missions singlehanded for so many years that considerable re-adjustment was needed on both sides before a *modus operandi* could be found. He soon discovered that the need to keep the Committee informed and to consult them on all decisions of any importance was an irksome cause of delay involving a great deal of correspondence. Nor was Coke's resentment the best of lubricants. He was quick to detect signs that they wished to limit his authority and even to come between him and the missionaries, with whom he had long enjoyed a relationship of benevolent oversight.

Coke was present at the first two meetings of the Committee, on 14th and 16th August, and all went smoothly; but by the time they met again, on 3rd September, he had left London and the first cracks were appearing on the surface. A letter was laid before them from William Black, explaining why he had been unable to proceed from New York to Bermuda, where he had been stationed by the Confer-ence.[2] The Committee was clearly dissatisfied and passed a rather brusque resolution to the effect that, 'Dr Coke shou'd be asked *why* Mr Black was *first* called to the United States, & whether he has re-turned any answer to Mr Black's Letter, & if he have, what that

[1] *Minutes*, ii. 239f. Cf. Findlay and Holdsworth, op. cit., i. 67f.

[2] *Minutes*, ii. 232. The appointment had, in fact, been made by Coke himself while still in America. His letter recommending Black to the Governor General of Bermuda is dated from Philadelphia, 28th May 1804 (Baltimore Methodist Historical Society).

answer is.' They went on to record their judgement, 'that they cannot possibly act agreeably to the decision of the last Conference, unless *all official* Letters from the Missionaries be sent to the Secretary of the Committee, and therefore it is *resolved*, to send a Circular Letter to the Missionaries informing them of it'. They also decided that money should be paid out only by the Treasurer acting on their instructions.[1]

Entwisle accordingly wrote to Coke, who was in Lincolnshire working on his *Commentary*. He reported the Committee's misgivings and their resolutions concerning official correspondence with the missionaries and the administration of the fund. 'The Brethren do not wish to clog the wheels of the Mission; but to co-operate with Dr. Coke to promote them to the utmost. But from the knowledge they have of the general dissatisfaction wch prevails in Town & Country for want of clear & accurate reports, they are fully persuaded that neither the Preachers nor the leading friends will, in future, exert themselves in favor of the Missions, if such accounts be not published.'[2]

Though written, no doubt, with the best of intentions, this letter had the effect of fanning the flame of Coke's resentment. The Committee's opinion 'that the utmost caution is necessary in the choice of missionaries' he took to be (what indeed it was) a criticism of his selection of candidates. For the rest, while welcoming their readiness to co-operate for the good of the missionary cause, he was clearly apprehensive of losing effective control. 'I do assure you', he wrote in reply, 'that I am thankful to God, that I have a Committee of finance and advice taken out of my own ministerial brethren, to assist me in the Missions. I am growing old and cannot live long, and there is some degree of uncertainty respecting my engagements and connections in the United States of America (not that there is anything new on the subject). Consequently, that my leading brethren among the Preachers should be led of God into the proper missionary spirit by the Providence of God and their own reflections (for it is a peculiar talent and however many good men may not see it in that light), is very desirable.' He was sure that they could find a way of working together, 'And it may be, that your very frugal spirit may be necessary to check my too ardent zeal.' He agreed that official correspondence should be directed to the secretary rather than to himself. 'Only let

[1] Missionary Committee minutes, 3rd September 1804.
[2] Letter from Entwisle to Coke, 4th September 1804 (M.M.S. Archives).

[the missionaries] be informed that they may correspond with me as (shall I say) their friend and father, in the most friendly and familiar manner. If this be not the case, I shall consider myself entirely laid aside.'[1]

Coke drafted a circular letter to be sent to all the missionaries, explaining the new arrangements, and this was considered by the Committee at their next meeting, on 11th September. They approved it, with the addition of a tactful hint on the need for economy and a reminder to those missionaries who had not submitted their accounts. 'It affords great satisfaction to the Brethren,' they wrote, 'as they perceive their valuable friend Dr Coke is disposed to everything to enable the Committee to act in their office in a proper manner.' Meanwhile, however, in his Lincolnshire retreat, Coke had been pondering over their previous letter, and was so disturbed by what he considered to be its implications that he sat down to write three further letters to the Committee. He protested that, whatever their intentions might be, he was in fact being ousted from the superintendency to which the Conference had appointed him. These letters, penned in a moment of emotional stress, throw much light on Coke's personality as well as on his relations with the Committee.

'I feel myself constrained by what I believe to be the will of God,' he began, 'to sit down again, and send you another answer to your official letter. Indeed, my health, my life (if they may be so preserved) call me to it. Your letter has already robbed me of three nights sleep . . . and if things go on in their present train you will probably not be troubled with me much longer . . . I really wrote in the fervour of affection and not with the recollection and the coolness of judgment, and whatever I advanced in that letter which implied a renunciation of my superintendency of the Missions, I did not design in that sense and must solemnly recall.' He went on to enumerate his objections and misgivings, and next day wrote a second letter elaborating these. If all official correspondence with the missionaries was to be addressed to the secretary, then except during his rare visits to London Coke's hands would be tied and the unofficial letters he received would simply increase his sense of impotence. 'Perhaps you will smile at my feelings, and say Why do you trouble yourself? I answer because the Missions we are adverting to, are mine under God, as far as anything of that kind can be ascribed to those who open new doors for the Gospel—and not yours; and you *seem* to want (though I have too

[1] Letter to the Committee, 7th September 1804 (M.M.S. Archives).

278

high an opinion of the goodness of your hearts, through grace, to suppose without further proof that you intend) to "kill and take possession".' The new arrangement, he protested, 'entirely annihilates my superintendency and makes me a mere shadow in the whole business, or only a mere tool to beg for you'.[1]

To these two letters Entwisle wrote an unofficial reply on 12th September, assuring Coke once more of the unanimous desire of the Committee to co-operate with him. He had been surprised and pained by the tone of Coke's last letters. 'All the Committee were pleased, at our last meeting, with the prospect of mutual co-operation between them and yourself, and hoped they would be enabled to *assist* you in the Missions to the general satisfaction of all concerned . . . I do not now write *officially*, but as a friend, and because I perceive your mind is considerably distrest. On the receipt of your next Letter, there will be a meeting of the Brethren, & the whole business will be fully considered, of wch you will have the earliest intelligence.'[2]

Coke's third letter, written on the 11th, has not survived, but can in part be reconstructed. He had undertaken to consider his third point, that the Committee's proposals were inconsistent with the will of God, and 'to make a few observations on the astonishing imperiousness' of their letter to him. He had promised, finally, to submit certain propositions to them, adding 'If you choose to accede to them, we may go on in amity, union and peace, and I trust with the blessing of God. If you do not, and are determined, without any authority from God or man, to wrench the whole out of my hands, I shall not divide the child, for I am the true mother, and *you are not*; though I have no doubt whatever but you are genuine and eminent ministers of the Gospel.'[3]

Unquestionably, Coke had so fully identified himself with the cause of the missions over the years, that it was impossible for him to consider the issue except as an intensely personal one. The child he had fathered seemed now to be threatened by those who would usurp the responsibilities of parenthood. Here are laid bare the defects of those very qualities which alone had brought the missions into being, in the face of indifference and even at times opposition from the rest of the Connexion.

The Committee duly considered Coke's eight propositions on 13th

[1] Letters to the Committee, 9th and 10th September 1804 (M.M.S. Archives).
[2] M.M.S. Archives.
[3] Letter of 10th September 1804 (M.M.S. Archives).

September and unanimously adopted each of them in turn. A letter was sent, informing Coke of their complete satisfaction with this basis of agreement, but denying the desire for power which he had imputed to them. The propositions themselves were embodied in a printed letter sent to all the missionaries over the names of the whole Committee headed by Coke as general superintendent.[1] Their very prolixity is an indication of the tense atmosphere they were designed to relieve. They laid down that all official letters were to be directed to Coke or, in his absence, the secretary, and must be laid before the Committee as soon as possible. No other letters were to be considered official, but there was to be no restraint on friendly correspondence with the missionaries either by Coke or by other members of the Committee. During Coke's absence, all official letters were to be forwarded to him, but he was to return them to the secretary without undue delay. The heart of the matter lies in the sixth and eighth propositions: 'That no step relating to the Missions, be taken either by Dr Coke or the Committee, but by the mutual consent of both parties . . .' and 'that no monies shall be paid on any account whatever, but by the Treasurer . . . with the consent of the Committee'. It is difficult to say what the missionaries themselves must have thought of so tediously-wrought an agreement when the circular letter reached them in the field: though it ends on a much more positive and heartening note: 'We wish to do our utmost by united councils and united exertions, to promote the interests of the Missions, and to aid you in your arduous undertaking.'

The working compromise thus achieved by mutual forbearance in love proved the basis of a co-operation that lasted through the ten remaining years of Coke's life. The tension was reduced, though not removed entirely. But from the moment agreement was reached on Coke's eight propositions, the tone of his correspondence with the Committee changed. Relieved of his anxiety about their intentions, Coke immediately gave himself afresh to matters of detail. His very next letter, after briefly mentioning the 'most perfect satisfaction' their last letter had afforded him, gets down straight away to arrangements for despatching Robert Johnston to the West Indies, and to the question of meeting the current expenses of the missions. Almost the only indication of what had recently passed between them comes at the close: 'Write to me when you do write very kindly. Don't

[1] A copy of this circular, dated 24th September, is inserted in the Committee minute book (M.M.S. Archives).

snub me, for I am very weak, and don't be afraid of a Want of money. The Lord bless you.'[1]

* * *

One reason for setting up the Committee of Finance and Advice was a growing feeling that the missions were not being administered as economically as possible. The rank and file of the Methodist people were far from wealthy and there were many demands on their generosity. Their chapels were built and their preachers maintained only by giving that was often sacrificial. The Kilhamite secession meant heavier financial burdens for those who remained in the Wesleyan fold.

Both as Wesley's lieutenant and later as secretary of the Conference, Coke had earned his share of unpopularity for discouraging indiscriminate appeals to the Methodists.[2] Consequently, there was a natural resentment in some quarters that his repeated missionary appeals were siphoning so much from the church at home. Any rumour that the missionaries were being too lavishly provided for added fuel to the fire. In 1807, William Myles was speaking for many others in condemning the current methods of equipping the missionaries as too costly. In contrast to Coke's policy, which we have already illustrated from his *Statement* of 1794, Myles advocated a far closer scrutiny of the needs of each missionary. 'A fair, impartial account should be taken of what a single Missionary wants; And what a married Missionary wants for his wife, on their first going out.

[1] Letter to the Committee, 17th September 1804 (M.M.S. Archives). Tension between the Superintendent and his Committee continued, even after this *modus vivendi* had been worked out. In November 1808, the Committee sent Coke a letter criticizing his letter to William Gilgrass as 'calculated to harrass the man's feelings' and reporting their decision 'That the word "us" in the Dr's Letters be expunged, and Mr T. Blanshard, Treasurer, be substituted.' (Minutes, 4th November.) Coke was still very sensitive to real or imagined snubs, as his reply on this occasion shows: 'When you differ with me in opinion, write to me very kindly, and not in the way of rough resolves. I lie at your feet, as it were, and have *no wish* on matters which conjointly concern us, but in everything to act with you in the most perfect harmony. I love you greatly, and am at a great distance from you, and you may very easily grieve me when you don't intend it.' (Letter of 15th November 1808 [M.M.S. Archives].) For the attitude of the Committee to the work among the French prisoners and in Sierra Leone in 1811, see below pp. 315f; and p. 298, note 5.

[2] E.g. his letter 'to our Brethren at Delph in Yorkshire', 10th October 1780 (Everett MS Book, Archives Centre).

These necessarys they should get, if they need other things, they should do as the brethren do at home, do without them, till they can get them for themselves.' He also considered that if all missionaries were fitted out by the Committee in London, money would be saved, if only because 'they would not be so urgent on the Committee as on an individual'.[1]

Even if he had been prepared to save money at the expense of the health or safety of the missionaries themselves, Coke did not believe that a committee could do things more efficiently or economically than he did himself. In 1802, he told George Whitfield, 'I always do things myself more economically in missionary matters than anybody else.'[2] He was able to boast that his administrative costs were far from excessive. 'A confidential friend of mine, a very leading man indeed in the London Missionary Society, confessed with surprise (when he and I candidly conversed concerning the expenses of the different missions) that their missions cost them *proportionately* (comparing similar cases) twice as much as ours. Please to tell the Committee this from me. A *Body* of men, however wise, excellent and holy, are in great danger of being too severe, especially about money matters.'[3]

The 'want of money' was a perennial preoccupation of both Coke and the missionary committee throughout these years of expansion. The committee, not unnaturally, were concerned lest their commitments should outstrip their resources and land the mission fund again in debt. They scrutinized with wary eyes every proposal for an extension of the work. Thomas Coke, on the other hand, was impatient of delays and hesitations, and longed only to respond to the challenge of each new opportunity as it arose. *Jehovah-jireh* is a recurring watchword in his letters. He was content to know that, if the work was of God, then 'the Lord would provide',[4] but it is only fair to add that this conviction was matched, not by a splendid inactivity, but by the most vigorous and persistent endeavours to assist in this provision. When his main point was won, he did go so

[1] Letter of William Myles to William Jenkins, 14th November 1807 (M.M.S. Archives).

[2] Letter to George Whitfield, 7th December 1802 (Archives Centre).

[3] Letter to Robert Lomas, 8th November 1804 (M.M.S. Archives). Inflation, caused by the Napoleonic Wars, was already one adverse factor in mission finance. Writing to Lomas in defence of the cost of equipping the missionaries, Coke observed in 1806 that '£10 now, is not more than £7 was at the beginning of the missions.' (19th October 1806 [M.M.S. Archives]).

[4] See, e.g., his letter to Johnson, 1st January 1810 (M.M.S. Archives).

far as to concede that 'in the movement of the great machine with the care of which God and the Conference have entrusted us, it is best to move slowly and surely'.[1] But the leisurely implementing of carefully considered decisions was contrary to his eager and impulsive nature.

He was convinced of their need to 'think big'. In his very first letter to the Committee, dealing with certain items of expenditure which might appear excessive, he argued that while they could not be 'too frugal, consistently with the interests of the work', on the other hand any 'meanness of spirit' would incapacitate them for so great an undertaking.[2] And this became a recurring theme in his official correspondence. They should not be dismayed, he said, at having so little in hand just after the Conference: it was always so at that time of the year, when all the major items of expenditure were incurred. But once the missionaries had all been sent out, everything would be smooth and he would ensure that they had an adequate balance by the next Conference. 'Don't be afraid. The General Collection throughout Great Britain will be, or ought to be, not less than £1,500, but we must, I think, mutually consider in a little time about sending a Circular letter to the Preachers to stir them up . . . Again, I will engage, *if necessary*, to raise £1,500 more for you and the Missions; I say, *if necessary*, because I never have begged and I believe never shall I beg, but on the ground of necessity. Besides, if really necessary for the Missions (though I am persuaded it will not be so) I will drop my tour through half of Ireland, . . . and that would be a great trial to me indeed, because the Lord owns my ministerial labours in Ireland vastly . . . We must not want to hoard money in missionary matters, but mind only the present *Now* —that is, the present year.'[3] 'You grieve', he wrote, 'because you have not *every moment* more in hand than is called for: that is, you will have no cross, no sacrifice, no reward. Well, be it so; we will endeavour, when I see you, to think of some other plan.'[4]

Above all, he was deeply concerned lest any bills of exchange drawn on him or the committee should not be honoured because of the temporary embarrassment of the fund. In September 1804 he

[1] Letter to the Committee, [16th September] 1804 (M.M.S. Archives).

[2] Letter to the Committee, 31st August 1804 (M.M.S. Archives).

[3] Letters to the Committee, 17th and 18th September, 1804 (M.M.S. Archives).

[4] Letter to the Committee, November 1804 (M.M.S. Archives).

was in an agony of apprehension over two such bills received from Dominica. 'I know the spirit of the planters well; and they would be [more] enraged at the protesting of a bill of exchange than at adultery or any sensual vice in the world.' Such an action, he was sure, would be 'a mortal blow to our work in Dominica'.[1] He made a determined effort to ensure that the necessary sum was found, and wrote in a frantic letter to Lomas, 'Pray do secure the Bills. I entreat you by the Blood of Christ.'[2] Even when his personal resources were seriously depleted, he was ready to find the necessary money himself rather than let the missions suffer. 'Whilst I live, the supplying of the missions with what they want (not to save the public, but to carry on the work) shall with me *supersede every other consideration*.'[3] To the end, this was his response whenever the Committee or the Conference hesitated to seize any opportunity for advance.

Coke's concern lest the functioning of the Committee should curtail his superintendency may be misconstrued unless we bear in mind the manner in which the missions had come into existence and his unique personal relationship with the missionaries. For nearly twenty years he had himself chosen, equipped and stationed them, supervised their labours and corresponded regularly with them. Their right of direct personal access to him he guarded jealously, as much for their sake as for his own, knowing well that no committee of preachers who had travelled only in home circuits was able to appreciate the difficulties and set-backs under which the West Indian work was carried on. Throughout this period he showed himself to be the faithful champion and friend of the missionaries. When they fell ill, he pleaded for them to be allowed to return home; when they fell foul of the authorities, he exerted all his influence with those in high office to relieve their distress; and when any of them fell by the wayside, he was as concerned to plead for mercy on their behalf as he was to uphold the necessary discipline of the ministry.

A single instance from among the many that occur in his correspondence with the Committee must suffice to illustrate this

---

[1] Letter to Entwisle, 25th September 1804 (cf. letter of 23rd September, to Lomas) [M.M.S. Archives].

[2] Letter to Lomas, 26th September 1804 (Duke University). (Cf. letter of 27th September to Entwisle [M.M.S. Archives]). As a further burden, he even had to contend with the moral scruples of some of the committee concerning the use of bills of exchange. See his letter to Lomas, 3rd December 1804 (M.M.S. Archives).

[3] Letters to the Committee, 1st and 3rd January 1810 (M.M.S. Archives).

paternal oversight. Robert Shepley had given faithful service in Dominica, but both he and his wife were repeatedly prostrated by fever. In 1804 he was set down for Barbados,[1] but sailed instead for home, under doctor's orders to return as the only way of saving his life. Hearing of his arrival in Bristol, the Committee deferred judgement on his case until further enquiries had been made; but they were obviously displeased at his anticipating their consent to his return.

As soon as he heard of this, Coke took up the matter on Shepley's behalf. 'I am very much against making any inquiry about Br. Shepley's former life, tho' I knew nothing of it till I received Mr. Entwisle's letter. But if I had time to enlarge, I could give many reasons for this opinion. He has brought the work in Dominica to a blessed state. You must either provide comfortably for him till the Conference, or give him a place in a Circuit. Simple justice requires one of these, and I submit to your choice. Do write kindly to him. He has been at death's door.'[2] Later he reverted to this in greater detail: 'Bro. Shepley has done more in the way and spirit of martyrdom than perhaps any other man in the connexion would have done. He nursed that blessed work in Dominica, till the Society sprung up from 50 to 1005. To do this he endured the yellow fever 4 times and his wife twice [sic]. When he was on the point of dying his physicians urged him to set off instantly with the fleet to his native country, or he must die quickly. He went off, instead of going to Nova Scotia. Very probably you would have done the same. We have no right to punish him with expulsion from the public exercise of the ministry of the Gospel.'[3]

To add to his distress, on reaching Bristol Shepley had got himself involved in a case of suspected smuggling and had to appear before the Quarter Sessions. Coke hastened down to Bristol from Yorkshire to find him living, with his family, in wretched, though expensive lodgings. In the past, Coke would have acted unhesitatingly. Now, with little of his own personal resources left, he felt the full force of the restrictions placed upon him by the existence of the missionary committee. He was reduced to pleading, 'He is very ill and very poor. Must I not advance to him what he wants?'[4] The

[1] *Minutes*, ii. 233.
[2] Letter to the Committee, 27th September 1804 (M.M.S. Archives).
[3] Letter to Lomas, c. 22nd October 1804 (M.M.S. Archives).
[4] Letter to Lomas, 29th October 1804 (M.M.S. Archives). Cf. letter to Entwisle of the same date, quoting Portia's 'Mercy' speech.

285

Committee did little more than exhort Shepley to live more frugally while in Bristol, and Coke returned to the attack with a series of indignant questions: 'And shall we treat with *severity*, with all the severity in our power, one who has already, I believe, shortened his life . . . twenty years by the unwholesome climate of the West Indies—by throwing him out of the ministry like a withered branch? Who would again that knew of this, go upon our missions?'[1] Despite Coke's pleas for Shepley's reinstatement as a missionary, the Committee would go no further than to propose that he be stationed in the Bath Circuit until the next Conference, and he was eventually lost to the ministry. Behind Coke's unwillingness to relinquish his authority over the missions lay something more than a love of power and prestige.

[1] Letter to the Committee, 18th(?) November 1804 (M.M.S. Archives).

CHAPTER 19

INTO ALL THE WORLD

During the last ten years of Coke's life, new fields of missionary activity were opened up in Gibraltar, in Sierra Leone and at the Cape of Good Hope; and plans were laid for the mission to India and Ceylon. In each case, the appeal for action came from abroad, and Coke was foremost in responding to it.

Although there had been Methodist preaching in Gibraltar since 1769, Conference did not take this officially under its wing until 1804. In 1800 Coke received a letter pleading for a preacher to be sent out to Gibraltar, where two local preachers and two class leaders were shepherding a society of fifty. He pleaded their cause in the Conference, and was authorized to send a missionary, but four years passed before James McMullen went out. Both he and his wife soon died from the yellow fever then raging in the colony, leaving a small daughter to be cared for by the Committee. No replacement was available at that time, but in 1807 it was resolved that another preacher should be sent immediately. Coke busied himself with finding a suitable man[1] and by the next Conference William Griffiths had gone out to take up the reins.

* * *

A more substantial venture undertaken during these years was the mission to Sierra Leone. It was not his first African venture. The proposal to send missionaries to Guinea, with which Coke was closely associated soon after becoming a Methodist, had come to nothing. But a new opportunity occurred in 1787, when Granville Sharp and the Committee for Relieving the Black Poor founded a settlement for negro refugees from the American colonies. Was it possible that Coke had heard of this plan when, in the spring of that year, after his first visit to the West Indies, he wrote in his *Journal*,

[1] Letters to the Committee, 23rd September and 18th November 1807 (M.M.S. Archives). Originally he had had young Jabez Bunting in mind, but this came to nothing (J. B. Dyson, *Methodism in Congleton Circuit*, p. 119).

'Since my visit to the islands, I have found a peculiar gift for speaking to the blacks. It seems to be almost irresistible. Who knows but the Lord is preparing me for a visit in some future time to the coast of *Africa*?'[1] Initial setbacks in the settlement led to the formation of the Sierra Leone Company in 1791, with Henry Thornton as its first president and Sharp, Wilberforce and Clarkson among its directors. The Company's twofold purpose was to reorganize the settlement and to combat the evils of the slave-trade by promoting legitimate trading on the Coast. The first party of 1,200 negro settlers from Nova Scotia sailed for Sierra Leone early in 1792.

Coke knew some of those responsible for the settlement, and took an active interest in it from the outset. 'We are going to send Missionaries to Sierra Leone in Africa,' he wrote in November 1791, 'where the English are establishing a very capital Settlement. The Company has chosen two Chaplains. One of them is a zealous Methodist Preacher of my Recommendation. Four of our young Exhorters are also going over.'[2] Of the young exhorters we know nothing more, but the chaplains were Nathaniel Gilbert (son of the pioneer of Antiguan Methodism) and Melville Horne. Horne was Coke's protégé and in later years, despite their doctrinal differences, used to pay tribute to the many kindnesses Coke had shown him from his youth up.[3] He was not content to serve as a chaplain to the settlers, but showed his missionary zeal by preaching to the Temne. After his return home he published his opinion that Africa needed missionaries who would live, not in the European settlements such as Freetown, but in African villages, going on circuit in the Methodist fashion. He also believed that they needed to be single men.[4]

Among the first Nova Scotian settlers were a number of Methodists, under the leadership of Moses Wilkinson, a Negro preacher. In the 1792 *Minutes* a membership of 223 'Coloured People' was returned for Sierra Leone,[5] and this figure recurs for several years. Later on, Coke wrote of the leaders of this group that, 'As their lives were exemplary, and their preaching regular, their congregations soon increased, and several others augmented the

[1] Coke's *Journal*, p. 93.
[2] Letter to Ezekiel Cooper, 21st November 1791 (Garrett Theological Seminary).
[3] Hamilton, *Faithful Servant receiving his Reward*, pp. 23f. For Horne's doctrinal controversy with Coke, see Appendix E, item 61.
[4] Fyfe, *History of Sierra Leone*, p. 52.
[5] *Minutes*, i. 268.

original number of the society.'[1] The truth is, unfortunately, less edifying. The diary of Zachary Macaulay, governor of the settlement from 1794 to 1799, depicts them as an ill-disciplined group deeply affected by extravagant notions, rabidly nonconformist, and all too ready to mingle religion and politics. The governor, himself a pious man, sincerely regretted the 'notoriously irreligious lives' of some members of the society and the growing discontent and rebellious-ness stirred up by a troublesome preacher named Beveshout. 'Per-haps it might be well', he wrote, 'if Dr Coke, or some delegate from him, were to visit Freetown, in order to establish some kind of discipline among the Methodists; for at present their government is a pure democracy, without subordination to anyone.'[2] It is not an endearing picture of primitive Methodism. The gospel proclaimed by the Wesleys, divorced from the discipline which they enforced on their societies, had rapidly degenerated into extravagance and licence. We must remember that these were men but recently emancipated from slavery and set down in a strange environment; they had been deprived of their spiritual pastors, except for one or two sincere but ill-equipped laymen and the Anglican chaplains whom, however unjustifiably, they deeply distrusted; and the spirit of revolution, then abroad, inevitably appealed to their simple minds.

Under the auspices of the Company's directors, several of the leaders among the negro settlers visited England, to plead for missionaries. Thomas Haweis blamed the bishops for obstinately refusing to sanction such a mission or to ordain the candidates recommended to them, despite their high qualifications for the work. If the history of the Church in the American colonies seemed to be repeating itself, Thomas Coke would certainly not be unaware of the parallel. 'I hope the Lord will yet open our way into Africa,' wrote Haweis. 'Never did the access seem more promising.'[3] Coke concurred in this view, and in the previous year had already been

[1] *Interesting Narrative of a Mission sent to Sierra Leone*, p. 18.

[2] Knutsford, *Life and Letters of Zachary Macaulay*, pp. 49ff. The entry quoted is under the date 15th September 1793. On 3rd October, commenting on reports of 'wildest extravagances' at Granville Town, Macaulay wrote, 'It were much to be wished for that some sober-minded and authorized Methodist preacher came out who might introduce more discipline and regularity among that sect, and correct the extravagant ebullitions of their spirit'.

[3] Haweis's diary, quoted by A. Skevington Wood in *Sierra Leone Bulletin of Religion*, Vol. 3, No. 1, 1961.

planning a mission to West Africa.[1] This came to nothing, however, and when he initiated an African mission, it was not to the settlers on the coast but to some of the tribes inland that his attention was directed. Early in 1794 an expedition had penetrated the Fula district of French Guinea as far as Timbo and been warmly received. Reports of this exploratory journey reached England in 1795 and inspired a 'Plan for establishing Missions in the Foulah Country in Africa'. The prime mover in circulating this plan seems to have been Macaulay, who was on leave in England at the time; but he immediately enlisted the help of Coke, particularly in the selection of the missionaries.

In April 1795 Coke told Ezekiel Cooper, 'We are going to plant a colony of Methodists in the Interior Parts of Africa, about 500 miles from the Coast, among a people lately discovered, who are Mild, peaceable & when Compared to Africans on the Coast tolerably Civilized.'[2] This estimate was clearly based on the account of the Fula in the journal of James Watt, one of the leaders of the recent expedition. He had reported that the people were 'ingenious, and comparatively well-informed, kind to Strangers, docile and tractable'. The King and his chiefs were eager to acquire agricultural skills from the Europeans, which opened the way for a Christian mission both to convert and to civilize the Fula people.[3]

Macaulay's 'Plan' set out in some detail what was proposed.

Some pious Families in the late Mr. Wesley's Connexion who are well instructed in several useful Branches of Husbandry and Mechanics, who reside in the same Neighbourhood, and have lived together in habits of social and religious Intercourse, and who appear to be well qualified for carrying into Effect the Objects of this Institution, have offered their Services.

2ndly. The means to be used for effecting the first Object, is the Preaching of the Gospel by itinerant Missionaries, whose labours will be

[1] Letter to William Black, 7th November 1793: 'I have strong invitations to Africa. I cannot say whether I must not accept of them before I see you'. (M. Richey, *Memoir of William Black*, p. 302). W. Harvard, *Narrative of Mission to Ceylon*, p. 18, says that Coke approached his father about going out.

[2] Letter to Cooper, 23rd April 1795 (Garrett Theological Seminary). Timbo is nearer 200 than 500 miles from the coast; but Africa was even more of an unknown continent then than when Livingstone arrived in 1840.

[3] Watt's journal is quoted in the 'Plan' of the proposed mission, a MS copy of which is in the British Museum (Add. MS 41263 fol. 116). The copy is undated and unsigned, but its style bears every indication of being, at least in part, from Coke's pen.

aided by those of [their fellow?] Settlers with whom they are connected.—
The Means to be used for effecting the second Object, viz. The civilization
of the Natives, are 1. [The example?] which the Establishment will afford
them, of conduct influenced by Christian Principles, and other patient
Perseverance and productive Industry. 2. The improvements in Agriculture and other useful Arts, which the Establishment will introduce. 3. The
erection of Schools, in which the Children of the Natives may be instructed
in the Knowledge of Letters and other useful Branches of Science.

3rdly. The Persons to be engaged on these Missions should be pious
Men, employed in Trades, suitable to the circumstances of the Country,
such as Farmers, Carpenters acquainted with House-building, Plough and
Cart-making, &c., who should be accompanied by one or more Mission-
aries. Their having Families should be no Objection, provided that their
Wives are pious, and their Families small.

4thly. It is thought that six Families will be a suitable Number in the
[first instance?] for this Undertaking.

In lending his support to this scheme, Coke acted in a private
capacity and in response to Macaulay's appeal, not as the agent of
the Conference or Superintendent of the missions. It was intended
from the first to conduct it on non-sectarian principles. A note
appended to the Plan asserts that the fact that those eventually
chosen to go out were Methodists was quite fortuitous: they 'were
not selected on account of their relation to any particular religious
Society, but because of their own Piety and evangelical principles,
and their apparent fitness for the different branches of this Service—
one essential part of which is the introduction of the Christian
religion into Africa, without . . . attending to any of the distinctions or Sections of it which prevail in our own Country'. This
assertion, like the fundamental principle adopted the following year
by the London Missionary Society[1] breathes the spirit that was
abroad in the dawn of the modern missionary movement, when men
of every Protestant denomination felt a common concern for world
evangelism. Unfortunately, this ecumenical mood was soon superseded by a spirit of rivalry which transferred to the mission field the
old theological argument between Calvinist and Arminian.

[1] 'As the union of Christians of various denominations in carrying on this
great work is a most desirable object, so, to prevent, if possible, any cause of
future dissention, it is declared to be a *fundamental principle of the Missionary
Society*, that its *design* is not to send Presbyterianism, Independency, Episcopacy,
or any other form of Church Order and Government . . . but the glorious
Gospel of the blessed God to the heathen . . .' (Quoted in R. Lovett, *History
of London Missionary Society*, i. 49f.).

The directors of the Sierra Leone Company, most of whom belonged to the Clapham Sect, gave the mission their official blessing and support. Wilberforce wrote to Coke, 'I shall certainly, among my brother Directors, recommend and enforce our duty, and the utility of forwarding the measure in the best way we are able, in propriety, in our official situations; and I dare say we could procure a large subscription towards the support of the mission in our individual capacities.'[1]

Coke's original intention had been to accompany the missionaries himself,[2] but he changed his mind, perhaps because of his other commitments. This made the choice of those who were to go out all the more crucial. Wilberforce spoke all too truly when he told Coke, 'Much must depend upon the qualifications and dispositions of the missionaries, not only for their success among the natives, . . . but also for the friends we might be able to raise for the general purposes of the establishment.'[3] The choice was left entirely in Coke's hands, and as he moved about the Connexion during 1795 he not only solicited subscriptions for the new venture, but kept an eye open for suitable personnel. A combination of piety and practical skill, rather than academic qualifications, was what he sought. Unlike Melville Horne, Macaulay and Coke were convinced that the advantages of marriage, as a safeguard against the temptations to which single men would be exposed, outweighed any disadvantages. They hoped, too, that 'families would have a far more civilizing effect, and make possible much greater influence on the women folk'. The wives, they thought, might be employed as teachers. Of the six men chosen, four were married, two single; and though it had originally been intended that the men should go out alone, to be joined by their wives when a settlement had been established, in the event all sailed together. The two single men, Giles and Yellalee, both local preachers, were ordained by Coke before they set out.

The initial cost of the expedition was estimated at about £1,000, to be raised by private subscriptions; and the hope was that, once established, the settlement would be self-sufficient. But the original

[1] Quoted by Drew, p. 265.
[2] This is implied by Wilberforce's words: 'It can hardly, however, be expedient for you to go to Africa so soon as you mention . . . it will be better . . . for you to wait till November or December' (ibid.). Cf. Asbury's *Letters*, p. 139: 'Dr. Coke writes me he now is about to sail for Timboo in Africa with six companions. One of the kings hath invited him.'
[3] Drew, p. 265.

estimate was soon exceeded. To the considerable expense of providing the missionaries with tools and equipment was added the cost of maintenance in England before their delayed embarkation. They were due to sail from Plymouth in December 1795, but eventually embarked at Portsmouth on 23rd February 1796, and reached Freetown after a swift passage on 18th March. This delay would have been a negligible setback, had not the missionaries already begun to reveal their true characters. Their sad degeneration cannot be blamed on the rigours of the African climate, any more than on the primitive conditions of life in the Fula territory, which they never reached. It began in fact before they sailed. On 12th February, Macaulay wrote to his fiancée from Portsmouth that he was 'pestered almost to death with Dr Coke and his Missionaries'.[1] Their squabbles among themselves gave him serious concern for the success of the mission and his misgivings increased as the voyage proceeded. The married missionaries seemed to him 'quite inoffensive people' who 'conducted themselves in general with great propriety'. The trouble here lay with their wives, some of whom were in poor health, and the rest 'unsuitable to the Mission from their bad tempers'. But it was the two single preachers who gave most cause for disquiet. Giles seems to have been well-intentioned but weak, and proved ineffectual in rallying the rest of the party when they reached Freetown. Yellalee, on the other hand, showed himself to be a positive trouble-maker. Macaulay expressed his surprise that Coke should have seen fit to ordain him. 'The man is vain, empty, assuming, and his levity and impudence are excessive. On board ship his disputatious temper has disgusted even his associates.'[2] What was worse, having been misled by their show of piety, Coke had imbued his chosen band with false hopes. Macaulay was always careful to impress upon prospective settlers the hardships and disadvantages of life in Sierra Leone, painting, if anything, too discouraging a picture of the colony. To be forewarned was to be forearmed. But they had scarcely reached Freetown before it became clear that Coke had singularly failed to forearm his missionaries and had given them far too sanguine an impression of the life they were going out to. 'This morning', wrote Macaulay, 'there was nothing to be heard among the Missionary ladies but doleful lamentations or

[1] Knutsford, op. cit., p. 110.
[2] Ibid., pp. 117f. For an entirely different assessment of Yellalee, apparently without foundation, see W. C. Barclay, *Early American Methodism*, i. 115.

bitter complaints. To their astonishment Freetown resembled neither London nor Portsmouth; they could find no pastrycooks' shops, nor any gingerbread to buy for their children. Dr Coke had deceived them; if this was Africa, they would go no farther, that they would not. Their husbands were silent; but their looks were sufficiently expressive of chagrin and disappointment. It was with real complacency I reflected that I had always used dissuasives in talking to them, that I had always endeavoured to dash every extravagant hope I observed them indulging, and that I had always coloured my paintings with the most dark and discouraging tints.'

Furthermore, they had been led to expect, or so they claimed, that once they reached Timbo they would no longer have to maintain themselves by manual labour. According to Giles, 'Dr Coke had told him the King was to provide the Missionaries with land, cattle, and servants, and that they would be under no necessity of labouring for a subsistence'. Macaulay reminded him of the conditions on which they had been engaged, namely that after receiving support during their first three months in Fula, they were to support themselves by agriculture and other manual skills; to which Giles replied, 'Yes, but Dr Coke said there would be no necessity for the latter expedient; besides, he told me that I should have a liberal provision arising from my situation as teacher, as the Foulahs would be so desirous of instruction in the English language as to be disposed to pay handsomely for it'. When reminded further that Macaulay himself had consistently discouraged such hopes, his answer was, 'But I could not possibly mistrust Dr Coke's assurances; they were very strong'. Macaulay found, in fact, that the missionaries had been forewarned of his discouraging representations and advised to discount them. 'I discovered that they had been taught to expect that I should make it a principle to paint gloomily, merely by way of trying the strength of their resolutions; what I said, therefore, was regarded merely as a sort of bugbear, which they believed to have no existence, and for braving which they should obtain the credit of undaunted courage at a cheap rate.'[1] In the event, the reality appeared to them worse even than Macaulay had represented it.

One very odd document, preserved among Macaulay's correspondence, is a letter written by Coke to the Fula King and entrusted to the missionaries. Macaulay saw it during the voyage and sent a copy back to Henry Thornton, chairman of the Company.

[1] Knutsford, op. cit., pp. 121ff.

The 'inflated language' in which it was couched seemed to him highly injurious in its effect upon the missionaries, 'who were already imbued with absurdly lofty ideas of their personal importance'. It began by stating that they 'will set forth an example of all the virtues and of all the graces, and are qualified to instruct his subjects in all the important arts of Europe'. These, according to Coke, included medical skill, on which Macaulay added the acid comment, 'Giles attended the London Hospital for one month'. The letter concluded with this pompous flourish:

I trust, O King, that my friends will be made a blessing, yea even to Ages yet unborn.

I have felt confidence, O King, in your clemency and goodness that you will show my friends every degree of kindness, and give them land, and men, and cattle. And I have also full confidence in my friends, that they will always prove worthy of the favours you bestow on them.

That all blessings may be your portion, O King, shall be the prayer of your willing servant,

Thomas Coke
Minister of the Most High God, and Teacher of the Law of Nations.

Written in England on the 13th day of February in the year 1796 of the Christian era.[1]

The truth was so far removed from this testimonial to the characters of the missionaries, that it was as well for both them and the Fula people that they never reached Timbo. Their bearing and conduct in Freetown were, if possible, more distressing even than they had been on board the *Calypso*. The women-folk quickly gave themselves up to their 'doleful lamentations or bitter complaints', and made no attempt to adapt themselves to their new environment. Worst of all, Yellalee lost no time in showing himself a trouble-maker, crossing swords first with a slave-trader, then with a Muslim. Later, he set the two groups of Methodists at odds with each other, and the Council was unanimous that, whatever happened to the others, he could not be allowed to proceed to Timbo. It was a great relief to them when he determined to take the next ship for America.

With Yellalee busy making mischief and the married men silenced by their wives' vociferous complaints, the only hope for the mission lay in Giles. But he was too faint-hearted to rally his companions, and drew back when confronted with the possibility of going on alone. The prospect of having to maintain themselves by their own

[1] Ibid., pp. 116f.

labours had already cooled their ardour very considerably, and they soon determined to return by the first ship sailing for England. All that was left to do was to compose an epitaph, which the governor did in these words:

Thus ended the Foulah Mission, and I think it fortunate that it has so ended. I tremble to think on the difficulties I should have had to encounter had I gone on to Teembo with such unstable subjects, and I cannot help being grateful for my escape. The crosses they have already met with are light compared with those they would have a likelihood of meeting in the Foulah country; and it is so far fortunate that they have been hindered from bringing Christianity into contempt among the Foulahs, as their miserable deficiency in the necessary qualifications for Missionaries, of patience under suffering, and perseverance in the face of danger and in spite of disappointments, leads one to suppose they would have done.[1]

While this incident undeniably spotlights Coke's weaknesses, particularly in his judgement of human nature, it is only fair to recognize them as the flaws in his more admirable qualities, and not the shortcomings of a nonentity. Most of his critics were content to criticize; by failing in the attempt, Coke had at least chosen the better part. No doubt, too, he acted on information which was both scanty and unreliable, and ought not to have dismissed so readily Macaulay's cautionary picture of conditions in West Africa. But the available evidence was, to say the least, conflicting. The report of the 1794 expedition into Fula territory had been warmly encouraging. Moreover, a few years before, Henry Smeatham had published his *Plan of a Settlement to be made near Sierra Leone*, which inspired the choice of that territory by those who pioneered the rehabilitation of American Negroes in 1787. Coke must have read Smeatham's glowing report, and was not the first to be misled by it. What pleasanter prospect could there be than this opening invitation: 'Any person desirous of a permanent and comfortable establishment, in a most pleasant, fertile climate, near Sierra Leone, where land may be purchased at a small expence, may have an opportunity of doing it on the following advantageous conditions'?[2]

---

[1] Ibid., pp. 121ff. Little has been written on this Fula mission, but see Fyfe, op. cit., pp. 67f.; Findlay and Holdsworth, iv. 76; W. Fox, *Brief History of Wesleyan Missions on Western Coast of Africa*, pp. 204–9; *Arminian Mag.*, 1797, pp. 83f. Coke's own *Interesting Narrative*, published in 1812, is studiously silent on the 1796 venture.

[2] *Plan of a Settlement to be made near Sierra Leone on the Grain Coast of Africa, by Henry Smeatham who resided in the Country near Four Years*, London, 1786.

Nor was Coke alone in his failure. Sierra Leone was at that time the focus of attention among missionary enthusiasts. In 1795 the Baptists had sent out two men, one of whom died of malaria, while the other fell foul of the authorities by meddling in local disputes. Then in 1797 two further attempts were made, with similar discouraging results; one by the Glasgow Missionary Society, the other a joint effort by the London, Glasgow and Edinburgh Societies. It can at least be said that Coke's missionaries were not the only ones to squabble among themselves or to succumb to the unaccustomed difficulties of the climate.[1]

To Samuel Drew, Coke's official biographer, it seemed that the root of the failure was not in his selection of personnel for the mission, but in the attempt to combine sacred and secular purposes in one scheme. Yet this is the one feature of the plan that commends itself to us today as being sound and far-sighted. 'How far it would have been proper', wrote Drew, 'for the Methodists, whose sole business is to preach the Gospel, to form any alliance with those arts which evidently belong to the department of civilization, may well admit of some serious doubts . . . It might have opened a way through which, in process of time, our foreign missionaries might have degenerated into a company of traders . . . through which the spirit of the world might have diffused its temporizing influence over that pure simplicity which distinguishes the principles of the Gospel.'[2] Fortunately, Coke's view of the purpose and methods of the Christian mission was both more biblical and more enlightened than that of the Cornish metaphysician. He did not, in this instance, divorce sacred from secular, but knew well that preaching and service are inseparable facets of the Church's witness.

News of the total failure of the mission reached Coke in time for him to report it to the 1796 Conference; with the result that, 'after prayer and mature consideration, the Conference unanimously judged, that a trial should be made in that part of Africa, on the proper Missionary plan'.[3] Two preachers, Archibald Murdoch and William Patten, volunteered for 'this important work' and were set down in the stations as 'Missionaries for Africa'. But the decision was never implemented because news was received of the similar ventures planned by other societies.[4] In the unsettled years that

[1] C. P. Groves, op. cit., pp. 207ff.; Fyfe, op. cit., pp. 75f.
[2] Drew, p. 270.   [3] *Minutes*, i. 352.
[4] In 1799, however, Coke and Mather were authorized to send out George

followed, the Methodists in Sierra Leone repeatedly begged that a missionary should be sent to them;[1] but only in 1808, after the abolition of the slave-trade, was it resolved that 'a suitable person' should be sought.[2] Even then, not until 1811 did Coke find such a person in George Warren.[3]

Coke had no doubt of the importance of establishing a Christian bridgehead on the African continent, and his vision of the potential harvest was a far-reaching one. He saw Africa, like America, as an emergent continent with the future at its feet:

On the importance of carrying the Gospel into Africa, and the magnitude of the undertaking, it is needless to expatiate. It is not a solitary island, nor even an archipelago, which we are about to visit, but a continent, peopled with nations of which we scarcely know the names. We have a promise, that 'Ethiopia shall stretch out her hands unto God' . . . During a series of years we have compelled Africa to weep tears of blood; let us now endeavour to brighten her countenance with the smiles of joy as some compensation for the injuries we have done her. Already has the legislature of our country shown us the way by putting an end to the slave-trade . . . Let us follow the bright example thus set before us by applying the balm of Gilead to heal her wounds.[4]

The first reports Coke received from Warren were most encouraging, and he wrote in March 1812 in glowing terms concerning the prospects.

I have recd. most pleasing accts. in Letters of seven sheets, concerning the African Missions. The Missionaries landed safe, after being pursued by a French Privateer. The Governor, Council, etc. recd. them most kindly. Our Society of 110 were overjoyed . . . A Neighbouring little king has visited the Missionaries, to invite them to his Country with encouraging promises. They are learning the language. They are establishing schools. I have great hopes of a glorious work in that quarter of the globe.[5]

Smith of the Horncastle Circuit, if they should 'judge it proper, after due investigation of the subject' (ibid., ii. 9f.).

[1] E.g. letter to Coke from Joseph Brown, a Negro preacher, in July 1806 (*Methodist Magazine*, 1807, pp. 283f.).

[2] *Minutes*, iii. 17.

[3] Ibid., iii. 209. The fact that Gibraltar and Sierra Leone are listed, as if by an after-thought, at the end of the circuits in the Aberdeen District is an indication of the uncertainty still prevalent in the Connexion about the exact status of these new mission stations.

[4] *Interesting Narrative*, p. 51.

[5] Letter to George Morley, 20th March 1812 (Wesley College, Bristol). The

Within eight months of his arrival, however, Warren fell victim to the climate; but two of his companions sustained the work until others were able to take it up. Thus were laid the foundations of a permanent Methodist work in West Africa, owing its existence to the dedicated persistence of Thomas Coke.

* * *

While he was thus engaged during these years in urging the Church to advance on so many fronts, Coke's concern for his first love, the West Indies, had in no way abated. As the years went by, missionaries were found for one new island after another. In 1796, William Turton began work in the Swedish island of St Bartholomew. Two years later it was the turn of the Bermudas, where, on Coke's instigation, John Stephenson was stationed.[1] His work among the slaves there aroused the hostility of the white population, and he quickly found himself under persecution. A law was passed prohibiting any except the Anglican clergy from preaching or teaching in the island. Coke made strong representations to the Privy Council through the Earl of Liverpool, against a measure which seemed entirely contrary to the provisions of the Toleration Act, as well as to 'the spirit of the British Constitution and the universal practice of the Illustrious House of Hanover'.[2] But the mission received a severe set-back, and not until 1808 was a fresh advance made possible.

A 'pressing invitation' to send Missionaries to Providence Island was declined by the Virginia Conference of 1797, on the grounds that, though so near the American mainland, the Bahamas were British colonies and should be supplied from Britain or Ireland.[3] But the British Connexion lacked the resources to take any immediate action. Early in the new century, however, William Turton was sent to open up a mission there.

---

best that the Missionary Committee could do by way of encouragement to Warren, was a letter warning him that unless his three companions could support themselves, they must return home. (Committee Minutes, 4th September, 1812).

[1] Letter to George Morley, 31st July 1798 (Wesley College, Bristol). The whole letter throws interesting light on Coke's methods of missionary administration.

[2] See his letters to Lord Liverpool, 7th April and 29th May 1801 (B.M. Add. MS, 38235, fol. 71-2, 101-3).

[3] Coke's *Journal*, p. 246.

Trinidad, which had been held by the Spanish until 1797, was the last of the larger islands to receive a missionary. Here the initiative was taken by Thomas Talboys in 1809, but Coke quickly followed it up and was soon badgering the Committee for missionaries to be sent. 'There is a Physician there, Dr Robinson, who was our Friend when he resided in Antigua; and who promised me, when I saw him in London, that he would be our Friend, if ever we should institute a Mission in Trinidad. Some hundreds of our dear Negroes have been removed to that Island from other islands in the Windward group since our capture of it, who are now as sheep without a shepherd.'¹ 'We have had invitation on invitation to Trinidad, but in vain.'² He was pressing at the same time for missionaries to be sent to the Danish island of Santa Cruz and to Demarara. And when, at long last, the door was unbarred in St Eustatius, he lost no time in renewing the work that had languished for so many years.

'O do all you can for the West Indies,' was his reiterated plea to the Committee.³ 'We want preachers . . . The West India work is dying or at least languishing for want of labourers.'⁴ And again, 'That great work (I mean, throughout the whole Archipelago) cries aloud for mercy and help. And in a proper way I am sure you will join me in giving it all the help in our power.'⁵ While the Committee still advanced step by step with the utmost caution and a proper regard for their slender material resources, Coke became more and more convinced that the West Indian mission had reached a critical stage. There was no standing still: not to press forward would be to fall back, a prospect which wrung from him this agonized reappraisal in 1810:

It is a melancholy observation, that for many years (I believe, for five or six) the work in the West Indies has been losing ground, and I ascribe this in a great manner to the want of a full supply of missionaries. If we do not keep up a full supply of missionaries, God will give up that great work to the Calvinists. A Calvinist missionary who was sent to Tobago (where, by the by, we ought to have had a missionary long before this) has been at Trinidad, and told the people [under Brother] Talboy's care, that if they ever stood in need of a missionary [and would] inform him, he would

¹ Letter to the Committee, 28th July, 1809 (New Room, Bristol).
² Letter to the Committee, 2nd October, 1809 (M.M.S. Archives).
³ Letter to the Committee, 28th July 1809 (New Room, Bristol).
⁴ Letter to Robert Johnson, 25th August 1809 (M.M.S. Archives).
⁵ Letter to the Committee, 2nd October 1809 (M.M.S. Archives).

immediately come among them . . . If we even keep our ground in the
[West Indies] we must have at least two in every Island. Antigua [will
never] I believe, flourish with fewer than three. Not a single [British?]
Colony in the West Indies has been opened to us for between twenty and
thirty years . . . Brother Talboys [in Trinidad], who has a Calvinistic
missionary on each side of him (at Demarara and Tobago) if not more than
those two by this time, should have a colleague sent to him by the Spring
Fleet; one also should be sent at the same time to the Virgin Islands, that
St. Thomas's may be supplied. Brother Marsden's place at Bermuda
should be supplied; & so should Brother Rutledge's at New Providence,
whether Brother Turton continues in the Bahamas, or not. Santa Cruz,
the largest of the Virgin Islands, a most important Island, is now open to
us: but it would be lost to us unless we had an establishment there, if
peace were to take place. If the Calvinists are determined to fight us, we
should send a missionary to the great colony of Demarara, but in *this*, we
should move on very slowly indeed at present.[1]

The presence of Calvinistic missionaries in the West Indies was
obsessing Coke's mind at this time. Ever since reading Fletcher's
works at South Petherton, he had been strongly opposed to the
Calvinistic doctrine of election. When the [London] Missionary
Society was formed in 1795, he gave it his support, in the confidence
that its interdenominational character would set it above sectarian
wrangles. He wrote to the Directors of the Society, urging them not
to enter into rivalry with the existing missions, and was assured by
them that their purpose was 'to act as brethren towards the missionaries from other denominations'.[2] The Society's first mission station
was in the South Pacific, where the Methodists had no plans for a
mission, and Coke was therefore able to welcome the news of its
early success.[3] But early in 1798 he was perturbed by the news
that the Society was planning to send men to the West Indies. Since
the doctrinal emphasis of the Society was by now clearly Calvinistic,
Coke feared a clash of rival enterprises, and wrote a hurried letter to
the Directors, drawing their attention to the extensive Methodist
work in the Caribbean and outlining his immediate plans for its
extension.

[1] Letter to the Committee, 1st January 1810 (M.M.S. Archives). Cf.
Etheridge, p. 445.

[2] Meeting of the Directors, 29th September 1795 (Lovett, op. cit., i. 44f.).

[3] Letter to Thomas Haweis, one of the founders of the L.M.S., 26th October
1798 (copy supplied by Dr F. Baker). Coke himself had contemplated a mission
to the South Seas as early as 1789, after reading Captain Cook's *Voyages* (*Journal*,
p. 138).

'Our Conference', he wrote, 'has hitherto furnished men and by public collections and private subscriptions money enough to embrace all the openings Providence has favoured us with. We move slowly, as all large bodies do. Our Conference sit only once a year, but whenever I am in these Kingdoms I endeavour in the intervals of Conferences to correspond regularly with the missionaries and to send them and the work all the assistance in men and money they stand in need of.' After a review of the West Indian Missions, he continued,

From these considerations I sincerely wish and request, Gentlemen, that you would be pleased to suspend your operations, or intended plan, concerning the West Indies, till after our next Conference, and I promise, Sirs, that if our Conference does not give the fullest assurance of their determination under the grace of God to support that work, with men and money according to all its wants, I will inform you of it with all possible candour; for God forbid that I should do anything or recommend anything which might obstruct the propagation of the Gospel . . .

I am deeply conscious, my dear respected gentlemen, that your view and the views of your Society purely regard the glory of God, and that propagation of the everlasting Gospel of Jesus Christ. But I am persuaded, that in the present instance you would expend so much of the spirit of prophecy and so much of the wealth of your fund, as would be necessary for the support of a work in the West Indies, merely that the Gospel might be preached by what are called Calvinistic ministers, instead of those with whom I have the honour of being connected. I cannot see any other end it would answer, for you to send missionaries to any part of that archipelago.[1]

The Directors of the Missionary Society did not respond to this plea for comity, but pressed on with their work in the West Indies. As a result, Coke felt impelled to take a less cordial view of the Calvinistic missions. Their existence furnished a further argument for the expansion of Methodist work in the Caribbean islands. 'We must endeavour to supply the West Indies well,' he told the Committee, 'or we shall lose them. There are, I think, five Calvinistic missionaries now in that archipelago. They do not preach where we have preachers, but watch every opportunity to seize on a vacancy.'[2] And in 1812, the news that the London Missionary Society was

[1] Letter to the Directors of the Missionary Society, 26th February 1798 (L.M.S. Archives).
[2] Letter to the Committee, 15th November 1809 (M.M.S. Archives).

seeking support for its work from members of the Methodist societies led him to put forward plans for ensuring that the Methodists subscribed first of all to the work of their own missions.[1] The eventual formation of the Methodist Missionary Society was thus brought another step nearer.

[1] Letter to the Committee, 29th October 1812 (M.M.S. Archives).

CHAPTER 20

BEGINNING AT JERUSALEM

The principle, already implicit in Coke's *Address* of 1786, that the Church's mission to the world is one and indivisible, governed his activities to the end. He was able to claim in 1806 that the Church had officially endorsed his view that the distinction between 'home' and 'overseas' was an arbitrary one. 'It was the unanimous judgment of the Conference,' he wrote, 'that the Foreign and Home Missions should be incorporated.'[1] So far was he from a one-sided concern for the foreign work, that in 1810 he was prepared to assert, 'Our home missions are of greater importance, I believe, than all our other missions put together.'[2] It was, perhaps, a recognition of the difference between the root and the fruit of the tree.

His advocacy of the Wesleyan home missions was as fervent as the pioneering work overseas for which he is chiefly remembered. Largely on his initiative, in 1805 a number of 'home missionaries' were appointed to circuits as widely scattered as Warminster, Liverpool and Sheffield.[3] The tentative nature of the experiment and the degree to which Coke was personally responsible for its supervision are shown by this letter to Jonathan Edmondson of the Stourport Circuit:

Nottingham, March 3. 1806.

Very dear Friend,

I request the favour of you to send Brother Millman, as soon as possible, to the Brough Circuit, in order to join the other Brother in the Mission. Messrs. Midgeley & Fairbourn have just written to me, to inform me of the great success of the Mission, and their great want of a second Missionary.

P.S. If Brother Millman wants money to go, please to advance what he wants & I will be answerable to you for it.[4]

[1] Letter to Robert Lomas, 5th October 1806 (M.M.S. Archives).

[2] Letter to Robert Johnson, 21st May 1810 (M.M.S. Archives).

[3] *Minutes*, ii. 273ff. Most of these appointments were to already existing circuits. But Warminster, to which Robert Shepley was sent, was new and appears to be the first attempt to establish a home mission circuit.

[4] Original at the New Room, Bristol.

The following Conference placed these Missions on a more official footing. The names of the missionaries disappear from the body of the English stations and in their place a separate list of eight Home Missionaries is given. A few weeks later Coke wrote to Robert Jenkins, 'These missions will be an extraordinary blessing to the nation. Help me in them. I intend to beg for them as well as for the other missions.'[1] He told the preachers of the Baltimore Conference early in 1807 that among other commitments in Europe, he was now 'General Superintendent of a new Institution—a Mission for breaking open new Ground in England; on which eight Missionaries are already employed'.[2]

In 1807, South Petherton made its appearance among the Home Mission stations. Coke, with his wife, had been revisiting the scene of his curacy. 'I made a visit to my old place South Petherton,' he told Lomas, 'and spent three nights there. One night I preached in the Church to, I suppose, 2000 people, who came, not only from the little town, but from all the villages round about, and I wept over them in a manner I never before, I think, wept over any congregation in my life, except two or three . . . The other night I collected most of those who had earnest desires . . . Sixteen of them appeared to prize Christian fellowship and therefore I united them in class, and got Brother Stuckey of Ilminster (5 miles off) to promise to lead them every Thursday evening, till the Lord shall raise a leader among themselves.'[3] Because the whole neighbourhood seemed ripe for the gospel, the Conference appointed Richard Smetham to establish a mission there, and the first chapel was built in 1809. Thus did Coke's earliest ministerial labours produce a belated harvest.

The 1808 mission report, in setting out the purpose of these new missions, depicts a secularized society oddly like our own: 'In numerous small towns, villages and hamlets, a very considerable part of the inhabitants attend no place of worship whatever, nor once think of entering a religious edifice, except when marriages, baptisms, or funerals occur. It is among people of this description that our missions have been chiefly established.'[4] Times have not changed, after all.

[1] Letter to Jenkins, 1st October 1806 (M.M.S. Archives).
[2] Letter to the members of the Baltimore Annual Conference, 6th January 1807 (Garrett Theological Seminary).
[3] Letter to Lomas and Jenkins, February 1807 (M.M.S. Archives).
[4] Quoted by Drew, p. 323.

The home missions grew rapidly, though in certain towns, such as York and Hull, some of the subscribers to the foreign work who were not members of society refused to support them.[1] In 1810 Coke wrote optimistically, 'Let us go on, and not regard any croakers, and God will be with us in spite of the Sidmouth's and all our enemies, and we shall, I believe, have a leaven in every Village in England in twenty years.'[2] But the mission outgrew its strength and after 1813, deprived of Coke's enthusiasm, became a drag on the connexional wheel. In 1817, in a pamphlet setting out his 'Thoughts upon the Finances, or Temporal Affairs, of the Methodist Connexion', Jonathan Crowther, Coke's earliest biographer, blamed the unstable finances of Methodism on the number of circuits dependent on connexional grants. Most of these circuits had begun as Home Mission stations. 'A few years ago,' he wrote, 'Dr. Coke boasted that by these Missions he had given us forty Circuits. But alas! in a temporal point of view, most of them have proved so many Mill stones hung about the neck of the Connexion, through which it has been sinking every year. And even in a spiritual sense, few of them have been very prosperous. But this was not owing to any want of integrity or zeal in the Doctor. In many instances, however, there has been a flagrant want of judgment, economy, and prudence.'[3]

Whether this comparative failure should be set down to Coke's want of prudence or to the Connexion's half-hearted support, it is hard to say. In at least one area, North Devon, the retrenchment which followed hard upon Coke's death seriously hindered the spread of Methodism in the villages. Though he did not live to see the rise of the Bible Christian movement, Coke would surely have understood the compulsion under which William O'Bryan was led to evangelize a neglected corner of the West Country at the cost of expulsion from the St. Austell Circuit. O'Bryan was, after all, attempting a task to which Coke had long been goading the Wesleyan Conference and one which it had only half-heartedly tackled through the Home Missions. Had the whole Connexion shared Coke's vision and perseverance, both the Primitive Methodist and the Bible Christian movements might have developed within the parent body and the mutual impoverishment of separation might have been avoided.

[1] Letter to Johnson, 15th November 1809 (M.M.S. Archives).
[2] Letter to Johnson, 26th May 1810 (M.M.S. Archives).
[3] Crowther, op. cit., p. 16.

These English mission stations were by no means the first-fruits of Coke's concern for the witness of the Church at home. In 1799 he had taken the initiative in establishing vernacular missions among the Irish Roman Catholics, and followed this in 1800 with a Welsh-speaking mission in North Wales.

In the course of his successive tours of Ireland, Coke became convinced of the need for a mission among the Irish-speaking section of the population. The way had been pioneered many years before by Thomas Walsh. Later, with Coke's encouragement, Charles Graham attempted to preach in Irish in Sligo, and the Irish Conference of 1790 acknowledged his unexpected success by receiving him as a preacher on trial despite his being a married man of forty.[1] These were no more than spasmodic and unco-ordinated experiments. In 1799, however, Coke proposed to the Conference an organized mission to the Irish-speaking Roman Catholics. His tour of Londonderry, Tyrone and Fermanagh prior to the Conference had convinced him that the time was now ripe for such a venture. With the rebellion over, the preachers were once more free to travel without fear of molestation or official suspicion. Moreover, the distress and disillusion under which many of the native Irish then laboured were seen as an opening for the Gospel. 'The minds of the people were subdued . . . and desolated homesteads ravaged by death and destruction kept before them the sad consequences of rebellion and sin, while the religious teachers who had led them on to ruin had in many instances lost their confidence.'[2] The Conference in Dublin doubted at first whether Coke's plan was practicable, for though the need was obvious and suitably qualified men were to hand, the lack of funds was a serious obstacle. However, Coke's fervent conviction that this work must be undertaken won the day, and when, as on similar occasions in England, he pledged himself to raise the necessary funds, the opposition melted away. Two missionaries were appointed and Coke had the highest hopes for their success. Two years later, in presenting to 'the Generous Public' copies of letters from the Irish Missionaries, he wrote: 'The native Irish have passions the most susceptible of impression of any people, I believe, in Europe: if, therefore, their warm affections can be engaged on the side of truth, they will probably become, from the most superstitious, one of the most virtuous and religious nations on the globe, and, in reality, correspond with the title which was

[1] Crookshank, *Methodism in Ireland*, i. 2f., 17.   [2] Ibid., i. 165f.

anciently bestowed upon their island, of "The Isle of Saints".'[1] If this was too sanguine a view by half, it was at least true that the mission developed rapidly, so that in ten years the two pioneers had grown to a dozen and their labours continued to be fruitful for many years. In a memorial sermon preached in the Whitefriar Street chapel in Dublin at the end of 1814, Andrew Hamilton spoke of his country's great obligation to Coke and the affection in which he was held by the Irish Methodists. To serve his Irish brethren and the cause of God in Ireland was 'one of the chief felicities of his life', and many remembered how often he had prayed from the pulpit 'that Ireland might flame with the glory of God'.[2] As always, Coke's prayers had been matched with strenuous action.

Only one year after successfully launching the Irish mission, Coke was steering a similar project for Wales through the British Conference. The idea had long been germinating in his mind, and was fertilized by a journey through North Wales soon after the 1799 Conference. If there were to be Irish-speaking missions, why not Welsh-speaking ones too?

In the earliest days, the Wesleys and Howell Harris had agreed on a plan of comity by which Welsh-speaking Wales was left to the Calvinistic Methodists, an arrangement which lasted for many years, despite the widening doctrinal breach in the ranks of Methodism. Nevertheless, there was some Wesleyan preaching in Flint and Denbighshire from at least 1750 onwards, and for many years, especially as he passed to and fro on his way to Ireland, Coke pondered the need of his native Wales and what might be done about it. The need as he saw it was twofold: to supplement the labours of both parish clergy and dissenting ministers by sending Welsh-speaking itinerants among those otherwise out of range of the Gospel; and to combat the insidious effects of Calvinistic preaching. Ironically, he was encouraged in his project in the autumn of 1799 by meeting with a 'pious person' in Anglesey, Griffith Owen, a Calvinist of Holyhead who was friendly towards the Wesleyan preachers and gave them his support.[3] On his return from America the following summer, Coke met Owen Davies, a native of Wrexham then stationed in Cornwall. Davies's thoughts were already running

---

[1] *Copies of the Letters from the Missionaries who are employed in Ireland*, p. 43.

[2] Hamilton, *The Faithful Servant*, p. 17.

[3] A. H. Williams, *Welsh Wesleyan Methodism*, pp. 73ff. Cf. references to Owen in John Hughes's *Journal* (printed in *Bathafarn*, 1956–7).

along the same lines and he spoke to Coke on the matter. 'He said, his mind had been influenced by a similar desire for some time, and that he intended making a proposal to this effect at the next Conference. At the same time he requested me to offer myself to this work.'[1]

It was about this time that Edward Jones formed his society in Ruthin, and Coke heard of this just soon enough for it to spur him on to win Conference approval for his latest scheme. He arrived in London late, having been delayed by contrary winds in the Irish Channel, and found the stations already settled. Nevertheless, he proposed that the Conference should appoint Owen Davies and John Hughes as Welsh-speaking missionaries, Davies as 'a Native of that Country' and Hughes 'as understanding the welsh Language'.[2] It had been decided that Davies should return to Cornwall and Hughes was already set down for Leek in Staffordshire. But to alter the stations even at that stage was a small matter to Coke when the furtherance of the Kingdom was involved. He moved the Conference by a speech in which he told how 'his heart was being consumed for his kinsmen, the Welsh of North Wales'. 'Did not darkness encompass the land and were not many being doomed through ignorance? For those preachers already in the country were not interpreting the Gospel broadly enough.'[3] Those who had at first thought the scheme too romantic were won over, and Coke's two nominees were appointed. Despite temperamental differences between Davies and Hughes, which sometimes strained their personal relationship, this work grew steadily. By the Conference of 1802, the Ruthin Circuit was able to support three preachers, and Coke was inspired by their success to undertake the support of two more from the mission funds.[4] The 1805 missionary report says that the work in North Wales has been 'successful beyond our most sanguine expectations', and adds, 'In about five years nineteen Welsh travelling preachers; about twenty local preachers, and a society of near four thousand have been raised.'[5] This encouraged Coke to contemplate an extension of the work into his native South Wales.[6] His interest was, as always, an intensely personal one. He wrote to Lomas early in 1806 that the preachers in North Wales were pressing

[1] *Methodist Magazine*, 1803, p. 537.   [2] John Hughes's *Journal*.
[3] Williams, op. cit., pp. 78f., quoting Hughes's *Journal*.
[4] John Hughes's *Journal*.   [5] Quoted by Crowther, p. 470.
[6] Letter to Joseph Entwisle, 2nd March 1805 (M.M.S. Archives).

him to make them a more extended visit and to preside at their quarterly meetings. 'They say it will be of great use . . . The work spreads rapidly in that country. But they are violently opposed by the numerous Antinomian preachers in that country, some of whom even go so far as to say that the missionaries do not act under the authority of the Conference.'[1] A suggestion at the 1806 Conference that the Welsh missions should be brought more directly within the control of the Conference so grieved him that it was dropped for the time being.[2]

For the most part Coke's impressions of the Welsh work were gleaned during his journeys to and from Ireland, but in the autumn of 1808 he and his wife made an extensive tour, from South to North via the Merioneth coast, and finishing in Denbigh and Flint, where the Welsh-speaking mission was centred.[3] When Coke preached to a crowded congregation at Ruthin, Hughes acted as his interpreter, and says, 'Several of the respectable inhabitants, and some members of the Calvinist society, attended the Doctor's ministry; and the discourse in the morning was in his most interesting style and manner. Mr Davies and his friend accompanied him to Denbigh, Holywell and Mold; at which places the people paid him great attention, notwithstanding the apathy that prevailed among many, and the hostility of others; while, as to the poor, the venerable man had it not in his power to address them.'[4]

*   *   *

Three further spheres of home mission activity must be noted. There was, in the first place, as an off-shoot of the work in Wales itself, a Welsh missionary stationed in London, the first being Edward Jones in 1808. The initiative once more lay with Coke. In July 1809, the missionary committee was of the opinion 'that the Welsh Mission in London ought to be discontinued, because the success, or even the probability of success, bears no proportion to the Expence'.[5] That the appointment continued for some years was

[1] Letter to Lomas, 12th February 1806 (M.M.S. Archives).
[2] John Hughes, in *Wesleyan Methodist Magazine*, 1832, p. 480.
[3] Hughes's *Journal*.
[4] *Wesleyan Methodist Magazine*, 1832, pp. 541f. For the detailed history of Welsh Wesleyanism, see: A. H. Williams, op. cit., *W.H.S. Proc.*, xviii, etc.
[5] Missionary Committee Minutes.

due chiefly to Coke's intervention. Arguing that much of the effectiveness of the Welsh missions depended on the stationing of a Welsh-speaking preacher in the metropolis, he wrote to the Committee, 'Do what you can for them. Don't let that work fall to the ground . . . Let us keep the ground we have. I join Brother Carter in praying your aid for my poor country men in London. May God incline your hearts to do something effective for them.'[1] During the same period, Coke was pressing on, under very considerable difficulties, with the publication of a Welsh translation of his New Testament commentary.

He was also a pioneer in the establishment of Sunday Schools, though it was always less important to him that the pupils should be educated than that they should have the gospel preached to them. In December 1798, he preached one of the first sermons in City Road Chapel on behalf of the new Sunday School Society, recently formed to co-ordinate the work of several schools that had sprung up in London.[2] A number of Sunday Schools in Cornwall, including Liskeard (1803) and Camelford (1805) owe their origin to his encouragement and financial support.[3] 'I consider the establishment of Sunday Schools', he wrote in 1797, 'as one of the greatest blessings that these nations have been favoured with. I most sincerely wish that every Methodist society in the world supported a Sunday School. We do much in this way at present; but if our exertions were unanimous and universal, we should, I believe, prepare the rising generation for a general revival.'[4]

Finally (if such a word is ever appropriate in dealing with anyone so indefatigable) in his closing years, with all the burden of the existing missions on his shoulders and plans for a mission to India already shaping in his mind, Coke took up the cause of the French prisoners of war then in England, and persuaded the Missionary Committee officially to adopt and extend a work already being carried on by William Toase in the Medway prison-ships.

This idea, too, had long been germinating. Coke was improving his French, with the possibility of a mission to France in mind, as early as 1786. He looked upon the work in the Channel Islands as a preparation for an eventual 'invasion' of the mainland. The Revolution was a serious blow to his hopes, but seemed in due course, by

[1] Letter to Johnson, 30th April 1810 (M.M.S. Archives).
[2] G. J. Stevenson, *City Road Chapel*, p. 154.
[3] *W.H.S. Proc.*, xxxii. 67f.   [4] Coke's *Journal*, p. 261.

breaking the power of the Roman Church in France, to be a providential opening up of the way for a Protestant mission.[1] Coke was not the man to weigh personal safety in the balance against an opportunity for evangelism. Soon after his hasty return from America in 1791, he heard that a plea for a preacher to be sent to Paris had gone unanswered because of the recent death of the Countess of Huntingdon. Taking this as a providential call, Coke set out on September 12th,[2] sailing via Jersey where he ordained Jean de Quetteville as a young preacher in every way suited for this mission. Landing at Granville, they travelled through Normandy to Paris. At Courseulles, Coke met and ordained William Mahy. Arriving in Paris, where the revolutionary spirit was at its height, they sought out the writers of the letter to Lady Huntingdon. These turned out to be two English schoolmasters whose motive, it subsequently appeared, was to stimulate the demand for English tuition. Coke lost no time in hiring a preaching-room near the river and began to negotiate the purchase of a disused church for £120. It very soon became apparent, however, that the possibility of establishing a mission there had been grossly exaggerated. At the first service held in the room, de Quetteville had no more than thirty-six hearers; while the announcement that next day the English doctor would read a sermon of his own composing in the French tongue produced a congregation of six. Even Coke began to see that the situation was not promising, and prepared to beat an honourable retreat. Through the timely intervention of an English acquaintance, Miss Freeman Shepperd, whom he found to be then living in a convent in Paris, he was able to extricate himself from the negotiations to purchase the church, and was soon on his way home.[3]

The people of Paris were clearly too preoccupied with their

---

[1] Coke may well have taken his cue in this matter from Wesley himself. Cf. Wesley's letters to Thomas Morrell, 4th February 1790, and to William Black, March 1790 (*Letters of John Wesley*, viii. 199f., 204). The letter to Morrell was forwarded by Coke with a covering letter of his own (*Christian Advocate & Journal*, 27th March 1851, p. 49).

[2] Letter to Mrs Charles Wesley, 11th September 1791 (W.H.S. Library, London).

[3] Drew, pp. 239ff., gives the most detailed version of this visit to France, based largely on Coke's own unpublished account. But cf. also William Toase, *The Wesleyan Mission in France*, pp. 14f. Crowther's account (p. 310) of the help given by Miss Freeman is substantially different and appears to be less reliable. Cf. Findlay and Holdsworth, iv. 445.

revolution to give any serious thought to their spiritual condition, least of all on the prompting of a well-bred Welshman. A less sanguine, or less zealous person than Coke would scarcely have seen the moment as an opportune one for such an experiment. They left Paris, in fact, under threat of being strung up on the lamp-posts if they remained.[1] It is hardly surprising that Coke never pursued his intention of publishing the journal of this escapade.[2] Nevertheless, he did not consider the venture a total failure. If Paris remained inviolate, he continued to cherish the hope that an opportunity to follow up this first visit would one day arise. Meanwhile, a seed had been sown in Normandy. He summed up the results in a letter to Ezekiel Cooper in November: 'Soon after the English Conference I found it in my heart to visit France: and the Lord went with me. We have already formed a few Societies in Normandy . . . I spent some time in Paris, and the Lord was with me there.'[3] Later a more detailed report went to Walter Churchey: 'I spent about five weeks in France, with two of our French Preachers: one from Jersey, and one from Guernsey. In Normandy we had some success. About eight hundred of the French Protestants, in the neighbourhood of Caen, put themselves under our instruction. Thirty of them, who manifested good desires, we united in Class: six of those were deeply awakened. I left the two Preachers to labour in Normandy. One of them I took with me to Paris; but our success in that dissolute city was not equal to our expectations. However, I have received some encouraging letters from thence, since I left it.'[4]

In the years that followed, the final stages of the Revolution led to the rise of Bonaparte and two decades of war between France and England. Undeterred by these events, Coke still hoped that the opening for a mission to a country so desperately in need of the Gospel would present itself sooner or later. He told his American friends in 1794 that amid his many other commitments he was finding time to improve his French, 'that we may exert our utmost efforts for the saving of Souls in France, when in the Providence of God

[1] Etheridge, p. 229, quoting de Quetteville's daughter. Drew nowhere hints that their lives were threatened.

[2] Drew, p. 241.

[3] Letter to Ezekiel Cooper, 22nd November 1791 (Garrett Theological Seminary).

[4] Letter to Walter Churchey, 23rd December 1791 (*Wesleyan Methodist Magazine*, 1826, pp. 387f.).

peace is established'.¹ But peace was long in coming and it was war which was to furnish the opportunity Coke sought.

In the spring of 1810 William Toase, then in the Sevenoaks Circuit, accepted an invitation to preach to the prisoners-of-war on board the prison-ship *Glory*. The success of his first visit encouraged him to repeat it as frequently as his circuit duties allowed. Coke came to hear of this opening early in the following year. On 18th April 1811, he wrote to a correspondent in Worcester, 'I shall be glad to do what I can in behalf of the French Prisoners; & shall undertake something in that business, or sincerely intend so to do, next week. If you can send me any further information on the business, do me the favour of doing so.'² He was quick to see in this an opportunity of re-establishing the mission to France, which had been languishing for so long because of the war. Not that it had ever entirely ceased: Coke had quite recently received letters from de Quetteville describing how William Mahy was still at his post in Normandy, despite many obstacles and privations.³

Coke was soon in contact with Toase and by 20th June, 1811, was ready to propose to the Committee that his work should receive official recognition and be extended. 'There are now, I suppose, 60,000 French prisoners in England. Br. Toase is remarkably useful among many of them. Should he not be set at liberty to devote himself to their salvation here and there? I could find a most excellent Frenchman, a most devout and able man, a local preacher, but married, in Jersey to join him, and could easily raise money enough for their support in a *separate* way, that is, distinctly from our fund. What a glorious thing it would be thus to send religion into France! It is our only way at present. Lord Liverpool *I am sure* would grant us power to visit all the French prisons.'⁴ On the Committee's recommendation, Toase was set apart at the next Conference to go as French Missionary in the Rochester Circuit; and possible local objections were forestalled by a note to the effect that the General Superintendent of the Missions, and not the Circuit, was to be re-

¹ Letter of 23rd July 1794 (Baltimore Methodist Historical Society and Garrett Theological Seminary).
² Letter to Miss Knapp of Worcester, 18th April 1811 (Archives Centre).
³ See especially de Quetteville's letter of 18th January 1810, published in the *Magazine* for that year, pp. 126f.; and cf. pp. 444f., of the same volume. Also, Toase, op. cit., pp. 18ff.; R. D. Moore, *Methodism in Channel Islands*, pp. 71f.
⁴ Letter to the Committee, via George Highfield, 20th June 1811 (M.M.S. Archives).

sponsible for his support. Once again, Coke's readiness to shoulder the financial responsibility had won the day, though before the end of the year we find him protesting that what he had undertaken was *not* to finance the mission personally but to raise the money by 'private applications'.[1]

The development of this work among the prisoners had in fact brought about a resumption of the old tug-o'-war between Coke and his committee. Towards the end of 1811 they wrote him a letter prefaced by a protestation that they desired to act in unison with him in all things and had the success of the various missionary undertakings deeply at heart. They then proceeded to raise objections to his recent begging in London for the missions to Sierra Leone and to the French prisoners—which they feared might jeopardize support for the general work; and also to his recruiting a missionary from Jersey for the work on the Medway without having consulted them.[2] On the understanding that he would raise the money, Conference had authorized him to call out two of the French-speaking preachers from the Channel Islands. Coke was particularly eager to extend the work to the depots and prison ships in Devonshire, especially as there were others preparing to step in if Methodism procrastinated; and he had several suitable preachers in mind. Coke's influence in official circles had won the Government's blessing and support, but only after some frantic correspondence with them was Coke able to carry the Committee along with him.[3] Even then in order to get his three French missionaries, he was obliged to relinquish the pioneer of this work. In 1812 Toase returned to circuit life, but was stationed at Rochester where he could supervise the work of Armand de Kerpezdron among the Medway prison-ships. Peter le Sueur jun. was sent among the prisoners at Plymouth and on Dartmoor where the work had been begun by Amice Olivier;[4] while William Beale laboured among

---

[1] Letter to the Committee, 26th December 1811 (M.M.S. Archives). Cf. letter to de Quetteville, quoted by Moore, op. cit., p. 81.

[2] Letter from the Committee to Coke, December 1811 (M.M.S. Archives), to which his letter of 26th December is a reply.

[3] See his letters to the Committee, 26th December 1811; 28th January, 13th February and 15th February 1812 (M.M.S. Archives) and the Committee minutes for this period. Also Toase, op. cit., pp. 32f.

[4] In March 1812, Coke himself spent some time at Plymouth Dock, lending his support to Olivier, who had come over from Jersey, despite the Committee's disapproval, to undertake this work. (Letters to R. C. Brackenbury, 20th March 1812 [Wesley's Chapel, London] and to John Holloway, 25th March 1812

those at Portsmouth, and James Etchells at Stapleton, Bristol. There were in all some 70,000 prisoners in these various depots, closely confined in squalid conditions, many of them illiterate and all of them spiritually unshepherded. It is little wonder that the very showing of concern for their plight met with a ready response. Coke did not live to see the end of hostilities, which restored them to their native land. But he had initiated a work in this instance whose effects were so widely disseminated that, for that very reason, they defy computation.

[M.M.S. Archives]; Committee minutes, 3rd January and 7th February 1812). The Committee refused to sanction a second missionary to assist Olivier, who soon handed over the work to le Sueur. Coke and the Committee were again at loggerheads over the conditions of le Sueur's appointment. In correspondence with le Sueur, the Committee virtually repudiated his appointment by Coke and gave him every encouragement to return to Jersey; despite this, he was set down once more for the Plymouth Mission at the 1813 Conference. (Committee Minutes, 4th September, 30th October, 4th December 1812; letter from le Sueur to the Committee, 17th November 1812, expressing his perplexity at the conflicting 'proposals, invitations, promises & encouragements' he had received first from Coke and then from the Committee (M.M.S. Archives).)

CHAPTER 21

MAN OF LETTERS

Although prayer was for him 'the great key to every blessing',[1] Thomas Coke's devotion to his Lord was active rather than contemplative. For many years, the prospect of death repelled him, not because he was unprepared to meet his God, but because he could not bear to relinquish cherished schemes and unfulfilled opportunities. Clinging precariously to the branches of a fallen tree amid the flood waters of an American river, he realized how imperfectly resigned he was to the divine will. 'I felt no fear at all of the pain of dying, or of death itself, or of hell, and yet I found an unwillingness to die. All my castles which I had built in the air for the benefit of my fellow-creatures, passed in regular array before my mind, and I could not consent to give them up.'[2] To be employed for Christ was his life-long delight: but to be laid aside for Him was something he came to accept only after a long struggle. The ill-usage he endured during the voyage to America in 1796 taught him greater resignation. 'O how was I weaned from the world and all its follies,' he wrote, 'and not only so, but became willing to be anything or nothing, as the Lord pleased; to be employed or laid aside, as he judged proper. This was a spirit I was but little acquainted with before. I had sincerely loved God for many years, and had no ambition but to be the instrument immediately and remotely of converting millions to him. I had been long willing to die, but not to be inactive while I lived.'[3]

Following closely upon this, another passage in his *Journal* reveals a different aspect of his nature—the contemplative disposition behind the life of activity. 'At Mr Myrick's I . . . spent much time engulphed in the woods, and reading the younger *Racine's* celebrated Poem *de la Religion*. Many might imagine, that my *natural* disposition leads me into busy life; but it is the very reverse. If the principle of duty did not carry me forth into scenes which call for activity and exertion, I should certainly settle in some solitary place, where I

[1] Coke's *Journal*, p. 119.   [2] Ibid., p. 56.   [3] Ibid., pp. 219f.

might enjoy the company of a very few select friends, and the pleasures of a retired rural life.'[1]

Throughout his other activities, Coke maintained a preaching ministry comparable to that of Wesley himself. But even his admirers tempered their praise with a recognition of his limitations in the pulpit. 'As a preacher', wrote Samuel Drew, 'his talents were always displayed to the greatest advantage, when he applied himself to the hearts of his hearers; and at this point he seemed invariably to aim . . . His public address, however, was too rapid for the tardy movements of sober theological discussion. Into a detail of argument he seldom entered; but he supplied the deficiency by a copious appeal, which he generally made to scripture authority, with which his mind was abundantly stored.'[2] Samuel Woolmer gives a similar verdict: 'His principal *forte* in preaching, was bold assertion and warm declaration. He was generally too warm for a theological reasoner. His subjects were seldom in an argumentative strain; but he was sound, sensible and lively, calculated to arrest the attention and captivate the heart. He was rather luminous than profound. His style was generally glowing and flowery; and often eloquent and sublime.'[3]

Coke's voice, which was normally soft and mellifluous, sometimes rose almost to a shriek in the more impassioned parts of a sermon.[4] Wesley once contrasted his pulpit manner with that of another preacher who was not only inaudible, but spoke in 'a dead, cold, languid manner, as if he did not feel anything which he spoke'.[5] Coke himself advised another preacher not to heed 'the poor old dry sticks that love to see a Preacher what they call cool and calm'.[6] But for his own as well as for his congregations' sake, he would have done well to heed Wesley's warning against screaming in the pulpit, for to the end of his ministry he found that preaching three times on a Sunday left him very hoarse.[7]

The effect of Coke's pulpit oratory on non-Methodists was not always what he intended. Dorothea Jordan, a famous actress and courtesan of the day, once went to hear him preach in Liverpool. 'The place was crowded beyond imagination. His doctrine was very

---

[1] Ibid., p. 236; cf. p. 146, quoted on p. 162 above.
[2] Drew, p. 381.   [3] Woolmer, op. cit., pp. 18f.
[4] Crowther, p. 511; Drew, p. 380.   [5] *Letters of John Wesley*, vii. 346.
[6] Letter to William Holmes, 12th October 1790 (Book Steward's Newsnotes, May, 1948).
[7] Letter to William M'Kittrick, 31st May 1810 (M.M.S. Archives).

good and perfectly orthodox as far as faith goes, and he commenced with a prayer for the King, Queen, Prince of Wales, Princess of Wales, and all the royal family, but his manner and delivery were so truly ludicrous that I was forced to pinch myself to keep from laughing.'[1]

His appeal to the heart rather than to the mind, his propensity for piling up one text of Scripture upon another, and his 'flowery' oratory were among the reasons why his sermons won few admirers among the dour Presbyterians of Edinburgh.[2] Another was his readiness to pluck other men's flowers, for his thinking was eclectic rather than original. He appears, too, to have sustained his roving ministry on a limited number of themes, among which one stood out —the world mission of the Church. His favourite text, from Psalm 68, 'Ethiopia shall stretch out her hands to God', was used over and over again in pulpits throughout the land, and it was when he discoursed on this theme that his eloquence became most persuasive. The Baptist minister, Samuel Pearce, soon after beginning his ministry in Birmingham, went to hear Coke preach from this text and his missionary interest was fanned into a flame. 'Then it was that 1 felt a passion for missions,' he wrote. 'Then I felt an interest in the heathen world far more deep and permanent than before.'[3] Through the zeal he kindled in Pearce, Coke added his influence to that of Carey in the formation of the Baptist Missionary Society, and the Holy Spirit once again showed Himself indifferent to denominational barriers.

Among the handful of other themes on which Coke regularly preached, the divinity of Christ was probably his favourite. It was the subject of one of his official sermons at the Christmas Conference in Baltimore, and this was afterwards published at the Conference's request. He preached it also at the Irish Conference of 1788, and again published it at their request. In 1811 it became his only sermon to appear in a Welsh translation. But the sermon had been in existence at least since 1779, when he sought to convert the Arians

[1] Quoted in *W.H.S. Proc.* xxx. 188. Mrs Jordan was mistress to the Duke of Clarence (later William IV).

[2] See above, pp. 139f. In the printed sermon Coke acknowledges his debt to Hoole's collection of scripture proofs.

[3] Andrew Fuller, *Life of Rev Samuel Pearce*, p. 108. Warren, *Sermon on Death of Coke*, p. 37, says, 'His uncommon ardour has been a means of giving animation to most other Missionary exertions in our Country, whether amongst the Dissenters, or in the Church of England'.

of Edinburgh. Since his own rescue from Deism, Coke had been a fervant opponent of all forms of heresy, within and without the Church. In 1805 he was on the track of Pelagian tendencies among some of the Cornish preachers, and declared that if the Conference failed to take a determined stand on the matter, he would leave the Connexion immediately.[1] But in this respect the very fervour with which he pleaded the missionary cause led him to intemperate denunciations of those he sought to refute. Early in 1807 he preached against Arianism and Socinianism in Taunton with such warmth that one of his hearers was stung into publishing an open letter rebuking him for the uncharitable spirit and intemperate language in which his 'indiscriminate abuse of professing Christians' was couched. The writer represents Coke as consigning 'all Arians and Socinians indiscriminately to *hell flames without the faintest hope of their salvation*' and declaring at the same time '*that he had more charity for heathen idolators, the worshippers of the sun, than he had for them*'. This contrasts very unfavourably, he claims, with the charitable spirit manifested by John Wesley; but he reserves his severest censure for Coke's manner in delivering his diatribe: 'The dogmatic and magisterial tone in which you conveyed your sentiments last evening; the *coarse, vulgar*, and *degrading epithets* you employed, . . . seem to strike me very forcibly that you at present stand on slippery and dangerous ground. Do you consider yourself infallible? Are you the centre of all wisdom, knowledge and piety? And are you commissioned to hold the keys of heaven and hell? If not, by what authority do you thunder out your anathemas against whomsoever you please, against all but your own party?'[2] Although written in the heat of the moment, this criticism reminds us that Coke's Welsh temperament could lead him seriously astray. There was perhaps wisdom as well as expediency in his concentration on missionary themes as he travelled around the country from year to year.

A handful of his sermons were published during Coke's lifetime. His earliest venture into print was the *Sermon upon Education*, published during his Somerset curacy in order to vindicate himself against

[1] Letter, apparently addressed to one of the Cornish Methodists, 21st August 1805 (*W.H.S. Proc.* i. 103). Cf. letter to Benson etc., 27th August 1805 (M.M.S.); also Etheridge, *Life of Adam Clarke*, p. 212. At the request of the 1806 Conference Coke drew up an annotated series of *Articles of Religion*.

[2] *A Letter to the Rev Dr Coke*, by Job David. For similar criticisms, see *A Key to Explore the Mystery* . . . by a Layman [George Booth]; and Melville Horne, *Investigation of the Definition of Justifying Faith*, 1809, p. 4.

misrepresentations of his critics. Among the others printed from time to time 'by request' are memorial sermons on John Wesley, John Richardson and Hester Ann Rogers, and the two sermons preached at the Christmas Conference of 1784. Of these, as of the few manuscript sermons that have survived, we may at least say that they are no more suggestive of 'dried seaweed' than those of many another preacher who, being dead, yet speaketh.

Coke's many administrative responsibilities and the constant travelling which he accepted as his lot, undoubtedly affected the quality of his preaching. 'Some fastidious critics', wrote Andrew Hamilton, 'thought meanly of the Doctor's abilities as a preacher; and it must be acknowledged, that when his multifarious employment prevented his studying for the pulpit, he did not always excel; but when he gave himself sufficient time to prepare for the work, his compositions were elegant, and his sermons ranked among the best pulpit performances of the day.'[1]

* * *

Even in his rare interludes of leisure, Coke was surprisingly active. Whether confined to a cabin on the high seas or in the retirement of a friendly home such as Raithby Hall, he was fully occupied with the affairs of the churches; and such time as might be left over from official correspondence was devoted to study and the writing of books.

For one so fully involved in administration, Coke was a widely-read man; and in this respect his numerous voyages furnished an opportunity that would otherwise have been lacking. Quite apart from his devotional and biblical reading, we find the mention of authors as diverse as Virgil, Spenser, and Louis Racine. Books of travel and missionary biographies were predictable favourites. It is more surprising to find listed among the volumes of his library stored at City Road a number of musical items, including Handel's *Messiah* and harpsichord concertos by Bach, Handel and others.[2] This must be set over against the disapproval of the musical concerts given by Charles Wesley's sons, which he expressed in the first flush of his evangelical fervour.[3] But if Coke himself had any musical accomplishments or inclinations, his later life must have allowed him few opportunities to exercise them.

[1] Hamilton, *The Faithful Servant* . . . , p. 22.
[2] Catalogue of Coke's books (Archives Centre). Sutcliffe mentions that Penelope Coke had some accomplishments in 'sacred music'.
[3] Letter to Wesley, 15th December 1779 (*Arminian Mag.*, 1790, pp. 50f.).

Coke shared Wesley's awareness of the value of Christian literature. In 1782, anticipating the Religious Tract Society by seventeen
years, Wesley formed a society 'to distribute religious Tracts among
the poor'. To the prospectus that was issued on that occasion, Coke
contributed this commendatory paragraph:

NEVER was an Institution established on a purer or more disinterested
Basis than the present. And surely all who wish well to the propagation
of divine knowledge must afford their Approbation at least, to so benevolent a plan. And, that God may incline the hearts of thousands, to
administer an *effectual* assistance thereto, is the ardent prayer of Thomas
Coke.[1]

Unlike the Wesleys, Coke does not occupy even a minor niche
in the history of English literature. As an author he has no claim
either to originality or lasting importance. Yet, when we bear in
mind the multitudinous demands upon his time, the very number and
variety of his publications remind us how largely he achieved his
purposes through the written and printed word. He became an author
in fact, not by design or aspiration, but almost accidentally and
with some reluctance. In complying with the request of the Baltimore Conference for the publication of his sermon on Asbury's
ordination, he wrote, 'There is nothing in the world, I think, about
which I find more reluctance than the becoming an Author, but they
force me into it.'[2] This reluctance diminished with the years, and he
came to take a certain pride in some of his more ambitious publications; yet to the end he was ready, however regretfully, to forsake his
latest literary project in the interests of the missions or the victims
of persecution. At least one work, his proposed *History of the Bible*,
remained unwritten for this reason. He had printed the first number
as a specimen in 1810, and intended that it should fill three quarto
volumes.[3] But the news, early in 1812, that the mission fund was
£4,000 in debt caused him to 'sacrifice' all his literary labours in
order to 'be nothing but a preacher and a beggar, and to beg morning and afternoon'. 'I felt the sacrifice very great', he told George
Highfield, 'because I am so foolish as to think that I could do some
good through the Press. But all is over. The History of the Bible is
over. I must return the money back to the subscribers for about half

[1] *W.H.S. Proc.* xii. 137; Green's *Wesley Bibliography*, no. 363. Cf. also Appendix E, item 58.
[2] Coke's *Journal*, American edition, p. 294.
[3] This is stated in a prospectus of his works issued in 1810 (copy at B.M.)

a quarto volume.'[1] When he sailed for India early in 1814, he had not entirely abandoned the hope of taking up the *History* on his return,[2] but it remained unfinished at his death.

A whole group of his more ephemeral writings was called forth by such utilitarian considerations as the need to vindicate the action of the Conference in the cases of the Birstall and Dewsbury chapels, or to defend himself from the defamations of Charles Wesley, William Hammet and others. His share in drafting the successive editions of the Book of Discipline was by no means the least part of American Methodism's indebtedness to him. Beginning with the *Plan* of 1784 and the *Address to the Pious and Benevolent* of 1786, a whole series of missionary appeals and reports was wrung from him by the needs of the work overseas. His appeal was always to the 'friends of humanity' as well as 'of religion'. Nor was his interest in men confined to the saving of their souls. The breadth of interest evidenced by the journals of his visits to America and the West Indies is confirmed by such diverse publications as *The Case of the Caribbs in St Vincent* and his three-volume *History of the West Indies*, each of which though focussed on the missions, takes in a much wider survey.

Among these ephemera, a handful of works stand out as those on which he lavished especial care; among them the *History of the West Indies*, the *Commentary*, and his revised edition of Samuel Wesley's poem on *The Life of Christ*. With these we might class the *Life of John Wesley*, were it not that the bulk of that work must have been drafted by his collaborator, Henry Moore. The intransigence of Dr Whitehead, the third of those to whom Wesley's papers had been entrusted, led to an unedifying wrangle and caused the official Conference biography to be compiled and issued with undue haste. Moore is said to have written it in about four weeks, after which Coke revised it for publication.[3] The resulting work bears all the marks of its hasty production.

[1] Letter to George Highfield, 28th January 1812 (M.M.S. Archives); quoted in part by Etheridge, p. 445.

[2] Letter to Samuel Drew, 22nd January 1814, quoted in the *Life of Samuel Drew*, by his eldest son, 1834, p. 184. Coke refers to having with him 'a set of the numbers which have been printed'. I know of no surviving copy of these. Drew, p. 375, says that the work was abandoned because of insufficient support and the transfer of his literary property to the Conference.

[3] G. J. Stevenson, op. cit., p. 133. Cf. MS note of Stevenson, quoted in *W.H.S. Proc.* iii. 53f., in which the information is said to derive from Moore himself. Candler, p. 225, states that at the time the book was being written, Coke

Next to his Commentary, the *History of the West Indies* was Coke's most ambitious literary undertaking, on which he lavished considerable time and care. It was germinating for at least ten years—from its conception in 1799. In December of that year he wrote to a Mr Jones of Fleet Street, outlining the work he had in mind and seeking his collaboration:

I find it highly necessary for me to publish a good History of the West Indies, with proper engravings, &c. of views & other things. The Leading Subscribers to the Missions importune me very much on this point. I mentioned this cursorily to you, when I was in your study in London; & you expressed your willingness to assist me. I will therefore beg of you to be so good (if you please, & if you can) to purchase all the Histories of the West Indies, general & particular, & all the other publications which can throw any light upon the subject, & to place the whole to my account: & if you can spare time, I request you to read them, & to make such remarks upon them as you judge proper, so as to form a Syllabus for a History, or to make any other progress you think proper . . . In respect to the time you employ in reading or writing for me, I will make you, Sir, satisfaction.

I have written to the West Indies, to desire the Missionaries in the different Islands, to collect all the materials they can, which cannot be procured in London, & all the information they can for this work . . . If possible, I should like that the History should make a Quarto volume: & I would interweave the history of the West-India Missions with it. I know that such a work, if executed in a masterly manner, would meet with the public approbation; & would greatly contribute towards the increase of subscriptions for the support of the Missions.[1]

The work Coke contemplated was an ambitious one, embracing, in the words of his title, 'the natural, civil and ecclesiastical history of each island: with an account of the missions instituted in those islands, from the commencement of their civilization'; so that it is

---

was suffering from a disabled right arm as a result of an accident. I do not know of any evidence to support this statement. During the autumn of 1791 he was handicapped by a badly scalded leg. (Letter to Ezekiel Cooper, 22nd November 1791 [Garrett Theological Seminary]). On 19th November, he wrote to Alexander Mather, 'The Lord (Blessed be his Name) is now raising me up. I have been enabled to sit up about half the day for three days past . . . We are going on with the Life of Mr Wesley. 32 pages are printed; and we hope it will not dishonour him that is gone.' (Wesley College, Bristol). Cf also letter to Walter Churchey, 23rd December, 1791 (*Wesleyan Methodist Magazine*, 1826, pp. 387f.).

[1] Letter to 'Mr Jones, No. 32, Fleet Street, London', 6th December 1799, (Archives Centre).

hardly surprising that the single volume eventually became three and their publication was considerably delayed. But by the beginning of 1808, the first volume was almost ready for the press, in spite of the other demands made on his time. 'I have been consulting Mr Jos. Taylor and other brethren', he told Lomas, 'concerning my History of the West Indies. A fortnight or three weeks will perfect my 1st volume, but it must be in *perfect* retirement, except on the Lord's Day. And they are all of the opinion that I ought absolutely to retire for this purpose.' Pride of authorship led him to add, 'The whole History of the West Indies is so far ready, that if I were to deliver the whole now to the printer, I flatter myself it would meet with approbation. But I know I can still improve on it. I have some good hopes that I can get two volumes out of the three out by Conference.'[1]

Though he found the needed retirement in Harrogate, where the season for taking the waters was over, only one of the volumes actually appeared that year. The news of the persecution in Jamaica soon summoned him from his retreat to London, with the result that the two remaining volumes of the *History* did not appear until 1810 and 1812.[2]

During the same period Coke issued, as a labour of love, two small volumes containing Samuel Wesley's poem on *The Life of Christ*, 'corrected, abridged, enlarged by much original matter, and presented to the public in an almost entirely new dress'. This represents his only excursion into the realms of poetry. As he himself admitted, he did not 'profess himself to be a particular favourite of the muses. Parnassus is a mount which he never intended to ascend'.[3] But he had stumbled across this half-forgotten work, whose merits seemed matched by its defects, and was so impressed by the Pindaric stanzas in Book VI on the theme of Christ's divinity that he

[1] Letter to Robert Lomas, 7th January 1808 (M.M.S. Archives). Cf. his letter to the same, 5th December 1807 (M.M.S. Archives): 'I shall soon have two volumes of my History ready for the press. Most people are fond of their own work; possibly it is owing to this that I am confident that my History will be well received . . .'

[2] The third volume is dated 1811, but does not appear to have been in print until the following year. In a letter to George Highfield, dated 28th January 1812, Coke states that, in view of the need for him to clear the debt on the mission fund by more intensive begging, 'The 3rd vol. of the West Indies must remain till after Conference' (M.M.S. Archives).

[3] *Life of Christ*, Vol. i, p. xv.

determined to rescue it from neglect. He was attracted in the first place by the importance and solemnity of the theme, but soon found that the noble design of the work was not matched by its execution. The task he set himself was that of 'separating the ore from the dross'. Chief among the defects which he notes were the 'barbarous accentuation', the frequent use of expletives, archaisms and abbreviations, the 'numerous triplets and unmeaning alexandrines' (which appear to have especially offended his eighteenth-century preference for heroic metre), and what he conceived to be a general lack of proportion. These he sought to remove by a thorough-going revision of the original, in the course of which his extensive excisions were balanced by the addition of some two thousand entirely new lines.

That this revision was begun and continued as a labour of love is revealed by a letter to Brackenbury, in which he asked, 'Have you seen my new versification (I think I may truly call it so) of Mr Samuel Wesley's Life of Christ? If you have, I shall be glad to be favored with your opinion of it. If my readers were to have as much pleasure in perusing it, as I had in preparing it for the press, it would be good indeed. And it was the present which you made me of the original at Raithby Hall, with Mr Thos Roberts' eulogy on it, which led me to the work.'[1]

Coke was sufficiently pleased with the results of his labours to contemplate a further venture in the realms of poesy. Reporting to Thomas Roberts that Samuel Wesley's poem would shortly reappear 'in a very new dress', he wrote, 'When you see it, I beg you will compare it with the original, & you will be able to judge of the labor I have bestowed upon it. I never expected that I should mount my little ambling Pegasus; but now he is moving on, and I have entered upon another Poem, which will be an original.'[2] That this second poem never materialized can scarcely move us to regret. The merits of Samuel Wesley's verse, even in Coke's 'enlarged and improved' edition, are much too slight to earn it a place even among the minor masterpieces of English poetry. It may have enjoyed a certain vogue in its own day and pleased enough of its readers to justify the labours Coke spent upon it, largely, no doubt, as he and his wife

---

[1] Letter to R. C. Brackenbury, 1st September 1810 (Wesley's Chapel, London).

[2] Letter to Thomas Roberts, 1st September 1809 (Historical Society of Pennsylvania). Possibly some fragment remains in the stanzas preserved in the Dodsworth Bequest at Wesley's Chapel (see *W.H.S. Proc.* xxv. 116).

travelled up and down the country in their coach. But despite the appearance of a second edition in America as recently as the beginning of this century, the poem will hardly appeal to the modern reader; and though he took great pleasure in the writing of it, Coke himself would no doubt have preferred that his achievements as an author should be assessed by a more important work, the six-volume Commentary on the Bible.

He began work on this in response to a request by the Conference of 1792 that he would compile a commentary 'neither so tedious as the expositions of Gill and Henry, nor so laconic as the annotations' of Wesley.[1] Three years later he was ready to begin publishing the first parts; but, with his other commitments constantly hindering him, the first volume was not completed till 1801.[2] By the autumn of 1803, when he sailed for the last time to America, the Old Testament volumes were in print and much of the New Testament was almost ready for the press.[3] The necessity of begging intensively for the mission fund resulted in further delays, so that although they were both dated 1803, the two New Testament volumes were not, in fact, completed till 1807, when Coke was still wrestling with the index.[4]

One reason for this protracted delay was the fact that what had been planned as three quarto volumes materialized as six, with an extensive appendix on the fulfilment of prophecy which was later reissued separately. This was one reason why the Conference declined to publish it, unless in abbreviated form, with the result that Coke undertook the printing of it personally.[5]

There were enough subscribers to the Commentary to bring in a substantial profit, which enabled him to pay his own travelling expenses and contribute to the mission funds even when his personal resources had dwindled.[6] In 1810 he announced a new edition of the Commentary with additional marginal references and plates,[7] but

[1] Drew, p. 246.
[2] Letter to Ezekiel Cooper, 23rd April 1795 (Garrett Theological Seminary); letters to Thomas Williams, 19th July 1799 (M.M.S. Archives) and 17th October 1799 (Wesley's Chapel, London); letter sent to George Roberts and other American preachers, 28th February 1801 (Drew University).
[3] Letter to Mr Moulton of Norwich, 11th May 1803 (Dr Elmer T. Clark); and other letters written during the autumn of that year.
[4] Letter to Lomas, 5th December 1807 (M.M.S. Archives).
[5] Drew, p. 246.   [6] Letter to Lomas: See note 4 above.
[7] See p. 322, note 3. About this time there was also a proposal to issue an American edition of the Commentary, which came to nothing (Drew, p. 322).

this did not in fact appear, partly because Coke still had a considerable number of copies of the first edition on his hands. Moreover, a rival publication had just begun to appear from the pen of Adam Clarke, whose claim to scholarship far exceeded Coke's. Clarke had been working on his *Commentary* for some years, but delayed its publication to avoid competition with Coke's work. Even so, Coke viewed the appearance of the first parts of the rival Commentary with some apprehension, if not with resentment, as appears from the letter which he sent out to superintendent ministers early in 1810:

My dear brother and friend,

I think it my duty, in the present circumstances of things, to lay before you the state of my commentary. In the year 1792, the Conference requested me to write or compile a commentary on the Bible. When I had so far advanced in the work, that the part finished might be put into the press, my brethren did not judge it proper to enter on so expensive a work, but voted unanimously, that they would undertake to recommend and sell the whole work for me, if I would risk the publication of it; and that they would take only *ten per cent* commission money for the whole. However, on the representation of our worthy friend Mr Lomas, I made the commission money *twenty per cent*, paying up the arrears, and thereby gave to the book-room not less than a *a thousand pounds* in all. The Conference was pleased to honour me twice with an unanimous vote of thanks for that work.

I have now about two hundred sets of my commentary on the Old Testament on hand, and about twelve hundred sets of my commentary on the New Testament. I have therefore, I think, a claim to your indulgence, and to your assistance for the sale of the remainder of my edition, prior to that of any other person whatever. I here except every thing that makes a part of your stock in the book-room. I would not choose to oppose any person upon earth. But justice, as well as mercy, seems to be in this instance so clearly on my side, that I have no scruple earnestly to entreat the favour of you to assist me in the sale of the remainder of my edition.[1]

Some of the preachers who received this letter were offended at being treated 'as if they were mere vendors of Books, ready to be employed by such as might offer them the greatest profits'. They complained to the Committee in London, on whose behalf Walter Griffith wrote to Coke asking for an explanation. 'I am desired to add', he wrote, 'that Committee do not object to you writing, & printing, & employing Booksellers to sell your Books. Nor do they object to the Preachers disposing of your books, coming to them

[1] Letter of 16th February 1810 (Drew, pp. 330f.).

through the Book-room. But they conceive that no member of the Body ought to avail himself of the advantages which his situation, & the love of his brethren afford him, to promote his own private emolument, to the injury of the sale of those books upon the sale of which so many of his brethren, good, holy, laborious & useful men only stationed upon small & poor circuits, are in part dependent for their support & the support of their families.'[1]

Probably as a result of this official reaction to his attempt to promote the sale of his works through the circuit preachers, in 1811 Coke offered to transfer to the Conference all remaining stocks of his publications, together with the warehouse in City Road in which they were stored. The Conference of 1812 agreed to this transaction at a fraction of the estimated value of the property and stock.[2]

The accusation of plagiarism was levelled at Coke's writing as well as his preaching, and particularly in connexion with the Commentary. This was criticized as being 'in the main a reprint of the commentary of the unfortunate Dr Dodd', who had been executed as a forger in 1777.[3] In fact, however, Coke's indebtedness was far more extensive than that. We have seen how he employed a period of enforced idleness in the Hague in 1794 by amassing material for the commentary. His method, as in other works he undertook, was to compile from the best sources at his disposal, and he made no claim to originality. The wrapper of almost every number of the Commentary, says Drew, bore the avowal that 'he had only been like the bee, culling honey from every flower'.[4] The title-page of the work, it is true, bears no indication of this indebtedness, but that seems to have been contrary to the author's intentions. A note in Coke's own hand, preserved at the Southern Methodist University, Dallas, appears to be the original draft of the title-page, in which the Commentary is described as 'compiled from the best authorities by Thomas Coke LL.D.'. On the same sheet is an 'Advertisement to the Reader', which, Coke instructed, was to be 'inserted either before or after the dedication, as Mr Preston judges best', and in which he acknowledges 'the great assistance I have received in the course of

[1] Letter from Walter Griffith to Coke, 19th March 1810 (W.H.S. Library). Coke had been employing travelling salesmen who, however, proved unprofitable (Drew, p. 322).

[2] G. J. Stevenson, *City Road Chapel*, p. 285. The property and stock were valued at £10,000, but the Conference paid only £3,150 for them.

[3] Crowther, p. 333f. For Dodd, see Tyerman, *John Wesley*, iii. 237ff.

[4] Drew, p. 372.

this work from the writings of Mr Henry, Dr Dodd, Dr Haweis, Bishop Hopkins, Mr McEwen &c. &c.'[1] The dedication 'to the Church of Christ, militant on earth' was duly printed in the opening volume, but for some reason the intended Advertisement did not appear either before or after it, as Coke had intended.

The Appendix to his commentary on the Apocalypse, later republished as a separate work, is the most sustained example of Coke's interest in the fulfilment of prophecy. He saw the political and theological turmoil of his day, and especially the tremendous event of the French Revolution with all its repercussions, as a clear indication that the 'great and terrible day of the Lord' was at hand. Between 1790 and 1810 his correspondence is marked by this recurring theme, and his millenarian convictions grew stronger with the passing years. 'Awful times, very awful times, you may depend upon it, my dear Sir, are at hand', he assured Brackenbury in 1808, 'and we, as a nation, have cause to tremble . . . The Lord Jesus is at this time peculiarly jealous for his own glory. He has drawn the glittering sword, and I am afraid it never will be sheathed till it has done its complete work. But why should we be afraid. The war, the dearth, the pestilence, all proclaim his coming. And is it not the cry of every pious soul, Come, Lord Jesus, O come quickly? If we be safe in the cleft of the Rock, we need not be afraid of anything that can happen.'[2] In the Appendix to his Commentary, he devoted considerable time and care to a survey of 'the great transactions which are at this moment passing before us in the world' and their relation to 'those prophesies which refer to *the latter days*, and as leading immediately to those awful commotions which should precede that reign of righteousness which Christ shall establish on the earth'. In this case he fully acknowledged his indebtedness to 'the most modern publications on the prophesies', particularly those of Bicheno, Dr Mitchell, Whitaker, Galloway, Kett and Faber. Following the calculations of the 'acute and ingenious' Mr Faber, he surmised that 'the final overthrow of the Mahometan, Papal and Infidel powers, will most probably take place about the year 1866'. It is only fair to add Coke's conclusion, that we can have no certain knowledge of how, when or where these prophecies are to be fulfilled. 'It is not knowledge, but goodness, that is held out before us in the present life as

[1] Original in the Bridwell Library, Southern Methodist University, Dallas.
[2] Letter to R. C. Brackenbury, 7th February, 1808 (Wesley's Chapel, London).

the primary object of our pursuit; and they who attain it, are made wise unto salvation, however ignorant they may remain of speculative facts and theories.' Some of those who shared his millenarian views would have done well to heed this note of caution. Again, we may note that millenarianism was one of the factors of his concern for the reunion of the Churches, since he believed that a 'complete external union' would take place during the Millennium and for this reason deplored the intransigent attitude of the American Baptists towards the other Protestant denominations.[1]

The publication which gave Coke more trouble than any other was an abridged edition of his Commentary translated into Welsh. Two volumes, covering the Old Testament and translated by Thomas Roberts of Corwen, Merioneth, appeared in 1806 and 1808. But the New Testament volume was not completed until 1813, after several changes of both translator and printer. During his tour of North Wales in the autumn of 1808, Coke tried hard to engage the services of the Calvinist poet and schoolmaster, David Thomas,[2] whom he described in a letter to Thomas Blanchard as 'an excellent translator, the best translator, as I am told, in all Wales, and a classic scholar'. The Welsh preachers, he added, were very eager for the translation to be made. 'And considering that . . . the Welch have very few well-written books in their own language, it becomes to me a call of duty which I dare not resist.'[3] The way was nevertheless fraught with pitfalls. Before the end of the year Coke had engaged not David Thomas but John Hughes, one of the pioneers of the Wesleyan mission in North Wales, who moved to London early in 1809 in order to supervise the work more adequately. Meanwhile, Joseph Hemingway of Chester, who had printed the Old Testament volumes, was superseded by A. Paris and Son, Coke's London printers. Hemingway's work had been far from faultless, but Hughes soon found himself in difficulties for lack of a compositor who understood the language. Severe criticism from some of the subscribers added to his frustration and led Hughes to resign after completing the four Gospels. Coke appreciated the difficulties under which he had been labouring, however much he regretted the necessity of finding yet

[1] Letter to Stith Mead, 31st January 1804 (Southern Methodist University, Dallas).

[2] Letter from David Thomas to Sion Lleyn, 29th November 1808, printed in D. E. Jenkins, *Thomas Charles of Bala*, 1908, iii. 122.

[3] Letter to Thomas Blanchard, 18th October 1808 (M.M.S. Archives).

another translator and a printer more qualified to wrestle with the intricacies of the Welsh language. The difficult conditions under which this New Testament volume was produced are mirrored in the letter Coke wrote on 1st September 1809, to his old friend Thomas Roberts, then at Carmarthen:

My very dear Friend,

My worthy Friend Mr Hughes has so much trouble, owing to my employing a Printer to print my Welch Commentary who does not understand Welch, that I design to employ a Printer who is a Master of the Welch Language to proceed with the work, and the character which has been given me of Mr Daniel as a man of talent in this way, & of integrity, inclines me to employ him, if Mr Daniel and I can agree . . .

Mr Paris, Took's Court, Cursitor Street, Chancery Lane, London, my Printer, bought a new type on purpose for the Welch Commentary. If Mr Daniel approve of this type from seeing the specimen, I should be glad if he would take the type off Mr Paris's hands. But I by no means intend this as a sine qua non between Mr Daniel and me.

As I sell at *five* sheets for a shilling, I was satisfied that I could not give a fine paper at the present expense of paper. But the paper which my London Printer bought has not given satisfaction to the Subscribers; and therefore I shall print no more of the Commentary on that paper. The Subscribers complain that the paper is too thin . . . I think that, if Mr Daniel and I can agree, it will be best for Mr Hughes with the assistance of my London Printer, to buy a lot of paper in London, in order to expedite business. Whether Mr Daniel consent to purchase Mr Paris's type, or will have one of his own, I shall expect that the type shall be *new* for so large a work, and very good.[1]

Such time-consuming difficulties were the price Coke paid for his part in promoting Christian literacy and scriptural holiness among his fellow-Welshmen. His concern that the Bible should be found in every home also led him in 1810 to begin publishing *The Cottager's Bible*, in which the text itself was accompanied by 'some practical reflections at the end of each chapter'.[2] At the same time

---

[1] Letter to Thomas Roberts, 1st September 1809 (Historical Society of Pennsylvania). (N.B. This is not the Thomas Roberts who translated the first two volumes of the Commentary.) For Hughes's part in the translation, see also Hughes's *Journal*, in *Bathafarn*, 1956–7, under the years 1808–9; *Wesleyan Methodist Magazine*, 1832, pp. 542f.; ibid., 1847, p. 215; A. H. Williams, *Welsh Wesleyan Methodism*, pp. 121f.

[2] Drew, p. 375.

he was planning on a more ambitious scale the *History of the Bible* which remained unfinished at the time of his death.

Most of Coke's major publications were concentrated into a dozen years towards the close of his life. In the midst of his other activities, this would have been impossible but for the assistance of Samuel Drew, whom Coke met in Cornwall early in 1805. This meeting led to a collaboration which saw through the press the closing numbers of his *Commentary on the New Testament* and the *History of the West Indies*.

The fact that Drew's name did not appear on any of the title-pages, and that no formal acknowledgment of his part in these works was made elsewhere, led to considerable criticism of Coke and a revival in new dress of the old accusation of plagiarism. Adam Clarke's comments were particularly caustic. 'What are you doing?' he wrote to Drew in 1807. 'Some tell me that you are writing Dr Coke's History of the West Indies! Can you make English of this speech? If I thought you were dull, I would explain it.'[1] And again, later in the year, 'Have you finished *Dr Coke's* Philosophy yet? It is said here [in London], that you are writing one for *him*.'[2]

There was never a shortage of tongues to wag behind Coke's back, all the more when rumour contained a grain of truth. The facts in this case appear to have been that Coke engaged the services of the Cornish metaphysician as editor, to work over the materials he had accumulated for the completion of his *Commentary* and other books he was contemplating. Coke's itinerant existence in the service of the missions made it virtually impossible for him to give the time and sustained attention which this required. Drew's son, in his biography of his father, gave the most explicit account of the relationship between the two men: 'Much material had been collected for the Commentary. The outlines were also sketched of the West Indian History, the History of the Bible, and other books which Dr Coke had either announced or contemplated. These outlines and materials were put into Mr Drew's hands; and it became his business to select, arrange and perfect . . .'[3] Drew himself gives a similar account of their collaboration, describing his own part in it as that of examining the papers entrusted to him, 'to notice defects, to

[1] Quoted in *Life of Samuel Drew*, by his son, p. 194.

[2] Ibid., p. 204. Cf. F. D. Leete, *Methodist Bishops*, which gives this item among the Coke bibliography: 'A Compiled System of Philosophy, unfinished, 1808'.

[3] *Life of Drew* by his son, pp. 180ff.

expunge redundancies, and to give on some occasions a new feature to expression'. Drew adds that in 1811, Coke 'proposed to incorporate the author's name with his own; but in the title-pages of the works that had already appeared, this could not be done'; and the proposal was thwarted by the subsequent transfer of his literary property to the Conference.[1]

Though the value he set on his own writings increased with time, and his literary projects accordingly became more ambitious, this aspect of his life is the one by which Coke would least have wished to be judged. His talents as an author were strictly limited; and with the exception of the *Journal* extracts, which still make lively and entertaining reading comparable to those of Wesley himself, there is little from his pen that is still of interest for its own sake. Coke would probably not regret this. With his pen, as with his life, he was content to serve his own day and generation. In 1810, he announced a number of new editions to the public with the moderate and justifiable claim that they were 'the result of much enquiry and investigation', to which he added the hope that they formed 'a consistent part with the aims and intentions that have accompanied him through life'.[2] As such, they are not unworthy by-products of a life well spent.

[1] Drew, pp. 371f.
[2] Prospectus, dated 13th April 1810: see p. 322, note 3.

CHAPTER 22

EOTHEN

The thought of a Methodist mission to the East had haunted Coke's mind ever since he wrote to Charles Grant early in 1784. Despite Wesley's backing, the plan had to be shelved because of the pressing calls from across the Atlantic, and for some years Coke was so pre-occupied both with the missions in the West Indies and with affairs at home that he took no further action. But the dream was not forgotten: Coke had heard the call of the East, and in the end the call became too clear and persistent to be denied any longer.

Meanwhile others were at work in India. The Danish missions, begun at Tranquebar in 1706 and sponsored for many years by the S.P.C.K., were reinforced in 1793 by the arrival of the first Baptist missionaries under Carey's leadership. Progress in British India was hampered, however, by several factors, including low moral standards among the European population and the hostility of both Hindus and Roman Catholics. Above all, the Directors of the East India Company were opposed to any kind of missionary work in the territory under their control. The renewal of the Company's charter in 1813 brought about a change of official policy, but until then the opportunities for missionary expansion were severely limited.

During the closing years of the century, public interest in Indian affairs was stimulated by the protracted trial of Warren Hastings. In 1800, the Methodist Conference went so far as to authorize Coke to send a missionary to Madras, but this resolution was never implemented.[1]

Coke was far from idle, however; he continued to collect information and to watch for an opportunity of putting it to use. By 1805 his ideas were beginning to crystallize. He was already in contact with Colonel William Sandys and, through him, with the Directors of the East India Company.[2] Sandys came to the Conference of that

[1] *Minutes*, ii. 59.
[2] Letter to Benson, Lomas and Entwisle, 27th August 1805 (M.M.S. Archives).

year and a small committee was formed to meet him and discuss the possibility of an Indian mission. As a result, an approach was made to the East India Company, and both Coke and Sandys began lobbying such influential figures as Wilberforce, Grant, Lord Teignmouth and Lord Castlereagh, President of the Board of India Control, in the hope of gaining their approval and support. The result was only partially encouraging. 'From comparing together all the information which both the Col. and myself collected on the business,' Coke wrote, 'we were fully satisfied that the Court of Directors for India Affairs would not consent to the Establishment of a mission to India for the conversion of the natives, whether instituted by us or by the Established Church itself. But we were fully satisfied, that neither the Court of Directors, nor the Government in India, would persecute us, if we established a mission in India, but would perfectly connive at our proceedings.'[1] In this spirit of cautious optimism, Coke and Sandys began to make more detailed plans, undeterred by the indifference of the East India Directors. Intimacy with the great did not blind Coke to their limitations. 'We must wait an age, if we wait, for the vote of the Indian Court of Directors. Those merchants are princes and quite above the gospel.'[2]

Towards the end of 1806, Coke had further conversations with Sandys in Helston, and both men wrote at length to the Missionary Committee, setting out their proposed course of action. In the first instance, two or three preachers should be sent to establish a mission among the Syrian Christians of Malabar, as recommended by Claudius Buchanan. Such a mission would be far enough from both the secular authorities in Calcutta and the existing Danish and Baptist missions, and would serve as a bridgehead for a wider work among the Hindus. Sandys estimated the cost of sending out each missionary as £250: £100 for his passage, £100 for fitting him out, and £50 for 'pocket money on landing'. The kind of man required was one who, like Swartz in India or Brainerd in America, 'leaving his Country and kindred and renouncing Honor and Emolument, embraces a life of Toil, difficulty and danger'.[3] Coke already had several suitable men in mind. 'Two will be enough, perhaps, for the first attempt,'

[1] Letter to the Missionary Committee, 18th December 1806 (M.M.S. Archives). Cf. his letter to Lomas of the same date.
[2] Ibid.
[3] Letter from Sandys to the Missionary Committee, 20th December 1806 (M.M.S. Archives).

he wrote. 'But if you think that it will be best to send three, considering the vast distance, and how slowly we can supply places on any accident, I will endeavour to get three.'[1] As always, he supported his plea by readiness to raise the necessary funds:

In respect to finance, Colonel Sandys will make us a very handsome present at the onset of the business, and contribute liberally afterwards. My dearest wife and I will, *if necessary*, save £50 per annum for this mission. If this be not sufficient we will lay out some of our Principal on joint annuities and give £100 per annum or £200 per annum to this mission. I have no doubt but many will join us liberally. I am fully satisfied that we shall be able to support the mission *distinctly* from the General Missions.[2]

This was but one of several abortive attempts by Coke to initiate an Indian mission during the opening years of the century. In 1809 his attention was diverted to the island of Ceylon which, being under direct British rule, displayed a more tolerant attitude than the intransigent East India Company, and seemed a promising base for evangelizing the Indian mainland. Sir Alexander Johnston, the Chief Justice of the island, returned home in that year and, in conversation with Wilberforce, spoke of the need for a Christian mission to Ceylon. Wilberforce commended to him the work of the Methodist missionaries, and put him in touch with Dr Adam Clarke, who raised the matter in Conference. Needless to say, Coke lent his support to the proposals, but again no immediate steps were taken.[3] By now, however, the ground had been thoroughly broken up and the seedtime was near.

Early in 1811, the death of his beloved Penelope plunged Coke into deeper distress of mind than he had yet encountered. 'I am quite shaken from every thing terrestrial. If God's will & Missions were out of the question, I should long to drop my Body, & be with my dear, dear Penelope.'[4] Declining the hospitality of his old friends at Raithby Hall, he drove himself to frenzied activity as a refuge from

[1] Letter to the Committee, 18th December 1806 (M.M.S. Archives).
[2] Ibid.
[3] W. M. Harvard, *Narrative of the Establishment and Progress of the Mission to Ceylon and India*, pp. 15f. Harvard mentions that Coke was also influenced by conversations with others recently returned from India, including a Mr Morton, an Army surgeon and father-in-law to the great Chinese missionary, Robert Morrison.
[4] Letter to R. C. Brackenbury, 16th February 1811 (Wesley's Chapel, London).

his distress. 'The unspeakable loss I have felt, has quite unhinged my whole soul,' he wrote in April. 'I have hardly been able to put pen to paper. I was obliged to fly from myself . . . I have travelled about 1500 miles in about ten weeks; but all nature has lost its beauty. I am happy when in the Pulpit; & can repose in God, when out of it. "I know that in faithfulness he hath afflicted me".'[1] Asbury was not far out when he suggested, in a spirit of gentle rebuke, that Coke had perhaps loved his wife more than his God.[2]

The Conference of 1811 authorized Coke to prepare the way for a mission to Ceylon, and this he proceeded to do. Three things were needed: suitable missionaries, financial support, and government protection. He considered that four missionaries would be sufficient for the time being, but they must be 'men of talent, of studious habits, & apt to learn languages'; by March 1812 he already had three such men in mind.[3] In financing the new venture, it was essential that the support for the existing missions should not be jeopardized. Hence the only way seemed to be by 'a large private subscription of a select number', and several well-to-do subscribers, including Colonel Sandys, had been found in the West Country.[4]

Meanwhile, before the year was out, Coke was married for the second time. Anne Loxdale, the second daughter of Thomas Loxdale of Shrewsbury and one of Wesley's intimate correspondents, was at this time living with a married sister, Sarah, in Crosby, Lancs.[5] She and Coke were already acquainted, and in the August following his first wife's death, he visited Liverpool, for the purpose, as the second Mrs Coke put it, 'of making me an offer of extending my usefulness, by uniting with him heart & hand, in his work of faith, & labour of love'.[6] Many years before, she had been disappointed in love with the result that she was now an eligible spinster of fifty-five and a

[1] Letter to Miss Knapp of Worcester (Archives Centre).

[2] Asbury, *Letters*, p. 450. Cf. Coke's *Memoir* of his first wife, in *Methodist Magazine*, 1812, pp. 211ff.; Harvard, op. cit., p. 17.

[3] Letter to R. C. Brackenbury, 20th March, 1812 (Wesley's Chapel, London). Cf letter of the same date to George Morley (Wesley College, Bristol); and Harvard, op. cit., p. 18. Coke's letter to John Hughes, in the *Methodist Magazine*, 1847, p. 216, appears to belong to this period.

[4] Letter to Brackenbury: See note 3 above.

[5] *W.H.S. Proc.* xxiv. 108. Sarah Loxdale married the Rev. Thomas Hill in 1797. She was opposed to her sister's marriage.

[6] Letter from Mrs Anne Coke to Mrs Fletcher, 28th December 1811 (M.M.S. Archives).

prominent member of the Methodist society in Liverpool. She did not immediately accept Coke's proposal of marriage, partly, no doubt, because some of her family opposed it on the grounds of her delicate health. 'I for some time declined,' she told her friend Mrs Fletcher, 'till all my objections were overruled, and removed by a satisfying conviction of the will of God respecting it.'[1] They were accordingly married on 16th December, in Trinity Church, Liverpool.

During the few months of their life together, Anne Coke proved a worthy helpmeet. Charles Atmore called her 'one of the excellent of the earth' and expressed the hope that Coke would find her to be 'a very great blessing to you and to the cause in which your whole heart has long been engaged'.[2] Coke himself had no doubt of her worth. A few days after their marriage he wrote this lyrical post-script in a note to Mrs Fletcher:

I could fill a Quire of paper with love & praises for my very dear Wife. God himself has brought her to me or me to her, by a series of wonderful Providences, &, I verily believe, by the *direction* of my *Penelope*. I am almost afraid to enter into this subject: & yet you have had such divine interviews with your blessed Saint, that, methinks, I could venture. How-ever, if it please God, that we have an interview here below, I intend to open my whole heart to you: & when Eternity & the Glory of our Jesus open upon us, we shall not only sweetly converse of what we know at present, but infinitely more.[3]

Though he had no reason to revise this estimate of his second wife's sterling worth, Coke seems to have felt the need to justify the apparent haste with which he had plunged a second time into matrimony. It was, after all, a fair topic for the gossiping tongues of Methodism. Accordingly, six months after the marriage, he told a correspondent, 'I bless God, he has given me the very counterpart of my late dear Wife in my present. I cannot possibly tell which of them is most excellent. But my present dear Wife is probably more extensively useful in the Church.'[4]

Like her predecessor, Anne Coke fully accepted the consequences of being married to a man who had no resting place on earth, and

[1] Ibid.

[2] Letter from Charles Atmore to Coke, 27th January 1812 (Emory University).

[3] Note appended to his wife's letter to Mrs Fletcher (see p. 338, note 6).

[4] Letter to John Dutton of Southport, 7th July 1812 (Archives Centre).

they lost no time in setting out together on their first 'pilgrimage'. But she perhaps underestimated the strain which such an existence involved. She wrote:

For my own part I shall esteem it an unspeakable privilege, if I can watch over the health, & contribute to the comfort of so highly esteem'd, & truly laborious a servant of Christ, and his Church, as my beloved Husband is.—As he travels in his own Carriage & by easy stages, having so many calls necessary to make, & I have a truly pious woman, as an attendant & companion, who has been much accustomed to travel, you will not wonder that I find my way of life very pleasant; & I think, greatly calculated to promote health & length of days.[1]

Alas, her words proved anything but prophetic. Though Coke was at pains to settle on her an adequate part of his remaining estate,[2] she was not destined to survive him, but died on 5th December 1812, within a few days of their first wedding anniversary, leaving him for the second time in two years deeply afflicted by his loss. Yet, whenever his grief overwhelmed him, he seemed to hear a voice, saying repeatedly, 'Don't weep: go to the East,' and was convinced that the call was from God.[3] When in due course he emerged once more from the valley of the shadow, it was to take up with renewed singleness of purpose the threads of his plans. Henceforth he declared himself 'dead to Europe' and before long had determined that he would accompany the missionaries in person when they sailed.

Amid these matrimonial vicissitudes, Coke had continued to exercise his mandate from the Conference of 1811 to prepare the way for a mission to the East. Several preachers, including William Ault and William Harvard, had offered for the work, and a number of subscriptions were promised. But the Conference of 1812 postponed its decision on financial grounds. Early in the New Year Ault wrote to ask whether the mission was still contemplated, and Coke roused himself sufficiently from his bereavement to reply:

I have a Ceylonese Mission most closely at heart: more so than ever. I hope you will go to Ceylon, if the Conference consent. I have now on my

[1] See p. 338, note 6.
[2] See especially his letter to John Holloway, 25th March 1812 (photostat at M.M.S. Archives); and cf his letter to the Missionary Committee, 26th December 1811 (M.M.S. Archives).
[3] William Fowler, in *Wesleyan Methodist Magazine*, 1848, p. 123. Cf. Coke's *Journal*, p. 264, Crowther, p. 509.

list several who are willing to pay £5 per annum for seven years for the support of a Ceylonese Mission. I made a visit to Dr Buchanan about three months ago; but it was only for a few hours . . . I intend to write to him in a few days: perhaps I may make him another visit.[1]

Coke had been deeply moved by Buchanan's *Christian Researches in Asia*, describing a tour through southern and western India. The book was his chief source of information on Hindu worship and customs, and on the Christian communities already existing on the West coast. He was particularly stirred by the account of the rites associated with the Juggernaut, an image of Vishnu in Bengal, and by the activities of the Inquisition in Goa.[2] During the period we are now considering he corresponded with Buchanan and in due course paid him the second, more extended visit anticipated in his letter to Ault.

As the engulfing tide of bereavement receded, Coke began to devote himself more and more to the Asian mission, exploring every possible avenue. All who were in close contact with him at this period bear witness to his being entirely absorbed in this one concern.[3] It so fully possessed him that during the spring of that year he committed the most serious of all his indiscretions by offering himself as a candidate for the proposed new Indian bishopric. Such a step can be defended (as distinct from justified) only on the grounds of his total absorption in the spiritual need of India. He revealed his secret in a letter to Wilberforce which, since it was to furnish such valuable ammunition for his critics, must be allowed to speak for itself.

At Samuel Hague's, Esq.
Leeds, April 14, 1813.

Dear and highly respected Sir,

A subject which appears to me of great moment lies much upon my mind; and yet it is a subject of such a delicate nature, that I cannot venture to open my mind upon it to anyone, of whose candour, piety, delicacy, and honour, I have not the highest opinion. Such a character I do indubitably esteem you, sir; and as such, I will run the risk of opening my whole heart to you upon the point.

For at least twelve years, sir, the interests of our Indian empire have lain very near my heart. In several instances I have made attempts to open

[1] Letter to William Ault, 18th February 1813 (Harvard, op. cit., pp. 19f.).
[2] S. Woolmer, *The Servant of the Lord*, p. 28.
[3] E.g. Benjamin Clough (*Wesleyan Methodist Magazine*, 1858, pp. 97f.; Crowther, p. 521); and Thomas Roberts (Buckley, *Memoir of Roberts*, p. 95).

a way for missionaries in that country, and even for my going over there myself. But every thing proved abortive.

The prominent desire of my soul, even from my infancy (I may almost say), has been to be useful. Even when I was a Deist for part of my time at Oxford, (what a miracle of grace!) usefulness was my most darling subject. The Lord has been pleased to fix me for about thirty-seven years on a point of great usefulness. My influence in the large Wesleian [*sic*] connexion, the introduction and superintendence of our missions in different parts of the globe, and the wide sphere opened to me for the preaching of the Gospel to almost innumerable large and attentive congregations, have opened to me a very extensive field for usefulness. And yet I could give up all for India. Could I but close my life in being the means of raising a spiritual church in India, it would satisfy the utmost ambition of my soul here below.

I am not so much wanted in our connexion at home as I once was. Our committee of privileges, as we term it, can watch over the interests of the body, in respect to laws and government, as well in my absence as if I was with them. Our missionary committee in London can do the same in respect to missions; and my absence would only make them feel their duty more incumbent upon them. Auxiliary committees through the nation (which we have now in contemplation) will amply supply my place in respect to raising money. There is nothing to influence me much against going to India, but my extensive sphere for preaching the Gospel. But this, I do assure you, sir, sinks considerably in my calculation, in comparison of the high honour (if the Lord was to confer it upon me in His Providence and grace) of beginning or reviving a genuine work of religion in the immense regions of Asia.

Impressed with these views, I wrote a letter about a fortnight ago to the Earl of Liverpool. I have either mislaid the copy of it, or destroyed it at the time, for fear of its falling into improper hands. After an introduction, drawn up in the most delicate manner in my power, I took notice of the observations made by Lord Castlereagh in the House of Commons, concerning a religious establishment in India connected with the established church at home. I then simply opened my situation in the Wesleian connexion, as I have stated it to you, sir, above. I enlarged on the earnest desire I had of closing my life in India, observing that if his Royal Highness the Prince Regent and the government should think proper to appoint me their Bishop in India, I should most cheerfully and most gratefully accept of the offer. I am sorry I have lost the copy of the letter. In my letter to Lord Liverpool, I observed, that I should, in case of my appointment to the Episcopacy of India, return most fully and faithfully into the bosom of the established church, and do everything in my power to promote its interests, and would submit to all such restrictions in the fulfilment of my office, as the government and the bench of bishops at home should think necessary—that my prime motive was to be useful to the Europeans in India; and that my second (though not the least) was to introduce the Christian religion among the Hindoos by the preaching of the Gospel, and perhaps also, by the establishment of schools . . .

I am not conscious, my dear respected sir, that the least degree of ambition influences me in this business. I possess a fortune of about 1200£ a year, which is sufficient to bear my travelling expenses, and to enable me to make many charitable donations. I have lost two dear wives, and am now a widower. Our leading friends through the connexion receive me and treat me with the utmost respect and hospitality. I am quite surrounded with friends who greatly love me; but India still cleaves to my heart. I sincerely believe that my strong inclinations to spend the remainder of my life in India originates in the Divine Will, whilst I am called upon to use the secondary means to obtain the end.

I would just observe, sir, that a hot climate peculiarly agrees with me. I was never better in my life than in the West Indies, during the four visits I made to that archipelago, and should now prefer the torrid zone, as a climate, to any other part of the world. Indeed, I enjoy in this country, though sixty-five years of age, such an uninterrupted flow of health and strength as astonishes all my acquaintance. They commonly observe that they have perceived no difference in me for these last twenty years.

I would observe, sir, as I did at the commencement of my letter, that I throw myself on your candour, piety, and honour. If I do not succeed in my views of India, and it were known among the preachers that I had been taking the steps I am now taking, (though from a persuasion that I am in the Divine Will in so doing,) it might more or less affect my usefulness in the vineyard of my Lord, and that would very much afflict me. And yet, notwithstanding this, I cannot satisfy myself without making some advances in the business . . .

I have reason to believe that Lord Eldon had (indeed I am sure of it), and probably now has, an esteem for me. Lord Sidmouth, I do think, loves me. Lord Castlereagh once expressed to Mr. Alexander Knox, then his private secretary in Ireland, his very high regard for me: since that time I have had one interview with his lordship in London. I have been favoured on various occasions with public and private interviews with Lord Bathurst. I shall be glad to have your advice whether I should write letters to those noblemen, particularly to the two first, on the present subject; or whether I had not better suspend every thing, and have the pleasure of seeing you in London. I hope I shall have that honour.[1]

The publication of this letter by Wilberforce's sons in 1840

[1] Printed in *The Correspondence of William Wilberforce*, ii. 256ff. The Earl of Liverpool became Prime Minister in 1812.

343

inspired a virulent and ill-informed attack on Methodism by no less a figure than Edward Pusey in an open letter to the Archbishop of Canterbury. His conception of Methodism as based on a doctrine of 'justification by feelings' which destroys all sense of penitence is such a travesty of the truth that it can be defended only on the grounds of culpable ignorance. Pusey proceeds, in similar vein, to instance Thomas Coke, as revealed in this letter to Wilberforce, as an outstanding example of worldly ambition and pride, which he conceives to be a hallmark of Methodists:

One need but refer to the case of the individual to whom Wesley deputed the organisation of their Missions. He was known to be ambitious, affecting high titles of honour, to which he had no claim; was consecrated to the Episcopal Office, and took its highest spiritual titles; since his death, it has been discovered, that he made application for a bishopric in the Church, being ready on such terms to abandon his Wesleyanism. All this is known, yet he is not disowned, but held in high repute as before.[1]

Pusey's attack produced in its turn a detailed reply by Thomas Jackson in which he defended both Methodism and Coke.[2] In particular, he vigorously refuted the charge of worldly ambition, one which, as we have seen, was far older than Pusey. It would be necessary to say little more on this matter were it not that subsequent writers, both Anglican and Methodist, have continued to reiterate the charge. No less an authority than William Warren Sweet, for example, writes that Coke's finer qualities were offset by 'an ambition to lead' and that 'the height of his ambition was to be a bishop'.[3] By reviewing the course of Coke's life of service to the

---

[1] Pusey, *Letter to the Archbishop of Canterbury*, Note F (pp. 17–21).

[2] Thomas Jackson, *Letter to Rev. Edward B. Pusey D.D.*, pp. 73–94.

[3] W. W. Sweet, *Religion on the American Frontier*, vol. iv, *The Methodists*, p. 17. Cf. Knutsford, *Life and Letters of Zachary Macaulay*, p. 50; A. Lunn, *John Wesley*, p. 360; R. Pyke, *Dawn of American Methodism*, p. 123; etc. Yet his critics have overlooked a passage of searching introspection penned by Coke in 1797: 'Lord, teach me to depend wholly upon thee. It is with thee alone I desire to forget all my trials, all the creatures. But alas! too often have I wished that the foolish projects of my own heart should serve as the rule of thine infinite wisdom. I have wandered and been lost in my thoughts; my imagination has formed a thousand flattering dreams; my heart has run after phantoms; I have desired more favour from men, more health of body, more talents, more glory, as if I had been wiser and better acquainted with my true interest than thou, Omniscient Lord God!' (Extract from Coke's *Journal*, printed in *Methodist Magazine*, 1814, pp. 125f.) But to quote such words against him as evidence of inordinate worldly ambition would be obtuseness indeed.

Church, Jackson has little difficulty in showing that such charges were based on a superficial knowledge of the man and his motives. On the charge of worldliness, Jackson comments:

To the cause of religion and humanity he devoted all that he had to give;—his property, his time, his intellect, his influence, his life . . . He might have purchased a rich living, and probably have obtained preferment in the Church, had he been so minded. Instead of this, he lived only to promote the spiritual interests of the most neglected of mankind.

On the letter to Wilberforce which supplied the main ammunition for Pusey's assault, Jackson makes a detailed reply. The object of Coke's proposals, he says, was in every respect noble and worthy, but the means he envisaged were admittedly unfortunate, the more so since they were not likely to achieve their purpose.

Everyone who knew him was aware that his judgment was not equal to his zeal. The ardour of his mind sometimes bordered upon impetuosity, and occasionally led him, especially in the absence of his ordinary advisers, into acts of indiscretion. This was his great failing; and he often confessed it . . . The letter was indiscreet. This is freely acknowledged; but more than this, to the writer's disadvantage, no man can prove.

In accusing Coke of seeking preferment for its own sake, Pusey overlooked the fact that the missionary bishopric he sought was no sinecure. 'If it was a post of honour, it was no less a post of difficulty and peril; and certainly, considered in itself, apart from the momentous object which the Doctor proposed, no very enviable situation for a man who had nearly arrived at the grave period of "threescore years and ten".' Jackson might well at this point have enlisted the support of Wilberforce himself, who years before had suggested to the Archbishop of Canterbury the need for an ordination for missionaries distinct from that of the clergy at home. 'It is obvious', he wrote, 'that the qualifications required in those who discharge the duties of the ministerial office in this highly civilized community, where Christianity also is the established religion of the land, are very different from those for which we ought chiefly to look, in men whose office it will be to preach the Gospel to the heathen nations . . .'[1] Coke's ill-advised offer of himself was inspired primarily by a desire for the conversion of India: we have the

[1] Wilberforce, *Substance of the Speeches of William Wilberforce, Esq., on the clause in the East-India Bill for promoting the Religious Instruction and Moral Improvement of the Natives of the British Dominions in India*, 1813, pp. 2f.

evidence not merely of his own words, but of the general tenor of his life from his first correspondence with Charles Grant in 1784 to his final embarkation for India thirty years later.

Jackson's reply to Pusey's insinuation that in order to gain episcopal honours Coke was ready to abandon his Wesleyanism is of particular interest in the light of the varying course of Coke's churchmanship which we have already plotted. The 'great and leading principle' of Wesleyanism, Jackson says, is 'the absolute and universal necessity of personal conversion to God'. 'Wesleyanism, therefore, subordinates everything to such conversion . . . Canonical irregularity is an accident of Wesleyanism, and does not enter into its nature and substance . . . Dr Coke had been irregular, as irregular as were the Apostles and primitive Evangelists. . . . His purposes were perfectly honourable. He sought not the Church's emoluments and influence, to innovate upon her doctrine and order; but to accomplish that which is the end of all ecclesiastical arrangements—the salvation of redeemed men.'[1] In fact, as in his correspondence with Bishop White, Coke's motive for returning to the Anglican fold was the same as for his initial irregularity—a readiness to subordinate all things to the cause of Christ's kingdom, which more than once blinded him to the imprudence of the steps he took.

For all his ill-advised impulsiveness, it is doubtful whether Coke would have presented himself in this way as a candidate for the Indian bishopric, had not the whole question of the Church in India been then under review. The renewal of the charter of the East India Company provided an opportunity to ensure that in future Christian missions would be free to operate within the Company's domain. During the spring of 1813 Wilberforce was in the thick of a campaign which succeeded in inserting in the new charter a clause 'for promoting Religious Instruction and Moral Improvement of the Natives'. Though the Methodists were now definitely estranged from the Established Church, men like Thomas Coke were still reluctant to be dismissed as Dissenters if it meant forfeiting the opportunities for Christian evangelism that seemed about to be offered in India.

At the same time, Coke was engaged in his own battle within the Methodist Connexion. On 30th April he persuaded a meeting of the Missionary Committee to recommend to the Conference the appointment of one missionary to the Cape of Good Hope and about six for

[1] Jackson, op. cit., p. 92.

346

Ceylon.[1] Coke himself was designated the General Superintendent of the Asiatic Mission, and at the London District Meeting soon afterwards pleaded for support for his plans.[2] Several of his friends sought to dissuade him from accompanying the missionaries; such a course at his age seemed to some to border on folly. 'Surely,' wrote one of them, 'the doctor is getting into a state of dotage.'[3] But Coke was adamant. He told Joseph Entwisle in June,

I am certainly going to India with the help of God, to Ceylon in the first instance. How far we may afterwards stretch our borders, must depend upon Providence. After thirty-seven years' attachment of the most inviolable kind to the Connexion, and attention both at home and abroad to the business in which I have been employed by Mr Wesley and the Conference, with incessant patience and perseverence, I believe that the Conference will not suffer me to go alone. And yet the will of God concerning me is so evident, that, so far as I know myself, I would rather be set down naked on the coast of Ceylon, to make my way from that spot, than not to go at all . . . I should have ten missionaries to go with me, inclusive of a secretary, and of another companion, as a half-servant, to travel with me . . . But I would go with eight, with six, with four, with two, with one, with none. . .[4]

And to Samuel Drew, who had sought in a long letter to dissuade him from going to India, he replied in similar terms:

I am now dead to Europe, and alive for India. God himself has said to me, 'Go to Ceylon'. I am as much convinced, that methinks I had rather be set naked on the coast of Ceylon, without clothes, and without a friend, than not go there.[5]

During the early summer, Coke travelled extensively, accompanied by 'a young man of cheerful piety', named Benjamin Clough. They visited both Scotland and Ireland, and everywhere Coke sought both funds and suitable volunteers for the new mission. The Irish Conference in Dublin encouraged him to press on with the project, and supplied three of the volunteers he needed, James

---

[1] Missionary Committee minutes (M.M.S. Archives).
[2] Harvard, op. cit., pp. 20–23.
[3] *Memoir of Joseph Entwisle*, by his son, p. 252.
[4] Letter to Joseph Entwisle, 18th June 1813 (ibid.).
[5] Letter to Samuel Drew, 28th June 1813 (Drew, pp. 350f.; Etheridge, pp. 376f.).

Lynch, George Erskine and John McKenny. Thus armed, he came to Liverpool for the English Conference of 1813, where the acceptance of his proposals was far from a foregone conclusion, even with the qualified support of the Missionary Committee. He had notable supporters in men like Richard Reece, Charles Atmore and Thomas Roberts,[1] but veterans such as Joseph Benson and Henry Moore were among the opposition. There were doubts about Coke's personal involvement in the mission and about the considerable expense.[2] When the matter was deferred for further consideration on the following day, Coke returned to his lodging depressed to the point of tears and spent a sleepless night largely in prayer for the India he longed to be allowed to serve. Next morning he was late in arriving at the Conference, but when the debate was resumed, made so moving a plea for authority to proceed with his plans that the opposition began to waver. Since money problems were the main cause of his brethren's misgivings, he offered if necessary to pay the initial cost of up to £6,000 from his own pocket. To this the Conference could not agree, but after further discussion they accepted his offer to guarantee the amount required for the equipping of the mission, on condition that the party should be reduced from twelve missionaries to seven, one of whom should be stationed at the Cape and one in Java. Of the remainder, three were for Ceylon, and two were to act as Coke's personal companions and attendants.[3]

Coke immediately wrote to a number of the preachers on his list, to ask if they were willing to accompany him to the East; so that by 11th August he had a full complement. In addition to Lynch, Erskine and McKenny, there were William Ault, William Harvard, Thomas Squance and Benjamin Clough.[4] They were summoned to London, and during the autumn months were busily engaged in kitting themselves out and in mastering the Portuguese language, which Coke declared to be one of the easiest in the world. A Portuguese priest was engaged as their tutor. Coke himself was rarely seen without some Portuguese book in his hand and made

[1] Buckley, op. cit., p. 96.

[2] T. P. Bunting, *Life of Jabez Bunting*, 1887 Edn., p. 396.

[3] Harvard, op. cit., pp. 25f. Printed circular letter of appeal, dated September 1813 and signed by Coke (copy in M.M.S. Archives).

[4] Letters to Thomas Ballinghall, 2nd August 1813 (M.M.S. Archives); to Thomas Squance, 7th August 1813 (R. Lee Cole); to George Banwell, 9th August 1813 (Wantage Methodist Church, Berks); to Squance, 11th August 1813 (Mr T. H. C. Squance, Brigsteer, Kendal). Cf. Harvard, op. cit., pp. 27f.

unexpectedly rapid progress. There was no instruction in either Singhalese or Tamil to be had in London.[1]

In a circular appealing for funds, Coke outlined his plans for making Ceylon the headquarters of a mission to the Indian mainland. The island contained, according to Buchanan, about half a million Christians, and both Portuguese and the Malabar language were widely spoken. The Syrian Church of Travancore in south-west India was within easy reach. Coke himself intended to concentrate his attention on Ceylon, where three of the missionaries would be stationed, but he also planned to visit Madras and Calcutta, and possibly Java, before returning home to report progress.[2]

In the event, they had to travel via Bombay, since there were no ships sailing direct to Ceylon at that season. Coke had influential friends, however, and the Directors of the East India Company proved unexpectedly co-operative.[3] Letters of introduction were obtained from Lord Bathurst, the Colonial Secretary, and from Lord Teignmouth, Wilberforce, Charles Grant, Dr Buchanan and others.[4]

Despite his readiness to be set down 'alone and naked' on the shores of Ceylon, Coke seems to have had misgivings about the restriction of his party to six. Later in the autumn he sought to increase the number by taking a young man, John Wesley Suter, as his personal attendant or secretary. Suter was a schoolmaster, the son of the Methodist preacher at Bradford, Yorks, who fully approved of the proposal. Coke wrote on 30th November to advise him that he should be ready to leave for Portsmouth as soon as he heard that the Court of Directors had authorized his passage.

I breakfasted with the Captain of the *Cabalva* this morning. He is to receive you as a *Gentleman* under the denomination of my *Secretary*. You are to dine with me and the Missionaries of course at his table. He will also provide for you a comfortable Cabin, &c. and I shall fit you out at Portsmouth, which will require only a few days. You shall want nothing. You will act as a Preacher, and as my Secretary, wherever we go. But you will not be considered as a *stationed* Missionary; but I am perfectly certain that you will be respected as much everywhere as any missionary whatever.

[1] Harvard, op. cit., pp. 30, 43.
[2] Letter of 26th December 1813, quoted in Hamilton, *The Faithful Servant*, p. 29.
[3] Letter to Jabez Bunting, 3rd November 1813 (M.M.S. Archives).
[4] Harvard, op. cit., p. 36.

I must pay 200 Guineas for your passage instead of one hundred; but that I shall not regard, if I have you for my Companion.

By engaging Suter as his secretary, Coke clearly intended to circumvent the decision of Conference to limit his party, without involving the Missionary Committee. Suter's appointment was to be on an entirely different footing from that of the other missionaries, as Coke made plain in the same letter:

Again, I shall most probably return, after I have seen the six Missionaries fully established, and have taken a tour of India,—in 2 years or two years and a half. My Letters of recommendation will make my way, & *your* way, easy. If then it appears best that you should return with me to England, you shall. In short, you shall not remain behind me in Asia, without our mutual consent . . .

You may consider yourself as a joint-Preacher with myself wherever I am, & wherever I go, and my Companion, and my Secretary, & my Friend . . . *You shall want nothing that is comfortable as my Fellow-Missionary.*[1]

On the following day, the Court of Directors gave their consent to Suter's travelling on the *Cabalva*; and the Missionary Committee, informed of Coke's intentions, unanimously agreed that he was right in taking a companion and confidant. The way now seemed clear, and Suter was instructed to give up his teaching post and set out for Portsmouth without delay.[2] But at this point there was an unexpected intervention by Richard Reece, another of the preachers stationed in the Bradford Circuit, who wrote to Coke protesting against Suter's appointment as detrimental to the success of the mission.[3] The precise grounds of his objection to Suter are not clear, but they were sufficient to cause Coke to reconsider the matter and then to withdraw his proposal. Alexander Suter was highly indignant at the way his son had been treated and wrote a letter of strong protest, to which Coke sent a conciliatory reply:

Dear Brother,

Notwithstanding your angry Letter, I must call you by that name. I will not enter into the particulars of our business . . . But *you* know, that I

[1] Letter to John Wesley Suter 30th November 1813 (Archives Centre).

[2] Letter to Suter, 1st December 1813 (Archives Centre).

[3] Reece's letter has disappeared, but Coke's reply, dated 3rd December, is at Drew University: 'I did not intend to take John W. Suter out as a Missionary. I had no right. The Conference limited me to *six*. I proposed, first, to take him as my Servant. I then proposed, to meet his dear Father's wishes, to take him out as my Secretary . . .'

never promised that your Son should be a *seventh* Missionary to the East. I had no power to do so.

However I acknowledge that your Son has suffered by this business; & I never suffer any one to be damaged on my account. You say that I ought to allow your Son a year's income for his losses. I enter not into the minutiae of the case. Tomorrow I will send to Mr Reece for you a Bill of Exchange on my agent—John Holloway, Esqr, at the Reduced Office, Bank of England, for £140 for your Son. I am your Friend T. Coke.[1]

Lacking the rest of this correspondence, we cannot determine exactly what were the shortcomings which caused Coke to change his mind about taking Suter to Ceylon at a time when it was too late to find a replacement. The whole idea of engaging a travelling-companion seems to have been rather hastily conceived, perhaps because another of his intentions had just been abandoned. This was nothing less than that of contracting a third marriage, before he sailed for the East. Drew is the only one of Coke's biographers who alludes to this little-known incident, and Coke himself, after his intentions had been providentially thwarted, was at pains to see that it was as little known as possible. In a letter to Jabez Bunting on 3rd November, he wrote, 'I find that a report has gone forth that I am married. But I am neither married, nor going to be married. I shall go to Asia, a single man and I'll beg the favour of you to contradict the report, whenever and wherever you hear it.'[2] But there was more truth in the rumours than Coke cared to admit. Since his second wife's death less than a year before, his sociable nature had more than ever shrunk from the prospect of solitude. For a time Benjamin Clough provided the constant companionship he needed in his bereavement. But as the voyage to India loomed ahead, the possible companionship of a wife more and more attracted him. During the autumn, while busy in London with preparations for the voyage, he met a young woman who convinced him that she was a suitable partner for such a venture. Drew speaks of 'piety, zeal, activity, an enterprising spirit, and a pleasing address' as the qualities Coke sought—and believed he had found—in her.[3] All of these qualities except the first she seems indeed to have possessed in her own way; but plausibility rather than piety was her hallmark. Coke's own piety was too spontaneous and sincere for him to suspect a show of it in

[1] Letter to Alexander Suter, 14th December 1813 (Archives Centre).
[2] Letter to Jabez Bunting, 3rd November 1813 (M.M.S. Archives).
[3] Drew, p. 354.

others; and he was even more deceived on this occasion than in the case of the Fula missionaries in 1796. A proposal of marriage was made and accepted, but his friends intervened in time to prevent a disastrous match.

The objections to the marriage were more serious than the discrepancy between their ages or the brief interval since his second wife's death. One of those who helped to prevent it was Richard Treffry of the Penzance Circuit, who wrote on 6th November:

We have very little Methodistical news here, unless you deem the following of that cast. Dr Coke has been on the verge of matrimony, & I may add without exaggeration on the verge of ruin, from which I hope he is now escaping. A woman of a very bad character (that is, if failing in business, not being able to pay 1s. in the pound; getting honest tradesmen to be bound for her; defrauding even her own mother, & cheating her out of all her property, going off to escape a jail with a married man &c. &c. be proofs of badness of character)—fell in his way, & he made love to her &c., & the business drew so near to a crisis that the woman wrote from London to her mother, who is a native of this circuit, that she was going to be married to Dr Coke in a few days & going out to India with him. This news shocked us all in this neighbourhood as the woman's character was so detestable we cd. not credit it though it came in such a shape that it would scarcely admit of doubt. However I immediately wrote off to London to Benson stating it as a report, hoping it was not true &c. This brought me an answer, saying that I must show just cause & impediment why those two shd. not be joined together in holy matrimony. This led me to be circumstantial & I detailed a list of black actions well authenticated which produced the desired effect, & Blanshard tells me that he believes the business is ended, & adds it was a narrow escape . . . The woman's creditors were exulting in the prospect of arresting the Doctor immediately on his marriage with her.[1]

In his present exalted state of mind, Coke was an easy victim to a designing young woman who had everything to gain and nothing to lose in the attempt to elude those she had already defrauded. Though Coke certainly showed himself gullible, others more worldly-wise had clearly been taken in before him. But for Treffry's timely intervention, Coke's career must have had an abrupt and disastrous end at this point.

Coke was aware that his absence in India might jeopardize the

[1] Letter from Richard Treffry to Isaac Clayton, 6th November 1813; copy at Archives Centre.

mission funds. He had tried for many years to win more support for the overseas work, but Methodism was poor and the response had been limited. In the Autumn of 1812, when the burden of the war with France was being widely felt, he warned the Missionary Committee that others were soliciting aid among the Methodist people and so jeopardizing the support given to their own work. 'Our people love to promote missions', he urged, 'and if we do not follow some Plan to counteract the above, many hundreds, if not thousands of pounds will be taken out of the pockets of our people to support the London Missionary Society.' The short-term solution he proposed was the launching of an annual subscription list; but he already had more far-reaching plans in mind: 'I have been reading some addresses from the London Missionary Society, and from the Awakened Clergy's Society, where they press the point of forming little connexions in each town to increase their annual subscriptions.'[1]

The Committee was reluctant to move in this matter, feeling that the Connexion was already over-burdened; but early the following year Coke took it up once more. Since he was about to leave for India, he planned to ensure that support from the Church at home should continue despite his absence. As he told Wilberforce in his letter of 14th April, he hoped that local auxiliary committees in the provinces might take over his role as money-raiser. He was soon busy pressing for this idea to be implemented.

The meeting of the Missionary Committee at the end of April which decided to commend the Asian Mission also passed resolutions aimed at organizing missionary support in every circuit. Each circuit was to have a missionary committee composed of the travelling preachers and lay representatives of the Quarterly Meeting, under the chairmanship of the Superintendent Minister and with the primary aim of raising funds.[2]

Conference that year was too busy debating the proposed Asian Mission to take any steps towards implementing these proposals. But in September the preachers of the Leeds Circuit, supported by a number of laymen, took the initiative by calling a great public meeting in the 'Old Boggart House', at which, on 6th October, the Methodist Missionary Society of the Leeds District was formed. Meeting on the same day in London, the Missionary Committee,

[1] Letter to the Missionary Committee, 29th October 1812 (M.M.S. Archives).
[2] Missionary Committee minutes, 30th April 1813 (M.M.S. Archives).

after a long debate, agreed to recommend that such societies should be established 'at large'.[1]

Coke was in close touch with the developments in Leeds, chiefly through Jabez Bunting, who had himself considered offering for India the year before. Coke apparently discouraged Bunting from this, possibly on the grounds that he could more usefully serve the missionary cause at home. Hearing of the success of the meeting in Leeds, Coke wrote to Bunting, 'The generality of our Committee *rejoices* in the steps you have taken in behalf of the missions. As to myself, I shall go to Asia with a glad heart indeed thro' the blessing of God. We have agreed on a Circular letter to be sent to the circuits . . . It is the Lord who has put into your hearts thus to step forth. There is nothing which you have done, which I do not most fully approve of.'[2] And from aboard the *Cabalva*, at the very moment of sailing, he wrote, 'Though we are now on full sail I must write one line to you by the Pilot, to express the joy and thankfulness to God which I feel that you have entered so zealously into the mission business. The Lord reward you a thousandfold for this.'[3]

With this encouragement from Coke and the Missionary Committee, the example of the Leeds District was quickly followed in Halifax, Hull, Norfolk and elsewhere,[4] so that there sprang up a number of District Missionary Societies whose activities were co-ordinated in 1818 by the formation of the General Wesleyan Methodist Missionary Society. Meanwhile, Coke sailed from England for the last time, in the knowledge that others were at last taking up his task of sustaining the missions.

[1] Ibid., 6th October 1813.
[2] Letters to Bunting, 15th October, and 3rd November, 1813 (M.M.S. Archives).
[3] Letter to Bunting, 31st December 1813 (M.M.S. Archives).
[4] Letter from Samuel Taylor to Joseph Benson, 30th November, 1813; letter from Bunting to Robert Smith, 11th October 1813; letter from Coke to Bunting, 3rd November, 1813 (M.M.S. Archives).

CHAPTER 23

CONSUMMATION

Amid both distractions and encouragement, preparations for the mission continued in London throughout the autumn. After several visits to the docks, two East Indiamen were chosen and passages booked on them. Coke spent much time on the equipping of the party. But some of the Missionary Committee felt that they were not being consulted sufficiently on these matters and there was talk of excessive expenditure. Coke had always been generous in providing for his missionaries, even though he knew better than most that every penny spent had to be raised. Among the major items of expenditure on this occasion, he included a printing press, so that Harvard and Squance might put their technical knowledge to good use.[1]

When the Committee met on 22nd November, there was a general feeling that Coke had spent too lavishly on clothing, books and other items, many of which were considered superfluous or in excess of the missionaries' needs. Coke was asked for a detailed account of expenditure; and when he learned of their dissatisfaction, he proposed that he himself should bear the expense of any purchases the Committee considered unnecessary. A list was accordingly prepared of those items whose provision the Committee approved, which amounted in all to £3,291 4s. 11d. Robert Smith was deputed to go to Portsmouth, where the missionaries were now waiting to embark, to present this list to Coke and come to an agreement over it.[2] So, on the eve of sailing, Coke found his attention occupied by the cost of such mundane items as hat-boxes, pillow-cases, towels, travelling expenses and custom house duties, for which he was answerable to the Committee.[3]

Such quibbling will seem an unworthy valedictory for a man so

[1] Harvard, *Narrative of . . . the Mission to Ceylon and India*, pp. 36ff.

[2] Missionary Committee minutes, 22nd November and 17th December 1813. The last meeting which Coke attended was on 8th December.

[3] The detailed memorandum on items of expenditure drawn up on the Committee's instructions by Robert Smith, together with Coke's annotations, is preserved at Wesley College, Bristol.

devoted to the missionary cause as Thomas Coke unless we remember the difficulties under which the Missionary Committee laboured. The mission to India was not their only commitment. In the face of increasing demands on limited resources, their attitude was fairly summed up in a letter written by William Myles at the beginning of November. After reporting that arrangements for Coke's party to sail were well in hand, he continued: 'We have four other Missionaries in Town, waiting to embark for the West Indies. We have a strong invitation from Botany Bay to send a Missionary there, and another from the Island of Demarara. But our finances are so low we cannot send Preachers to these places. My own opinion is, we must lessen our sails: we cannot support the work we are engag'd in.'[1] It is nevertheless a check on any tendency to glamorize the circumstances in which Coke sailed on his last voyage, to find that one of his last official communications with the Committee ends with this half-apologetic note: 'I have been obliged to buy Pewter Chamber pots, pewter-bottles, pewter wash-hand Basons, & pewter-tumblers, for the Missionaries, & a cheap deal table, & a cheap chair for each. You shall know all about it before we sail.'[2] Nor does it make much difference that on the day the party sailed from Portsmouth, the Committee, meeting in London, decided that the cost of the pewter wash-basins and other articles purchased in Portsmouth for the missionaries' cabins should be borne by the funds and not by Coke himself.[3]

If the Committee's duty was to put a necessary curb on Coke's enthusiasm, fortunately there were others ready to speed him on his way with encouragement. The news from Leeds and other districts was a source of comfort and hope during these trying weeks of final preparation. And in the closing days of the year, as the moment of farewell drew steadily nearer, the Methodists of Portsmouth took him and his party to their hearts. The missionaries forgathered there in the Bush Inn on Saturday, 12th December, and the relief and joy with which Coke presided over the supper-table that evening, with all his companions about him, was long remembered by those present. 'At this time,' wrote Clough, 'he seemed as though he had

[1] Letter from William Myles to Robert Blunt of Frome, 1st November 1813 (W.H.S. Library).
[2] Note in Coke's hand at the end of the memorandum referred to, p. 355 note 3.
[3] Missionary Committee minutes, 31st December 1813.

not a dormant faculty about him; every power of his soul was now employed in forwarding the work in which he had engaged.'[1]

On the remaining Sundays of the month, the missionaries preached in the chapels of the neighbourhood. Coke's final sermon was in St Peter's Chapel, Portsea, on the text from Psalm 68 which had long been his favourite, 'Ethiopia shall stretch out her hands'. As in the farewell sermon he had preached in Hinde Street Chapel before leaving London,[2] the proximity of death was in the forefront of his mind and he seemed fully aware that he might not live to see his native land again. 'We go forth', he said, 'in the name of God, trusting solely to Him for the success which we hope to realize . . . For my own part, I am fully persuaded, that we, who are about to leave you, are in the path of duty; and I am perfectly convinced that God will bless our labours, although to what extent and in what manner may be unknown.' Then, in words that must in retrospect have seemed strangely prophetic, he continued: 'It is of little consequence whether we take our flight to glory from the land of our nativity, from the trackless ocean, or the shores of Ceylon. "I cannot go where universal love not smiles around, and where he vital breathes, there must be joy" . . . We can appeal to heaven for the purity of our motives, and we look into eternity for our final reward.'[3] Those present on this moving occasion were not likely to forget such words.

Early on 30th December, the signal guns were heard, indicating that the fleet was preparing to sail, and the missionary party hastened to embark. Jonathan Edmondson, who helped Coke into the boat, gives this description of the moment, for which Coke had so long waited: 'I watched him carefully all the way to the Pilot-boat, with mingled feelings of love and fear. He sailed backwards, with his face towards me; his hands were clasped, his eyes were closed, and he seemed to be engaged in deep devotion all the way to the vessel. When he bid us farewell on the shore, he appeared to have done with us altogether; for he never looked at us, nor turned his head to observe anything.'[4] From long years of experience, Coke had learned

---

[1] *Methodist Magazine*, 1815, p. 32; cf. Harvard, op. cit., p. 48.

[2] Telford, *Two West End Chapels*, p. 155. This sermon has sometimes been wrongly described as the last Coke preached before sailing for India.

[3] Harvard, op. cit., pp. 52f.; Drew, pp. 389ff. (Cf. letter to Drew, 22nd January, 1814, in *Life of Drew* by his son, pp. 180ff.)

[4] *Wesleyan Methodist Magazine*, 1850, p. 114.

to take leave of his friends with less outward emotion than when he first visited America in 1784. Had he perhaps some premonition that on this occasion he was bidding farewell to his countrymen for the last time? His mood was expressed by the words of William Cowper's verses which had long been familiar to him, but which now seemed charged with fresh meaning, so that he quoted and sang them frequently during these closing days:

> To me remains nor place nor time,
> My country is in every clime;
> I can be calm and free from care
> On any shore, since God is there.
>
> Could I be cast where Thou art not,
> That were indeed a dreadful lot;
> But regions none remote I call,
> Secure of finding God in all.

* * *

For reasons of economy, the party was divided between two of the East Indiamen; Mr and Mrs Ault, Lynch, Erskine and Squance sailed in the *Lady Melville*, while Clough and Mr and Mrs Harvard accompanied Coke in the *Cabalva*. (John McKenny did not sail for the Cape until later.) The fleet consisted of eight Indiamen and a number of merchant ships bound for various parts of the world, with an escort of warships because of the war still raging on the Continent.[1] (Some of the merchantmen were supply vessels bound for Lisbon with stores for Wellington's army.) 'The sight of such a floating city is very agreeable,' Coke wrote. 'On a calm, the boats are passing and repassing from ship to ship.' The *Cabalva* carried a complement of over 400, nearly half of whom were soldiers, chiefly recruits from Ireland. There were a number of Portuguese-speaking Indians on board, and, among the crew, about fifty Lascars.

With all the speed of a seasoned traveller, Coke lost no time in settling down on board ship, calling attention to himself by the ease with which he fell into his usual routine when at sea. 'I have a most charming study,' he wrote. 'It has two large windows that open from the stern to the sea; and my elbow-chair and my table are placed in the most convenient situation possible. . . . Here I employ almost all my time and nearly the whole of it in reading and writing

[1] Coke, *Journal*, pp. 262ff.; *Methodist Magazine*, 1815, p. 29.

Portuguese . . .'[1] His chief study was the Portuguese Bible, an edition of which he planned to publish immediately on arrival in Ceylon, but he also busied himself with preparing hymns, sermons and prayers in the language.[2]

They were destined to have a slow and stormy voyage. The winter gales began to buffet them on 6th January and continued till they were well past Madeira, with consequent damage and loss of life. 'Many of our ships were more or less dismasted. The *Cabalva* suffered very little: a single little mast at the end of one of the booms alone was broke. On the 19th of January one of the merchant-ships was missing, and was not afterwards seen or heard of. What made this incident still more melancholy was that she had been firing guns of distress for some time before; but the gale was so violent that no relief could be afforded her.'[3] By 24th January, six ships were missing, including one of the Indiamen, the *Fort William*, in which Coke had originally considered booking passages. Though distressed that some at least of these must be feared lost, Coke was too experienced a sailor for the storms to disturb his studious routine. The *Cabalva* was a fortress compared with the much frailer vessels in which he had so often braved the Atlantic. 'When we came into the Bay of Biscay,' wrote Clough, 'and had to contend with gales of wind, and tempestuous seas, the Doctor seemed alike unmoved, and pursued his labours of prayer, study, reading and writing, with as much settled composure of mind, as though he had been on land.'[4] This was a source of comfort and encouragement not only to the other missionaries, none of whom had ever ventured on the high seas before, but also to others on board. 'When at any time the weather was stormy, or when on any occasion there appeared any fears or alarm, he would encourage the passengers by observing in what small ships he had frequently taken long voyages, what distressing scenes he had witnessed, and how far short these came of what he had witnessed; then he would remind them of our fine large ship; our comfortable accommodation, &c. . . .'[5] The delays caused by the weather were opportune, rather than irksome, to one so bent on redeeming the time and preparing himself thoroughly to meet the challenge of Asia. 'We have had hitherto a very slow voyage,' he wrote to Bunting on 24th January. 'But it is right. We must, if possible, be perfect masters of the Portuguese Language before we

[1] Coke's *Journal*, p. 263.   [2] Clough, *Methodist Magazine*, 1815, p. 33.
[3] Coke, *Journal*, p. 265.   [4] Clough, loc. cit., p. 32.   [5] Ibid., p. 34.

reach Asia . . . I had some apprehensions that at my advanced age my present voyage would prove tedious to me, and on that account oppress the body, and through it the mind. But it is just the contrary, praised be God. Perhaps the vile but glorious drudgery in which I was almost continually engaged in England might help on this occasion. I am sure that God is with us!'[1]

The tedium of the daily round during so protracted a voyage was relieved by even the slightest variation of their normal routine. One of the soldiers was brought for trial before the captain for beating his wife; Coke was disposed to believe that she deserved less pity than her husband. Another was flogged for abusing a Major who was travelling among the passengers. Such passing incidents as these and the death of a sailor who fell from the top gallant-yard into the sea were important enough to be entered by Coke in his *Journal*— alongside his observation of the methods of catching sharks and boneta-fish and their food value; while the sight of another fleet of some forty ships which crossed their path ranked as a major event.[2] For the rest, the passengers were driven back on their own resources. One device was the compilation of a weekly newspaper, which was read out at the dinner-table each Saturday evening. Harvard's comment on this seemingly innocuous relief from boredom is: 'The perfect delicacy with which this otherwise hazardous amusement was conducted, reflected high honour on its managers.'[3] If Harvard is representative of the missionary party as a whole, they appear to have found it difficult to unbend even in the close proximity necessitated by conditions aboard ship. Their apprehension seems to have reached its climax as they approached the Equator. To quote Harvard again: 'The usual ceremonies were performed by the sailors on those who now crossed the line for the first time . . . The ceremony was by no means a desirable one; and the passengers were of course not expected to submit to it. A low-minded captain, in some inferior line of maritime service, may sometimes be met with, who will rank his *passengers* with his *crew* on such an occasion; but this will never be suffered by any commander of respectability. The sailors, however, expected a gratuity from the passengers, in order to defray the expenses of their merriment; and when we had Neptune in our cabin, for the purpose of giving him our donation, we endeavoured to direct his mind to higher things.'[4] Unfortunately

[1] Letter to Jabez Bunting, 24th January 1814 (M.M.S. Archives).
[2] Coke, *Journal*, pp. 267f.   [3] Harvard, op. cit., p. 66.   [4] Ibid., p. 71.

no record has come to light of what Neptune said to his comrades on returning from the Harvards' cabin, so that it is impossible to hazard more than a guess at the success of their exhortation.

Though their fellow-passengers showed them the utmost politeness, the missionaries aboard the *Cabalva* seemed to have less prospect of being a leavening influence than those on the *Lady Melville*. On Sundays, whenever the weather allowed, passengers, soldiers and crew assembled on deck for prayers read by the Captain. Coke's offer to give a short address was not taken up, but the captain subsequently was at pains to explain to the other missionaries that in this he had been acting under instructions from the owners to 'go on just as usual'. On Sunday evenings, however, a number of the passengers gathered to hear Coke reading extracts from the introduction to his Commentary and occasionally one or other of them asked permission to attend the evening prayer meetings held in Harvard's cabin.[1] Coke particularly hoped to influence the military recruits, many of whom had enlisted because, though well-born, they had fallen into poverty and disgrace at home. Some of them had Methodist associations and used to meet Coke in Clough's cabin, which was the nearest to their part of the ship.[2]

The stormy passage caused Coke serious concern for the health of some of his fellow-missionaries. Mrs Harvard suffered from prolonged sea-sickness, from which she did not recover until they had won through to the Tropics. Later in the voyage Harvard's own health occasioned some anxiety, and he once overheard Coke in agonized intercession on his behalf, praying that he might be spared for the sake of Asia.[3] The two halves of the party were always eager for news of each other's welfare and arranged a signalling code of their own for use whenever their two ships came near enough: a white handkerchief signifying health, and a coloured one sickness.[4] On 10th February, came the sad news that Mrs Ault was dead. This was not unexpected, since she was found, before embarking, to be in an advanced stage of consumption; though her doctor considered that, should she reach the Tropics, she had some chance of recovery.

On 5th February, during a period of calm near the Equator, Ault and Squance had borrowed a boat and visited the *Cabalva*; and a

[1] Harvard, op. cit., pp. 6of., 63f.; Clough, loc. cit., pp. 32f.
[2] Harvard, op. cit., pp. 72ff.
[3] Coke, *Journal*, p. 268; Harvard, op. cit., pp. 76ff.
[4] Coke, *Journal*, p. 269; Harvard, op. cit., p. 67.

little later Harvard and Clough had an opportunity of paying a return visit to the *Lady Melville*. Coke confessed himself too old to venture up and down the sides of ships more than was absolutely necessary, and did not leave the *Cabalva*.[1] But his distress at the news of Mrs Ault's death was augmented soon afterwards by concern for the health of Thomas Squance. 'Mr. Squance is ill—very ill indeed,' wrote Ault in a letter home at the end of February. 'I am afraid that he will not be able to stand the climate; nay, I am doubtful whether he will be able to reach Bombay. The Doctor thinks that he is consumptive. He is, however, very happy and resigned.'[2] In the event, these fears proved groundless: Squance lived to serve in Ceylon and India until 1822, and though his health then compelled him to return home, he continued to itinerate until 1862 and by the time of his death in 1868 had outlived all the others who accompanied Coke in 1814. At the time however, his illness was none the less a matter for concern, coming so soon after Mrs Ault's death; and Coke's fatherly care for the young man he was taking out to India is evident in every line of this note which he wrote to Squance inviting him to the *Cabalva*.

My dear Squance,

I am *excessively* concerned in respect to you. Come to me. Come to me this afternoon. Bring your Cot with you. Bring with you of wearing apparel what you can immediately lay your hands upon. I will at all events make you comfortable. Trust me. You may stay here *as long* a time, or as little a time as you please. I will lend you wearing apparel, if you have a deficiency. Come without delay. I don't know what to say more.[3]

While on board the *Cabalva*, Squance recovered sufficiently to be able to join the group that met in Harvard's cabin, though forbidden, on pain of Coke's severe displeasure, to join in the singing or prayers. At one stage, Coke proposed to leave him at Mauritius, to establish a mission there, but his health had by then improved sufficiently for him to remain with the party.[4]

* * *

[1] Coke, *Journal*, pp. 269f.
[2] Letter from Ault to Thomas Wood, 26th and 28th February, 1814, in *Methodist Magazine*, 1814, p. 718. Cf letter from Joseph Benson to Bunting, 19th August, 1814 (W.H.S. Library).
[3] Letter to Squance, 15th March 1814 (Mr T. H. C. Squance).
[4] Harvard, op. cit., pp. 69ff.

The violence of the gales prevented the fleet from putting in to Madeira for a few days' respite, so that Coke was unable to despatch the letters he had prepared for England. Shortly afterwards, on 25th January, they had a tantalizingly brief glimpse of one of the Canary Islands. Not until 19th February, however, when some of the merchantmen left the main fleet to sail to the Brazils, did he have an opportunity of sending off his letters by the captain of the brig which escorted them. Later he despatched further letters via St Helena and the Cape, each reiterating his main plea, that the Conference would lose no time in reinforcing the mission by seeking permission to establish a mission on the Indian mainland and by sending out at least two more preachers. The prolonged gales, which had driven them well to the west of their intended course, were followed by periods of calm as they neared the Cape, so that it became clear that they could not expect to reach Bombay until early June, by which time the monsoons would prevent their proceeding to Ceylon before the end of the autumn. In the light of this enforced delay, which he saw as a divine opportunity, Coke was already modifying his plans. The numerical inadequacy of his party, reduced to six by Conference decision, now appeared more painfully obvious than ever. He intended to leave the Harvards with two other missionaries in Bombay, and take the rest on to Surat. Among their military converts on board were men who were to be stationed in these two garrison towns, in both of which were many Portuguese-speaking natives. 'If we form societies in these places (as I have no doubt but we shall) we dare not leave the lambs to the mercy of wolves. If God be pleased in this wonderful but unexpected way . . . to give us a double footing on the *Continent* of Asia, it must be our bounden duty to keep it.' He proposed, therefore, to station a missionary in each of these places, and another among the Syrian Christians in Travancore. This would leave him only two for Ceylon and one for Java. Having established these, he planned a tour of the east coast of India, the scene of Swartz's apostolic labours, in the course of which he hoped to visit Tanjore, Madras and Calcutta. Unless they granted his plea for two further missionaries licensed for India to meet him in Calcutta, he would have no one to leave behind in any of these places. 'In respect to expense, I will *lend* the money for the outfit. Or rather than return home without having any to second my labours along the coast of *Coromandel* to Rajamaughl, I will *give* the money necessary for the outfit. O *embrace* the opportunity, while I am over there, and don't let me return home grieved to the heart, that I have left societies on the Continent as lambs among wolves.'[1]

Such was the final appeal to the British Conference of the man who had set all else aside that he might bring the light of the Gospel to India. The last letter he is known to have written, almost identical copies of which were addressed to the Missionary Committee in London and to Bunting and his colleagues in Leeds, repeated this plea. They had rounded the Cape at last and were in the neighbourhood of Madagascar, so that India began, figuratively speaking, to loom ahead. 'The Lord will bless me on the Continent, at Bombay and elsewhere,' he wrote, 'and to have nobody to leave behind me at the place (Bombay and its vicinity excepted) where the Lord may own me most upon the Continent will be very heart-breaking.'[2] But sadder news was destined to follow hard on the heels of these pleading letters.

Further storms were encountered early in April, as they entered the Indian Ocean, and these continued throughout most of the month. On the evening of the 23rd they had a view of a volcanic eruption as they passed the island of Bourbon. In general, Coke had so far enjoyed better health than most of the other passengers, largely through being so experienced a sailor. But his companions feared the effects of his long and intensive application to his studies, and Clough in particular did his best to encourage him to take adequate exercise. Sometimes he would agree to take a turn on deck, if enticed by the prospect of some such curiosity as a shoal of flying fish chased by a dolphin or the sight of a whale; and, as always when at sea, he particularly enjoyed the spectacle of the sunset clouds. At other times, however, he could not be prevailed upon to leave his books, in which he took such great delight, and the very intensity of his studies in such a climate, coupled with his advanced age, told on his health more than he was prepared to recognize. He had been unwell as they approached the Equator on their way south, but soon recovered his usual health and spirits. Now that they were again entering the Tropics, however, there were further disturbing signs. On Sunday, 1st May, Mrs Harvard, taking a turn on deck for the

[1] Letter to the Conference via Richard Reece, 14th March 1814 (M.M.S. Archives); another copy, addressed to Walter Griffith, is at the Archives Centre.
[2] Letter to the Missionary Committee, 13th April 1814 (M.M.S. Archives); cf letter of the same date to Bunting, Morley, Reece etc., printed in *W.H.S. Proc.* ii. 91f.

first time since her illness, was immediately struck by the alteration in Coke's appearance. 'In the evening,' says Harvard, 'the Doctor, as usual, came into our cabin and prayed. He would hardly acknowledge that he was ill, but spoke of taking some tincture of rhubarb, which he did. He had complained of cold, from the chilling effects of his own fine linen shirts, when damp from excessive perspiration, and had consulted Mrs Harvard on having some made of calico, when we should reach Bombay.'[1] Meanwhile, he borrowed some of Harvard's.

Next morning Mrs Harvard found him sitting abstractedly in his cabin 'with his head on one of his hands'. Though he made a show of cheerfulness he admitted that he felt 'rather poorly', but hoped it would soon wear off. He proposed to take a walk on deck, but appeared too weak to be able to support himself. In the evening, however, he paid his usual visit to the Harvard's cabin. 'We perceived the langour of disease, notwithstanding his evident effort to conceal it. He sat for a short time in occasional conversation, but evidently in a state of great relaxation and debility.'[2]

Clough accompanied him back to his cabin and did his best to ensure his comfort and well-being; but Coke declined his offer to sit up with him, assuring him that he would be better in the morning. The servant who later took him a glass of brandy and water was the last to see him alive. Early the following morning, 3rd May, when he went to call him as usual about 5 o'clock, he found him on the cabin floor. He had been dead for some hours, and from the position of the body it appeared that he had probably risen to fetch something he wanted. The Doctor readily ascribed his death to apoplexy, brought on by undue concentration on his beloved studies under tropical conditions. From the fact that neither the Captain nor the Harvards heard anything through the thin partitions separating their cabins from his, it appeared that the end must have been swift and painless: his fellow-missionaries noted the placid smile which still rested on his features when they entered the cabin.[3]

Captain Birch broke the news to Clough, who was apprehensive of the effect of the shock on Mr and Mrs Harvard, but undertook the task of telling them as gently as he could. They then wrote a note to their brethren in the *Lady Melville*, who at first were almost unable to take in the news. The leaderless party lost no time in gathering

[1] Harvard, op. cit., pp. 78f.   [2] Ibid., p. 79.
[3] Ibid., p. 82; *Methodist Magazine*, 1815, p. 30.

on board the *Cabalva* and determined to ask the Captain to arrange for Coke's body to be preserved and transported back to England. But he convinced them that this was quite impossible, and arrangements were soon made for burial at sea later on the same day.

The funeral accordingly took place at 5 o'clock that afternoon in the presence of the entire complement of the ship. 'The awning was spread, the soldiers drawn up in a rank on deck, the ship's bell called together the passengers and crew, and all seemed struck with silent awe.'[1] Harvard read the burial service; Ault delivered an address on the life and character of their lost leader; Lynch then read the hymn, 'Hark a voice divides the sky', and offered a concluding prayer. The heavy deal coffin, weighted with cannon-shot, was then committed to the deep, within three weeks' sailing distance of the country he had so ardently longed to serve. It seems fitting that this man, so long homeless, should lie in an unmarked grave beneath the waters of the Indian Ocean.[2]

Despite their earlier apprehensions of the state of Coke's health, the missionaries were at first too stunned and bewildered to take in the full reality of their loss and the practical implications of his death. Only when they reached Bombay did they begin to realize the serious obstacles in their path, now that they themselves were leaderless and their resources jeopardized. But the difficulties were surmounted and the mission Coke had so eagerly planned went forward despite his death. As Joseph Benson remarked, when reading to the City Road congregation the first reports from Ceylon, 'The death of Dr. Coke, instead of proving the ruin of the Mission, seems to have been overruled greatly for the furtherance of it.'[3] Similarly, when the news of his death first reached England towards the end of the year, a shocked Connexion was stirred into greater efforts to support the world-wide mission which Coke had personally sustained for so many years. In this case, at least, the good was not 'interréd with his bones'. 'Dr Coke is removed from us,' wrote Joseph Entwisle when the news reached him. 'God's thoughts are not our thoughts, nor his ways our ways. We must still say, The Lord doth all things well. He buries his workmen, and carries on his work.'[4]

[1] *Methodist Magazine*, 1815, p. 31.
[2] The accounts differ as to the exact latitude and longitude at which the burial took place.
[3] G. J. Stevenson, *City Road Chapel*, p. 182. The letters referred to were no doubt those printed in the *Magazine*, 1815, pp. 150ff.
[4] *Memoir of Entwisle* by his son, p. 312.

APPENDIX A

(i) *Coke's 'Certificate of Ordination'*

To all to whom these Presents shall come, John Wesley, late Fellow of Lincoln College in Oxford, Presbyter of the Church of England, sendeth greeting.

Whereas many of the People in the Southern Provinces of North America who desire to continue under my care, and still adhere to the Doctrines and Discipline of the Church of England, are greatly distressed for want of Ministers to administer the Sacraments of Baptism and the Lord's Supper according to the usage of the same Church: And whereas there does not appear to be any other way of Supplying them with Ministers:

Know all men, that I John Wesley think myself to be providentially called at this time to set apart some persons for the work of the ministry in America. And therefore under the Protection of Almighty God, and with a single eye to his Glory, I have this day set apart as a Superintendent, by the imposition of my hands and prayer, (being assisted by other ordained Ministers,) Thomas Coke, Doctor of Civil Law, a Presbyter of the Church of England, and a man whom I judge to be well qualified for that great work. And I do hereby recommend him to all whom it may concern as a fit person to preside over the Flock of Christ. In testimony whereof I have hereunto set my hand and seal this second day of September, in the year of our Lord one thousand seven hundred and eighty four.

John Wesley

(Original in M.M.S. Archives)

(ii) *Wesley's letter to 'Our American Brethren'*

Bristol, September 10, 1784

1. By a very uncommon train of providences many of the Provinces of North America are totally disjoined from their Mother Country and erected into independent States. The English Government has

THOMAS COKE

no authority over them, either civil or ecclesiastical, any more than over the States of Holland. A civil authority is exercised over them, partly by the Congress, partly by the Provincial Assemblies. But no one either exercises or claims any ecclesiastical authority at all. In this peculiar situation some thousands of the inhabitants of these States desire my advice; and in compliance with their desire I have drawn up a little sketch.

2. Lord King's *Account of the Primitive Church* convinced me many years ago that bishops and presbyters are the same order, and consequently have the same right to ordain. For many years I have been importuned from time to time to exercise this right by ordaining part of our travelling preachers. But I have still refused, not only for peace' sake, but because I was determined as little as possible to violate the established order of the National Church to which I belonged.

3. But the case is widely different between England and North America. Here there are bishops who have a legal jurisdiction: in America there are none, neither any parish ministers. So that for some hundred miles together there is none either to baptize or to administer the Lord's supper. Here, therefore, my scruples are at an end; and I conceive myself at full liberty, as I violate no order and invade no man's right by appointing and sending labourers into the harvest.

4. I have accordingly appointed Dr. Coke and Mr. Francis Asbury to be Joint Superintendents over our brethren in North America; as also Richard Whatcoat and Thomas Vasey to act as elders among them, by baptizing and administering the Lord's Supper. And I have prepared a Liturgy little differing from that of the Church of England (I think the best constituted National Church in the world), which I advise all the travelling preachers to use on the Lord's Day in all the congregations, reading the Litany only on Wednesdays and Fridays and praying extempore on all other days. I also advise the elders to administer the Supper of the Lord on every Lord's Day.

5. If any one will point out a more rational and scriptural way of feeding and guiding those poor sheep in the wilderness, I will gladly embrace it. At present I cannot see any better method than that I have taken.

6. It has, indeed, been proposed to desire the English bishops to ordain part of our preachers for America. But to this I object: (1) I

368

desired the Bishop of London to ordain only one, but could not prevail. (2) If they consented, we know the slowness of their pro-ceedings; but the matter admits of no delay. (3) If they would ordain them now, they would likewise expect to govern them. And how grieviously would this entangle us! (4) As our American brethren are now totally disengaged both from the State and from the English hierarchy, we dare not entangle them again either with the one or the other. They are now at full liberty simply to follow the Scriptures and the Primitive Church. And we judge it best that they should stand fast in that liberty wherewith God has so strangely made them free.

[Printed in the *Letters of John Wesley*, vii, 238f. Etheridge, p. 105, gives the letter a longer form of heading, thus: 'To Dr. Coke, Mr. Asbury, and our Brethren in North America'. Cf. the British Minutes, 1785.]

(iii) *Asbury's 'Ordination' Certificate*

Know all men by these presents, that I, Thomas Coke, Doctor of Civil Law, late of Jesus College, in the University of Oxford, presbyter of the Church of England, and superintendent of the Methodist Church in America, under the protection of Almighty God, and with a single eye to His glory, by the imposition of my hands and prayer, being assisted by two ordained elders, did on the twenty-fifth day of this month, December, set apart Francis Asbury for the office of a deacon in the aforesaid Methodist Episcopal Church. And also on the twenty-sixth day of the said month, did, by the imposition of my hands and prayer, being assisted by the said elders, set apart the said Francis Asbury for the office of elder in the said Methodist Episcopal Church. And on this twenty-seventh of the said month, being the day of the date hereof, have, by the imposition of my hands and prayer, being assisted by the said elders, set apart the said Francis Asbury for the office of a super-intendent in the said Methodist Episcopal Church; a man whom I judge to be well qualified for that great work. And I do hereby recommend him to all whom it may concern, as a fit person to preside over the flock of Christ. In testimony whereof I have here-unto set my hand and seal, this 27th day of December, in the year of our Lord 1784.

Thomas Coke

APPENDIX B

(i) *Address to President Washington, 1789*

New York, N.Y.
May 29, 1789[1]

To the President of the United States

Sir:

We the bishops of the Methodist-Episcopal church, humbly beg leave, in the name of our society collectively in these United States, to express to you the warm feelings of our hearts, and our sincere congratulations, on your appointment to the presidentship of these states. We are conscious from the signal proofs you have already given, that you are a friend of mankind; and under this established idea, place as full a confidence to your wisdom and integrity, for the preservation of those civil and religious liberties which have been transmitted to us by the providence of God, and the glorious revolution, as we believe, ought to be reposed in man.

We have received the most grateful satisfaction, from the humble and entire dependence on the Great Governor of the universe which you have repeatedly expressed, acknowledging him the source of every blessing, and particularly of the most excellent constitution of these states, which is at present the admiration of the world, and may in future become its great exemplar for imitation: and hence we enjoy a holy expectation that you will always prove a faithful and impartial patron of genuine, vital religion—the grand end of our creation and present probationary existence. And we promise you our fervent prayers to the throne of grace, that God Almighty may endue you with all the graces and gifts of his Holy Spirit, that may enable you to fill up your important station to his glory, the good of his church, the happiness and prosperity of the United States, and the welfare of mankind.

Signed in behalf of the Methodist-Episcopal church,

Thomas Coke,
Francis Asbury

[1] The original, in the Manuscript Division of the Library of Congress, is wrongly dated the 19th.

(ii) *Washington's reply*

New York, New York
May 29, 1789

To the Bishops of the Methodist Episcopal Church in the United States

Gentlemen:

I return you individually, and through you to your Society collectively in the United States, my thanks for the demonstration of affection and the expression of joy offered in their behalf on my late appointment. It shall be my endeavor to manifest the purity of my inclinations for promoting the happiness of mankind, as well as the sincerity of my desires to contribute whatever may be in my power toward the civil and religious liberties of the American people. In pursuing this line of conduct, I hope, by the assistance of the Divine Providence, not altogether to disappoint the confidence which you have been pleased to repose in me.

It always affords me satisfaction when I find a concurrence of sentiment and practice between all conscientious men, in acknowledgments of homage to the great Governor of the universe, and in professions of support to a just civil government. After mentioning that I trust the people of every denomination who demean themselves as good citizens will have occasion to be convinced that I shall always strive to prove a faithful and impartial patron of genuine vital religion, I must assure you, in particular, that I take in the kindest part the promise you make of presenting your prayers to the throne of grace for me; and that I likewise implore the Divine benediction on yourselves and your religious community.

George Washington

APPENDIX C

During Wesley's lifetime, Coke exercised his episcopal power of ordination not only in America, but also in England on at least one occasion sanctioned by Wesley. On 24th October 1785 he ordained Robert Johnson deacon for work in Scotland, thus anticipating Wesley's ordinations for Scotland in the following summer. (*W.H.S. Proc.* xxiv. 79. The ordination certificate is at the Archives Centre.) Wesley showed his approval of this by ordaining Johnson elder on 27th May 1786. The case of the twelve young men on whom Coke laid his hands at the 1790 Conference is discussed in the text above.

After Wesley's death, Coke continued to ordain, chiefly but not exclusively for the mission field. The following is a list of those ordinations for which there is definite evidence. Unless otherwise stated, all were for overseas work.

Date	Place	Name	Authority
22nd Sept. 1791	Jersey	Jean de Quetteville	Letter from Pawson to Atmore, 9th Dec. 1791 (Archives Centre) Drew, pp. 239ff.
24th Sept. (?) 1791	Courseulles, France	William Mahy	Ibid.
17th Oct. 1791	—	Richard Pattison	Etheridge, p. 436
6th Oct. 1793	Liverpool	Thomas Dobson Francis Thursby	Letter from Pawson to Atmore, 9th Oct. 1793 (Archives Centre) Copy of certificate in M.M.S. Archives
early 1794	—	John Pawson (as bishop)	Letter from Pawson to Atmore, 21st Jan. '94 (A.C.)
15th April 1794	—	James Alexander	Certificate at Wesley's House, London
1796	—	Robert Yelalee Giles	Knutsford, *Zachary Macaulay.* pp. 117f.
Sept. (?) 1802	Hull (?)	Edward Thompson	Letter to John Brownell, 27th Sept. 1802 (in private hands; copy in M.M.S. Archives)
25th July 1804	—	John Remington	Certificate at Drew University
Sept. (?) 1804	Hull (?)	George Johnstone	Letter to the Missionary Committee, 17th Sept. 1804 (M.M.S. Archives)

APPENDIX C

Date	Place	Name	Authority
24th May 1808	—	William Griffith	Certificate in Archives Centre
10th Aug. 1808	—	John Ogilvie	For the *Chester* Circuit. Certificate at Wesley College, Bristol
10th Oct. 1809	Liverpool	Myles Dixon George Poole	W.H.S. *Proc.* xxx. 188; letter to the Missionary Committee, 10th Oct. 1809 (M.M.S. Archives)
11th Oct. 1809	Liverpool	John Charrington	Letter to the Missionary Committee, 10th Oct. 1809 (M.M.S. Archives)
22nd April 1810	London	William Jewett William Dowson	Dowson's *Journal* Dowson's *Journal*
Dec. 1813	London	William Ault Benjamin Clough George Erskine William Harvard James Lynch John McKenny Thomas Squance	All except McKenny, for Asia. Harvard's *Narrative*, p. 46. Lynch's certificate, in Candler, p. 381

APPENDIX D

Coke's Will

Thomas Coke's will was signed on 27 November 1813 and proved on 18 November 1814. A copy may be inspected at the Probate Registry, Somerset House.

The largest single bequest was the sum of £2,000 from his personal estate to John Holloway; in the event of his prior decease, this was to be invested in the name of his widow, Louisa, or divided among his children. A further sum of £100 was left to Samuel Drew.

To John and Louisa Holloway, their sons and daughters, their sons-in-law and daughters-in-law; to Thomas Holloway of Hampton, Middlesex; to Robert Carr Brackenbury and his wife Sarah; to the Rev. Thomas Roberts, his wife and son Thomas; and to Samuel Drew, he left 'a ring not exceeding two guineas in value'. (One of these memorial rings turned up mysteriously in a Truro gutter early in the present century and is now in the possession of the Cornwall District of the Methodist Church.)

To Samuel Drew were left 'all my printed books which may be in his possession at the time of my decease, but not my Manuscripts'.

The whole of his real estate was left to John Holloway, Robert Carr Brackenbury and Thomas Roberts, who were appointed his executors. The residue of his personal estate was left to the 'Itinerant Methodist Preachers Annuity' (the Preachers' Fund, established in 1799 to assist superannuated and supernumerary preachers and their widows). Details of this bequest may be gained from a folded sheet in the Lamplough Collection, Archives Centre, on which Coke has listed annunities totalling £1,055 7s 0d p.a., adding instructions that all but £42 of this shall be given to the Preachers' Fund.

(Etheridge's statement, p. 381, is too sweeping and needs to be qualified in the light of the above information.)

APPENDIX E

Much of Coke's writing was of an ephemeral nature and has survived only in a few scattered copies. The present list is as exhaustive as enquiry on both sides of the Atlantic can make it; but other items are likely to turn up from time to time. Each section is arranged according to date of publication.

(a) *Journals*

1. *An extract of the Rev. Dr. Coke's Journal, from Gravesend to Antigua, in a Letter to the Rev. J. Wesley.* London, 1787. 12mo, pp. 12. Another edition: Bristol, 1787.
2. *A continuation of Dr. Coke's Journal: in two Letters to the Rev. J. Wesley.* London, 1787. 12mo, pp. 12.
3. *A farther continuation of Dr. Coke's Journal: in a Letter to the Rev. J. Wesley.* London, 1787. 12mo, pp. 11.
4. *Some account of the late missionaries to the West Indies; in two Letters from the Rev. Dr. Coke, to the Rev. J. Wesley.* London, 1789. 12mo, pp. 12.
5. *A farther account of the late missionaries to the West Indies: in a Letter from the Rev. Dr. Coke, to the Rev. J. Wesley.* London, 1789. 12mo, pp. 12.
6. *A journal of the Rev. Dr. Coke's visit to Jamaica, and of his third tour on the continent of America.* London, 1789. 12mo, pp. 16.
7. *An extract of the Rev. Dr. Coke's first Journal to North America.* Philadelphia, 1789. Printed in the American edition of the *Arminian Magazine*, Vol. I, 1789, pp. 237ff., 286ff., 339ff., 391ff. Another edition, 'carefully conformed to the original by Jno. J. Tigert', 1896.
8. *Extracts of the journals of the Rev. Dr. Coke's three visits to America.* London, 1790. 16mo, pp. 120. A collected edition of the *Journals* covering the years 1784–9.
9. *A journal of the Rev. Dr. Coke's Third Tour through the West Indies: in two Letters to the Rev. J. Wesley.* London, 1791. 12mo, pp. 12.

10. *A continuation of the Rev. Dr. Coke's third tour through the West Indies: in a letter to the Rev. J. Wesley.* London, 1791. 12mo, pp. 16.

11. *A journal of the Rev. Dr. Coke's fourth tour on the continent of America.* London, 1792. 12mo, pp. 23.

12. *A Letter from the Rev. Dr Coke to Mr Thompson.* London, 1793-4. The Journal of Coke's fifth visit to America and fourth tour of the West Indies. Printed in the *Arminian Magazine*, 1793, pp. 218ff., 385ff., 439ff., 543ff.; 1794, pp. 47ff.

13. *Extracts of the journals of the Rev. Dr. Coke's five visits to America.* London, 1793. 12mo, pp. 195.

14. *Dr. Coke's sixth tour of the continent of America and his last tour through Ireland.* London, 1798. Printed in the *Arminian Magazine*, 1798, pp. 313ff., 395ff., 448ff., 500ff., 551ff. The extracts cover the period from 6th August, 1796 to early May 1797.

15. *Copy of a letter from the Rev. Dr. Coke to Mr. J. Pawson.* London, 1814. Printed in the *Methodist Magazine*, 1814, pp. 125f. The letter is dated, 'Norfolk, Virginia, Nov. 10, 1797', and the journal extract covers the period of his voyage to America from 29th October, 1797. This extract is not included in the collected edition of 1816.

16. *Extracts of the journals of the late Rev. Thomas Coke, L.L.D.; comprising several visits to North-America and the West-Indies; his tour through a part of Ireland, and his nearly finished voyage to Bombay in the East-Indies: to which is prefixed A Life of the Doctor* [by Joseph Sutcliffe]. Dublin, 1816. 12mo, pp. 271. A collected edition of all his extant journals, with the exception of the extract dated 1797 and listed as no. 15 above.

(b) *Biblical*

17. *A Commentary on the Holy Bible.* London, 1801-3. 4to. Four vols. on the O.T., two (with the title *A Commentary on the New Testament*) on the N.T. Vols. 1-2, 1801; Vol. 3, 1802; Vol. 4, 1803; Vols. 5-6, dated 1803, but not completed until 1807.

17a. An abridgment of the Commentary was issued in Welsh: *Y Bibl Sanctaidd; gyd a Sylwiadau Eglurhaol a Defnyddiol, yn cynnwys Esponiad Cyflawn o'r Hen Destament a'r Newydd. Wedi eu cymmeryd allan o Esponiad Thomas Coke, LL.D. O Brif Ysgol Rhydychen.* Cerlleon [Chester]: Argraphwyd ac ar werth, gan J. Hemingway. 1806. Three volumes: 1. pp. xiv, 882

(1806); 2. pp. iv, 862 (1808); 3. pp. x, 842 (1813). Vol. 3 was printed partly in London by Paris & Son, and partly in Carmarthen by D. Rees, 'for the Editor of the *Carmarthen Journal*' (i.e. John Daniel) (note in N.L.W. Catalogue).

18. *The Recent Occurrences of Europe, considered in relation to such prophecies as are either fulfilling or unfulfilled.* London, 1809. 12mo, pp. 318. A reissue of the appendix to the Commentary.

19. *The Cottager's Bible, with copious References, &c.* London, 1810. 4to. Cf Drew, p. 375. I have been unable to trace a copy of this work.

20. *History of the Bible.* Begun in 1810, the parts to comprise three quarto volumes; but left unfinished at Coke's death.

(c) *Sermons, etc.*

21. *A sermon upon Education: preached at the Anniversary of a Public School, at Crewkerne, in the County of Somerset, On Tuesday, September 14, 1773.* Sherborne, 1774. 8vo, pp. 31. (Text: Proverbs 22:6.)

22. *The Substance of a Sermon on the Godhead of Christ, Preached at Baltimore, in the State of Maryland, on the 26 day of December, 1784, before the General Conference of the Methodist Episcopal Church.* By Thomas Coke, LL.D. Superintendent of the said Church. Published at the desire of the Conference. Baltimore, Maryland: Printed by Goddard and Langworthy. MDCCLXXXV. pp. 22. (Text: John 1:1.) English edition, London, 1785; also 1810 under title 'A Sermon on the Supreme Godhead of Christ'. Other editions: Dublin, 1788 ('published at the desire of the General Conference, held in Dublin, July 1788'); New York, 1815.

22a. A Welsh translation, *Pregeth ar Dduwdod Crist*, translated by H. Carter, London, 1811; second edition, 1815.

23. *The Substance of a Sermon preached at Baltimore, in the State of Maryland, before the General Conference of the Methodist Episcopal Church, on the 27th of December, 1785 [1784], at the ordination of the Reverend Francis Asbury, to the office of a superintendent.* By Thomas Coke, LL.D. Superintendent of the said church. Published at the desire of the conference. Baltimore, Maryland: Printed by Goddard and Langworthy. M.DCC.LXXXV. pp. 24. (Text: Revelations 3:7-11). A second edition corrects the date of the sermon to 1784. Another edition,

printed by Shepard Kollock, New York, 1785. English edition, London, 1785, pp. 22. Another edition, New York, 1840.

24. *A letter to the author of Strictures on Dr. Coke's Ordination Sermon, preached at Baltimore, in the State of Maryland, December 27, 1784.* London, 1786. 12mo, pp. 18. (Coke's reply to Charles Wesley's attack on him.)

25. *The Substance of a sermon preached in Baltimore and Philadelphia, on the First and Eighth of May, 1791, on the Death of the Rev. John Wesley.* London, 1791. 8vo, pp. 20. (Text: 2 Kings 2:12.) Second edition, 12mo, London, 1791.

26. *A sermon preached at the New Chapel, in the City-Road, London, Feb. 19, 1792, On the Death of the Rev. John Richardson, A.B.* London, 1792. 8vo, pp. 24. (Text: Psalm 116:15.)

27. *A sermon on the Witness of the Spirit. Preached at Baltimore before the General Conference of the Methodist Episcopal Church, On Sunday, November 4th, 1792, by Thomas Coke, Bishop of the same Church. Published at the Request of the Conference.* Philadelphia, 1793. 8vo, pp. 22. (Text: Romans 8:16.)

28. *A funeral sermon, preached in Spitalfields-Chapel, London, on Sunday, October 26, 1794, on the death of Mrs. Hester Ann Rogers; . . . Also an appendix, written by her husband . . .* Birmingham, 1795. 12mo, pp. 72. Various later editions, including Birmingham, 1796, under the title *The Character and Death of Mrs. Hester Ann Rogers . . .*

29. *Four discourses on the duties of a Minister of the Gospel.* London, 1798. 8vo, pp. iv, 74. (Based on 2 Timothy 4:1–5 and Acts 6:4.) Another edition, 1810.

30. *Four discourses on the duties of the Gospel Ministry.* Philadelphia, 1798. 12mo, pp. 109. (An American edition of the above.) (Another American edition, New York, 1821, under the English title and bound in with Adam Clarke's *Preacher's Manual.*)

31. *A sermon on the Doctrine of Illumination.* London, 1810. 8vo, pp. 16. (Text: Matthew 2:1–12.)

32. *A sermon on the all-sufficiency of Christ to save sinners; with the prevelancy of his intercession.* London, 1810. 8vo, pp. 27. (Text: Hebrews vii. 25.)

(d) *Missionary*

33. *A Plan of the Society for the Establishment of Missions among the Heathens,* 1783/4. Folio, pp. 4.

34. *An Address to the pious and benevolent, proposing an annual subscription for the support of the missionaries in the Highlands and adjacent islands of Scotland, the Isles of Jersey, Guernsey and Newfoundland, the West Indies, and the Provinces of Nova Scotia and Quebec.* London, 1786. pp. 12.

35. *The case of the Caribbs in St. Vincent.* 12mo, pp. 24. No date or place of publication, but apparently issued in 1787. Subsequently incorporated in Coke's *Journals*, this account originated as a letter from Dr George Davidson to John Clarke. The introductory section was apparently written by Coke.

36. *An Address to the Generous Subscribers and Contributors for the Support of the Missions carried on by the Methodist Society, among the Negroes and Caribbs in the West Indies.* London, 1788. F'cap, pp. 4. (Extracts from letters of William Hammet, prefaced by letter from Coke dated 8th August 1788.)

37. *To the benevolent subscribers for the support of the missions carried on by voluntary contributions in the British Islands, in the West Indies, for the benefit of the negroes and Caribbs.* London, 1789. 12mo, pp. 20.

38. *An address to the subscribers for the support of the missions carried on by voluntary contributions for the benefit of the negroes in the British Islands, in the West Indies.* London, 1790. 12mo, pp. 17.

39. *An account of the great revival of the work of God in the city of Dublin which commenced on the 4th of July, 1790.* London, 1790. 12mo, pp. 12. Introductory paragraph by Coke, followed by extracts from letters reprinted in the *Methodist Magazine* (Philadelphia, 1798), vol. 2, pp. 28–36, 72–78.

40. *A statement of the receipts and disbursements for the support of the missions established by the Methodist Societies for the Instruction and Conversion of the Negroes in the West Indies, addressed to the Subscribers.* London, 1794. 12mo, pp. 94.

41. *An Account of the Missions established by the Society late in Connexion with the Rev. John Wesley, for the Conversion of the Negroes in the West Indies.* Dated: Bristol, 13th August, 1798. 4to, pp. 2.

42. *To the Methodist Societies and Congregations and all other friends of humanity and religion.* 1799. An appeal for support for the West Indian work; signed by Coke and dated 6th October, 1799.

43. *Copies of letters from the Missionaries who are employed in Ireland, for the instruction in their own language, and for the conversion, of the native Irish: with a short address to the general public.*

London, 1801. 18mo, pp. 44. Another edition, Leeds, 1801. 18mo, pp. 48. Reprinted by W. G. Campbell, under the title, *The Secret of Ireland's Genuine Regeneration*, Newry, 1883.

44. *An account of the rise, progress, and present state of the Methodist Missions.* London, 1804. 8vo, pp. 39.

45. *An Account of the Progress of the Methodist Missions in the West-Indies, and the British Dominions in America, In Ireland, and in North Wales. With a Statement of the Receipts and Disbursements.* London: 1805. pp. 35. The account itself, written by Coke, fills the first six pages.

This was the first of the reports issued annually by the Missionary Committee and signed by Coke; e.g.:

45a. *The Annual Report of the Spiritual and Financial State of the Missions carried on in the West-Indies, Nova-Scotia, New-foundland, Ireland and Wales, under the Direction of the Methodist Conference.* London, 1806, pp. 45.

45b. *The Annual Report of the State of the Missions which are carried on both at home and abroad by the Society late in connexion with the Rev. John Wesley; addressed in particular to those generous subscribers who have contributed to their support. And to the benevolent public at large.* London, 1808, pp. 43. (Further reports with the same title appeared in 1809, 1811, and 1812.)

46. *Llythyrau a anfonwyd at Dr. Coke ac eraill; yn dywedyd am lwyddiant yr Efengyl yn nhlith yn Wesleaid yn America a llefydd eraill yn y flwyddyn ddiwaechaf, 1806.* Caerlleon [Chester]: arg. gan J. Hemingway. Letters to Coke and others from missionaries in the West Indies, originally printed in the *Methodist Magazine*; reprinted separately in Welsh translation.

47. *A History of the West Indies, containing the natural, civil and ecclesiastical history of each island: with an account of the missions instituted in those islands, from the commencement of their civilization; but more especially of the missions which have been established in that archipelago by the society late in connexion with the Rev. John Wesley.* Vol. 1: Liverpool, 1808, pp. 459; Vol. 2: London, 1810, pp. 463; Vol. 3: London, 1811, pp. 543. 8vo.

48. *An interesting narrative of a mission, sent to Sierra Leone, in Africa, by the Methodists, in 1811; to which is prefixed an account of the rise, progress, disaster and present state of the colony. The whole interspersed with a variety of particulars.* London, 1812. 8vo, pp. ii, 51.

(e) *Administrative*

49. *An address to the inhabitants of Birstal and the adjacent Villages.* Leeds, 1782. 12mo, pp. 12.
50. *Minutes of Several Conversations between the Rev. Thomas Coke, LL.D. The Rev. Francis Asbury, and Others, At a Conference Begun in Baltimore, in the State of Maryland, On Monday, the 27th of December, In the Year 1784. Composing a Form of Discipline For the Ministers, Preachers and Other Members of the Methodist Episcopal Church in America.* Philadelphia, 1785. pp. 35. Bound up with Wesley's *Sunday Service of the Methodists.* This was the first of numerous editions of the *Discipline.* It is not clear in how many of these Coke had a hand; but he certainly assisted in the preparation of the following:
50a. *The Doctrines and Discipline of the Methodist Episcopal Church in America. Revised and Approved at the General Conference Held at Baltimore, in the State of Maryland, in November 1792: In Which Thomas Coke and Francis Asbury Presided: Arranged under proper Heads and methodized in a more acceptable and easy Manner.* 8th edition. Philadelphia, 1792.
50b. *The Doctrines and Discipline of the Methodist Episcopal Church in America. With Explanatory Notes, By Thomas Coke and Francis Asbury.* 10th edition. Philadelphia, 1798.
51. *An address to the annual subscribers for the Support of Cokesbury-College, and to the Members of the Methodist Society to Which Are Added the Rules and Regulations of the College, by Thomas Coke, LL.D., and Francis Asbury, Superintendent of the Methodist Episcopal Church.* New York, 1787. Another edition was printed in the 1788 edition of the *Discipline.*
52. *The State of the Dewsbury-House, in Yorkshire: being a Vindication of the Conduct of the Conference respecting it.* 12mo, pp. 11. [No proper title-page;] dated at end, 'London, September 5th, 1788'.
53. *An Address to the Methodist Society in Great Britain and Ireland on the Settlement of the Preaching Houses.* Edinburgh, 1790. pp. 12. Another edition, Liverpool, 1795; 12mo, pp. 24.
54. *An Address to the Preachers lately in Connexion with the Rev. J. Wesley, containing strictures on a pamphlet published by Mr. W. Hammet.* London, 1793. 8vo, pp. 22. A reply to Hammet's *Impartial Statement,* 1792.

55. *Address to the Preachers.* Liverpool, 1795. pp. 6. Published at the beginning of Pawson's *Chronological List of Preachers.*

56. Copy of a Circular Letter to the Preachers in America. London, June 1, 1805. pp. 3.

(f) *Miscellaneous*

57. *The Life of the Rev. John Wesley, A.M. including an account of the great revival of religion, In Europe and America, of which He was the first and chief instrument. By Dr. Coke and Mr. Moore.* London, 1792. 8vo, pp. x, 542. 2nd edition, idem. Many subsequent reprints.

58. Various Tracts, printed for Coke by Williams and Smith, London, and by A. Paris, London. At least 38 titles, though many of these can no longer be traced. Some of these may have been written by Coke himself. London, 1806–8.

59. *Articles of Religion for the Preachers late in Connexion with the Rev. John Wesley, proposed, agreeably to a vote of Conference, for the consideration of the District Committees: To which are added, Scripture Proofs, and Testimonies from the Writings of Mr. Wesley, in defence of each article.* Dublin, 1807. folio, pp. 7. Reprinted as W.H.S. Publication No. 2, 1897.

60. *The Life of Christ, a Poem: Originally written by the Rev. Samuel Wesley, Vicar of Epworth in Lincolnshire, Father of the late Rev. and venerable John Wesley: corrected, abridged, enlarged by much original matter, and presented to the public in an almost entirely new dress, by Thomas Coke, LL.D. of the University of Oxford.* London, 1809. 12mo, pp. 304, 290. Another edition of this, together with a 'sketch of the author' by the Rev. Frank Crane, edited by Edward R. Roe, Chicago, 1900.

61. *A series of Letters addressed to the Methodist Connection, explaining the important doctrines of Justification by Faith, and the direct witness of the Spirit, as taught by the preachers of that body; and vindicating these doctrines from the misrepresentations and erroneous conclusions of the Rev. Melville Horne, minister of Christ Church, Macclesfield, in five letters, written by that gentleman.* London, 1810. 12mo, pp. xii, 382. A reply to Horne's *Investigation of the Definition of Justifying Faith,* 1809.

62. *Memoir of Mrs. Penelope Goulding Coke, by her husband . . . Revised by the Editors.* 1840; originally published in the *Methodist Magazine,* 1812, pp. 120ff., 211ff.

BIBLIOGRAPHY

(A) *Biographical Studies of Thomas Coke, etc.*

Thomas, John, Curate of Shepton Beauchamp, *Two Letters to the Rev. Thomas Coke, LL.D., Curate of South Petherton: Written with a friendly Intention of convincing him of some gross Errors in his Clerical Conduct*, London, 1777

A Layman [George Booth], *A Key to Explore the Mystery enveloped in Dr. Coke's Sermon, Preached in Tullamore, 26th September 1801, upon 2d Timothy, iii.5. Wherein a straight Line is drawn between the Christian Religion, and the religious Polity of Methodists, as opposite Extremes. To which is added, A comparative View of the Analogy between the Church of Rome, and the System established by John Wesley*, Dublin, 1802. [The Advertisement is signed: 'George Booth. Tullamore, 1st December 1801']

David, Job, *A Letter to the Rev. Doctor Coke, occasioned by a sermon which he delivered at Taunton Jan. 26, 1807*, Taunton, 1807

Horne, M., *An Investigation of the Definition of Justifying Faith, the Damnatory Clause under which it is enforced, and the Doctrine of a Direct Witness of the Spirit, held by Dr. Coke, and other Methodist Preachers. In a series of Letters*, London, 1809

Hamilton, Andrew, *The faithful servant receiving his reward: a sermon* [on Luke 12, 42–3] *preached on Nov. 6, 1814, on the death of the Rev. T. Coke*, Dublin, 1814

A Missionary [Joshua Marsden], *Lines on the Much Lamented Death of the Rev. Thomas Coke, LL.D.*, London, 1815. [Ascribed to Marsden in the catalogue of the Garrett Theological Seminary]

Crowther, Jonathan [Senr.], *Life of the Rev. Thomas Coke, LL.D., a Clergyman of the Church of England . . . Written by a Person who was long and intimately acquainted with the Doctor*, Leeds, 1815. [There appear to have been two separate printings of this: one by 'A. Cummings', issued anonymously; the other by Edward Baines, bearing Crowther's name on the title page.]

Roberts, Thomas, *The Burning and Shining Light, a Sermon occasioned by the death of the Rev. Thomas Coke, LL.D. Preached November 13, 1814, in New King-Street Chapel, Bath*, Bath, 1815.

Warren, Samuel, *A Sermon preached in the Methodist Chapel, Northwich, on Sunday, the 5th of February, 1815; on the occasion of the death of the late Rev. Thomas Coke, LL.D.: and published at the request of the congregation*, Chester, 1815

Woolmer, Samuel, *The Servant of the Lord. A Sermon occasioned by the Death of the late Rev. T. Coke, LL.D., preached at Sheerness and Brompton, Kent*, London, 1815. [Woolmer says that he had been 'brought to a knowledge of the truth under the Doctor's ministry in the island of Barbadoes' twenty-one years before]

Sutcliffe, Joseph, *Memoirs of the late Rev. Thomas Coke, LL.D.*, Dublin, 1816. [Prefixed to the collected edition of Coke's *Journals*]

Drew, Samuel, *Life of the Rev. Thomas Coke, LL.D., including in detail his various travels and extraordinary missionary exertions . . . with an Account of his Death . . . interspersed with numerous reflections; and concluding with an abstract of his writings and character*, London, 1817. [The official biography, commissioned by Coke's executors]

Anonymous, *Life of the Rev. Thomas Coke, LL.D., abridged from Authentic Sources. By a Friend of Sabbath Schools*, New York, 1830

Etheridge, J. W., *The Life of the Rev. Thomas Coke, D.C.L.*, London, 1860

Anonymous, in *Wesleyan Methodist Magazine*, 1860, pp. 769ff. [Review of Etheridge's *Life*, apparently by someone who remembered Coke]

Moister, W., *The Father of our Missions: the story of the life of the Rev. Thomas Coke, D.C.L., &c.; with an Introduction by the Rev. William Arthur, M.A.*, London, 1871

Punshon, W. M., *Thomas Coke*; in *Lives of Methodist Bishops*, edited by T. L. Flood and J. W. Hamilton, New York, 1882

Davies, Samuel, *Thomas Coke*, in *Y Geninen*, 1885 and 1886

Upham, F. E., *Thomas Coke*, London and New York, 1910

Evans, W. O., *Thomas Coke y Cymro a'r cenhadwr*, Bangor, 1912

Candler, W. A., *Life of Thomas Coke*, Nashville, 1923

Baker, F., *Thomas Coke, the St. Paul of Methodism*, London, 1947. [An address delivered in Wesley's Chapel, London, 9 September 1947]

Davey, C. J., *The Man who Wanted the World*, London, 1947

Davey, C. J., *The Significance of Thomas Coke*, in *London Quarterly and Holborn Review*, July 1947

Lawrence, G. E. and Dorsett, C., *Caribbean Conquest, the Story of Dr. Coke and Methodism in the West Indies*, London, 1947

Roberts, G. T., *Thomas Coke*, in *Bathafarn*, 1950, pp. 23–34

(B) *General Works*

(i) *European Methodism*

Addison, W. G., *Renewed Church of the United Brethren*, 1932

Arminian Magazine, 1778–97, continued as *Methodist Magazine* and *Wesleyan Methodist Magazine*

Baker, F., *Charles Wesley as revealed in his Letters*, 1948
Representative Verse of Charles Wesley, 1961

Blackwell, J., *Life of Alexander Kilham*, 1838. [Published anonymously; but ascribed to Blackwell in the British Museum catalogue]

Bowmer, J. C., *Sacrament of the Lord's Supper in Early Methodism*, 1951

Buckley, J., *Memoir of Thomas Roberts*, 1838

Bunting, T. P., *Life of Jabez Bunting*, 2nd edn., 1887

Crookshank, C. H., *History of Methodism in Ireland*, 1885–8

Drew, J. H., *Life, Character and Literary Labours of Samuel Drew*, by his eldest son, 1834

Edwards, M. L., *After Wesley*, 1935

Entwisle, *Memoir of Joseph Entwisle*, by his son, 1848

Guiton, F., *Histoire du Méthodisme Wesleyen dans les Iles de la Manche*, 1846

Harrison, A. W., *Evangelical Revival and Christian Reunion*, 1942
Separation of Methodism from the Church of England, 1945

Jackson, T., *Life of Charles Wesley*, 1841
Lives of Early Methodist Preachers, 3rd edn., 1865

Lawson, A. B., *John Wesley and the Christian Ministry*, 1963

Lelièvre, M., *Histoire du Méthodisme dans les Iles de la Manche*, 1885

Macdonald, J., *Memoirs of Joseph Benson*, 1822

Minutes of Conference, Collected edition, 1862, Vols 1–3

Perkins, E. B., *Methodist Preaching-houses and the Law*, 1952

Pusey, E. B., *Letter to his Grace the Archbishop of Canterbury, on some Circumstances connected with the Present Crisis in the English Church*, 1842

Simon, J. S., *John Wesley and the Religious Societies*, 1921
John Wesley, the Master Builder, 1927
John Wesley, the last Phase, 1934

Smith, G., *History of Wesleyan Methodism*, 1857–61
Stevenson, G. J., *City Road Chapel*, 1872
Swift, W. F., *Methodism in Scotland*, 1947
Taylor, E. R., *Methodism and Politics*, 1935
Thompson, E. W., *Wesley, Apostolic Man*, 1957
Toase, William, *The Wesleyan Mission in France*, 1835
Towlson, C., *Moravian and Methodist*, 1957
Warner, W. J., *Wesleyan Movement in the Industrial Revolution*, 1930
Wearmouth, R. F., *Methodism and the Common People of the 18th Century*, 1945
Methodism and the Working-Class Movements of England, 1800–1880, 1937
Wesley, John, *Journal*, Standard Edition, ed. N. Curnock, 1909–16
Letters, Standard Edition, ed. J. Telford, 1931
Works, 3rd Edition, ed. T. Jackson, 1829–31
Lives of Wesley by: Coke and Moore, 1792; Whitehead, 1793–6; Southey, 1820 etc.; Moore, 1824–5; Tyerman, 1870–1
Wesley Historical Society, Proceedings of, 1897–present
Williams, A. H., *Welsh Wesleyan Methodism*, 1935
Williams, C. W., *John Wesley's Theology Today*, 1960

(ii) *American Methodism*

Addison, J. T., *Episcopal Church in the United States, 1789–1931*, 1951
Arminian Magazine, American edition, printed in Philadelphia, 1789–90
Asbury, F., *Journal and Letters*, 1958
Barclay, W. C., *History of Methodist Missions*, Vol. 1, *Early American Methodism*, 1949
Bangs, N., *History of the Methodist Episcopal Church*, 1839
Bucke, Emory Stevens (editor), *The History of American Methodism*, 1964
Chorley, E. C., *Men and Movements in the American Episcopal Church*, 1946.
Cross, A. L., *Anglican Episcopate and the American Colonies*, Harvard Historical Studies, Vol. ix, 1902
Drinkhouse, E. J., *History of Methodist Reform*, 1898
Emory, J., *Defence of 'Our Fathers' and of the Original Organization of the Methodist Episcopal Church against Alexander McCaine and Others*, 1827

Manross, W. W., *History of the American Episcopal Church*, 1935

Paine, R., *Life and Times of William M'Kendree*, 1874

Stevens, A., *History of the Methodist Episcopal Church*, 1864-7

Seaman, *Annals of New York Methodism*, 1892

Sweet, W. W., *Methodism in American History*, 1933
Religion on the American Frontier, 1783-1840, Vol. iv, *The Methodists*, 1946
Virginian Methodism, 1955

Temple, S. A., *The Common Sense Theology of Bishop White*, 1946

Tigert, *Constitutional History of American Episcopal Methodism*, 1894

Wakeley, J. B., *Lost Chapters Recovered from the Early History of American Methodism*, 1858 and 1880

White, W., *The Case of the Episcopal Church in the United States Considered*, 1782
Memoirs of the Protestant Episcopal Church, in the United States of America, 1820

Wilson, B., *Memoir of the Life of the Rt. Rev. William White, D.D.*, 1839

(iii) *Overseas Missions*

Findlay, G. G., and Holdsworth, W. W., *History of the Wesleyan Methodist Missionary Society*, 1921-4

Fox, W., *Brief History of Wesleyan Missions on the Western Coast of Africa*, 1851

Fyfe, C., *History of Sierra Leone*, 1962

Groves, C. P., *Planting of Christianity in Africa*, Vol. 1, 1948

Harvard, W. M., *Narrative of the Establishment and Progress of the Mission to Ceylon and India*, 1823

Knutsford, Viscountess, *Life and Letters of Zachary Macaulay*, 1900

Lovett, R., *History of London Missionary Society*, 1899

Moister, W., *History of Wesleyan Missions*, 1871

Richey, M., *Memoir of William Black*, 1839

INDEX

Knox, Alexander, 226, 343

La Trobe, Benjamin, 107ff.
Lambert, Jeremiah, 99, 149
Le Sueur, Peter, 315f.
Lee, Jesse, 96, 118, 175, 234, 240
Leeds, 353f.
'Legal Hundred', 44, 63ff.
'Lichfield plan', 199f.
Life of Christ, poem, 325ff.
Life of John Wesley, 323
Liskeard, 311
Liverpool, Lord, 314, 342
Liverpool, 263, 318, 338f., 348
Lomas, Robert, 275
London, 39f., 262, 263f., 273f., 310f.,
  355; City Road Chapel, 39, 102,
  366; Hinde St Chapel, 357
London, Bishop of, 202f.
London Missionary Society, 282, 291,
  301ff., 353
Loxdale, Ann: see Coke, Mrs Ann
Loyal Address, 218f.
Lumb, Matthew, 155, 157, 165f.
Lynch, James, 348, 358, 366
Lyons, James, 161

M'Allum, Duncan, 141
Macaulay, Zachary, 289ff.
M'Geary, John, 145
M'Kay, Hugh, 142
McKendree, William, 257
McKenny, John, 348, 358
McMullen, James, 287
McNab, Alexander, 51f.
Maddocks, John, 62f.
Madras, 349
Magaw, Dr Samuel, 81, 183
Mahy, William, 201, 312
Maryland, 103, 125, 187
Mason, William, 103, 129
Mather, Alexander, 194f., 198f., 210,
  219, 221
Maxfield, Thomas, 39, 40
Medway, 314f.
Mevagissey, 265
Missionary Committee, 202, 249f.,

264ff., 271ff., 310ff., 336, 342, 346,
  353, 355ff., 364
Montego Bay, Jamaica, 163, 167
Montserrat, 158, 162
Moore, Henry, 61, 194, 199, 206ff.,
  221, 323, 348
Moravians, 107ff.
Morrell, Thomas, 126ff.
Moss, Dr Charles, Bishop of Bath and
  Wells, 34
Myles, William, 281, 356

Netherlands, 168
Nevis, 153f., 160, 162
New England, 246
New York, 80f., 91, 93, 122, 123,
  126ff., 255
Newcastle, Del., 184, 191
Newcastle upon Tyne, 205
Newcombe, William, 14
Newfoundland, 114, 144ff.
Newport, I.O.W., 53
Normandy, 313
North, Lord, 17, 29
North Carolina, 91, 94, 95f., 125
North Shields, 58
Norwich, 65f.
Nova Scotia, 98f., 114, 145ff.

Ogilvie, John, 202
O'Kelly, James, 87, 175f., 180, 232,
  236
Olivier, Amice, 315
Ordinations, Methodist, 197ff., 372ff.
Otterbein, Philip, 86
Oxford, 9ff., 20, 167

Paris, 213, 312f.
Parker, Thomas, 133
Patillo, Henry, 94
Pawson, John, 107, 112, 198, 210,
  213f., 218, 251
Pearce, Benjamin, 155, 166
Pearce, Samuel, 319
Penzance, 352
Perry Hall, Md., 86
Persecution: in Bermuda, 299; in
  Channel Islands, 143, 223ff.; in